TRANSATLANTIC ECHOES

Also by the authors:

COSMOS AND COLONIALISM:
Alexander von Humboldt in Cultural Criticism

TRANSATLANTIC ECHOES

*Alexander von Humboldt
in World Literature*

Edited By

Rex Clark and Oliver Lubrich

Berghahn Books
New York • Oxford

Published in 2012 by

Berghahn Books

www.berghahnbooks.com

©2012 Rex Clark and Oliver Lubrich

Library of Congress Cataloging-in-Publication Data

Transatlantic echoes : Alexander von Humboldt in world literature / edited by Rex Clark
and Oliver Lubrich.
    p. cm.
    Includes bibliographical references and index.
    ISBN 978-0-85745-265-8 (hardcover : alk. paper)
  1. Humboldt, Alexander von, 1769–1859—In literature. 2. Humboldt, Alexander von,
1769–1859—Influence. I. Clark, Rex Marvin, 1954– II. Lubrich, Oliver, 1970–
    Q143.H9T68 2012
    509.2—dc23

                                       2011037464

British Library Cataloguing in Publication Data

A catalogue record for this book is available from the British Library

Printed in the United States on acid-free paper

ISBN 978-0-85745-265-8 (hardback)

Contents

Illustrations

Acknowledgments

We would like to thank a number of people and institutions that helped us in various ways during our work on this project: Michael Strobl, first and foremost, for his resourceful research and valuable editorial contributions. For the efforts of the lead translators: Steven Sidore and Richard John Ascárate; for additional translations: Joshua Clemente Bonilla, James Adam Redfield, Naomi Lubrich, Daniel Charles Thomas, Luisa Elena Ruiz Pulido, Cathrine Blom, and Odile Cisneros. For references, suggestions, and discussions: Adrián Herrera, Justus Fetscher, Tobias Wimbauer, Dieter Lohmeier, and the participants of a workshop at the University of Kansas on the project (in April 2006). The writers Hans Magnus Enzensberger, Hans Christoph Buch, Peter Schneider, Rainer Simon, Luis Armando Roche, and Ibsen Martínez personally allowed us to use their works and supported the editorial process. Several publishing houses credited in the bibliography granted us permission to reprint or translate their licensed material. The Alexander von Humboldt Stiftung provided generous financial support through its "Transcoop Program." Additional means were contributed by the Hall Center for the Humanities and the Max Kade Center for German-American Studies at the University of Kansas and by the Peter Szondi Institute of Comparative Literature at Freie Universität Berlin. And, finally, we are grateful to Berghahn Books, for their commitment, patience, and cooperation.

Editorial Method

The texts for this collection were selected on the basis of their connections to Alexander von Humboldt. These connections are the result of various types of reference or intertextuality. The texts are direct variations and retellings of scenes or excerpts from Humboldt's works (for example, William Herbert and Adelbert von Chamisso); they are explorations of his biography and historical person based on personal or mediated acquaintance and in more or less fictional form (for example, Johann Wolfgang von Goethe and Hans Christian Andersen, Ibsen Martínez and Daniel Kehlmann); at times, the relation may even be of a rather indirect nature following patterns of discursive transmission and literary adaptation (as with José María Heredia, Mário de Andrade, or Pablo Neruda).

Genre and text types. The texts are drawn from many different genres and styles of writing: poetry, drama, novels, novellas, letters, essays, newspaper articles, scholarly papers, film scripts, comic books, and works of non-fiction. (This volume on the literary reception of Alexander von Humboldt, in the larger sense of the word, is complemented by a second one that assembles fifty essayistic texts that document a more factual, theoretical, or critical approach.)

Quality. The texts show great differences in literary quality. It has not been the goal to select the 'best' pieces or the most historically 'accurate' testimonies, but to find the most significant, representative examples in the reception of Alexander von Humboldt. The documents exhibit the idiosyncratic character of their authors, they show the signs of their times, and some even have the flaws of ideological prejudice.

Research goals. This collection is an attempt (by translating and assembling the texts in English) to make available to a broad international public a set of materials that have in the past been isolated by national and academic boundaries. It is hoped that the works can be read as literature and as cultural history, and that they also create the incentive to explore the variety of topics they touch upon, be it the history of science, the decolonization of Spanish America, or the social life of Berlin in the 1830s. Scholars from cultural studies, postcolonial theory, history, politics, art history, rhetoric, and aesthetics, as well as the disciplines closest to the materials, such as travel writing, comparative literature, German Studies, Latin American Studies and Hispanic Literature, and North American and British literature should find new directions to explore.

Organization. The ordering of the texts is chronological according to the date of their publication. In the case of letters and diary entries not necessarily conceived to be published, the date of the manuscript is used, regardless of its later publication date. In the case of memoirs and autobiographies, by contrast, the date of the publication is used, presumably closer to the date of composition than the remembered (or refashioned) events that may well be dated in the respective excerpts. The chronological organization makes it possible to draw connections between contemporaries, reconstruct individual reception patterns, and review larger historical trends.

Sources. The source texts that have been used as the basis for reproduction, with only a few exceptions due to unavailable archive copies, are the original first versions and not later modern republications, or annotated standard editions. For a number of texts the first printing was in newspapers or magazines prior to book publication. For this reason many of the texts exhibit the particular character of publication and conventions of historical spellings.

Bibliography. The bibliography includes citation of the first printing, often a second reference of the first standard edition, and generally a citation of the standard modern edition for easy access and reference.

Translations. Forty-eight newly translated texts, out of the one hundred items in this collection, have been created by our collaborating translators and are published here for the first time. All of the new translations have been done from the original language of publication into English. Where historical or modern translations were available, they have been used. Where needed due to inaccuracies, the translations have been corrected or rewritten by the editors and a note of the revision made in the bibliography.

Languages. This collection represents the international interest in Alexander von Humboldt. There are thirty-eight German-language authors (with forty-eight texts), twenty from the United States and Britain (with twenty-two texts), eighteen from Latin America (with nineteen Spanish and Portuguese texts), two from France (with eight texts), and one each from Denmark and Sweden (with three texts).

Publication history. Given the number of languages, the long period of time that this collection covers with the typical shifts in interests and focus, and the variety of publication forms, a large number of the collected texts are reproduced for the first time since their original publication. In addition a few of the contributions are original texts that have not yet been made available in any standard edition or have only been published in newspapers or magazines, and thus their inclusion amounts to their first publication in book form.

Text conventions, corrections, editorial additions. For historical texts printed in English, either original source or contemporary translation, the text conventions of the original have been strictly maintained, including variations in grammar, usage, orthography, punctuation, and differences in American and British English. The only exception to this practice has been to standardize dates and the spelling of names and place names as well as the conversion of footnotes to endnotes continuously numbered. For all translations that were produced for this anthology standard American English conventions have been followed. Obvious mistakes and typographical errors have been silently corrected; some of the typographical conventions (dashes) have been standardized. Omissions within the selected texts are noted as [...]. Extracts from the same text that do not immediately follow one another in the original are separated by the symbol ⌒. Divisions of paragraphs that appear in the original sources are represented by the symbol *. All use of emphasis in the original (italics, bold, underlining, German *Sperrung*) has been standardized to italics. Square brackets have been reserved for this edition's occasional editorial interventions, additions or explanations; any original use of square brackets has been changed to parentheses. For the sake of readability there are no added editorial comments or explanations of references in footnotes. The introduction offers commentary to the texts and authors and suggestions for the interpretation of the materials.

Original illustrations and additional illustrations. In the case of original texts that contained illustrations (comic book, photographic essay) the pictures or illustrations have been reproduced (in black and white and not necessarily in the original size). Selected pictures relevant to or referenced by the texts have been added by the editors, for example, drawings by Alexander von Humboldt or illustrations from his work, or items of interest to the text such as stills from a movie have likewise been included in the respective chapters.

INTRODUCTION
IMAGINING HUMBOLDT

Alexander von Humboldt's expedition through the Spanish colonies in the New World (1799–1804) is the most significant phenomenon of cultural contact between Germany and the Americas. The scientist, his travels, and the body of works that resulted generated an enormous echo—especially in literature. Political, scientific, and artistic factors, as well as those of personality, shaped the reception.

The Berlin traveler (1769–1859) was an important historical witness who obtained the seldom-granted permission to travel for years within the Spanish colonial lands where he came into contact with all social and ethnic groups. With the foreign gaze of the participating observer he experienced an empire shortly before the revolutions of independence. Humboldt's writings display a nuanced analysis and outspoken critique of the colonial system that not only motivated the *Libertador* Simón Bolívar but also inspired numerous writers to become involved with the history and politics of Latin America. Alexander von Humboldt stands for a transatlantic exchange at a significant moment. He initiated a worldwide intercultural dialogue. And he opened an early postcolonial perspective under the conditions of developing globalization, which today is increasingly a current topic of interest.

With the publication of Humboldt's *Ansichten der Natur* (Views of Nature, 1808), *Vues des Cordillères* (Views of the Cordilleras, 1810–1813) or the two thousand–page *Relation historique du Voyage aux régions équinoxiales du Nouveau Continent* (Personal Narrative of Travels to the Equinoctial Regions of the New Continent, 1814–1831) and their subsequent translations, as well as numerous reports and essays that appeared in newspapers or journals, international authors could draw upon vivid first-hand accounts for their inspiration. Humboldt's travel narratives offer canoe trips on the Orinoco and mountaineering in the Andes, earthquakes and volcanoes, El Dorado and Amazons, pyramids and cannibals, jaguars, mosquitoes, and electric eels. They contain dramatic scenes and meaningful motifs that were taken up and elaborated upon by numerous writers: the episode of the abducted Guahiba mother who struggles to find her way back to her children (*Relation historique* 2: 409–12), for example, was transformed by Adelbert von Chamisso into the narrative poem "Der Stein der Mutter oder der Guahiba-Indianerin" (The Rock of the Mother, or the Guahiba Indian, 1828) as well as by William Herbert in the verse epic *The Guahiba* (1832); the descent into the ominous grotto of the Guácharo (*Relation historique* 1: 409–31) was used by Jules Verne in the adventure novel *Voyage au centre de la terre* (Voyage to the Interior of the Earth, 1864), and by Erich Fried in his environmentalist poem "Der Guacharo" (The Guácharo, 1969); or the legend of the Atures parrot, the only living being that speaks the language of a destroyed and extinct tribe (*Relation historique* 2: 598–99), appears in the study by Charles Darwin on evolutionary theory, *The Descent of Man* (1871), as well as in the epilogue to Brazil's modernist 'national epic,' *Macunaíma* (1928), by Mário de Andrade.

As a traveling scholar Humboldt had a talent for moving creatively across the fields of various forms of knowledge that at the time were rapidly being differentiated from one another. In multifaceted works he achieves a unique poly-disciplinarity that fascinated his contemporaries and perplexed subsequent generations, but which, since the end of the twentieth century, is again being recognized as an original approach to traveling, to writing, and to scholarship that bridges the assumed oppositions between the natural sciences, the social sciences, and the humanities.

Alexander von Humboldt can therefore be related to the most divergent of interests. As a zoologist he studied apes and alligators. As an anatomist he researched the skin and nervous systems of the human body. As a medical observer he inspected the effects of insect bites or lack of oxygen in high altitudes. And as a pharmacologist, he experimented with deadly *curare* poison or the powerful *niopo* narcotic. He developed the theory of climate change caused by human behavior and established a project for worldwide observatories. As a botanist he described orchids and plants that produce milk. As an archeologist he visited Mexican temples and Peruvian fortifications. As an ethnologist he observed the customs of indigenous peoples; as a linguist he researched their languages as a record of their history; as a semiotician he interpreted their symbols and writing systems. As a mythologist he explicated native legends and recorded accounts of oral history. As an anthropologist he compared cultures from all over the world, equating pre-Columbian civilizations with those of classical antiquity. As a cultural theorist he conceptualized life forms in interaction with natural environments. As a cartographer he collected maps and reconstructed their development. As a historian he concerned himself with the events of the *Conquista* and the legacy of colonialism. Urbanization interested him as he noted how the ruined sites of Aztec Tenochtitlán became reconstructed into the capital of New Spain. As a social critic he saw a connection between constitutional freedoms and economic justice. As an economist he pondered the future of world trade and advanced the project of a canal through the isthmus of Panama. As a geologist he knew that the 'New

World' was by no means any less 'mature' than the 'old' one. And as a geopolitical visionary he thought about the future relationship between Europe and America.

Alexander von Humboldt has been located in dozens of disciplines—or at their intersections. He integrated as many perspectives as seemed suitable when he followed his questions, for example, on the meaning of indigenous pictorial codices that represented historical events, mythical characters, and cultural artifacts, but also plants and animals as well as different types of symbols. He stimulated the dialogue between cultures and disciplines. As the reputed 'universal scholar' he inspired intellectuals and artists, theoretical as well as literary writers. Thus the range of responses to Humboldt is unusually wide. An analysis of his literary reception must review material from many areas, eras, and languages. Thereby, it must critically examine processes of myth building, the construction of knowledge as culture, and the changing desires for either praise or disenchantment of an exemplary personification of science.

But Alexander von Humboldt was a scientist and a politician as well as an artist and a writer. How can a journey be narrated and the traveled reality most appropriately be represented? This question is a recurrent theme that occupied him throughout his work. In each of his books he attempts to answer it with a new approach—in the form of narratives, essays, fragments, or manifestos; with techniques of description, dialogue, and montage; or with illustrations, statistics, and tables of data. Humboldt tried experimental methods, found innovative solutions, and provided a new poetics for the authors who succeeded him.

The personality of the world traveler from Berlin must have had a fascinating effect on his contemporaries and later writers: the revolutionary enthusiasm of the young aristocrat, the charm of the urbane diplomat, and the biting irony of the sarcastic social observer; the resolute Francophile who stayed in Paris during the Napoleonic wars, a life on the move between different cultures and continents, travels full of hardship; the extreme erudition, his dedication to the abolition of slavery, for the emancipation of the Jews, or for the promotion of young researchers. Alexander von Humboldt became the protagonist of a large number of historical novels or plays that fictionalized his colorful biography, be it in the heroic, the sentimental, or the satirical mode.

The present anthology is a selection of literary texts inspired by Alexander von Humboldt across many genres: travel reports, poetry, novellas, essays, memoirs, letters, autobiographies, plays, film scripts, popular novels, and even comics. The more or less factual and fictional texts connect Humboldt with Napoleon and Simón Bolívar, Carlos IV of Spain and Thomas Jefferson, Goethe and Hegel, François Arago and Madame de Staël.

While numerous questions could be explored with this extensive material, a connected set of relevant themes will be outlined here:

1. How did Alexander von Humboldt influence the genre of the travel narrative? 2. What can we learn about the development of world literature by using the example of his reception? 3. What were the early reactions towards the German explorer in the nineteenth century? 4. How was he perceived as a narrator by other writers? 5. What role did he play in the formation of a Latin American identity? 6. Which modern poetical forms did he influence the most? 7. What was the reception process among North American intellectuals? 8. How and why did he occasionally become the object of hero worship? 9. How did the scientist become part of popular culture? 10. How did socialist intellectuals deal with his legacy?

1. Travel Writing

The reports of previous travelers often mediate the experience of subsequent journeys. The travel literature of the past filters new observations. Impressions are preformed, expectations fulfilled or disappointed. A framework is created for evaluating the other, or for recognizing the familiar. The two hundred–year reception of Alexander von Humboldt by generations of travelers—especially in Latin America—provides a case study for analysis of the foreign gaze, techniques of literary representation, and changing intercultural interests through time.

Does a reading of Humboldt promote a unitary colonial attitude or inoculate against it by recognizing decentered, multivoiced realities? How have different types of travelers made use of him and his writings? How did, for example, a US president, Theodore Roosevelt, an English gentleman, Aldous Huxley, a Jewish exile, Egon Erwin Kisch, or critical intellectuals of the '68 generation, such as Hans Christoph Buch or Peter Schneider, see Latin America through the Humboldtian lens? What consequences do his methods of appropriation have for writers of the travel genre and for authors of intercultural fiction more generally?

On his own expedition around the globe (*Reise um die Welt*; Voyage around the World, 1817) the poet Adelbert von Chamisso, a French *émigré* in Berlin and participant as a botanist on an ocean tour of discovery, met an indigenous man who told him of his encounter with Alexander von Humboldt. The Mexican cleric José Servando Teresa de Mier moved in the opposite direction and recalled in his *Memorias* (Memoirs, 1818) how he met Humboldt after the explorer had triumphantly returned from America in Paris. The Cuban dissident writer Reinaldo Arenas further fictionalized Mier's peregrination in *El mundo alucinante* (Hallucinations, 1966), raising doubts about who, in fact, travels when, where, and why.

Through the years travelers both in the field and in their accounts turned to Humboldt and his descriptions as a guide and imaginative companion for their own explorations. Charles Darwin used Humboldt's works as a frequent authoritative reference during his expedition to South America (Letters, 1831–1836; Diary, 1831–1836; *Voyage on the Beagle*, 1836; *Autobiography*, 1887). Cuba's national poet José Martí fashioned his "Voyage à Venezuela" (A Voyage to Venezuela, 1881) with Humboldt's narrative in mind. Aldous Huxley described in *Beyond the Mexique Bay* (1934) a visit to the pyramid of Cholula, which Humboldt depicted with two illustrations in his *Vues des Cordillères* (chapters VII and VIII, "Pyramide de Cholula" and "Masse détachée de la pyramide de Cholula"). Ernst Bloch described in his miniature "Erstaunen am Rheinfall" (Astonishment at the Rhine Falls, 1933) a completely different, non-exotic scenery while adapting Humboldtian methods of landscape representation. Ernst Jünger reflected on Humboldt's writings in his travel diaries (1966, 1970), sharing his interest in natural science as an entomologist, and his endurance of physical hardships as a war veteran. Redmond O'Hanlon (*In Trouble Again*, 1988) read Humboldt on his trip on the Amazon. He saw the same kind of native huts ("as Humboldt described them"), identical petroglyphs, and he even remembered the suffering of the Guahiba mother. But he also satirized the habit of using historical accounts as templates or guides by quoting the dry remark of his companion: "Redmond says some crazy Kraut and his sidekick came this way 184 years ago. Get that for a bundle of fun."

In the afterword to his collection of reports from Latin America, *Karibische Kaltluft* (Caribbean Cold Breeze, 1984), Hans Christoph Buch compares his methods as a travel writer and journalist with those of his famous precursor. Is a panoptic 'Humboldtian' vision, he asks, still possible? Or is the idiosyncratic field journal, documenting subjective observations, the only appropriate form that modern travelers have at their disposition?

Egon Erwin Kisch relied on Humboldt during his exile in Mexico in political terms, defending the great humanist against representatives of Nazi ideology (1942). East German movie director Rainer Simon compared his experience with indigenous extras when filming on site in Ecuador to Humboldt's collaboration with their ancestors almost two centuries ago in *Meine Chimborazo-Tagebücher* (My Chimborazo Journals, 1987–1988). Günter Herburger published a volume of *Travel-Novellas* with the programmatic title *Humboldt* (2001).

Like the author of *Vues des Cordillères* who created new methods of graphic visualization—combining, for example, a mountain profile with images and text—Herburger designed his work as a photo essay. Frederic Edwin Church is an earlier instance of visual, artistic influence. Inspired by Humboldt's descriptions and sketches of tropical nature he carefully revisited the exact locations as a source for some of his most famous paintings ("Cotopaxi," "Heart of the Andes"). In his letters (1853) he reported of his visit to the falls of Tequendama, which Humboldt had described and sketched in *Vues des Cordillères* (chapter VI, "Chute du Tequendama"). César Aira wrote a novella about the German artist Johann Moritz Rugendas, who wanted to realize in Argentina the Humboldtian program of physiognomic landscape depictions that were artistically composed and at the same time scientifically exact. *Un episodio en la vida del pintor viajero* (An Episode in the Life of a Landscape Painter, 2000) becomes, however, a story where personal adventure collides with artistic imagination when Rugendas is struck by lightning and loses his sanity.

A counter-example to romanticism and exoticism is Theodore Roosevelt's gentle deflation of Humboldt's achievements. In his account of his expedition to explore an uncharted river in Brazil (*Through the Brazilian Wilderness*, 1914), Roosevelt talks about three types of travelers in order to focus on the only important effort—the "work of the true wilderness explorers who add to our sum of geographical knowledge and of the scientific men who, following their several bents, also work in the untrodden wilds." Roosevelt is diplomatic in saying that it is hard to "define the limits" between the categories, but he judges that for Humboldt "his trip was one of adventure and danger; and yet it can hardly be called exploration proper." Roosevelt clearly wants to surpass his illustrious predecessor.

Theodor Fontane's excursions bring the Prussian novelist back to the origins of Humboldt's journeys. In his *Wanderungen durch die Mark Brandenburg* (Travels through the Mark of Brandenburg, 1862), the castle of the Humboldt family in Tegel, north of Berlin, may be considered the ideological center. The subdued burial site with its plain gravestones devoid of Christian symbolism and a statue of "Hope" towering above them is described by the Berlin author as a place of enlightened liberality and a "determined genteelness." The philosopher Hans Blumenberg remarked that with this comment on the home of the Humboldts' Fontane has actually expressed the "sum" of his own works.

Alexander von Humboldt's narratives served as points of departure for a number of factual as well as fictional explorations. The French writer Jules Verne used his motifs in several of his adventure stories (1860s–1890s). It is not a coincidence that his Captain Nemo takes along Humboldt's 'complete works' (which do not exist as such) in the submarine "Nautilus" in *Vingt mille lieues sous les mers* (Twenty Thousand Leagues Under the Seas, 1870).

There are numerous examples for the intersections between travel writing and literary production—even in drama and poetry. Humboldt's travels represent either enlightenment and natural science or romanticism and aesthetic exoticism, either colonialism and exploitation or humanism and liberty, either suffering and adversity or the pleasures of the tropical sublime.

One particular episode from Humboldt's *Personal Narrative*, which has been repeatedly retold over the years, is the above-mentioned story of the mother from the Guahiba tribe and her attempts to regain her children captured by the Spanish missionaries. A comparison of Humboldt's own first draft in his manuscript journal with the published version shows a careful repositioning of the narrative voice to emphasize the courage and intelligent tenacity of the indigenous woman's struggle against the colonial system of religious excess and arbitrary injustice. For William Herbert, an English church official, amateur botanist, and minor literary talent, the episode seems ideal for combining his enthusiasm for the tropics with the ideological task of Christianizing the natural world of the inscrutable apostate Humboldt. Added to this is the political criticism of Spanish religion and state, and a chance for a gendered gaze upon a native woman escaping alone in the jungle with dangerous animals (including lurid speculation on the mythical *salvaje,* the forest ape-man). We see the writer in his workshop, documenting the sources in extensive annotations (Herbert's footnotes, with extensive quotes from Humboldt's narrative, are much longer than the poem itself). Herbert exploits the potential for melodrama, popularization, and literary exoticism of that era. Adelbert von Chamisso, perhaps inspired by the Prussian explorer returning from Paris to Berlin in 1827 and by other parallels with his life, such as those recorded in his own travelogue, creates a Guahiba poem that might be more closely aligned with the spirit of the original. It is a judgment on the morality of European civilization when confronting subjected natives—a reception of Humboldt's cultural criticism that will take on many more forms in multiple contexts.

2. World Literature

The reception of Alexander von Humboldt as a global phenomenon is an instructive example for a brief history of cultural contact in world literature. The traveler precipitated an intensive literary communication between the 'old' and the 'New World.' Roughly, this history has the following chapters: a first period of interest in the travels and stories focuses on the tropes of tropicalism; in the first half of the nineteenth century 'foundational' writers of Latin America literature begin a sustained conversation in reaction to Humboldt's concepts of landscape, history, and identity; around his death in 1859 and centennial of his birth in 1869 there is a short period of hagiographic celebrations of Humboldt's role as a cultural icon; from the onset of German imperialism in the 1880s until the defeat of fascism in the 1940s a long period follows with relatively few documents of actual engagement with his texts; many writers of the Latin American 'boom' years turn again to Humboldt as inspiration for their baroque descriptions of nature and magical images of history; an East German appropriation is marked by a revision of the Enlightenment and ideological issues of 'third-world solidarity'; postcolonial debates include vehement attacks on Humboldt (Eurocentrism, imperial appropriation, discourse of power) as well as attempts at refining methods of interpretation (ambivalence, deconstruction, hybridity); recently, there is also a return to the text and an analysis of Humboldt's aesthetics, poetics, and rhetoric; in current popular culture the reception expands to new media, internet artists, filmmakers, writers of pot-boiler paperback historical novels, museum exhibits, and sound installations. A diachronic view of Alexander von Humboldt's reception reveals a metric of discursive change and shifting artistic interests in the representation of cultures, nature, and science.

The literary imaginings inspired by the works of Alexander von Humboldt over the past two hundred years surprise with the deep reach into the identity building of several nations, whether Latin American ("Segundo Descubridor"), US-American ("Napoleon of Science"), or German ("Deutscher Kolumbus"). Traditions of Humboldt reception have waxed and waned over the centuries across the globe, from the foundational myths surrounding Simón Bolívar and the South American liberation movements; the intellectual independence of Emerson, Thoreau, Poe, and Whitman in the United States; the ideological discourses in Imperial, Weimar, Nazi, as well as post-war East and West Germany; to the creation of modern Latin American 'marvelous realism' and a recent and unlikely bestseller from a unified Germany that has been exported to a global market. Humboldt's literary reception leads us to question the role of travel writing and natural science in forming cultural programs and national projects.

Of the one hundred texts in this collection, forty-eight are from German-speaking and twenty-two are from English-speaking authors, followed by nineteen from Latin America (writing in Spanish as well as Portuguese), eight from France, and three from Scandinavia. A national view opens up comparative perspectives that show different interests as well as shifting points of disinterest and ideological prejudice, the transfer of attention according to philosophical concepts or artistic contexts.

There are various theories for selective receptions. The 'Americanization' of Humboldt, for example, can be described as a process of denationalizing or de-Germanizing him in order to appropriate him into the American pantheon. General contributions to the study of nature (such as the focus on interconnectivity and the aesthetics of landscape) and prominent political attitudes (such as the opposition to slavery) defined his reputation in nineteenth-century North American and English culture. But toward the end of the century the overwhelming enthusiasm for Humboldt was largely forgotten.

Alexander von Humboldt is of immense cultural significance in South America where he receives a persistent and active reception not only from academic but also from popular audiences. But here as well, views and associations are transformed, for example, as Humboldt the heroic mountain climber (which appeals to a conquering spirit and nascent national identity) is supplanted by the reality that his expedition to Chimborazo failed to reach the summit (which shows limits of individualism and opens up the opportunity for surreal or satirical representations).

An early German reception where Humboldt appears as a social and cultural icon (portrayed in salon accounts and referenced by characters in novels to prove their cultural attainments) becomes problematic in the era of Wilhelminian Empire. In the twentieth century Humboldt turns into an object of national controversy and is contested as an item of propaganda (Nazi appropriations, exile reactions, communist ideology). At the end of the century he is involved in postmodern debates on colonialism and cultural identity but also in renewed discussions of his writing practices and a reevaluation of his contributions to a poetics of travel literature and ethnography. In each of these contexts authors engage with Alexander von Humboldt within their own cultural and intellectual traditions, but also within trans-Atlantic debates.

3. Initial Responses

The initial response was to a certain degree inspired by personal acquaintance with the charismatic explorer. Contemporary writers saw Alexander von Humboldt as a symbol of travel, a witness of otherness and a representative of modern science. Within a few years of his return, major European authors merged and appropriated Humboldt with exotic images and a rhetoric of intellectual and political progress to contest contemporary discourses or the limitations of national ideology.

Goethe's reference to Humboldt in his novel *Wahlverwandtschaften* (Elective Affinities, 1809) combines the wish to hear the traveler speak with the voice of the diary entries of the female protagonist, Ottilie, who looks to another world beyond the landscaping projects her husband has planned for their country estate. The quote places Humboldt's South America within a context of vague exoticism and an ambivalent desire for jungles and wild animals. We hear of apes, parrots, moors, elephants, tigers, and palm trees—which connects the new continent with the standard iconography of the Middle East, and Humboldt's American venture with Gotthold Ephraim Lessing's *Nathan der Weise* (Nathan the Wise, 1779) and the orientalist gazes of subsequent German authors. But here Goethe introduces at the same time a concern of the psychological contamination that may result from such contact, with what has become a standard German aphorism: "Es wandelt niemand ungestraft unter Palmen" (No one wanders under palm trees unpunished). It is not the external dangers of travel, but the changes in the self triggered by exposure to things unfamiliar that might disturb the serenity of aristocratic society.

In the play *Ein Gespräch im Hause Stein über den abwesenden Herrn von Goethe* (A Conversation in the House of Stein about the absent Herr von Goethe,

1975), Peter Hacks problematizes the influence Alexander von Humboldt had on Goethe's thinking ("He understands people and now loves skeletons"). At the same time in a poem ("Wilhelm von Humboldt") the East German author pours on the satire toward the elder of the two brothers whose statues guard the entrance to Berlin's Humboldt University: "Wer gab so Seichtes so in Form der Tiefe?" (Who has put out such drivel in such a form of profundity?).

In a cold Berlin winter Ludwig Achim von Arnim gives the dynamic of looking to Humboldt for utopian change a somewhat more urgent political twist in the humbled atmosphere of Prussia after the Napoleonic invasion of 1806. In his novel *Der Wintergarten* (The Winter Garden, 1809) a panorama is displayed with Humboldtian images of the tropics—Chimborazo, colorful birds, "the whole vegetation nonsense of those zones," which tolerate "no winter." The evocation of a warmer climate and a political rhetoric of uprising associate Humboldt with new departures and new beginnings.

After Napoleon's defeat, a satirical Lord Byron contrasts the traveler and bourgeois society. With the constant trips and changes in residence during his self-imposed exile from Britain after 1816 Byron's experiences gave him reason to appreciate Humboldt as a traveler. But Byron chafes at having to please what he considered the conservative literary judgment of groups of upper-class women, the "bluestockings." In an elaborate positioning of the poetic and the scientific, Byron's *Don Juan* (1821) mocks the armchair criticism of those women and spoofs Humboldt's penchant for instruments by analyzing the bluestockings with the cyanometer, a measuring scale that he applied to the intensity of blue in the sky: "Oh, Lady Daphne! let me measure you!"

4. Salon Culture

Humboldt himself performed a narrative of his travels before countless audiences throughout his life. Many of his books grew out of talks that he gave, from academic, popular, or private lectures. Goethe had in mind such an oral presentation when he mentions in *Wahlverwandtschaften* the wishful thinking of Ottilie: "Nur der Naturforscher ist verehrungswert, der uns das Fremdeste, Seltsamste mit seiner Lokalität, mit aller Nachbarschaft, jedesmal in dem eigensten Elemente zu schildern und darzustellen weiß. Wie gern möchte ich nur einmal Humboldten erzählen hören" (Only the naturalist deserves admiration, who knows how to describe and to represent to us the strangest and most exotic things in their locality, always in their own special element, with all that surrounds them. How much I would enjoy just once hearing Humboldt talk!).

What can reports on his performances reveal about Humboldt's narrative practices? And what do they tell us about what his listeners were interested in? Standard images of Humboldt as a writer—one who measures, collects, and inscribes nature in the field or who imagines, designs, and traverses the cosmos in his old age from his study—fail to capture the riveting presentations of the darling of the societies of Paris and Berlin, and the possible effects of performance on his literary and scientific prose. Perhaps the concept of Humboldtian writing should move from the explorer-scholar model to the narrator-essayist persona cultivated during the time when he completed his major Americanist works.

Humboldt's participation in salon life in Berlin and Paris is well documented. As a young man in the 1780s he visited the Henriette Herz salon and conversed in the Mendelssohn house with the daughter, later well known as Dorothea Schlegel. In the more than twenty years he spent residing in Paris after returning from America in 1804, Humboldt frequented many of the most celebrated salons of the French capital, including those of Germaine de Staël, Juliette Récamier and François-René de Chateaubriand, the painter François Gérard, Claire de Duras, and Sophie Gay. After taking up residence in Berlin in 1827, during the next three decades until his death at the age of ninety, Humboldt was seen at any number of social gatherings in the Prussian capital, most famously the salons of Rahel von Varnhagen (and its continuation by her husband Karl August Varnhagen von Ense and niece Ludmilla Assing), Bettina von Arnim, the Pückler-Muskau meetings, along with the more formal audiences and dinners at the royal court, which he attended as part of his duties as personal advisor to the king.

What were the characteristics of Humboldt as a performative narrator? One type of salon visit often practiced by the author of *Ansichten der Natur* was a presentation of anecdotes or set monologues rather than sustained conversation or development of a position. Heinrich Laube describes this phenomenon in his *Erinnerungen* (Memoirs, 1875): "Humboldt would go on and make his regular visits in the vicinity and would pour out his cup of wisdom from place to place. On his way from one visit to another, he continued to mull these themes through silent monologues, which were constantly on his mind." Laube continues to mock the style of the older Humboldt who was not able or willing to follow the conversational conventions—in fact, he had the habit of taking the floor and delivering a lecture. A touch of satire is not uncommon in these portraits when the focus is on Humboldt's style as when Karl Gutzkow in a portrait from the 1840s in *Rückblicke auf mein Leben* (Looking Back on my Life, 1875) notes the relief when the guests are released from their captive role at the end.

Several witnesses, accordingly, captured Humboldt's knowledgeable and talkative nature in the metaphor of the 'fountain'—from Goethe ("He is like a fountain with many outlets") and Karoline Bauer ("a fountain of Cologne water") to Alexander Pushkin who supposedly met him in St. Petersburg ("It's true, isn't it? Humboldt is like the marble lions in the fountains. Fascinating speeches just spout from his mouth").

Honoré de Balzac's "Aventures administratives d'une idée heureuse" (Administrative Adventures of a Wonderful Idea, 1834), a short sketch published in a periodical covering salon life in Paris, spins a fantastic tale of ideas extracted from the brain and stored in jars as a parody of academic categorizations around "a certain Prussian savant known for the unfailing fluidity of his speech." In a different text, "Les comédiens sans le savoir" (The Involuntary Comedians, 1846), the writer who portrayed the social world of Paris in his monumental *Comédie humaine* even alluded to Humboldt's *coiffeur.*

The aging 'star' of urban society was often depicted as having a series of fleeting encounters, leaving a fragmented impression of movement, the flurry of activity, the hurried broadcast of his message of the day, and on to the next reception, the next audience that is only a step away in a crowded room, or perhaps, across town in a different salon. Again this communication style of Humboldt resists the idealized intellectual exchange of sympathetic discussions. In an account by the actress Karoline Bauer in *Aus meinem Bühnenleben* (My Life on the Stage, 1876), the emphasis is on movement and speed, yet a balanced politeness to all involved: "Da war Humboldt so recht in seinem Element: wie mit Zaubergeschwindigkeit durch den Saal irrlichterirend, bald hier, bald dort an einem Theetischchen auftauchend, mit einer flüchtigen Causerie, einer Schmeichelei, einem Witz – und husch! husch! weiter!" (Humboldt was indeed in his element there: he flitted about the hall at a seemingly enchanted pace, now here, now there surfacing at one tea table, with fleeting small talk, a compliment, a joke—and whoosh! whoosh! onward!).

A description of Humboldt from 1824 by the geographer Carl Ritter focuses mostly on the style of delivery, but also looks at Humboldt's information sources and collection habits. In the word choice we see how the composition methods of the travel journals can be applied to a narrative of the daily gathering of news in Paris. We note the role of the "Beobachter" (observer), the collector activity, "mit vollen Taschen" (with filled pockets), and the production of well-segmented pieces, "Anecdoten", that are crafted to meet the taste of the audience "mit Witz und Laune" (with wit and humor). Rather than a composition of blocks of larger coherence, the restless activity reflects the narrative performance of the ever-curious traveler, the collector of ideas and information, and these practices reflect and inform the strategies of Humboldt the travel writer.

At least since Hannah Arendt's biography of Rahel Varnhagen, *Lebensgeschichte einer deutschen Jüdin aus der Romantik* (Rahel Varnhagen: The Life of a Jewess, written 1929–1938, published 1957) and the study of Jürgen Habermas, *Strukturwandel der Öffentlichkeit* (The Structural Transformation of the Public Sphere, 1962), salon culture has been depicted often with a great deal of idealism. Yet Alexander von Humboldt's salon performances are of an ambivalent political nature. He represents the aspirations of the enlightenment at social reform in a repressive state; but at the same time a younger generation of progressive intellectuals increasingly seems to have its problems with his towering presence.

Ludwig Börne's letters to Jeanette Wohl (1828–1830) show the development in the views of a representative of *Junges Deutschland* (Young Germany) toward the 'father figure' of the liberals as his attitude slowly changes from admiration to disengagement. In 1828 a hopeful Börne says, "Humboldt is supposed to be an exceptionally kind companion and is known to talk continuously. Our paths will cross yet." But just two years later, he agrees with someone in Paris who calls him a "windbag" ("il parle comme un moulin") and his judgment has turned harsh: "I find him an unbearable chatterbox. When he is in the room no one else can say a word" ("Für mich ist er ein unerträglicher Schwätzer. Wenn er im Zimmer ist, kann kein anderer zu Worte kommen"). In a similar vein, Heinrich Heine's *Lutezia* (1854) has reduced Humboldt to nothing more than a painting on the wall, part of a package of Beethoven and "a small glass of beer" to comfort homesick exiles in Paris. A visitor from Austria, the playwright Franz Grillparzer, also finds reasons to praise and criticize both of the Humboldt brothers in his journals.

The stream of visitors who wanted to see the celebrity included the Danish fairy-tale creator Hans Christian Andersen, who came to Berlin seven times. His letters and diaries mention Humboldt in eight places; the most interesting are the first and the last. In the first passage Andersen is inspired to a poem by the combination of a dream, a landscape, and the poetic quality of Humboldt's writing. (The Dane notes: "aras or alas (Humboldt's Travels) that is an excellent subject for a poem.") In the later passage we see Andersen perform a reading in a salon setting with Humboldt and the Prussian King at Potsdam.

The concept of the performative can be extended to Humboldt's expedition and to his interactions with the natives. Naturally enough, this aspect is most easily shown by film adaptations that dramatize rather than verbalize their material. In Luis Armando Roche's *Aire Libre* (Out in the Open, 1996), when Humboldt wants to communicate with a group of Yanomami on the Orinoco, he overcomes his limited repertoire of linguistic tools with performance. He changes identity markers by painting his body like the locals and responds in kind to their theatrics. As the East German director Rainer Simon describes in his memoirs, *Fernes Land* (Distant Land, 2005), the unscripted improvisations of the actor playing Humboldt with the local people cast in his film, *Die Besteigung des Chimborazo* (The Ascent of Chimborazo, 1989), become identical with the imagined performance of the historical explorer: "Jan Josef Liefers knew as little as the nonprofessional actors what dialogue would develop out of that and had to improvise just as they did. It would become the most beautiful scene of the film and for me one of the best from all of my films."

The improvised nature of Humboldt's communication in the field as well as in the salon corresponds to the fluid concepts and open forms of his works.

The account of a soirée at the Princess Pückler house by Heinrich Laube gives an impression of the fragmentation of salon conversation and highlights Humboldt's ability to follow comparisons and combine knowledge from any domain: "Discreetly gliding over the floor, slightly bowing, left, then right, he spoke right from his entry in an uninterrupted flow of words to the Princess. He did not speak loudly, yet his words were comprehensible, in well constructed sentences. Whenever the Princess managed to slip a polite word in edgewise between his sentences, this single word would spark in him an entirely new string of thoughts, which expanded in every direction." This practice, the penchant for analogies and excursions is a major characteristic of Humboldt's travel writing. The musical instruments of the Orinoco tribes are compared to those of Greece and Egypt, and the Mayan and Inca calendars are associated with date systems from India and China. Humboldt's addiction to digressions and indulgence in footnotes find a counterpart in the dispersive discourse, the interjections, asides, and comments of the salon banter. When salon narrative becomes writing practice, every annotation can take on a life of its own. The structure of the *Relation historique* follows the rhetoric of the salon, where interruptions can be included and a successful performance becomes a pastiche of many voices.

A more politically momentous salon encounter is celebrated by Reinaldo Arenas, which if it is true, shows the force of Humboldt's personality and communication changing the course of history. With his comment, overheard in a salon in Paris that "Spanish America is ripe for its freedom, though still it lacks a great man to set it on the move," Simón Bolívar is famously inspired to take up the fight for the liberation of South America.

5. Foundational Myths

Humboldt's journey and its descriptions resonated in collective memory, popular culture, and literary discourse in Paris and in Berlin, and particularly in the countries he traveled through: in Venezuela, Cuba, Colombia, Ecuador, Peru, and Mexico. His writings, furthermore, also found an echo in all of Latin America, even in Brazil, that he was not allowed to enter (in 1800). For a long period of time Alexander von Humboldt was more famous in Latin America than in Germany.

His impact was highly political. Numerous authors have condensed the *Independencia* to scenarios in which Alexander von Humboldt plays an important role. They arrange them to take place in venues of his American travels and so in a double sense make them memorial sites: for example, the landing in Cumaná (Venezuela), the river trip on the Río Magdalena (Colombia), or the ascent of Chimborazo (Ecuador).

The arrival in America described in Humboldt's travel narrative (*Relation historique* 1: 214–24) is enacted by the Venezuelan Luis Armando Roche in his densely symbolic film *Aire Libre* (Out in the Open, 1996) not as the discovery of a *terra incognita* but rather as an encounter between European naturalists and local intellectuals that marks the beginning of the revolution. Significantly, a local teacher who is holding his class outdoors and is using the beach as a blackboard, has already filled the white sand with letters before the Europeans step onto it in order to measure with instruments the temperature of a ground that, in a figurative sense, is heating up. The pregnant wife of the teacher who is about to bring, with the all pains of birth and power of allegory, the new America to the world must later be helped by Humboldt's companion Bonpland using 'violent' Caesarean surgery. An earthquake shatters the foundations of colonial society. The script by Luis Armando Roche and Jacques Espagne contains a scene in a pool in the jungle in which the travelers are literally 'immersed' in tropical nature. Alexander von Humboldt is 'Americanized' and integrated in a narrative of national identity formation.

The ascent of Chimborazo, which was literally and figuratively the highpoint of Humboldt's journey, evoked a tremendous mythopoetical fascination—'progress' and 'climbing' bring a man of the Enlightenment to unprecedented heights. Simón Bolívar celebrates it as a revolutionary triumph in his visionary prose poem "Mi delirio sobre el Chimborazo" (My Delirium on Chimborazo, 1822). (The authenticity of the text is controversial, but its imaginary significance is unquestioned. The Oxford edition does not consider it apocryphal.) Bolívar described, fictitiously, how he "daringly follows" Humboldt's footsteps in the culmination of his "marcha de la libertad" until he finally "left them behind" and independently treads new ground. At the summit, which his exemplar twenty years earlier had not quite reached, he experiences a revelation: he hears the voice of the Daemon of Colombia and the spirit of Time. The *Libertador* takes ownership for Latin America of its supposedly highest peak—and thus brings to completion the work of his German mentor, whose critique of colonialism had legendarily inspired him. The storm at the peak becomes an allegory of liberation and the founding myth of an independent continent that can be surveyed from the summit—from a perspective set forth by Alexander von Humboldt.

The motif of mountain climbing, rich in connotations, was also elaborated by José María Heredia. His short prose works "En el teocalli de Cholula" (On the Teocalli of Cholula, 1820) and "Viage al Nevado de Toluca" (Journey to the Mountain of Toluca, 1838) correspond in many details with the famous climbs of Alexander von Humboldt—from Teide on Tenerife to the heights of Mexico. (The panels VII and VIII of *Vues des Cordillères* are dedicated to the pyramid of Cholula). The choice of a travel destination initially established by Humboldt, the same physical and perspectival positioning, the reports of the vegetation zones: all are typical of the Latin American acquisition of landscape through the eyes of the Prussian researcher.

In his English-language epic published in Caracas, *The Spirit of Chimborazo Speaks* (1930), Jordan Herbert Stabler framed Simón Bolívar's liberation struggle by two slightly varied phrases that place the *Libertador* literally in the "footprints" left by Alexander in Humboldt in the eternal snow of the Andean volcano. First, during the ascent, "up the Humboldt trail he trod," and finally again along the same path, on the way to deification, "he mounts up the Humboldt path again." Stabler stresses the importance of political identity in the symbolic conquest of the mountain when he speaks of the "crown" of the Chimborazo ("my Crest") that Bolívar had reached, where the word *crest* in a double sense refers both to the mountainous peak and a heraldic emblem that is activated in effect by reaching it.

Eduardo Galeano of Uruguay has expanded the historical perspective. The second volume of his monumental *Memoria del fuego* (Memory of Fire, 1985), a chronological series of prose miniatures on Latin American history, includes twelve episodes about Alexander von Humboldt, each of which is dated and localized. One of them is dedicated to the Chimborazo, "En las cumbres del mundo" ("On top of the world"). Here, Galeano discretely links Humboldt with Bolívar by using the word *delirio*. The Uruguayan writer stages the peregrination, once again, as a near-mystical experience, this time, however, not as an apotheosis, but as a moment of illumination ("plenitud de luz"), and, moreover, the onset of mythopoiesis. Galeano's Humboldt is seized, spontaneously, with a desire to tell his story: "he feels a tremendous urge to tell it right away to brother Goethe, over there at his home in Weimar" ("siente tremendas ganas de contárselo ya mismo al hermano Goethe, allá en su casa de Weimar"). Ironically, Humboldt resisted the demand for a narrative about his most famous episode for a long time. And when he finally told it, in 1837, he ironically disappointed all those who had expected a heroic discourse.

To portray the failure of the Bolivarian dream of a united America, Gabriel García Márquez describes in his novel *El general en su laberinto* (The General in his Labyrinth, 1989), the motion of tracing Humboldt's route *in the opposite direction*—as a process of disillusionment. As the hopes for a Pan-American republic collapsed, Bolívar and his followers are on the Río Magdalena, which Humboldt had traveled to open up the continent, boating down toward the sea, on the way into exile, which for the title character is also the journey to his death. On their way, they meet a German who has been stranded on a sand bank because he had abused his rowers. He pretends to be an astronomer and botanist, but he is exposed as an imposter. Although he tries to make Humboldt's myth his own, he turns out to be the exact opposite. He fantasizes of people with chicken claws, which he intends to exhibit in Europe as curiosities, and thus embodies the ideological and exploitative version of Europeans in foreign lands. The German tells tasteless jokes about the sex life of the famous Baron. Bolívar is disgusted: "We should leave him on the beach again" ("Debimos dejarlo otra vez en el playón"); "That motherfucker isn't worth a single hair on Humboldt's head" ("Ya quisiera ese coño de ser una madre del cabello hebra de Humboldt"). This encounter causes the *Libertador* to reflect on the importance that Humboldt had for him and for America and to conclude with a broad admission: "Humboldt opened my eyes" ("Humboldt me abrió los ojos").

Authors such as Bolívar, Roche, and García Márquez tell the story of the *Independencia* by speaking of Alexander von Humboldt. They stage important events of their countries' history as episodes of his journey. The famed expedition becomes an allegorical independence movement.

6. Poetic Spaces

While the journey offered itself to political interpretations, its descriptions resonated poetically. The artistic influence of Alexander von Humboldt is especially apparent in the poetics of 'marvelous realism' (*lo real-maravilloso*) as it was set forth by the Cuban Alejo Carpentier in the now famous preface to the novel, *El reino de este mundo* (The Kingdom of this World, 1949).

Alejo Carpentier's novel *Los pasos perdidos* (The Lost Steps, 1953) was directly modeled on the route of Humboldt's journey. An academic scholar flies from a metropolis (New York) to Venezuela. From Caracas he penetrates further and further into the interior of the country and thus recreates the passage of the historic explorer from coastal civilization into the mythic world of the jungle where time seems to stand still. Even in the details the Cuban novelist describes phenomena that are borrowed from Humboldt's narrative, for example, the stone carvings on very high cliffs that indicate a prehistoric deluge. Carpentier's protagonist receives a gift of the *Odyssey*, he encounters, not coincidentally, Greeks, experiences an Archaic utopia, and continually references—like his role model—allusions to antiquity.

Many scenes in Humboldt's reports from the jungle can be taken as 'marvelous realism' *avant la lettre*. The technique of *real-maravilloso* corresponds well with the approach of the German explorer: to perceive reality (nature) realistically (in scientific terms), while at the same time, aesthetically, appreciating its marvelousness in order to gain a comprehensive understanding of its specificity (physiognomy).

Along with David Hernández, we may regard Alexander von Humboldt's travel writing as a "harbinger of the Latin American novel." Precedents for the modern Humboldt reception appear in epic and lyrical poetry of South America throughout the nineteenth century. Joaquim de Sousândrade tells the epic story of the mythical *Guesa* (1884) by using Humboldt's *Vues des Cordillères* (chapter XLIV, "Calendrier des Indiens Muyscas, anciens habitans du plateau de Bogota," Calendar of the Muyscas Indians of Colombia), which he quotes at length at the beginning as a model and source for his work: "Humboldt more scientifically writes the story thus."

The lyrical appropriation of Alexander von Humboldt ranges from Andrés Bello to Pablo Neruda. Andrés Bello had met the explorer in Venezuela and published various texts about him during his exile in London (translations, adaptations, reviews). His lyrical "Alocución a la poesía" (Allocution to Poetry, 1823) declares independence from European poetic themes ("Time it is to abandon Europe") and discovers "the heights of Quito," "the valleys / of the Magdalena," and other "equatorial wonders" introduced into literary discourse by Humboldt. Pablo Neruda's poem "El pájaro Colorario" (Corollary Bird, 1966), even though a direct reference is not made explicit, continues these tropes, with specific attention to avian themes.

In the epilogue to *Macunaíma* (1928) Mário de Andrade retells a legend from Humboldt's travel narrative, which is almost an ideal example of 'marvelous realism.' It is the story of the Atures parrot, the last living creature that speaks the language of an extinguished tribe. (In fact, we know that Mário de Andrade's main sources for the history of Macunaíma were the travel accounts of a German researcher who followed the route of Humboldt on the Orinoco.) After Macunaíma has moved from the jungle to the big city, returned again and received a revelation, the question arises as to who could actually deliver his story. How can we preserve the memory of the victims of progress? Mário de Andrade's answer to this question is complicated and paradoxical. The whole book, the song of the nation's 'hero,' is the translation of the speech of the parrot into a new Brazilian idiom: from a language that nobody understands (anymore), into a language that no one (yet) writes. And then we read: "One day a man went there." The parrot entrusted him with the legacy of the extinct tribe, the story of its destruction. Mário de Andrade's narrator identifies himself with this nameless man, whom we can take to be Alexander von Humboldt (who wrote about the parrot just after the extinction of the tribe in his *Ansichten der Natur* as well as *Relation historique* and brought the legend to international attention) when he proclaims momentously in the epilogue: "And that man, dear people, was myself, and I stayed on in order to tell you this story."

It is Mário de Andrade's national epic, of all things, which requires the ethnographic reports of Germans (Alexander von Humboldt, as well as Theodor Koch-Grünberg). Ironically for the Brazilians, the programmatic fiction of their own nation is inspired by foreign representations. But the American author, in his assertion of cultural autonomy, where even the language is meant to create its own new expression, has concealed the prominent original. He has silently, and perhaps unconsciously, appropriated—or 'cannibalized' it.

7. American Abstractions

The reception of Humboldt in North America begins, appropriately enough, with Ralph Waldo Emerson. Emerson started his career as a public writer giving lectures and the title of only his second lecture sounds rather Humboldtian: "On the Relation of Man to the Globe" (1833). Under the topic of "hazards" and the "adjustment between man and external nature" Emerson mentions two stories from Humboldt on confrontations with a jaguar and a crocodile. Although Emerson begins with the topic of the adventuresome traveler, it is noticeable at what a late date, and how rare this is in comparison to the German and Latin American sources, where there are many examples of the heroic Humboldt.

Shifting the focus, in his *Thoughts on Modern Literature*, Emerson moves from the heroic explorer to an abstraction of Humboldt as a knowledge producer: "Send Humboldt and Bonpland to explore Mexico, Guiana, and the Cordilleras."

Henry David Thoreau makes a similar use of Humboldt in *A Walk to Wachusett* in 1842. While the lofty comparison implicit in Thoreau's list of Homer, Virgil, and Humboldt is a marker of his reputation, the focus on the act of measurement in this passage fits with the images of the outdoor scientist.

In the later 1860 reference from Emerson, *The Conduct of Life,* he sees a contrast between true knowledge, the abstract values of science exemplified by Humboldt, and practical knowledge that is tainted by commerce and greed. Thus throughout his active life Emerson tested his ideas of the idealized modern thinker using Humboldt as a paradigm.

If the North American reception had ignored the personal Humboldt in order to create an abstraction, then the arrival of *Kosmos* (beginning in 1845) started a new wave that carries distinctive contours not quite matched elsewhere. Emerson writes in his *Journals* (in 1845): "Kosmos. The wonderful Humboldt, with his extended centre and expanded wings, marches like an army, gathering all things as he goes. How he reaches from science to science, from law to law, tucking away moons and asteroids and solar systems in the clauses and parentheses of his encyclopaedic paragraphs!"

It is, however, the younger generation of Edgar Allen Poe and Walt Whitman who created a type of *Kosmos* mysticism that is only distantly related to Humboldt's scientific prose. In the year before his mysterious death in 1849, Edgar Allen Poe (whose *Arthur Gordon Pym* also has a number of Humboldtian motifs) put together a prose poem, *Eureka,* describing the universe that shows similarity today with the Big Bang theory. The universe is expanding from a single source of energy and will at some point retract again to a single unity. Poe dedicates his work to Humboldt, but his lyrical essay remains obscure and unknown.

But it is Walt Whitman's most famous proclamation of the self, changed a number of times over the years, yet in every case retaining the word *kosmos*—always spelled with a (Greek or German) *k*—that most clearly brings the cult of Humboldt into the self-definition of a US-American: "Walt Whitman, an American, one of the roughs, a kosmos" or "Walt Whitman, a kosmos, of Manhattan the son" (*Leaves of Grass,* 1855 edition).

In the 1860 version of *Leaves of Grass,* Whitman adds a complete poem titled "Kosmos" as a paean to Humboldt, completing the abstracting, depersonalizing, denationalizing nature of the American reception, proposing an author who overcomes all boundaries in a vision of intergalactic detachment. It repeats nine inquiries beginning with "Who" followed by the conclusion. These are the last lines:

> Who believes not only in our globe, with its sun and
> moon, but in other globes, with their suns and moons;
> Who, constructing the house of himself or herself, not
> for a day, but for all time, sees races, eras, dates, generations,
> The past, the future, dwelling there, like space, inseparable together.

The image of Humboldt as the author of *Kosmos*—what could be more of a contrast with a particular national character than this international or even extraterrestrial timelessness?

In *The Crisis* (1901), Winston Churchill, the American writer of best-selling historical novels (not to be confused with his somewhat younger contemporary namesake, the later prime minister of England), creates a scene where Abraham Lincoln meets for the first time a young newspaper journalist from Boston. To counter the impression that "this rail-splitter, this postmaster, this flat-boatman" has a limited intellect, Churchill has Lincoln correctly identifying Humboldt's concepts being peddled as the journalist's own in conversation. Even at this late date in the United States, the name and the concept of Humboldt as a figure of cultural importance was still part of the popular imagination and could still be used as a quick test of cultural literacy.

For the whole twentieth century, however, North Americans have only a couple of toss-away references for the reception of Humboldt. One example is Saul Bellow's *Humboldt's Gift* from 1973 where the main character, Charles Citrine, has a long and complex friendship with the older poet, Von Humboldt Fleisher. Toward the end of the novel, Citrine visits Fleischer's uncle, Waldemar Harlequin, where he hears (and the reader learns for the only time in the novel) about Von Humboldt Fleisher's namesake: "When his dad took off it was a houseful of women and it was up to me to make an American boy out of him. Those women did plenty of damage. Look at the names they gave us—Waldemar! The kids called me Walla-Walla. And he had it rough, too. Humboldt! My goofy sister named him after a statue in Central Park."

Lauren Gunderson in *Wide World* (2004) uses the format of a drawing room play to bring to life Humboldt and his short visits in Philadelphia and in Washington on his return trip to Europe in 1804. Witty dialogues with President Jefferson and other contemporaries including two fictitious women, Dolley and Annabelle, highlight Humboldt's positions, and the contradictions of the American ideals, that have become mainstays of US academia's reception of Humboldt—his fervent opposition to slavery, his contributions to the mapping of the American West and motivations for the war between Mexico and the United States, the conflicts between the study and the control of nature within the ideology of "Manifest Destiny," and the fascination with Humboldt's flamboyant personality, not the least of which is the focus on his ambiguous sexuality.

8. Hagiographic Excesses

With the ongoing publication of *Kosmos* beginning in 1845 and Humboldt's sometimes influential but often marginalized position as personal advisor, if not court intellectual, to the king of Prussia, the 1840s saw literary responses that reached new heights of adoration and hyperbole. In the complex calculation of cultural politics in an era marked by censorship and repression, praise of the celestial abstractions of a prince's favorite could be the clever apolitical positioning of a conservative. Or attempts to elevate an unabashed and outspoken liberal into a national literary pantheon could also be a safe cover for advocating political change.

Bettina von Arnim's *Dies Buch gehört dem König* (This Book Belongs to the King, 1843) creates in the introduction an elaborate symbolic construct that draws Humboldt into the literary dedication. With the revolutionary criticism of social conditions in the body of the book, an interpretation has to weigh the balance between cynical flattery of the leading cultural advisor of the Prussian king and a targeted elevation of style to gain acceptance of the message—publication politics being mixed with admiration for an old friend and his methods of writing.

Bernhard von Lepel's Ode "An Humboldt" (To Humboldt, 1847) overwhelms with the scale of its metaphors reaching across time and space and the association of Humboldt with literary ideals of German Classicism such as unity, harmony, and beauty. "A grand law in mind, he ascends / Today the peak of Chimborazo," and the opposing four elements of nature find "the quiet balance of all forces" and become sublimated in a literary vision: "The steps of poesy, fervently moved, O aged sir; / They roam in the orbit of your unveiled world / And rise up, just as your intuition, / Above the limits of the grand enigma."

Friedrich Adolf Maercker's poems (1858, 1862) continue the creation of a national leader based on intellectual achievements—"Genius, lift me to the light from Earth's surging mists"—but also give a rare acknowledgement to Humboldt's civic engagement in a number of controversial issues, showing him participating in an election several months before his death: "The right of freedom to protect, here comes an old man."

In the year of Humboldt's death in 1859 and again on the centennial of his birth in 1869 there was a wave of commemorations, especially in the United States. The events and resulting literary productions show a full range of Humboldt images, but it is often apparent that the authors are working from a laundry list of topics rather than creating authentic connections to contemporary concepts of culture. In one of the dedication poems for the Central Park statue, William McJimsey's *The Memory of Humboldt* (1869), wooden rhymes provide some comic relief: "With Telescope his eyes did see afar, / The Solar System and each shining star; / He saw the Planets blaze and did rehearse, / The glory of the expansive Universe!"

Here, in addition to the science and universal *kosmos*, we also have mention of advocating "Freedom's onward cause." This and another commemorative poem by Oliver Wendell Holmes, *Humboldt's Birthday* (1869), which is a much more forceful praise of liberty, compares the atrocities of Napoleon with the peaceful conquests of science: "Tear up the despot's laurels by the root, / Like mandrakes, shrieking as they quit the soil! / [...] / Heap with full hands the peaceful conqueror's shrine / Whose bloodless triumphs cost no sufferer's tear! / Hero of knowledge, be our tribute thine!"

The cross-Atlantic political meanings of freedom for the German-American community are shown in the "Fest-Gedicht für die Humboldt-Feier in Amerika am 14. September 1869" (For the Humboldt Festival in America, 1869) by Emil Rittershaus, who considered Ferdinand Freiligrath his mentor, a long-exiled member of the 1848 generation whose daughter is the translator of this side-by-side German-English pamphlet. The creation of personality-based national myth and identification figures is evident as the Schiller cult of liberty is modernized and updated with Humboldt: "'Art' was the fiery sword of one, 'Science' the rapier of the last!" Humboldt is further identified with the New World and the call is made to export the lessons of the Germans in America back to the old country: "Old World! Dash off thy fetters bold, and hold communion with the Free!"

9. Popular Culture

As adventuresome and colorful as Alexander von Humboldt's life was, popular forms of literature depend on an excess of fantasy and sensationalism to exploit the benefits of association with fame. The techniques of using Humboldt are as varied as the genres, from sedate novels of social manners to science fiction and swashbuckling adventures. German novels of social realism find ways to incorporate Humboldt into middle-class discourse as a domestic cultural figure. Other popular works aiming more for entertainment than reinforcement of middle-class norms appropriated travel reports and foreign descriptions into adventures, escapism, exotic landscapes, and convoluted storylines. As postcolonial analysis has shown, especially for the nineteenth century, such imaginings of European contacts with other cultures are also a process of negotiating difference and domesticating otherness. Thus we see Humboldt linked with orientalist themes, with colonial tales of romance that reconcile Europeans and natives, and with wish fulfillment of utopian travel and conquest.

Name dropping, reading Humboldt out loud, or a discussion of reading plans, especially for women, are markers for a certain level of intellectual achievement or the cause for irony and subtle mocking of fictional characters in a number of relatively short references in nineteenth-century German social novels. In a three thousand–page novel with numerous characters endlessly discussing contemporary life after the failed revolution of 1848, Karl Gutzkow's *Die Ritter vom Geiste* (Knights of the Spirit, 1850–1851) uses Humboldt to align arguments with culture or its breakdown. In the same author's *Ein Mädchen aus dem Volke* (A Girl of the People, 1852) a parlor reading for a blind princess becomes part of a secretive dance of reacquaintance for two lovers. The ability to read Humboldt without "making a false step over the difficult expressions" shows gained maturity for the young lady, while a momentary faltering voice betrays the tension of recognition. Julius Stinde's *Die Familie Buchholz* (The Buchholz Family, 1884) also uses Humboldt as a test by an uncle for his young nieces on summer vacation, but they repeatedly fall asleep as they attempt to work through the borrowed tomes. Adalbert Stifter's *Der Nachsommer* (Indian Summer, 1857) has the narrator thumbing through Humboldt's works as he walks around the German countryside to "follow scientific pursuits," looking at clouds and getting plenty of sleep as he competes with his host to accurately predict the next rain. Are the parallels between these domesticated wanderings and Humboldt's travels based on ironic humor or the self-satisfaction of middle-class pettiness? August Strindberg's "Triumfatorn och narren" (Conquering Hero and Fool, 1903) works with the contrasts of authentic travelers and the perceptions of those whose horizons are more limited.

Eugen Hermann von Dedenroth's *Ein Sohn Alexander's von Humboldt oder der Indianer von Maypures* (A Son of Alexander von Humboldt, or the Indian from Maypures, 1858) could be dismissed as preposterously contrived and trivial, even if there is humor in the absurdities. The connection to Humboldt is tenuous, even within the terms of the popular novel. The protagonist is in Berlin only in a framing narrative at the very beginning and the end of the story. His scribbled notes on his life, which become the text of the main part, are eagerly copied by an ambitious writer determined to cash in on any sensation. But finally the exotic visitor has to admit that he hardly believes his own claim that he might be the son of the famous man. The colonial dynamic of romantic relations that overcome racial difference is linked to Humboldt, improbable as it may be, playing with the homosexual's role in a heterosexist paradigm of erotic conquest. Within the story it forms the basis for the illusion of the 'son' as he grows up with this belief, but it also allows him to fall in love with the daughter of a European planter. Within the framing narrative set in Berlin it openly suggests paternal connections between Prussia and the distant jungles.

Wilhelm Raabe's *Abu Telfan* (1868) continues the trend of colonial themes in the opposite geographic direction. The main character has returned to Berlin after spending so many years in the Orient that he has become a foreigner and lost his German identity. Humboldt—who initially wanted to travel to Egypt before Napoleon's invasion foiled his plans—at least provides a figure of comparison and reference for the isolated migrant as Raabe imaginatively explores the meaning of an oriental space for Germans.

Frances Calderón de la Barca in *Life in Mexico* (1840–1841) and Artemio del Valle-Arizpe in *La güera Rodríguez* (The Fair Rodríguez, 1949) make use of the sentimental genre when they ascribe, of all things, a heterosexual romance to the homosexual scientist: "De lo humano de la ciencia a lo divino del amor." "Fanny" Calderón grew up in Scotland, Baltimore, and New York, married a Spanish diplomat and consequently resided in Mexico for a number of years. As is the case with a number of twentieth-century Germans, such as Egon Erwin Kisch or Hans Christoph Buch, whose reception is based on encountering Humboldt's legacy in Latin America, Calderón's use of Humboldt's works as a travel guide and the stories of his supposed fascination with a famous beauty might be seen more as a re-importation of Mexican reception than an original North American reading.

Jules Verne turned to Humboldt repeatedly over the more than forty-year run of his *Voyages extraordinaires* series, which established modern science fiction. Not only was Humboldt mentioned and referenced as an important scientist and explorer, it can be argued that some of Verne's main conceptual inspirations are related to specifics of Humboldt's works. In *La Jangada. Huit cent lieues sur l'Amazone* (The Giant Raft. Eight Hundred Leagues on the Amazon, 1881) Humboldt's observations on actual locations are frequently quoted to lend the adventure credibility. In the early *Voyage au centre de la terre* (Voyage to the Interior of the Earth, 1864) the narrator references Humboldt's description of the cave of the Guácharo, which the natives took for the entry to the underworld, as the fantastic journey to the interior begins. Ironically, in *Voyages et aventures du capitaine Hatteras* (Adventures of Captain Hatteras, 1865) a character congratulates Humboldt for having dismissed the idea of undertaking a voyage to the center of the earth himself. Humboldt's contributions to the research on volcanoes are acknowledged in *Les enfants du capitaine Grant* (The Children of Captain Grant, 1865–1867) when the travelers wistfully note, approaching the Pic de Tenerife, that there is actually nothing more to discover since Humboldt was there before them. And at the end of his career, Verne's *Le superbe Orénoque* (The Mighty Orinoco, 1898) is a full-length homage to the most famous of Orinoco travelers. The turtle episode shows the typical mixture of fact and wild fantasy that is a case study in Verne's appropriation methods. Humboldt's estimate of the nesting turtle population based on the egg harvest, which today is still referenced by biological studies, is dramatized into a conversation by Verne's characters using almost verbatim quotes from the original. After this introduction of the topic and lesson in science, Verne amplifies the excitement by creating a calamity of stampeding turtles: "After circling the base of the hill, the slow and irresistible chelonian avalanche approached La Urbana, some two hundred meters away. Everything within the village would be flattened, crushed, obliterated!"

The cultural memory of Humboldt is still deemed popular enough to attempt commercialism in the present day. Berndt Schulz, using Mattias Gerwald as his pen name for *Der Entdecker* (The Explorer, 2001), does not shy away from embellishing deeds with melodramatic dialogue and death-defying escapes. The overnight entrapment in a snow cave on Chimborazo is a worthy addition to scenes of the overexcited imagination so typical of the genre of popular Humboldt literature.

A comic book from the German Democratic Republic is an attempt to find an updated version of Verne's didactic intention and popular format. Theo Piana and Horst Schönfelder's *Alexander von Humboldt* (1959) has a chapter on his second grand voyage across imperial Russia to the outposts of China. It tells a story of knowledge acquisition, criticism of social conditions, and surveillance in the czarist police state that is compatible with a socialist agenda—but may also be applied to the oppressive reality of East Germany itself.

10. Socialism

The political and literary debates in Eastern and Western Europe that focused on social movements in Latin America during the 1960s and 1970s brought about a rethinking of the image of Humboldt. For example, a growing interest in the new society of post-revolutionary Cuba contributed to an interest in Humboldt's two sojourns (1800, 1804) and extensive writings (1826) on the island nation. The Salvador Allende government and the Pinochet coup d'état of 1973 in Chile heightened the politics of socialist 'solidarity' of the Eastern Bloc toward Latin America, of which Humboldt could be considered a forerunner. However, literary constructions of political alternatives abroad were both an engagement with the needs of the 'Third World' and at the same time a proxy exploration of how to bring about reforms at home.

Against this background Volker Braun enacts a satirical reversal of the Humboldt myth. Yet even in the caricature, a postcolonial world opens up, which is rather different from traditional Humboldt images. The opening scene of Braun's *Guevara oder Der Sonnenstaat* (Guevara, or the Republic of the Sun, 1975) condenses associations for Alexander von Humboldt that only decades later began to enter academic discourse. The figures of "Bumholdt," an academic archeologist only interested in the past, and "Bedray," a parody of philosopher Régis Debray and empty idealism, are contrasting characters to the main focus of the play on Guevara's Bolivian campaign, but their function as ridiculous representations of Eurocentrism adds a general discussion of cultural difference to the polemical purpose of their grotesque scenes, which serve as interludes to the retrograde restaging of Che's final fight.

Volker Braun links the Humboldt figure by various symbolic associations with topics of today's postcolonial theory. Bumholdt problematizes the effects of travel—phenomena of distancing and disorientation—by diagnosing Bedray with "Fernweh." He mentions cross-cultural comparisons based on expectations of the Spanish conquerors when they saw the superior Inca road construction. The myopia of academic science is lampooned when a clump of clay that is evidence for a complex theory of Andean civilization turns out to be a Coca-Cola bottle. The same Coke bottle evokes modern practices of US American cultural imperialism on indigenous cultures. Finally a discussion of cannibalism is introduced, and a progressive speculation on why the Incas suppressed it. Here Braun mocks the ultimate legitimization of Empire—since the days of the conquest accusations of cannibalism as proof of barbarity were a standard excuse for the imposition of Christian religion and Western civilization. At the end of the play the inversion of symbolic action that drives the Bumholdt figure reaches its grotesque finale when he shoots and casually makes a meal out of his philosopher friend, thus demonstrating the inherent capacity of the civilized world for barbaric cannibalism. The opposing symbol to Bumholdt's nihilistic anthropophagy, evoked by Che Guevara right before his death, is the volcano, allegory of revolution: "I see only a world that is bloody. / That of a volcano before it erupts, I / look into the crater. No longer fighting, I can / still die, falling into the opening."

Where Volker Braun works with cryptic or exaggerated imagery to analyze the topic of revolutionary change, the play by Claus Hammel, *Humboldt und Bolívar oder Der Neue Continent* (Humboldt and Bolívar, or The New Continent, 1980), is an encyclopedic discussion of the historical origins of the South American revolutions and wars of liberation in the context of Paris of 1804. Numerous characters, from Quasimodo and a wandering spirit arising from the Seine, and of course, Napoleon, Humboldt, and Bolívar, along with many others, give voice to competing political strategies and positions on the future of colonial America. The play begins with the suggestion of a volcano on an allegorical stage and the opening scene ends when the figures disappear into the crater. With the enthusiasm of young Bolívar, and science provided by Humboldt and Bonpland, the didactic message will highlight the inevitability of social transformation as a quasi-natural force that can be treated with scientific accuracy.

Between the predictable endpoints of the play, a specific dynamic demands analysis, a dynamic always close to the writing practice of authors working within the East German system, marked by the coercive pressure and self-imposed reactions to state surveillance and censorship. As Bolívar listens to Humboldt's public lecture on seismic activity and earthquakes, and whether society becomes accustomed to minor tremblings, Bolívar interrupts and tries to get Humboldt to openly stand for social change. Bolívar is shown the door as he insults Humboldt for being a "tourist." Somewhat later, however, recognizing the rules of distrust, secrecy, and intimidation under which both Humboldt and he must operate, he begins to consider the following interpretations: "Is an earthquake to him truly an earthquake? Does he not conceal behind appearances an essence of a completely different nature? And does 'to become accustomed' perhaps not mean the pride of the unflappable, who for three hundred years have coped with every disturbance, in that they have pushed it back into the earth by virtue of their magnificence? Does the 'shaking of the earth' perhaps not mean the perpetual threat from the depths of the ancient people?"

With this process enacted on stage by Bolívar, which arose from the necessity of the realities well known to everyone in the GDR, we see the interpretive practice of creating messages that can leak through the censor to reach the intended audience. Humboldt in the GDR functioned as a proxy figure, displaced in time, for the positioning of a German writer within a repressive state apparatus. But the process of decoding that is hinted at in Bolívar's statement: "Is an earthquake to him truly an earthquake?" goes beyond the immediate context. Emerging for one of the few times in the previous one hundred–year period of German reception is a specific form of literary analysis that opens the writings and texts of Humboldt for symbolic and stylistic interpretation. In order for this question to be posed, the supposedly purely scientific writings of Humboldt are not to be taken at face value. The assumption of a neutral rhetoric is no longer the operative paradigm. Humboldt's text has become a literary artifact that is open to critical analysis. Science is metaphor, landscape descriptions are symbolic systems, reading Humboldt's prose becomes an act of construction or deconstruction.

Christoph Hein's novella *Die russischen Briefe des Jägers Johann Seifert* (The Russian Letters of the Huntsman Johann Seifert, 1980) radically increases Humboldt's role as a critic of surveillance and censorship. The voice of Humboldt comes through a dizzy filter of narrative perspectives. The text is composed of the (fictional) letters of Humboldt's domestic servant from Berlin, Johann Seifert, who is writing home to his wife while accompanying Humboldt on the expedition through Russia during 1829. They have been opened by the Russian secret police, handed over to their Prussian counterparts, inherited by the Gestapo, glued behind wallpaper, and retrieved with the help of the Stasi. Adding to the complexity of the narrative voice and textual transmission is the fact that Humboldt is long accustomed to his own correspondence being routinely read and copied by the authorities. Throughout the story, Seifert is being recruited, pressured, and in the end brutally blackmailed, to spy upon his master and produce written reports on his activities. Obviously, with this structure, Hein prevents the illusion of a flat narrative perspective in his presentation of Humboldt's travels—the retrieval of any meaning requires a series of contested negotiations. Within Seifert's letters we see Hein moving toward postcolonial perspectives when Humboldt, always working against the foil of his opinionated servant, engages him in discussions on 'otherness' (Russian, American, or Jewish). He lectures him on social injustice and satirizes public expectations and the genre restrictions of travel literature that render its value for social change essentially nonexistent.

Hein's Humboldt is highly concerned with the process of writing. He works through with Seifert the methods of revealing and hiding just enough of your true opinions in order not to become overly suspicious for the professional spies who will read every word of your correspondence. He discusses the compromised position of the intellectual within a state-controlled system— rather transparently applicable to the position of writers in the GDR. Hein's dismantling of the modern Humboldt myth is complete. The great scientist is constricted by court intrigues, the self-censored author creates a compliant identity for his spying observers, impotent travel literature cannot effect social criticism or change, and the act of writing itself is hopelessly twisted by compromise and in any case requires intensive interpretation to create meaning within multiple narrative structures. In the final crisis, Seifert is held hostage by the police and his last letter to his wife makes clear that the blackmail has forced him to capitulate and betray Humboldt to the authorities—he has finally written his report and the expedition is released to return to Berlin. Rather than the producer of knowledge for publication, Humboldt is the source of information that will serve authority or at best be kept secret. The basis of Enlightenment travel, and a constitutive part of any Humboldt reception, which is to return home and transmit insights gained from afar that could not have been experienced in the native country, is perverted by the secret police.

The film project of Rainer Simon, *Die Besteigung des Chimborazo* (The Ascent of Chimborazo, 1989), builds on and expands the modern reception of Humboldt in the more contested public medium of movie production. Again Humboldt serves several ideological roles now familiar within the GDR reception—coded statements make him a time-displaced regime critic, and he problematizes structures of exploitation of the colonial system. Humboldt is also personalized to a high degree, his personality living out the contradictions inherent in the Enlightenment, rather than harmony and universality. But after the Humboldt project was chosen to be the first (and as it turned out, also the only) East/West German film coproduction, the GDR team had the unique opportunity to travel and film in South America. After a first trip to Ecuador in 1987 and contact with the people and landscape around the Chimborazo, Paul Kanut Schäfer and Rainer Simon rewrote the script with a shift in focus (1988). More emphasis was placed on explorations and cultural exchange. The measuring and surveying activities of the natural world are framed both as common learning activity done by Humboldt and the locals and this is also put on equal footing with rituals of indigenous sages. The travelers have more to learn from the natives than vice versa. Humboldt's relation to nature is far from a sovereign campaign of collection or a grand aesthetic experience, but also a struggle with failure, pain, and tortured physical exertion. The facile categories of the scientific conquest of the nature, culture, and people of the Americas is thus resisted and problematized. The ideological battle against reactionary forces in the colonies with the corresponding modern political parallels is present but muted. Where colonial issues are raised, the analysis is often contested between several positions. In one scene where simple vocabulary words are exchanged, German and indigenous, Humboldt is directly engaged to model encounters with cultural alterity. The scene attempts to create simple communication exchanges, which respect the possibility of difference without hegemony, but which also show each side trapped within the limits of their language and culture.

In a poignant manner, the movie is also a commentary on German history. It was released in the GDR in September 1989, just weeks before the Berlin Wall fell. The story of an eccentric traveler, whom the film shows as a youthful rebel revolting against the Prussian stiffness and paternalism, prompted Simon to question East Germany's travel restrictions and censorship. When he has to seek permission from the Spanish ruler to enter his colonies, a furious Humboldt asks, rhetorically: "Why must I ask a king, where I can travel to?"

From the rigid and academic reception of the figure of Alexander von Humboldt in the German Democratic Republic during the 1960s, these four works by Volker Braun, Claus Hammel, Christoph Hein, and Rainer Simon and Paul Kanut Schäfer established during the 1970s and 1980s a creative renewal of Humboldt's legacy. The modern representation of Humboldt is now associated with a number of contentious and critical debates on colonial structures, authoritarian regimes, censorship, personal freedom, theories of travel, cross-cultural exchanges, and postcolonialism. While Humboldt was often used as a historical figure for discussions of contemporary issues specific to GDR audiences, these works also reinvented the literary reception of Alexander von Humboldt in a more general way.

Tankred Dorst added a satirical touch to Alexander von Humboldt's greatest episode, the ascent of the Chimborazo, when he displaced the volcano to the border between the two Germanys. In Dorst's comedy *Auf dem Chimborazo* (On the Chimborazo, 1974) the mountain becomes a metaphor for the divided country. An elevation on the West side offers a view of the East. The Chimborazo, which is reduced to a mere hill, stands for the assumed destination of many East Germans, who want to go to the West. "I think of the poor people," one character says, "who are over there in the East. They look at our beautiful mountain, and it is unreachable for them."

Epilogue: Humboldt our Contemporary

Some of the great modernist writers interested in Alexander von Humboldt have problematized the relationship between civilization and barbarism, science and imperialism: Euclides da Cunha, José Lezama Lima, or Robert Musil. (The reception of Alexander von Humboldt in cultural theory, essays and critical studies, rather than in literary works, is documented in a companion volume, *Cosmos and Colonialism: Alexander von Humboldt in Cultural Criticism.*)

In Canto LXXXIX (1956), Ezra Pound makes a somewhat enigmatic reference: "Guadalupe ('48) Hidalgo / Out of von Humboldt." Pound thus brings Humboldt in connection with the *Tratado de Guadalupe Hidalgo* of 1848, by which Mexico had to cede a third of its territory to the United States, arguably one of the most controversial effects of Alexander von Humboldt's voyage. During his sojourn in New Spain, the traveler had gathered information about the geography, natural resources, and political topography, which he freely gave to President Jefferson on his way back to Europe, thus unwillingly whetting his appetite for an expansion of the United States toward the southwest.

In his poem "A. v. H. (1769–1859)" (1975) Hans Magnus Enzensberger puts the German explorer in the context of a dialectic of progress, focusing on the unwanted consequences of Humboldt's actions. "Ein Gesunder war er, der mit sich die Krankheit / ahnungslos schleppte, ein uneigennütziger Bote der Plünderung, ein Kurier, / der nicht wußte, daß er die Zerstörung dessen zu melden gekommen war, / was er, in seinen *Naturgemälden*, bis daß er neunzig war, liebevoll malte" (A healthy man he, an unwitting carrier / of the disease, a selfless harbinger of plundering, a courier / who didn't realize he had come to announce the annihilation / of what he lovingly painted until ninety, in his *Views of Nature*).

Thirty years later Enzensberger's character dialogue, *Alexander von Humboldt und François Arago* (Alexander von Humboldt and François Arago, 2004), was staged in Berlin and the scientist is seen as a progressive force in the politics of his time. The occasion of the play was to celebrate the publication of a "Humboldt Project" that created a sensation in Germany. A one-volume complete edition of *Kosmos* and the first German version of *Ansichten der Kordilleren* appeared in the book series selected and managed by Enzensberger, "Die Andere Bibliothek." Both editions became bestsellers and the news weekly *Der Spiegel* devoted a title cover story to the "Rediscovery of Alexander von Humboldt."

This editorial coup was followed a year later by a literary one. Daniel Kehlmann's novel, *Die Vermessung der Welt* (Measuring the World, 2005), which has now become one of the bestselling literary works in post-war Germany, brings together the loquacious and cosmopolitan geographer Humboldt with the socially awkward and travel-adverse mathematician Gauss. Using the dry form of indirect quotation Kehlmann ridicules the weaknesses of his protagonists and reduces the intellectual giants to an all too human level.

That Kehlmann is just continuing a rich tradition, as Alexander von Humboldt has often been the object of satirical treatment of intellectuals and academics, is shown in this volume with several examples. In the absurd play of Ibsen Martínez, *Humboldt & Bonpland, taxidermistas* (Humboldt & Bonpland, Taxidermists, 1981), the experts wander around lost in the jungle. In Denzil Romero's novel, *Recurrencia equinoccial* (Equinoctial Recurrence, 1998), there are bizarre scenes of jealousy.

Maybe Gabriel García Márquez wanted to warn from an over-intensive occupation with the German scholar, perhaps from an overdose of Humboldt, when he tells a tragicomic episode in *Cien años de soledad* (One Hundred Years of Solitude, 1967). As the old Melquíades falls into a delirium, in the end he is only able to articulate two understandable words: "equinoctial" and "Alexander von Humboldt."

Chapter 1

JOHANN WOLFGANG VON GOETHE

Elective Affinities

1809

After an important conversation which provides the participants with much to reflect upon, there commonly follows a sort of pause, which resembles general embarrassment. They walked back and forth in the parlor. The Tutor leafed through various books, and came at last to the folio of engravings which had been lying there since Luciana's visit. As soon as he saw that it contained nothing but apes, he quickly closed it again. This incident may, however, have given occasion to a conversation of which we find traces in Ottilie's diary.

From Ottilie's Diary

"How anyone can bear to portray with such care these nasty monkeys. We demean ourselves enough when we look at them as animals, but we become really vile when we follow the inclination to try to find people we know behind such masks."

"It takes a certain amount of quirkiness to take pleasure in caricatures and distorted sketches. I have to thank our kind Tutor that I have never been tormented with natural history; I was never comfortable with worms and beetles."

"This time he admitted to me, that he felt the same way. 'Of nature,' he said, 'we should know nothing except what is living immediately around us. With the trees which blossom and put out leaves and bear fruit, with every shrub which we pass by, with every blade of grass on which we tread, we have a real relationship, they are our true compatriots. The birds which hop up and down among our branches, which sing among our leaves, belong to us; they have

Revised translation by Rex Clark and Oliver Lubrich, based on Johann Wolfgang von Goethe, *Elective Affinities*, trans. James Anthony Froude, in *Novels and Tales*, trans. R. Dillon Boylan and James Anthony Froude (London: Henry G. Bohn, 1854), 170–172.

spoken to us since childhood, and we learn to understand their language. Is it not so, that every strange creature, torn out of its natural environment, at first sight makes a certain uneasy impression upon us, which is only deadened by habit? One has to live a noisy, colorful life to put up with monkeys, and parrots, and Moors all around.'"

"At times when a longing and curiosity about these strange things has come over me, I have envied the traveler who sees such marvels in living, everyday connection with other marvels. But he, too, becomes another person. No one wanders under palm trees unpunished; and attitudes are certain to change in a land where elephants and tigers are at home."

Only the naturalist deserves admiration, who knows how to describe and to represent to us the strangest and most exotic things in their locality, always in their own special element, with all that surrounds them. How much I would enjoy just once hearing Humboldt talk!

A cabinet of natural curiosities we may regard like an Egyptian burial place, where the various animal and plant gods stand about embalmed. It may be fitting for a caste of priests to busy itself with such things in a mysterious semi-darkness, but this has no place in general education, so much the less, since that which is nearer to us, and more valuable, may be so easily thrust aside.

A teacher who can arouse our feelings for one single good deed, for one single good poem, accomplishes more than he who fills our memory with row upon row of lower natural objects, classified by name and form. For the result of all this, which we already could know, is that the human figure is most perfectly and uniquely made in the image of divinity.

Individuals may be left to occupy themselves with whatever amuses them, with whatever gives them pleasure, whatever they think useful; but the proper study of mankind is man.

Chapter 2

Ludwig Achim von Arnim
The Winter Garden
1809

At this moment the tall doors opened which up to now had blocked the right wall of the room, warm air and the aroma of flowers wafted towards us, it was a wonderful enchantment, that no one had expected. We thought we were look-ing in the light of day into the distance, so splendidly transparent the sky was painted and set back in regions far beyond the Chimborazo, there it was before us in a glorious morning blue and behind it rose the sun, which was aban-doning us. The plain was wonderfully interspersed with unfamiliar gigantic plants, our fellow countryman Humboldt sat in the foreground and sketched, a condor lay at his feet. This well-done panorama was furthermore wonderfully supported by a *winter garden,* which our magnificent lady of the house had de-signed in secret with devoted care. Towards the bright panorama led a trail that grew wider, like a shaded path which is darker; both of its sides were covered with a thick row of embedded tropical plants which tolerate no interruption of growth, no winter; there stood luxuriant the tentacles, half-leaning pillars, palm trees, wrapped with vines, tree-like fern growth, the whole vegetation nonsense of those zones, among this secretly hidden the full abundance of our fragrant flowers. The width of the hall was only interrupted by several groups of those notorious voluptuous plants that are nothing but a few leaves growing on top of each other, armed with a few spikes. A number of birds, especially canary birds, swarmed through the air; several parrots with colored plumage climbed very majestically on the palms and aloes; an Indian raven drank from the pool of the fountain which, not far from the panorama, spouted its stream into a marble basin. Several lambs with red ribbons around the neck jumped towards our lady; the canary birds flew onto her head; in this world man was yet the God of creatures. The canary birds kept their balance on her head with

Translation by Rex Clark and Oliver Lubrich, from Ludwig Achim von Arnim, *Der Wintergarten. No-vellen* (Berlin: Realschulbuchhandlung, 1809), 481–485.

outstretched wings and received sugar, the lambs got bread. Thus she walked slowly to the fountain and basked in our amazement and delight.

~

A short officer entered the room, the envoy bowed and greeted him as did his princess; she enthusiastically announced to him the new hopes for her family and right away designated him for travel to an important appointment. The envoy assured her of his complete loyalty, but he warned her not to trust too much the emotions of the people, who were still half in the confusion of impassiveness. She however passionately called out: "My people have awakened, nothing will put them to sleep again, gone is the time of the pleasant dream that doubt concealed from us. Bold it was to wake the giant, the people's spirit, for when he awakes, he flails about, with clouded mind mixing friend and foe and realizing first by a scream that he awakens. Then he jumps up, looks surprised and asks: 'where is my wife, where are my children, where are the abundant provisions that I struggled to collect so that I sank down from effort and slept?' Then he sees his ring, his wife there on the hand of his enemy wandering afar, the children lie crushed at his feet, the bottom is smashed from the old wine cask, the goblets lie about in pieces. His house is burning, gone is the appeal of the quiet domestic life, he hurries to his neighbor to find comfort and finds him starved to death already. Now he thinks of everyone and forgets himself alone, choosing the hard fight for freedom for all; then he gathers himself together and feels his weaknesses and the power from above. 'Oh Lord, only a breath of fortune that swells all sails of vice,' so he sinks pleading before the rocky crag. Just then from the rocky heights a torrent spills onto him in a fog, and he cries, deeply enraptured: 'not a drop too much, not a drop too little, how bright and how bold, I act, I don't sound off.' — The gloom that had paralyzed him lifted from his head and whatever he had ever felt and found as joyful was nothing to compare to this bliss, to be fully *whole;* now he stood free, a strong pious hero, he gazes upward, a thousand colors shine toward him, days of hope for the new earth and now announcing to the world, forever shall be sealed the confederation." — As vividly as the last words reminded us of a farce which we often played with each other in those days about the deluge, yet none of us could laugh; it was as if every passion to begin a new world had the right, while the old lost at once its general significance.

Chapter 3

ADELBERT VON CHAMISSO
A Voyage Around the World
1817

Don José de Medinilla y Piñeda had known Alexander von Humboldt in Peru
[...] and was proud to have once lent him his own hat when the explorer
sought one so that he might appear before the Viceroy's court. Later in the
Philippine capital of Manila, which had always enjoyed lively dealings with the
New World, we often heard our countryman's world-renowned name spoken
with reverence. We also came across many, especially clergy, who were proud
of having seen or met him.

Translation by Richard John Ascárate, from Adelbert von Chamisso, *Werke*, vol. 1, *Reise um die Welt,
erster Theil* (Leipzig: Weidmann'sche Buchhandlung, 1836), 375–376.

Chapter 4

JOSÉ SERVANDO TERESA DE MIER

Memoirs

1818

The celebrated bishop of Blois, Grégoire, was [...] the pillar of religion in France. [...] He has written many works, among them the *History of Religious Sects in the Eighteenth Century,* which is very curious. Nearly all the entries in *The Annals of Religion,* a very substantial work, are his, as is everything attributed to an anonymous "bishop of France." He told me that it was highly probable that Saint Thomas the Apostle had preached in America, now that he had seen the Latin letter on the subject that I wrote to Langlès, the renowned Orientalist who in my opinion wrote the notes to Carli's American letters, in which the author, though a Deist, says that obviously America was Christianized at a very early date. The notes to Carli, like others to Ulloa, are by señor Wite-Brune [Villebrune]. After he had read the brief dissertation on the subject that I placed at the end of my history of the revolution in New Spain, Grégoire urged me to investigate the subject in greater depth when I returned to America, for the glory of religion and the refutation of unbelievers. Baron Humboldt also told me in Paris: "I believed that it was an invention of the friars, and said as much in my statistics; but after I saw your curious essay I see that this is not so."

The Memoirs of Fray Servando Teresa de Mier, trans. Helen Lane, ed. Susana Rotker (New York/Oxford: Oxford University Press, 1998), 32. Used with permission.

Chapter 5

JOSÉ MARÍA HEREDIA
On the Teocalli of Cholula
1820

How beautiful is the land where they lived,
Those valiant Aztecs! In their heartland
Concentrated within a narrow zone
With astonishment are seen all the climates
Which exist from the pole to equator. Their plains
Cover at par with golden fields and
Delicious sugarcane. The orange,
The pineapple, and the sounding banana,
Children of equinoctial soil, are mixed with
The exuberant grapevine, to the wild pine,
And the majestic tree of Minerva.
Eternal snow crowns the heads
Of purest Iztaccíhuatl, Orizaba,
And Popocatépetl, without winter
Ever touching with destroying hand
The most fertile land, where the distant
Indian looks at them in light purple
And tinting gold, reflecting the brilliance
Of the occidental sun, who serene in
Eternal ice and perennial green
Poured out its golden light in torrents,
And saw Nature moved with
Her sweet boiling heat in life.

It was evening; its light breeze
Was already folding its wings in silence,
And sleeping among the grass and trees,
While the wide sun sank its disk
Behind Iztaccíhuatl. The eternal snow,
As if dissolved in a sea of gold, seemed
To tremble around it; an immense arch
Ending on the zenith of heaven,
Like a splendid portico from the sky,
Clothed in light and scintillating glory, was
Receiving the richest colors from
The last rays. Its brilliance went
Fading away; the white moon
And solitary star of Venus
Appeared in the deserted sky.
Happy twilight! Most beautiful hour
Whether of soul's night or brilliant day,
How sweet is your peace on my soul!

I found myself seated on the famous
Cholula Pyramid. The immense
Prairie spread wide before me,
Inviting my eyes to wander.
Such silence! Such peace! Oh! Who would say
That in these beautiful fields barbarian
Oppression rose to rule, and that this land
Brought forth such rich fields, fertilized
With the blood of men, in which it was
Flooded because of superstition and war … ?

So the night went down. From the sphere
The light blue went turning darker
And darker; the movable shadow
Of serene clouds, floating in
Space on wings of the breeze,
Was visible on the wide prairie.
Purest Iztaccíhuatl returned
From the silver ray of the moon
A peaceful glow, and in the east,
Like points of gold, sparkled thousands
Upon thousands of stars. … Oh! I salute you,
Fountains of light, who in shadowy night

Illuminate the veil, and
Make poetry from the firmament!

While the moon was declining,
Descending toward its glowing set,
Slowly the shadow was extending
From Popocatépetl like some
Colossal phantom. The dark arch
Came to me, covered me, and its greatness
Got larger and larger, until at last it
Veiled the land in universal shadow.

I turned my eyes back to the sublime volcano
Which, veiled in transparent vapors,
Was drawing its immense contour
Onto the occidental sky.
Giant of Anáhuac! How can the flight
Of rapid ages not imprint some
Mark upon your snowy face?
Time runs quickly, carrying away
Years and centuries, like the fierce north wind
Knocks down before itself the crowd of
Ocean waves. You saw peoples and kings
Seething at your feet, who were fighting
Like we fight now, and called their
Cities eternal, and believed they
Wore out the earth with their glory.
They were: no memory remains of them.
And you shall be eternal? Maybe one day
Unhinged from your deep roots
You will fall; your great ruin will overwhelm
The barren Anáhuac; proud new
Generations shall be raised up there, who
Will deny you ever were.

All things perish
By universal law. Even this world
so beautiful and brilliant where we live
Is the pale and deformed cadaver
Of another world which was ...
Absorbed in such contemplation,
Sleep surprised me. A long dream

Of glories engulfed and lost
In the deep night of time
Descended upon me. The rude pomp
Of the Aztec kings unfolded before
My astonished eyes. I saw
Among the silent throng of
Feathered lords the savage
Despot uplift on rich throne
Of gold, pearls, and embroidered feathers;
And at the sound of warlike conch shells
The vast procession went slowly walking
To the temple where horrible priests
Awaited them with faces and vestments
Splattered in human blood.
With profound stupor the slave people
Sank their low foreheads into the dust,
Not even daring look at their lord
From whose fervent eyes broke forth the
Fury of power.

Such were your
Monarchs then, Anáhuac, and their pride; their
Vile superstition and tyranny were
Sunk in the abyss of nothingness.
Indeed, death, universal lady,
Wounding equally the despot and the slave,
Writes equality over the grave.
Oblivion with its charitable cloak
Hides your madness and fury
From the present and the future race.
This immense structure saw the
Most inhumane superstition
Enthroned upon it. It heard the cries
Of agonizing victims, while the
Priest, without pity or fear,
Ripped out their bleeding hearts;
It watched the thick vapor of blood
Rise up warm toward offended heaven,
To spread on the sun a mournful veil,
And it heard the awful howls
With which the priests suffocated
The cry of pain.

Mute and empty you
See yourself now, pyramid. Better
That weeks of centuries you lay deserted,
And the superstition you served
Sleep in the abyss of hell!
To our last grandchildren, however,
Be a healthy lesson; and today to the man
Who blind in his futile and vain knowledge
Thunders proudly at heaven, like a Titan,
Be the ignominious example
Of human madness and fury.

Illustration 5.1. Pyramid of Cholula.

Chapter 6

GEORGE GORDON BYRON

Don Juan

1821

Canto IV, Stanza 112

Humboldt, "the first of travellers," but not
    The last, if late accounts be accurate,
Invented, by some name I have forgot,
    As well as the sublime discovery's date,
An airy instrument, with which he sought
    To ascertain the atmospheric state,
By measuring "the *intensity of blue*:"
    Oh, Lady Daphne! let me measure you!

George Gordon Byron, *Don Juan,* vol. 2, *Cantos III, IV, and V* (London: Thomas Davison, 1821), 127.

Chapter 7

WILLIAM HERBERT
The Guahiba: A Tale
1822

The principal circumstances of this lamentable story, the particulars of the scenery, climate, and Indian superstitions, are taken from Humboldt's *Personal Narrative*. I fear that the facts which he has recorded concerning this barbarous transaction, and the manner in which Indian children have been hunted by the orders of some of the South American missionaries, must be authentic; at the same time we should remember that he writes (as he himself states) with the feelings of a Calvinist, of course not very favorable to the establishments he visited; and as he tells us that any written attestation in favor of the monks which he might have left amongst them would have been considered as extorted from him under circumstances that made him dependant upon them, so he must allow us to believe that his depositions against them after his return may have been a little colored by prejudice. With the exception of the modes occasionally employed for obtaining converts or neophytes, I apprehend that the government of the Spanish missions has been mild and patriarchal, though probably indolent and neglectful of stimulating the Indians sufficiently to industrious occupations. The exertions of the persecuted Jesuits were much more effective, and, since the dissolution of that illustrious brotherhood, civilization has undoubtedly retrograded in the South American wilderness. Although the particular transaction here recorded cannot be read without indignation, nothing can be farther from my intention than to excite any general odium against the Spanish missionaries, whose meritorious and patient endurance is not to be forgotten, while we lament the faults of their education. Of course it will be understood that the speech of the Guahiba expresses the sentiments natural to an Indian under such circumstances, not those of the writer.

I have in preparation, though little advanced, a work of greater magnitude, the style of which, according to my present intentions, will probably bear some

William Herbert, *The Guahiba. A Tale* (London: John Murray, 1822).

resemblance to that of the Guahiba, but may be modified in deference to whatever judgment may be passed on the lines which are now submitted to the
public.

The Guahiba

O COULD I lie by Oroonoko's bank,
Where Uniana's[1] isolated peak
Shoots thousand fathom towards the cloudless sky,
Dreaming myself in Paradise, embower'd
By some stupendous tree, whose outstretch'd arms
Seem in themselves a world, on either front[2]
Displaying different seasons, bud or fruit,
Springtime or summer, and its glorious trunk
Wreathed and perfumed with odorous parasites
That clothe it like a meadow! while the sound
Of the far waters from Atures' fall[3]
Comes on the breathless moonlight, stealing slow
Like some aërial strain! O could I view
The wonders of that realm! deep rayless chasms,
Where fire-plumed birds[4] hold empire unapproach'd;
Cleft rocks, ingulphing the all-powerful flood
In their fantastic caves; and numberless,
With arrowy boughs emerging from the foam
Amidst a cloud of spray, islets palm-crown'd,
Seeming to float in mist! still herbs, that slope
Their glossy leaves, with thousand living lamps[5]
Resplendent, from whose ray the light serene
Over the deafening water-chaos streams,
As from an angel's smile! There let me lull
Life's passions in delight, and thus reclined
Think peace on earth unbroken, and forget
That violence and guilt can scare the charm
Of such calm solitudes! Does nature view,
In all her wide extent of good and fair,
Scene liker Eden, than the flowery site
Of some mild mission in that stormless clime!
The plain's green carpet, and the leaf-built huts
Mantled with sweet lianas,[6] in the shade
Of plantains spreading wide and graceful palms!
The light mimosa's air-spread canopy,

Which seems depictured on the azure vault
Glowing behind it! and beneath the gloom
Of some majestic Ceïba,[7] that lifts
Its silky cotton into middle air,
The Christian father, with his docile group
Of feather-cinctured Indians, just reclaim'd
From perilous wanderings to the Shepherd's flock!
There, by vast waters, which give back their banks
As from a mirror, of their limpid depth
Revealing to the eye each secret form,
Celestial truth is cherish'd, which imparts,
In that still wilderness, midst earthly joys,
Hope of a brighter Eden. Wo to man,
Who mars that glorious vision, giving scope
To lawless rape, unto his perverse will
Likening his Maker's! and, for gentle lore
Breathed by the unadulterate voice of truth,
Yields force the reins, and makes his zeal the law
Oppressing nature, and hopes so to stand
Pure before God!—O for a Seraph's might
To whelm the mother's rock[8] beneath the depth
Of Atabapo, and wipe out the blot
From Christian annals! the stain stamp'd in gore,
Love's purest drops! or rather let it stand,
As, on some awful heath, the accursed tree
Which beacons to posterity the spot
Where guilt once triumph'd! Will the plume-crown'd chiefs
Bow at the shrine of Christ, in whose great name,
Blasphemed by his disciples, deeds were wrought,
That, whisper'd, turn Religion's cherub cheek
To deathlike hue, and, blurring her chaste form,
"Make angels weep"? The trees are in their prime
Which waved their green arms o'er the ruthless scene,
The rock of the Guahiba. It shall stand
A dark memorial till the wreck of worlds;
The opprobrious name shall to the granite cling,
While Pity hath a tear and Mercy shrinks
Back to her throne in heaven, as blood-stain'd zeal
With murder desecrates the font of Christ.

    O thou vast continent, where nature seems
A wondrous giant on his cradle lull'd

By the hoarse lapse of torrents; in the shade
Of thine immeasurable woodlands, stretch'd
To the utmost Cordillera's snowy peaks,
Where noontide's hottest splendors dart in vain
From the meridian! In thy loneliest wilds
How great, how glorious is thy majesty!

   Girded by torrents, San Fernando[9] stands
Surveying from her walls the mingled swell
Of three huge waters, singly which outvie
Danau or Nile. There in fierce eddy blends
The turbid Guaviare's[10] powerful stream
With stately Atabapo crown'd with palms;
And thee, renown'd of rivers, whose clear strength
Comes roaring from the East, foredoom'd to give
Thy name, great Oroonoko, to each flood
That rolls its thunder from the Western ridge,
Lofty Granada. Thence with proud excess
Shall thy broad deluge rush, wider than range
Of cannon shot, in a long line of foam
From Parima's[11] dark buttress hurrying down,
Till, join'd by Meta and Apure's tide,
It flows, like one vast ocean, thro' the plain
Of Barcelona to the Mournful gulf[12]
Right against Trinidad, that bars its mouth
Four hundred leagues aloof. There cultured scenes
Await thee, regal pomp, and busy cares,
And the mixt hum of commerce ever rings
Thro' burnt Cumana. Here, in wilds scarce trod,
An awful silence thro' thy forest reigns,
Save where the snowy bird[13] of loneliness,
The doleful Campanero, seems to toll
The dirge of solitude. In these rude wastes,
Tranquillest scenes, where Art has never rear'd
Her mimic shapes, stands most reveal'd the might
Of One benign, by whose prolific will
The plain is like a cultured garden gemm'd
With shrubs and flowers; who lifts the towering tree
Unto the sky serene, loaded with fruits
By his spontaneous bounty. Savage minds
Know this, and own their God in loveliness.
Guiana's Indian, underneath the palms,

Which o'er his thicket wave their feathery heads
E'en like a second forest in mid air,[14]
Sees God in all his works, and, thankful, bends
To one great source of life, whose genial power
For him bids plantain and cassava yield
Their sure encrease, filling each swollen brook
With teaming wealth. No sounds, save sounds of peace,
Break on his solitude; the wailing winds
Stir not, thro' that wide forest,[15] in their birth
Spell-bound. The unseen Genius of the wild
From out its vast interminable depth
Seems to cry "Peace, peace!" Peace to nature's works,
And glory to their Maker! Ebb and flow
Of seasons come not here; the fiery sun,
Once robed in mist, sleeps in that quiet shroud,
As if he waited till the Archangel's trump
Should rend heaven's curtain. Spring, perpetual spring,
Wafts incense; high o'er the Guahibo's hut
Wave plumy heads surcharged with fruit,[16] that shame
Persia or Babylonian gardens. There,
Lord of the waste, he casts his palm-string net[17]
Where, far removed from billowy ocean, sport
Huge dolphins,[18] spouting in their noisy play
Water and foam, or lurking by the shade
Of other greens than wreath old Nereus' hair.

Infants and wife, secure beneath their hut,
Expect his coming, when at fall of day
He and his sturdy boys shall bear the spoil
Of those lone floods. Wo waits his next return;
Silence profound and desolation reign
Where welcome should resound. His frugal meal
Lies half prepared; and gaudy parrot-flowers[19]
That sooth'd his fretful child, and leaves, and plumes,
Upon the sod confused. What force profane
Hath made the echoes of the forest mute?
Jaguar,[20] or Boa, or the wily strength
Of scale-arm'd crocodile hath ne'er approach'd
This tranquil dwelling. Wo! wo! Christian hands
At one fell swoop have made thee desolate!
The priest of San Fernando and his crew
Of red barbarians! in the faith baptized

Of Him who died to save, yet left not here
Peace but a sword! So works the ruthless zeal
Of man against his God, making that name
A curse amongst the heathens, which should breathe
Infinite bliss, unheard beatitude,
Bidding the wilds rejoice, thro' all their depth
Proclaiming social love, benevolent laws
That bind man to his fellows. Swiftly glides
Down Guaviare's flood, freighted by force,
The holy reaver's barque. Maternal shrieks
Die on the distance, and the fruitless wail
Of those rapt infants. Past the limpid mouth
Of Atabapo mingling its dark wave,[21]
They shoot amain, to where the Eastern stream
Winds round Fernando's walls its gorgeous strength,
Rushing from Cerro Duïda,[22] whose front
Abrupt mocks emerald's and diamond's blaze.

      Lorn parent, gaze on the unfathom'd whirl
Of those impetuous waters, and the trees
Which round thee rear their tall and barren trunks
Obscure and boundless! In that solitude
The flood, the desert, are thy prison walls,
Danger and Famine the stern sentinels!
Between thee and thy home two giant streams,
With all their tributary train, deny
Regress or hope. The southern cross[23] scarce gleams
Thro' that unchanging veil, the eternal cloud
That wraps the horizon; from thy calm abode
Thou art divorced by more than human power,
Nature's impediments. Yet hope still lives,
The unconquerable throb, the inborn spring,
That swells a mother's heart. Dauntless she mark'd
The rite baptismal, to her tender brood
Suspected badge of thraldom. They the while
Unconscious mourn'd, by cruel force estranged
From their dear native liberty; so will'd
The Christian ravisher, misnamed of Him,
Who, robed in gentleness, forbad his own
Outrage or e'en resistance. In her soul
Determined courage reign'd; the firm resolve
To barter life for freedom, or reguide

The nestlings to her hut. Their toil-burnt sire,
Brothers, and fatherland, were all to her;
All else without them, nought; or worse than nought,
Loath'd circumscription, tenfold servitude.

Night wrapp'd Fernando's fane; beneath their cots
Mantled with sweets umbrageous, slept secure
Christians, and neophytes by Christian rites
Regenerate, but heathen still in mind.
Not so the sad Guahiba; she forlorn
Watch'd each still hour, forecasting from those bonds
Escape, and thro' that untrod wilderness
Return to her dear home. Beside her lay
The unfledged captives, from a father's love
By zealous rapine sever'd; one, just skill'd
To lisp his name; one, conscious of her fate,
Joy of his hopes. "My child," with cautious breath
She whisper'd, "night is mirksome, but these wilds
Are not without their guide; well have I mark'd
Each globe of fire that studs the firmament;
And that huge orb, which from the east each morn
Rolls its illumined bulk to those dark hills
Whence comes the rain. Behold yon star; it gleams
Behind thy father's dwelling, a sure lamp
In trackless deserts. Better to confront,
Exposed and lone, that shaggy savage form,[24]
Half-man, half-brute, wide-famed for cruel rape
In woody solitudes, than bide the curse
Of this our prison-mansion! Better wade
Thro' flooded groves obscure, and stem the force
Of Guaviare in his turbid wrath,
Tempting the scaly crocodile! Its waves
Have seen thee, fearless infant, in thy sport,
Their glittering dolphins chase, and wreathe thy brows
With river-lilies; thy life link'd to mine
Together shall we sink, or burst our chain
Free as free-born. Dread nothing; thro' the waste
A mother's strength shall aid thee, little charge!
Father and brothers from thy native bank
Shall strive thro' the deep tide, breasting its foam
To rescue us. Myself thro' swampy shades
Will bear thy tender limbs, warding the harm

Of thorn-arm'd brake, or the nut's ponderous fall,[25]
Serpent or jaguar's fang." Forth stretch'd her arms,
Smiling, the lovely maid, and press'd her cheek
Against a mother's bosom, hiding there
The fearful tear. "Shall we indeed behold
Our sire," she murmur'd, "and our brothers? Haste,
Ere our fell guards awake." Behind her back
The mother slung love's lesser burthen, hush'd
By kisses into silence; that sweet girl,
Strain'd with firm sinew to her heart, she bore
Fearless of toil. Rise, floods, and trackless brakes,
And swamps not trodden by the step of man,
Alone she would o'erpass ye! Her fleet course
Would mock pursuit! But, ah! those infant limbs
Dread the rough bindweed, with its thorny ropes
Barring their path. Famish'd they cry for food,
Which, on the tree's high spire, eludes the grasp,
Or shrink from the coil'd snake. Behind them swell
Nearer and nearer on the breathless air,
The voices of their ravishers. She speeds
Phrensied with love, till close beneath her feet
She sees majestic Atabapo glide,
Pellucid, deep, and strong. Loud and more loud
The Christians come. With living cordage, pluck'd
From the green stem, she lashes to her flanks
Her timid cherubs, kissing from their eyes
The starting tear; then fearlessly she springs
Into that chrystal gulph, her grave, if not
Her path to freedom. Gurgling o'er them closed
The liquid volume. Soon she breasts the wave;
Her sinewy limbs throw back the glassy tide
Triumphantly; amazed the Christians view.
Their barques are on the water, and swift oars
Shall intercept her, ere the perilous course
Be half atchieved. Matron, thy foes prevail,
And thou once more art captive! Hearts of stone
Shall sever thee from thine! The plunderer's boat
Shoots down the torrent to Fernando's keep.
Thou, widow'd, childless, bound, must stem the flood
To lone Javita, where of thy beloved
Nor sound, nor sight shall cheer thee. Slow and still,
Laboring against the current's might, they pass

The tiger's rock,[26] the rapid's foaming chain,
The cataract Guarinuma. On her view
Plains open vast and drear, part thickly clothed
With giant grasses, thro' whose bosom wind
Streams tributary, part by forest hid;
And ever and anon rise castled rocks[26]
In ruin'd form, pillars and pyramids,
Quaint work of nature, mocking human art;
And oft-times on their summits towering stand
Yucca or palm. Next where the crumbling walls
Of Mendaxari, once the fane of Christ,
Frown o'er the waters, they suspend the oar,
Hymning a strain to its protecting saint;
Then striving fast by Kemarumo's crag
See culture smile, and pause beneath the boughs
Of that far-venerated tree,[27] whose trunk
Enormous, born what time the deeps were staid,
O'erbrows the Indian gardens; next descry
The Christian hamlet, deck'd in beauteous guise,
Balthasar, where the fig and lemon vie
With Americ's treasures. Onwards still they pass,
By toil undaunted. Thrice the sun had sloped
His ray thro' feathery trees that fringe the bank[27]
Laving their slender trunks; aloft the clouds[27]
Floated swift-borne; beneath, mute calmness reign'd,
And voiceless solitude. The monkey's howl[27]
Came not from far; the screaming vulture's wing
Was not upon the air; and dark, yet clear,
The glassy depth reveal'd no living form;
The crocodile[27] had shunn'd it, pleased to dwell
In turbid floods. Alone around the barque,[27]
Cleaving the surface with resplendent scales
Dolphins kept pace, or bounding by the prow,
Or in the silver wake. Her eye survey'd
Far hills and mountains in pale distance, oft
Measuring in thought the weary way between
Her and her husband. Moonlight fell so soft
On the transparent volume, its pure stream
Scarce seem'd to flow: and those who laboring pull'd
The frequent oar, to the blest Virgin raised
Their hallow'd chorus; the soul-melting notes
Seem'd to ascend unto the cope of heaven

By tranquil airs upborne. The slacken'd bonds
Dropp'd unperceived from the sad mother's limbs;
Hope fired her thoughts, as, gliding by, she mark'd
A stony buttress thro' the swampy fringe
Shelve down into the torrent. Heedless pass
That rock the Christians, which man never more
Shall pass unheeded. With impetuous plunge
Down the deep gulph she goes. They see her dive
Five fathom deep; and, near, the water-snake
Writhes his stupendous[27] folds, fierce, yet amazed
To see his haunts invaded: but secure
She rises, floating down the rapid stream,
Till, whirl'd in the swift eddy, lost in foam,
She grasps the dangerous ledge; with wounded limbs
Then labors to its summit, and gains quick
The river's lofty bank. Ere long, pursuit
Rings on her steps. To holy strains succeed
The unhallow'd war-cry and the hunter's shout,
Fierce and discordant. Morning sweetly dawn'd,
Lighting the lonely plain. They found her, spent
By toil and bleeding wounds, bay'd by their dog
Beneath the thickest jungle; the loud voice
Of triumph echoed, thro' that silent waste,
The death-whoop o'er their quarry. Her they led
Faint, hopeless, unresisting, to the rock;
That rock! late witness of her faith, and more
Than Roman valour! Every leaf was still
In the mute forest; on the umbrageous bank
There was no sound, save of the ceaseless flood
That foam'd against the granite, where her foot
First trod the stone. The deed, the damning deed,
Was done in silence. On that rock they scourged
The wife, the mother, while her innocent blood
Fell drop by drop,—reeking to Heaven, which saw
And yet withheld its thunder. Merciful God,
And those were Christians! Those had press'd the cup
Of thy salvation! with their bloody rites
Mingling thy praise, and casting on thy name
The curse of their own hellish outrage! This,
This weak and helpless woman, had no guide
But thy wide book of nature, from each page
Breathing the voice of love; and yet she trod

The steps of our great Savior, like a lamb
Led to the sacrifice, thro' pious love
For those her little ones. Will not her blood,
Spilt by thy hoary priests, rise against Spain
E'en to thy thunderous threshold? and the stain,
Fixt on that granite, like a furnace glow
Unexpiated in thy day of wrath!

    Once more chain'd down and bleeding, in that barque
She sees her hard oppressors plough their way
Thro' Temi's winding[28] and the auxiliar course
Of Tuamini to the Lusian bounds
Where stands remote Javita. There forlorn
She chews the bread of grief; but high resolve
Still nerves her courage, unextinguish'd hope.

    O fell tormentors, think ye to have quell'd
That spring unquenchable of holy love
Which fires the mother, while her infant brood
Pines in captivity! Floods, torrents, wastes,
And fearfullest vicissitudes of clime,
Unheeded vanish from the thought of her,
Who seeks home, husband, children. Long she watch'd
Occasion meet for flight, thro' pathless tracts
Deem'd unimaginable. No foot of man
Girded in fittest season for such toil
Had e'er traversed them. Weak, alone, uncheer'd,
She, while rains pour'd their deluge, and the brakes
Yielded no fruit, committed her frail strength
To God and to the desert. Night and day
Wading or swimming, torn by bristled cords
Which serpent-like around her wound their folds,
Defying toil and famine, still she press'd
To one dear goal, her children's prison; fed
With loathsome insects, gathered from the stem
Of barren trees, that knit their cumbrous arms.
Nor ceased the while that lesser plague, blood-fed
Zancudoes,[29] and the countless winged tribes,
Morning and eve and in noon's sultry hour
Successive, trumpeting their endless war:
And oft, when twilight's shadows were abroad,
High on some tortuous bough, with obscene grin,

She saw (or dream'd she saw) the man-like form
Of hairy savage, the wild's dreaded fiend,
In whose rude haunts, tho' scaped from human wrong,
Worse rape might seize her, brutish violence.
Before, around, unbounded forests rose,
Waters and woods illimitably stretch'd;
But Nature's might was stronger in the breast
Of one lone woman, than in all her works
Gloriously array'd in that wide solitude.

　　She reach'd Fernando's threshold; and, first seen,
A vengeful spectre deem'd, found way unblench'd
To her own innocents, and sunk foredone
In that last, fondest, loveliest embrace.
They tore her from her children, unappeased,
And steel'd by bigot zeal. From the sweet trance
Aroused to chains, serene her holy judge
She fronts, and thus with fearless majesty:

　　"I stand not here in judgment, haughty priest!
Nature forbids. Against a mother's love,
Against a wife's firm faith there is no law,
Not e'en to fellest nations gorged with flesh
Of mangled captives. Whence should we adore
Thy Deity, who mew'd, like one infirm,[30]
In that low fane, sends forth his ministers
To deeds of pitiless rape? Our God bestows
Harvest and summer fruits, chaining the winds
Which never lash our groves. Ye bend the knee
To the carved crucifix in temples wrought
By human hands; ye lift the hymn of praise
By torches' glare at noonday: but the God
We serve, best honor'd by the glorious ray
Of his great luminary, dwells not here
Prison'd midst walls, frail work of mortal skill.
We worship him abroad, under the vault
Of his own heaven; yon star-paved firmament,
The wilderness, the flood, the wreathed clouds
That float from those far mountains robed in mist,
The summits unapproach'd, untouch'd by time,
Snow-clad, are his; too vast to be confined
He fills his works. Bow ye the trembling knee

To your own idols and that murd'rous law
Which bids you seize a mother's callow brood
In hour of peace! The Carib doth not this,
The man-devouring Cabre![31] Are ye slaves
To the dread spirit of ill who wars with God,
Iolokiamo, fellest foe to man?
If there be one great Being, who hears our prayer,
When that sonorous trump[32] (which but to view
Were death to woman) thro' each leafy glade
Ten leagues aloof sends forth the voice of praise,
O tremble at his wrath! My little ones,
If e'er, to bliss restored, ye reach your sire's
Loved hut, tell him I live but while the hope
Of freedom and reunion with my own
Leaves life its worth. That lost, I welcome death."

    She ceased; and, had one heart midst all that crew
Beat worthy of its Savior, not in vain
Had spoke that proud appeal. Relentless chains
Are thrown on her worn limbs. Again they waft
Her bound, up ceaseless waters, far away
To Esmeralda, by the sparkling foot
Of Cerro Duïda's huge precipice,
Restrain'd with iron there, in guarded cell
Confined, her eye dwells fixt upon the flood
Of Oroonoko hurrying to the walls
Where rest immured her children. Scorn'd, the food
Lies at her feet. She speaks not, sad and stern.
She had braved famine in the desert, now
She woos it. Death in most abhorred guise,
By frightful inanition, with its train
Of loathsome and disgusting sympathies,
Smiles to her fancy; Death, her comforter.
She views the stream, as who, in burning climes
Where reigns the calenture, misled by love
Of his dear native meadows and the green
Delicious landscape, dreams of leafy glades
Umbrageous, sparkling with fresh morning dew,
Midst the calm ocean fever-struck, and dies
In that sweet error, sinking in the wave
As on a couch of herbage. She, deceived,
Sees in that flood, as fancy fires her brain,

Her hut, her husband, her blithe boys, and those
Two ravish'd innocents, from prison freed
To share that last delight. Her hollow cheek,
Foreshowing death's approach, wears yet a mien
Of such ecstatic rapture, that her eye
Seems lit by saintlike bliss. Silent and still,
As life beat slow and faint, she look'd away
Her soul upon the waters, and it pass'd
In that illusive dream without a sigh.

    Peace rest upon her ashes! May the God,
Who sent His Own to gather his stray'd flock
And light the path to heaven, forgive her what
She knew not! and, by his all-saving power,
Guide her to living streams, there to abide
With her beloved by mercy's hand upraised,
Where want, and sorrow, and force shall never come,
Nor voice of her oppressors! May the wilds
Where those foul deeds were wrought, erewhile resound
To purer hymns of praise, and social love
In that huge continent exalt to heaven
Christ's worthiest temple, deck'd with freedom's crown!

Notes

1. *Uniana.* "The northernmost of the great cataracts of the Oroonoko is the only one bounded on each side by lofty mountains. The left bank of the river is generally lower, but makes part of a plane which rises again west of Atures toward the Peak of Uniana, a pyramid nearly three thousand feet high, and placed on a wall of rock with steep slopes. The situation of this solitary peak in the plain contributes to render its aspect more imposing and majestic."—*Humboldt's Personal Narrative*, vol. V, p. 43.

2. *On either front*, &c. "Near Atures the old trees were decorated with beautiful orchideas, yellow bannisterias, blue-flowered bignonias, peperomias, arums and pothoses. A single trunk displays a greater variety of vegetable forms, than an extensive space of ground contains in our countries. Close to the parasite plants peculiar to burning climates, we observed, not without surprize, in the centre of the torrid zone, and near the level of the sea, mosses resembling those of Europe."—*Humb. P. N.*, vol. V, p. 49.
   "On quitting the village of Turmero (near Caraccas) we discover a single tree, the famous *zamang del Guayre*, known throughout the province for the enormous extent of its branches, which form a hemispheric head five hundred and seventy-six feet in circumference. The zamang is a fine species of mimosa, the tortuous branches of which are divided by bifurcation. Its delicate and tender foliage displayed itself agreeably in the azure of the sky. We stopped a long time under this vegetable roof. The trunk of the zamang del Guayre which is found on the road from Turmero to Maracay is only

sixty feet high and nine thick; but its real beauty consists in the form of its head. The branches extend like an immense umbrella, and bend toward the ground, from which they remain at an uniform distance of twelve or fifteen feet. The circumference of this head is so regular, that having traced different diameters, I found them one hundred and ninety-two and one hundred and eighty-six feet. One side of the tree was entirely stripped of its foliage, owing to the drought, and on the other side there remained at once leaves and flowers. Tillandsias, lorantheæ, cactus, pitahayas, and other parasite plants, cover its branches and crack the bark. The inhabitants of these villages, but particularly the Indians, hold in veneration the zamang del Guayre, which the first conquerors found almost in the same state in which it now remains. Since it has been observed with attention, no change has appeared in its thickness or height. This zamang tree must be at least as old as the Oratava dragon tree (*in Teneriffe*). There is something solemn and majestic in the aspect of aged trees, and the violation of these monuments of nature is severely punished in countries that are destitute of monuments of art. We heard with satisfaction that the present proprietor of the zamang had brought an action against a farmer, who had had the temerity to cut off a branch. The cause was tried, and the tribunal condemned the farmer. We find near Turmero and the Hacienda de Cura other zamangs, the trunks of which are larger than that of Guayre, but their hemispherical head is not of equal extent."—*Humb. P. N.*, vol. IV, p. 116.

3. *Atures' fall.* "It remains for me to speak of the rapids of Atures, which are found in a part of the valley where the bed of the river, deeply ingulfed, has almost inaccessible banks. It was only in a very few spots that we could enter into the Oroonoko to bathe between two cataracts, in coves where the waters have eddies of little velocity. Persons who have dwelt in the Alps, the Pyrenees, or even the Cordilleras, so celebrated for the fractures and the vestiges of destruction which they display at every step, can scarcely figure to themselves from a simple narration, the state of the bed of the river. It is traversed, in an extent of more than five miles, by innumerable dikes of rock that form so many natural dams, so many barriers like those of the Dnieper, which the ancients designated by the name of *Phragmoi.* The space between the rocky dikes of the Oroonoko is filled with islands of different dimensions; some hilly, divided into several paps, and two or three hundred toises in length, others small, low, and like simple shoals. These islands divide the river into a number of torrents that boil up as they break against the rocks; they are all furnished with *jaguas* and *cucuritos* with plumy leaves, and seem a mass of palm trees rising amid the foaming surface of the waters. The river is every where ingulfed in caverns, and in one of those caverns we heard the water roll at once over our heads and beneath our feet."—*Humb. P. N.*, vol. V, p. 53–55.

"The cataracts of Atures and Maypures are the only cataracts which, situate in the equinoctial region of the New World, are decorated with the noble growth of palm trees. At all seasons they exhibit the aspect of real cascades."—*Humb. P. N.*, vol. V, p. 58.

"When this noise (the noise of the cataracts of Atures and Maypures) is heard in the plain that surrounds the mission, at the distance of more than a league, you seem to be near a coast skirted by reefs and breakers. The noise is three times as loud by night as by day, and gives an inexpressible charm to these solitary scenes. What can be the cause of this encreased intensity of sound in a desert, where nothing seems to interrupt the silence of nature?" &c.—*Ib.,* vol. V, p. 67.

"The calm of the atmosphere, and the tumultuous movement of the waters, produce a contrast peculiar to this zone. Here no breath of wind ever agitated the foliage, no cloud veils the splendor of the azure vault of heaven. A great mass of light is diffused in the air, on the earth strewn with plants with glossy leaves, and on the bed of the river, as far as the eye can reach."—*Ib.*, vol. V, p. 139.

"The *raudal* (rapid) of Maypures is easier to pass than that of Atures. To take in at one view the grand character of these stupendous scenes, the spectator must be stationed on the little mountain of Manimi, a granitic ridge that rises from the Savannah. We often ascended this mountain, for we were never weary of the view of this astonishing spectacle, concealed in one of the most remote corners of the earth. Arrived at the summit of the rock, the eye suddenly takes in a sheet of foam, extending a whole mile. Enormous masses of stone, black as iron, issue from its bosom. Some are paps grouped in pairs, like basaltic hills; others resemble towers, strong castles, and ruined buildings. Their gloomy tint contrasts with the silvery splendor of the foam. Every rock, every islet is covered with vigorous trees, collected in clusters. At the foot of those paps, far as the eye can reach, a thick vapor is suspended over the river, and through this whitish fog the tops of the lofty palm trees shoot up. What name shall we give to these majestic plants? I suppose, &c. The leafy plume of this palm tree has a brilliant lustre, and rises almost straight toward the sky. At every hour of the day the sheet of foam displays different aspects."—*Humb. P. N.*, vol. V, p. 137. "The river is 800 toises broad above the cataracts."—*Ib.*, vol. V, p. 130.

4. *Fire-plumed birds.* The cock of the rock, or rock manakin, with splendid orange colored plumage.

"We ventured to pass in our canoe through the latter half of the Raudal of Atures. We landed here and there to climb upon the rocks, which, like narrow dikes, joined the islands to one another. Sometimes the waters precipitate themselves over the dikes, sometimes they fall within them with a hollow noise. A considerable portion of the Oroonoko was dry, because the river had found an issue by subterraneous caverns. In these solitary haunts the rock manakin, with gilded plumage, (pipra rupicola,) one of the most beautiful birds of the tropics, builds its nest. The Raudalito of Carucari is caused by an accumulation of enormous blocks of granite. These blocks are piled together in such a manner as to form spacious caverns. We entered one of these caverns. The spot displayed one of the most extraordinary scenes of nature that we had contemplated on the banks of the Oroonoko. The river rolled its waters turbulently over our heads. It seemed as if it were the sea dashing against reefs of rocks: but at the entrance of the cavern we could remain dry beneath a large sheet of water that precipitated itself in an arch from above the barrier. In other cavities, deeper but less spacious, the rock was pierced by the effect of successive filtrations. We saw columns of water, eight or nine feet broad, descend from the top of the vault and find an issue by clefts that seemed to communicate at great distances with each other."—*Humb. P. N.*, vol. V, p. 630.

5. *Living lamps.* "An innumerable multitude of insects spread a reddish light on the ground, loaded with plants and resplendent with these living and moving fires, as if the stars of the firmament had sunk down on the savannah. On quitting the cavern, we stopped several times to admire the beauty of this singular scene."—*Humb. P. N.*, vol. V, p. 623.

6. *Lianas.* Liana, *liane* in French, is the general name for twining or trailing plants which require support. The same extensive signification appears to be given by our colonists to the word *vine*, bind-weed having a more confined application; a word exactly analogous to liana is wanting in our language.

7. *Ceiba.* Bombax ceiba. Silk cotton tree. A tree of the first magnitude, with five-fingered leaves, somewhat resembling those of the horse-chesnut, and very large solitary white flowers.

8. *The mother's rock.* "Before we reach the confluence of the river Temi, a granitic hummock that rises on the western bank (of the Atabapo) near the mouth of the Guasacavi fixed our attention; it is called the rock of the Guahiba woman, or the Rock of the Mother, Piedra della Madre. If in these solitary scenes man scarcely leaves behind him any trace of his existence, it is doubly humiliating for a European to see perpetuated by the name of a rock, by one of those imperishable monuments of nature, the remembrance of the moral degradation of our species, and the contrast between the virtue of a savage and the barbarism of civilized man. In 1797, the missionary of San Fernando had led his Indians to the banks of the Rio Guaviare, on one of those hostile excursions, which are alike prohibited by religion and the Spanish laws. They found in an Indian hut, a Guahiba mother with three children, one or two of whom were still infants. They were occupied in preparing the flour of cassava. Resistance was impossible; the father was gone to fish and the mother tried in vain to flee with her children. Scarcely had she reached the savannah, when she was seized by the Indians of the mission, who go to *hunt men,* like the Whites and the Negroes in Africa. The mother and her children were bound, and dragged to the banks of the river. The monk, seated in his boat, waited the issue of an expedition, of which he partook not the danger. Had the mother made too violent a resistance, the Indians would have killed her, for every thing is permitted when they go to the conquest of souls (*à la conquista espiritual*), and it is children in particular they seek to capture, in order to treat them in the mission as *poitos,* or slaves of the Christians. The prisoners were carried to Fernando, in the hope that the mother would be unable to find her way back by land. Far from those children who had accompanied their father on the day in which she had been carried off, this unhappy woman showed signs of the deepest despair. She attempted to take back to her family the children who had been snatched away by the missionary; and fled with them repeatedly from the village of San Fernando, but the Indians never failed to seize her anew; and the missionary, after having caused her to be mercilessly beaten, took the cruel resolution of separating the mother from the two children who had been carried off with her. She was conveyed alone towards the missions of the Rio Negro, going up the Atabapo. Slightly bound, she was seated at the bow of the boat, ignorant of the fate that awaited her; but she judged by the direction of the sun, that she was removing farther and farther from her hut and native country. She succeeded in breaking her bonds, threw herself into the water, and swam to the left bank of the Atabapo. The current carried her to a shelf of rock which bears her name to this day. She landed and took shelter in the woods, but the President of the Missions ordered the Indians to row to the shore, and follow the traces of the Guahiba. In the evening she was brought back. Stretched upon the rock (*la piedra de la Madre*) a cruel punishment was inflicted on her with those straps of manatee leather, which serve for whips in that country, and with which the Alcades are always furnished. This unhappy woman, her hands tied behind her back with strong stalks of Mavacure, was then dragged to the mission of Javita. She was then thrown into one of the caravanseras that are called *Casa del Rey.* It was the rainy season, and the night was profoundly dark. Forests till then believed to be impenetrable separated the mission of Javita from that of San Fernando, which was twenty-five leagues distant in a straight line. No other path is known but that of the

rivers; no man ever attempted to go by land from one village to another, were they only a few leagues apart. But such difficulties do not stop a mother who is separated from her children. Her children are at San Fernando de Atabapo; she must find them again, she must execute the project of delivering them from the hands of the Christians, of bringing them back to their father on the banks of the Guaviare. The Guahiba was carelessly guarded in the Caravansera. Her arms being wounded, the Indians of Javita had loosened her bonds, unknown to the Missionary and the Alcades. She succeeded by the help of her teeth in breaking them entirely, disappeared during the night; and at the fourth rising sun was seen at the mission of San Fernando, hovering around the hut where her children were confined. 'What that woman performed,' added the missionary who gave us this sad narrative, 'the most robust Indian would not have ventured to undertake.' She traversed the woods at a season when the sky is constantly covered with clouds and the sun during the whole day appears but for a few minutes. Did the course of the waters direct her way? The inundations of the rivers forced her to go far from the banks of the main stream, through the midst of woods where the movement of the waters was almost imperceptible. How often must she have been stopped by the thorny lianas, that form a net-work around the trunks they entwine! How often must she have swam across the rivulets that run into the Atabapo! This unfortunate woman was asked how she had sustained herself during four days. She said, that, exhausted with fatigue, she could find no other nourishment than those great black ants called *vachacos,* which climb the trees in long bands, to suspend on them their resinous nests. We pressed the missionary to tell us, whether the Guahiba had peacefully enjoyed the happiness of remaining with her children; and if any repentance had followed this excess of cruelty. He would not satisfy our curiosity, but at our return from the Rio Negro we learnt that the Indian mother was not allowed time to cure her wounds, but was again separated from her children, and sent to one of the missions of the Upper Oroonoko. Here she died, refusing all kind of nourishment, as the savages do in great calamities. Such is the remembrance annexed to this fatal rock, to the Piedra de la Madre."—Humb. *P. N.,* vol. V, p. 233.

9. *San Fernando.* "San Fernando de Atabapo is placed near the confluence of three great rivers, the Guaviare, the Atabapo, and the Oroonoko."—*Ib.,* vol. V, p. 200. "The missionary of San Fernando has the title of President of the missions of the Oroonoko. The twenty-six ecclesiastics settled on the banks of the Rio Negro, the Cassiquiare, the Atabapo, the Caura, and the Oroonoko, are under his orders."—*Ib.,* vol. V, p. 200.

"We found at San Fernando, as well as at the neighbouring villages of San Balthasar and Javita, pretty parsonage-houses, covered by *lianas,* and surrounded by gardens. The tall trunks of the pirijao palms formed in our eyes the most beautiful ornament of these plantations. In our walks, the President of the Mission gave us an animated account of his incursions on the river Guaviare. He related to us how much these journeys, undertaken 'for the conquest of souls,' are desired by the Indians of the mission. All, even women and old men, take part in them. On the vain pretext of recovering neophytes who have deserted the village, children above eight and ten years of age are carried off and distributed amongst the Indians as serfs."—*Ib.,* vol. V, p. 215.

10. *Turbid Guaviare, &c.* "The Rio Paragua (or Upper Oroonoko), that part of the Oroonoko which you go up to the east of the mouth of the Guaviare, has clearer, more transparent, and purer water than the part of the Oroonoko below San Fernando. The waters of the Guaviare, on the contrary, are white and turbid."—*Ib.,* vol. V, p. 221.

11. *Parima.* "In the Oroonoko it is not near the origin of the river that the great cataracts are found. After a tranquil course of more than 160 leagues from the little *Raudal* of Guaharibos, east of Esmeralda, as far as the mountains of Sipapu, the river, augmented by the waters of the Jao, the Ventuari, the Atabapo, and the Guaviare, suddenly changes its primitive direction from east to west, and runs from south to north; and in crossing the land-strait (formed by the Cordilleras of the Andes of New Grenada and the Cordillera of Parima), in the plains of Meta, meets the advanced buttresses of the Cordillera of Parima. This obstacle is the cause of cataracts, &c."—*Ib.,* vol. V, p. 42.

12. *Mournful gulph.*—Golfo Triste.

13. *Snowy Bird.* The carunculated chatterer.—*Latham Synopsis,* vol. II, p. 98, plate 40. Cotinga blanc.—*Brisson* and *Buffon.* "These birds inhabit Cayenne and Brazil, and are said to have a very loud voice, to be heard half-a-league off, which is composed of two syllables, *in, an,* uttered with a drawling kind of tone, though some have compared it to the sound of a bell. The Brazilian name is Guira-panga."—*Latham.* It is called Campanero, or bell-man, and delights in lonely parts of the forest.

14. *Second forest in mid-air.* "Clusters of palm-trees (of the species called *el Cucurito*), the leaves of which, curled like feathers, rise majestically at an angle of seventy degrees, are dispersed amidst trees with horizontal branches, and their bare trunks, like columns of 100 or 120 feet high, shoot up into the air, and appearing distinctly against the sky, resemble a forest planted upon another forest. When the moon was going down behind the mountains of Uniana, her reddish disk was hidden behind the pinnated foliage of the palm-trees, and again appeared in the aërial zone that separates the two forests."—*Humb. P. N.,* vol. V, p. 46.

15. *The wailing winds Stir not thro' that wide forest, &c.* "When you have passed the latitude of three degrees north and approach the equator, you seldom have an opportunity of observing the sun and stars. It rains almost the whole year, and the sky is constantly cloudy. As the breeze is not felt in this immense forest of Guyana, and the refluent polar-currents do not reach it, the column of air that reposes in this wooden zone is not renewed by drier strata."—*Ib.,* vol. V, p. 248.

16. *Surcharged with fruit, &c.* The fine pirijao palm bears fruit like peaches in flavour.—*Ib.,* vol. V, p. 239.

17. *Palm-string nets.* The nets of the Indians are made of the petioles of palm leaves.—*Humb.*

18. *Huge dolphins.* "In the thickest part of the forest we were astonished by an extraordinary noise. On beating the bushes a shoal of fresh water dolphins four feet long surrounded our boat. These animals had concealed themselves beneath the branches of a fromager or bombax ceiba. They fled across the inundated forest, throwing out those spouts of compressed air and water which have given them in every language the name of *blowers.* How singular was this spectacle in the middle of the land, three or four hundred leagues from the mouths of the Oroonoko and the Amazon!"—*Humb. P. N.,* vol. V, p. 240.

19. *Parrot-flowers.* Heliconia Psittacorum, which bears scarlet and black flowers. The leaves of some species of Heliconia and other Scitamineous plants furnish covering for the Indian huts.

20. *Jaguar.* The South American tiger. "The jaguars, or tigers, come into the village of Atures and devour the pigs of the poor Indians."—*Humb. P. N.,* vol. V, p. 76. The name of Boa for the largest snakes is universally known.

21. *Its dark wave.* "The waters of the Oroonoko are turbid and loaded with earthy matter; those of the Atabapo are pure, agreeable to the taste, without any trace of smell, brownish by reflected, and of a pale yellow by transmitted light."—*Humb. P. N.,* vol. V, p. 227. "What proves the extreme purity of the black waters is their limpidity; their transparency, and the clearness with which they reflect the images and colors of surrounding objects. The smallest fish are visible in them at the depth of twenty or thirty feet; and most commonly the bottom of the river may be discovered, which is not a yellowish or brownish mud, like the colour of the water, but a quartzose and granitic sand of dazzling whiteness. Nothing can be compared with the beauty of the banks of the Atabapo. Loaded with plants, among which rise the palms, crowned with leafy plumes, the banks are reflected in the waters; and the verdure of the reflected image seems to have the same vivid hue as the object itself directly seen, the surface of the fluid is so homogeneous, smooth, and destitute of suspended sand and decomposed organic matter which roughens and streaks the surface of less limpid rivers."—*Humb. P. N.,* vol. V, p. 218.

22. *Cerro Duïda.* The river Cassiquiare, according to Humboldt, is as broad as the Rhine, or three times broader than the Seine opposite the Jardin des Plantes, and, running out of the Upper Oroonoko into the Rio Negro, forms a wonderful natural junction between the immense rivers Oroonoko and Amazon, which flow in different directions, the Rio Negro falling into the Amazon.—"Opposite the point (of the Upper Oroonoko) where the bifurcation takes place, the granitic group of Duïda rises in an amphitheatre on the right bank of the river. This mountain, which the missionaries call a volcano, is nearly 8000 feet high. Perpendicular on the South and West, it has an aspect of solemn greatness: its summit is bare and stony; but wherever its less steep acclivities are covered with mould, vast forests appear suspended on its flanks. At the foot of Duïda is placed the mission of Esmeralda, a little hamlet with eighty inhabitants; surrounded by a lovely plain, bathed by rills of black but limpid water."—*Humb. P. N.,* vol. V, p. 502. "A mineralogical error gave celebrity to Esmeralda. The granites of Cerro Duïda and Maraguaca contain in open veins fine rock crystals, some of them of great transparency, others colored by chlorit or blended with actinote, and they were taken for diamonds and emeralds."—*Ib.,* p. 506.

23. *The Southern Cross.* A conspicuous constellation in the southern hemisphere.

24. *Savage form.* "It was among the cataracts that we began first to hear of the hairy man of the woods, called *salvaje,* that carries off women, constructs huts, and sometimes eats human flesh. The natives and missionaries have no doubt of the existence of this anthropomorphous monkey, which they singularly dread. Father Gili gravely relates the history of a lady in the town of Carlos (in Venezuela) who much praised the gentle character and attentions of the man of the woods. She lived several years with one in great domestic harmony, and only requested some hunters to take her back 'because she was tired, she and her children (a little hairy also), of living far from the church and the sacraments.'"—*Humb. P. N.,* p. 81. "We will not admit, with a Spanish author, that the fable of the man of the woods was invented by the artifice of Indian women, who pretended to have been carried off, when they had been long absent from their husbands, we rather counsel travellers who shall visit the missions of the Oroonoko, to continue our researches on the *salvaje* or *great devil* of the woods; and examine whether it be some unknown species of bear, or some very rare monkey analogous

to the simia chiropotes, or simia satanas, that can have given rise to such singular tales."—*Ib.*, p. 84.

The absurdity of Humboldt's suggestion that the *salvaje* might be an unknown species of bear is too great to be passed over in silence. The accounts of this creature and its violence to women are exactly consistent with the habits of the African ourang-outang, and it cannot reasonably be doubted that they are referable to some analogous species of monkey. He adds, "We were every where blamed, in the most cultivated class of society, for being the only persons to doubt the existence of the great anthropomorphous monkey of America."—*Ib.*, p. 82.

25.   *The nut's ponderous fall.* The fall of the great nuts of the palm, called the juvia tree (*bertholletia excelsa*), which contain the triangular nuts known in England by the name of Para nuts, is mentioned by Humboldt as very dangerous to those who walk in the forests.

26.   *The tiger's rock, &c.* A granitic pass known by the name of Piedra del Tigre. "This solitary rock is only sixty feet high, yet it enjoys great celebrity in these countries. A little to the South of the mountains of Sipapu, we reach the southern extremity of the chain of cataracts, which I proposed to call the Chain of Parima. The whole of the land extending from the mountains of Parima toward the river of Amazons, which is traversed by the Atabapo, the Cassiquiare, and the Rio Negro, is an immense plain, partly covered with forests and partly with grasses. Small rocks rise here and there like castles."—*Humb. P. N.*, vol. V, p. 227. "After having passed the rapids of Guarinuma, the Indians showed us, in the middle of the forest, on our right, the ruins of the mission of Mendaxari which has been long abandoned. On the East bank, near the little rock of Kemarumo, in the midst of Indian plantations, a gigantic Bombax Ceiba attracted our attention. This enormous effort of vegetation surprised us the more, as we had till then seen on the banks of the Atabapo only small trees with slender trunks."—*Ib.*, p. 228. "It was night when we arrived at the mission of San Balthasar. A Catalan missionary had planted a fine garden where the fig-tree of Europe was found in company with the persea, and the lemon tree with the mammee. The village was built with that regularity which in the North of Germany, and in protestant America, we find in the hamlets of the Moravian brethren."—*Ib.*, p. 230. "The ground from the mouth of the Guaviare constantly displays the same geological constitution. It is a vast granitic plain, in which from league to league the rock pierces the soil and forms not hillocks, but small masses that resemble pillars or ruined buildings."—*Ib.*, p. 242.

27.   *Trees that fringe the bank.* "The river Atabapo displays every where a peculiar aspect. You see nothing of its real banks formed by flat lands, eight or ten feet high: they are concealed by a row of palms and small trees with slender trunks, the roots of which are bathed by the waters. There are many crocodiles from the point where you quit the Oroonoko to the mission of San Fernando, and their presence indicates, as we have said above, that this part of the river belongs to the Rio Guaviare and not to the Atabapo. In the real bed of the river above the mission of San Fernando there are no longer any crocodiles: we find some bavas, a great many fresh water dolphins, but no manatees. We also seek in vain on those banks the thick-nosed tapir, the araguates or great howling monkeys, the Zamuro or vultur aura, and the crested pheasant. Enormous water-snakes, in shape resembling the boa, are unfortunately too common, and

are dangerous to the Indians who bathe. We saw them almost from the first day, swimming by the side of our canoe: they were at the most twelve or fourteen feet long."—
Humb. P. N., vol. V, p. 225.

"The night was beautiful, dark clouds passed from time to time over the zenith with
extreme rapidity. Not a breath of wind was felt in the lower strata of the atmosphere,
the breeze existed only at the height of a thousand toises."—*Ib.,* p. 226. "Unaccustomed
to those forests which are less inhabited by animals than those of the Oroonoko, we
were almost surprised no longer to hear the howlings of the monkeys. The dolphins or
toninas sported by the side of our boat. According to the relation of Mr. Colebrooke,
the delphinus Gangeticus, which is the freshwater porpoise of the ancient continent,
in the like manner accompanies the boats that go up toward Benares."—*Ib.,* p. 227.

28. *Temi's winding.* "Above the mouth of the Guasucavi we entered the Rio Temi."—*Ib.,* p.
    238. "We remained in the bed of the river till day, afraid of losing ourselves amongst
    the trees. At sun-rise we again entered the inundated forest, to avoid the force of the
    current. Arrived at the junction of the Temi with another river, the Tuamini, the waters
    of which are equally black, we followed the latter toward the south-west. This direction
    led us to the mission of Javita, which is founded on the banks of the Tuamini."— *Humb.
    P. N.,* vol. V, p. 243.

29. *Zancudoes.* "After a few minutes repose, you feel yourself stung by Zancudoes, another
    species of gnat with very long legs. The Zancudo, the proboscis of which contains a
    sharp-pointed sucker, causes the most acute pain and a swelling that remains many
    weeks."—*Ib.,* p. 94. "At fixed and invariable hours, in the same season and the same
    latitude, the air is peopled with new inhabitants, and in a zone where the barometer
    becomes a clock, where every thing proceeds with such admirable regularity, we might
    guess blindfold the hour of the day or night by the hum of the insects, and by their
    stings, the pain of which differs according to the nature of the poison that each insect
    deposits in the wound."—*Ib.,* p. 96.

30. *Like one infirm.* "The Indians of the upper Oroonoko, the Atabapo, the Inirida, have no
    other worship than that of the powers of nature. They call the good principle Cachi-
    mana; it is the Manitou, or Great Spirit, that regulates the seasons and favours the
    harvests. There is an evil principle, Iolokiamo, less powerful, but more artful, and in
    particular more active. The Indians of the forest, when they visit occasionally the mis-
    sions, conceive with difficulty the idea of a temple or an image. — 'These good people,'
    said the missionary, 'like only processions in the open air. When I last celebrated the
    patron-festival of my village, that of Antonio, the Indians of Inirida were present at the
    mass. 'Your God,' said they to me, 'keeps himself shut up in a house as if he were old
    and infirm; ours is in the forest, in the fields, and on the mountains of Sipapo, whence
    the rains come.'"—*Humb. P. N.,* vol. V, p. 272.

31. *The man-devouring Cabre.* The Cabres, or Caveres, celebrated for their long wars with
    the Caribs, are much addicted to anthropophagy.—*Ib.,* p. 13.

32. *Sonorous trump.* "There are but a small number of these sacred trumpets. The most an-
    ciently celebrated is that upon a hill near the confluence of the Tomo and the Guainia.
    It is pretended that it is heard at once on the banks of the Tuamini and at the mission
    of San Miguel de Davipe, a distance of ten leagues"—"Women are not permitted to see
    this marvellous instrument, and are excluded from all ceremonies of this worship. If a
    woman have the misfortune to see this trumpet, she is put to death without mercy."—
    Ib., p. 274. "The trumpets are made of baked earth, and called Botutos."—*Ib.,* p. 232.

Chapter 8

SIMÓN BOLÍVAR

My Delirium on Chimborazo

1822

I was coming along, cloaked in the mantle of Iris, from the place where the torrential Orinoco pays tribute to the God of waters. I had visited the enchanted springs of Amazonia, straining to climb up to the watchtower of the universe. I sought the tracks of La Condamine and Humboldt, following them boldly. Nothing could stop me. I reached the glacial heights, and the atmosphere took my breath away. No human foot had ever blemished the diamond crown placed by Eternity's hands on the sublime temples of this lofty Andean peak. I said to myself: Iris's rainbow cloak has served as my banner. I've carried it through the infernal regions. It has ploughed rivers and seas and risen to the gigantic shoulders of the Andes. The terrain had leveled off at the feet of Colombia, and not even time could hold back freedom's march. The war goddess Bellona has been humbled by the brilliance of Iris. So why should I hesitate to tread on the ice-white hair of this giant of the earth? Indeed I shall! And caught up in a spiritual tremor I had never before experienced, and which seemed to me a kind of divine frenzy, I left Humboldt's tracks behind and began to leave my own marks on the eternal crystals girding Chimborazo. I climb as if driven by this frenzy, faltering only when my head grazes the summit of the firmament. At my feet the threshold of the abyss beckons.

A feverish delirium suspends my mental faculties. I feel as if I were aflame with a strange, higher fire. It was the God of Colombia taking possession of me.

Suddenly, Time appears to me as an ancient figure weighed down by the clutter of the ages: scowling, bent over, bald, his skin lined, scythe in hand. ...

"I am the father of the centuries, the arcanum of fame and secret knowledge. My mother was Eternity. Infinity sets the limits of my empire. There is no tomb for me, because I am more powerful than Death. I behold the past, I see

Simón Bolívar, *El Libertador: Writings of Simón Bolívar*, ed. David Bushnell, trans. Frederick H. Fornoff. Copyright © 2003 by Oxford University Press, Inc. Used by permission of Oxford University Press, Inc.

the future, and the present passes through my hands. Oh, child, man, ancient, hero, why such vanity? Do you think your Universe matters? That you exalt yourself merely by scaling one of the atoms of creation? Do you imagine that the instants you call centuries are enough to fathom my mysteries? Do you believe you have seen the Holy Truth? Are you mad enough to presume that your actions have value in my eyes? Compared to my brother, Infinity, everything is less than the tiniest point."

Overcome by a sacred awe, I answered: "Oh, Time, how can a wretched mortal who has climbed so high not simply vanish in thin air? I have surpassed all men in fortune, because I have risen to be the head of them all. I stand high above the earth with my feet; I grasp the eternal with my hands; I feel the infernal prisons boiling beneath my footsteps; I stand gazing at the glittering stars beside me, the infinite suns; I measure without astonishment the space that encloses all matter, and in your face I read the History of the past and the thoughts of Destiny."

"Observe," he said to me, "learn, hold in your mind what you have seen. Draw for the eyes of those like you the image of the physical Universe, the moral Universe. Do not conceal the secrets heaven has revealed to you. Tell men the truth."

The apparition disappeared.

Absorbed, frozen in time, so to speak, I lay lifeless for a long time, stretched out on that immense diamond serving as my bed. Finally, the tremendous voice of Colombia cries out to me. I come back to life, sit up, open my heavy eyelids with my own hands. I become a man again, and write down my delirium.

Illustration 8.1. Chimborazo, seen from the Plain of Tapia.

Chapter 9

ANDRÉS BELLO
Allocution to Poetry
1823

Fragments of a Poem entitled "América"

Divine Poetry,
you who dwell in solitude
and wrap your songs
in the silence of the shaded forest;
you who lived in the green grotto,
the mountain echoes your company.
Time it is to abandon Europe,
no lover of your native rusticity,
and turn your fancy to the great setting
unveiled by the New World.
There too heaven reveres the laurel
with which you crown excellence;
there too the blooming field,
the entangled forest, the twisting river
give colors galore to your brush;
and Zephyr gently stirs the roses;
stars gleaming bright
adorn the chariot of night;
and the king of the sky rises
between nacre-lined clouds
and a sweet little bill
warbles unlearned songs of love.

Anthology of Andrés Bello, trans. Barbara D. Huntley and Pilar Liria, ed. Pedro Grases, Washington, 1981. Copyright © Organization of American States. Reprinted with permission of the General Secretariat of the Organization of American States.

What care you, O rustic nymph,
for the pomp of royal palaces?
Will you too go with the courtesan crowd
to render the torpid incense of flattery?
You were not thus in your noblest days
when in man's infancy,
teacher of nations and kings,
you proclaimed the world's first laws.
Be not detained, O goddess,
by this region of wretchedness and light
where your ambitious rival, Philosophy,
submitting virtue to discretion,
has usurped your scepter;
where the crowned hydra threatens
to bring back the night of crime and barbary
to man enslaved by thought;
where freedom is vain delirium,
faith servility, greatness pomp,
culture corruption.
Take down from the withered oak
your sweet golden lyre where once
you sang to spellbound men
of meadows and flowers, the whisper
of dense wood, the peaceful
murmuring of the brook
the allure of nature's innocence.
And opening your restless wings
cross over the vast Atlantic
to another sky, another world,
another people, where the earth
is still in primitive array,
unsubdued by man,
and America, young bride of the Sun,
last daughter of the ancient Ocean,
breeds in her fertile breast
the wealth of every clime.

What dwelling awaits you? what peak,
what comely meadow, what replenished forest
shall be your home? What beach
shall first feel the tread
of your golden sandal? Where the river

that saw the heroes of Albion humbled,
where the blue pendons of Buenos Aires
now flutter, and proudly
bears the tribute of a hundred currents
down to the astounded sea? Or where the double crest
of the Ávila[1] breaks through the clouds
and the city of Losada[2] is reborn?
Or shall the valleys of Chile blessed
with their suave fruits and golden harvests,
where the innocence and candor
and hospitality of the Old World
blend with patriotism and valor,
smile upon you more, O Muse?
Or the city[3] shown the errant Aztecs[4]
by the eagle in the nopal,
with its soil of measureless ores
that almost sated Europe's greed?
The queen of the southern ocean
whose daughter's grace was Nature's dowry,
provides a haven under her mild sky
untouched by wind or rain.
Or will your home be the heights of Quito,
perched between white peaks,
listening to the roar of tempests at its feet,
with its clear air propitious
to your celestial inspirations?
Yet listen as the churning Bogotá
thunders its way
between walls of groomed rock,
and, wrapped in a cloud of rainbow mist,
boldly leaps towards the valleys
of the Magdalena.
Where memories of early days
await your lyre;
when Cundinamarca in sweet idleness
and native innocence gave easy sustenance
to her dwellers,
the first offspring of her generous breast,
before the curved plough broke the soil
or foreign vessel touched the distant shores.
Ambition had not yet stirred
the atrocious iron;

still undegenerate men
sought refuge in dark-roofed
forests and caves;
the land still had no master,
fields no fences, towns no wall.
Freedom flourished without law;
peace, contentment, joy abounded;
when a jealous Huitaca,[5]
goddess of the waters,
deluged the valley with the swollen
torrents of the Bogotá.
Some took refuge in the hills;
others were swallowed in the voracious abyss.
You shall chant the wrath of Nenqueteba,
child of the Sun,
at the havoc of his almost extinct race;
who parted the mountain with his scepter
to make a channel for the waves;
and the once vast lake of the Bogotá,
whose dominion reached from peak to peak,
scorned its prison and
pounding on its narrow banks
with mighty fury plunged through the gap.
You shall sing of Nenqueteba, the pious,
who gave laws, art, and religion
to the new nations,
after turning the naughty nymph
into the light of the night
and the silver moon first ploughed the Olympus.

Go extol the equatorial wonders;
sing of the sky made joyous
by the chorus of the stars,
where at once the dragon of the north
with its golden tail
encircles the north star,
and the dove of Arauco
dips its wings in the southern seas.
Grind your richest colors
and take your finest brushes
to portray the climes
preserved in pristine vigor

with which the omnipotent voice
swelled the earth freshly created
from the abyss of chaos
and covered it with vegetation and life.
Eternal forest, who dare name or number
the multitude that peoples your labyrinths
proudly boastful of their many forms
and heights and dress?
Silk-cotton trees, acacias, myrtles
intertwined, reeds, vines, grasses;
branches striving to reach the light
and the sun, in endless struggle;
the ground can ill contain so many roots.

O could you but take me, cherished Poetry,
to the shores of the Cauca
and let me inhale the gentle breath
of the eternal spring air
in its kingdom there!
O could I but carefree wander
along the shores of the Aragua
or, haply stretched under a palm tree on the plain,
watch in the heavens your four stars,
O Southern Cross, that measure the nocturnal hours
of the errant traveler
through the night's vast solitude.
Or see the trail of the firefly
cutting the gloam,
or hear from the far-off hostel
the sounds of the yaraví![6]

There will come a time
when an American Virgil
inspired by you, O Goddess,
will sing of the crops and cattle
of a land tamed by man
and the fruits of a region
beloved of Phoebus;
where cane bears sweet honey,
and the tuna bright carmine,
where cotton waves its snowy head,
and pineapple ripens its ambrosia;

the palm tree bears its varied abundance,
the naseberry its sweet buds,
the avocado its butter, the indigo brings forth its dye,
the banana tree droops under its sweet burden,
coffee concentrates the aroma of its white blossoms,
and the cacao jells its beans in purple urns.

*

    Yet, alas, would you rather chant the terror
of a merciless war, and depict hosts
hurrying to destruction, bent on filling the land
with mourning, to the beat of drums
that make every mother cow and tremble?
O if only you offered, land of mine,
less themes for songs of war!
What cities, what fields have not been deluged
with the blood of your sons and Spain's?
What wasteland has not fed human members
to the condor? What rustic homes
were spared the fury of civil strife?
But love of country worked no such
wonders in Rome or Sparta or Numancia.
Nor does any page of history give deeds
more glorious for your song, O Muse.
What province or man will earn your tribute
in your first hymn of praise?

Notes

1. Mountain near Caracas.
2. The founder of Caracas.
3. Mexico, founded by Aztecs, a native people of America.
4. American nation, founders of Mexico.
5. Huitaca, wife of Nenqueteba or Bochica, lawmaker of the muiscas. Humboldt, *Vues des Cordillères,* vol. 1.
6. Yaraví, melancholy music native to Peru and the Plains of Colombia.

Chapter 10

CARL RITTER
Letters
1824

17 September 1824

At nine o'clock it was now the time that I set out to visit my soirée at M. Arago's to which I had been invited. The customs are so mixed up here, that one just now goes to the gathering that one stays with until midnight. [...] Around eleven Alexander von Humboldt finally arrived and everyone looked forward to his stories and reports—as no one here observes things as he does, he has seen everything, he is already out at eight in the morning to make his excursions; he was just informed of the death of the king, he spoke with all the doctors, several of the best of the land, he was there at the viewing of the body, at the excesses which occurred in the palace, at the inquiries, he knows what happened in the circles of the ministers, in the family of the king, today he was in St. Germain, in Passy, with so many official persons, and he now returns with pockets filled, full of the most interesting anecdotes, which he plucked out with wit and whimsy; it was eleven thirty, we moved to the tea table; a stranger arrived bringing a leaflet by Chateaubriand, acquired in a dark alley, with *Le Roi est mort, vive le Roi*—it was read aloud, appraised, debated, it was past midnight, the conversation became even more animated, escalating until one o'clock, when suddenly everyone broke off and hurried home. At first I rode a distance with Humboldt, it was a splendid, starry, moonlit night, then I threw myself in my cabriolet [...] and hurried home, after one I retired.

Translation by Rex Clark and Oliver Lubrich, from Gustav Kramer, *Carl Ritter: ein Lebensbild nach seinem handschriftlichen Nachlaß dargestellt*, vol. 2 (Halle: Buchhandlung des Waisenhauses, 1864–1870), 185–186.

Chapter 11

ADELBERT VON CHAMISSO

The Rock of the Mother, or the Guahiba Indian

1828

(Humboldt: "Voyage aux régions équinoxiales."
Liv. 7. Ch. 22. Ed. 8. V. 7. p. 286)

In the place on the plains of that hot zone
    Where the Orinoko and the Amazon
    Their proud flow together run,
When rainy times their currents swell
    Inhospitable, inaccessible, awesome,
    Where jungle rises from the waves;
There the dreaded jaguar rules the wood,
    Crocodiles the flooded lea,
    And mosquito clouds darken the day.
Man arises, disappears without a trace
    A poor, thoughtless guest to rich,
    To mammoth, to unruly nature.
The missionary sews symbols of salvation
    High up on the river's bank, a spot
    That the free sons of the wild shy away from.
At Atabapo's bank there rises toward the sky,
    A stone, the Mother's Stone, likely familiar
    To the skipper who chose the spot to rest.
This is how our Humboldt learned it as well
    As he rode upon this current of the wilderness,
    Thirsty for knowledge and hungry for grand deeds.

Translation by Steven Sidore, from Adelbert von Chamisso, "Der Stein der Mutter oder der Guahiba-Indianerin," *Der Gesellschafter oder Blätter für Geist und Herz. Ein Volksblatt* (Berlin: Maurer, 1817–1850), vol. 12, no. 64 (21 April 1828), 317–318.

"The Mother's Stone? Tell me of it now:
    What bespeaks this stone with muted mouth?
    What memory should it possibly hold?"
All fell silent in the round,
    Only later, when to San Carlos they had come
    Did a missionary unveil the grisly lore:
"Once from San Fernando there came
    A raid seeking souls for the Holy Word
    And slaves to serve us as well.
Ministrations hard they do allow,
    The statutes of the Holy Order, for salvation,
    Let the heathens on the Guaviar be taken.
There where smoke from the shores arise,
    One, the padre, stayed praying in the boat
    Leaving the roughness for his men to do.
They overran, no guard or protector,
    A helpless dame; her man, sons at his side,
    Was likely chasing jaguars through the wood—
The fool had not thought of Christians;
    And so they bound the Guahiba mother
    And brought her in, her two small children too;
Resisting would have meant her death,
    Surrounded she was, left no room for flight;
    She was easily overpowered in her despair.
It was painful to her as scarce another
    Among the captured to gaze back unwavering
    As her native forest's rim fell away.
Estranged from her home, unknown
    In San Fernando, hardly were the binds free
    When, frantic, she sought to flee.
Swimming o'er the river, toward her ancestral land
    Her two young babes she sought to bring along;
    But she was chased and caught on opposing shore.
For this a hard penance she did pay;
    Yet still bloodied in form she tried again
    To return to the heathens' side;
And harder still the scourge was plied;
    Yet once again the deed was tried;
    Death or freedom her sole choice to make.
And so seemed to the missionary the best advice:
    Her children must be taken far away,
    That no shimmer of hope remain to her.

On the Rio Negro her doom was to be found.
    She was cast down bound, and the boat glided on
    Up the river, she spied the stars.
She felt not her own bitter need,
    She felt maternal love, the core of life,
    And her binds as well, and she wished for death.
The knots she broke with sudden burst of strength,
    There, where one sees the stone from the shore,
    And she hurled herself in the flow and swam—alas!
She was chased, captured, and cast
    Upon that stone, named now for the poor thing,
    Whose blood of anguish flecked its face.
She was whipped, lashed without mercy,
    Thrown in the boat for the trip's remainder
    With her arms tied firm behind her back.
And so she reached Javita;
    Wounded, bound, barely able to move,
    Stored at night in a boarding house.
It was the rainy time, it must be remembered,
    And in rainy times, even the boldest man
    Dares not wager the next town o'er country roads;
Where without banks the rivers run to the wood,
    Woods that, taxed of all nourishment,
    Can barely offer ants to feed the hungry;
Where, for those pushing into the jungle's heart,
    Even should they dare the jaguar's path,
    And should they manage to break a trail,
Would find themselves sunk into a shadow realm,
    Fully abandoned by the starless sky,
    Like a blind man lost without his guide.
That which even the brashest hunter to think
    Would blanch, that was what the women performed;
    Nigh thirty miles the stretch runs.
Just how she freed herself the binds,
    That is known to the darkness alone,
    But sometime in the night she was gone;
San Fernando she reached on the fourth morn
    Wringing her hands keenly around the house,
    Where her children lay, and her thoughts with them."
"O tell me, let loose the words, that we may know
    That this heroine maternal, not again, not again,
    So inhumanely from her children was torn!"

But mute he stayed, his eyes cast down,
    And lost in silent prayer he seemed. Words no more
    Would he find, however his asker beseeched them.
Yet what was not spoken there, Humboldt
    In his book let gruesome resound;
    Reports he elsewhere heard.
By force, away to the east they took her,
    Ending forever any last chance
    That she regain what was her all.
They parted her from her children!
    So the flame of hope went cold inside,
    And they could not prevent her dying.
And, as the Indians are wont to in despair,
    She could not be moved, from that hour of hope expired,
    To take nourishment into her body.
Thus she starved herself to death! This is the witness
    To the Guahiba and the Christians' image
    Told by that stone with mute mouth
On Atabapo's shore in the wilderness.

Chapter 12

LUDWIG BÖRNE

Letters to Jeanette Wohl

1828–1830

Berlin, 22 February 1828

Yesterday morning at 11 o'clock I picked up my Hans and we went to Humboldt's lecture. What a dish that would be for my sweet little Barbara! Imagine the most beautiful, the most magnificent room (belonging to the choral academy and just recently built) filled with 800 to 900 spectators, more than half of them women, with Berlin's upper classes, the king, all of the princesses, the entire court, hundreds of officers—before such a public I as well long to speak. The lectures begin after twelve, but the room is already crowded by eleven. Great attentiveness reigns, especially among the women, who surreptitiously take notes beneath their scarves and hats, whatever they can catch. Physical geography is the subject of the lectures, which is, of course, Humboldt's specialty. I, poor, deaf soul who sat somewhat removed from Humboldt, heard absolutely nothing. My wretched ears caused me no end of grief. In Frankfurt I always believed I would be indifferent to that infirmity. And so I was then, for so little there is spoken that deserves to be heard. Here, however, such is not the case. Nevertheless, everywhere I go I introduce myself as somewhat deaf, which makes my situation more bearable. At Mendelssohn's, when I brought up in conversation which the greater misfortune was, to be deaf or blind, Zelter remarked that deafness straight away bestowed upon one the great advantage of not having to go to church.

Translation by Richard John Ascárate, from Ludwig Börne, *Gesammelte Schriften. Neue vollständige Ausgabe,* vol. 12, *Briefe aus Paris* (Hamburg/Frankfurt a. M.: Verlag der Börne'schen Schriften, 1862), 360, 363–364, 371.

Berlin, 1 March 1828

I attended the Humboldtian lectures again on Thursday. Had you but seen the rush of people and coaches! Mounted gendarmes and police commissioners stood before the hall. But again, I heard nothing. Humboldt does not deliver a clear, certainly not a beautiful, lecture. My hearing impairment makes things difficult, and I suspect there is little to be done about it.

Berlin, 7 March 1828

I have a great desire to meet Humboldt, but there is no one to make the proper introduction. He is also often at court and seldom at home. How curious that only the Jews or the baptized Jews establish houses here and the Christians hardly at all. There are few wealthy Christian merchants and the remaining classes—the civil servants and such—have no money. I notice this most pointedly in a noble Viennese gentleman who, attached to the Austrian legation, came here fourteen days ago and who cannot be wanting a multitude of recommendations. Wherever and as frequently as I enter the social circle of my acquaintances, I find him also—proof that he is not invited elsewhere. Gans promised to introduce me at Hegel's, but the blowhard has yet to keep his word. It may also be that this gentleman wants nothing to do with me because of my piece against the Critical Society, whose director he is. The gentlemen have been very angry with me because they felt, yes, have even confessed, that I make an impression.

Berlin, 17 March 1828

This week I received an invitation to dine where Humboldt was also to come. But I was already promised elsewhere. That upset me very much. Humboldt is supposed to be an exceptionally kind companion and is known to talk continuously. Our paths will cross yet.

Berlin, 24 March 1828

Yesterday I finally became acquainted with Humboldt. He came to Mendelssohn's in the evening. He speaks without pause and very pleasantly. The entire company—comprised of more than thirty persons, men and women—encircled him and listened. He seems accustomed to such. He delivers extremely sharp and stern judgments. He singles out Schlegel in Bonn for endless ridicule, amongst society as well as in his lectures. A few days ago, Schlegel had a pamphlet printed here in which he defended himself far too long and strenuously against a short accusation of his Catholic sympathies, which a French paper recently related. Humboldt took that as the theme of a half-hour long satire, which was very amusing. I sat beside him and he asked me how Madame Wohl was. I told him that she presently grieves because a pair of trousers was stolen from her sweetheart. Yes, he remarked, that is no small matter. And he thereupon related to me a story about how in Peru a descendant of Hernán Cortés once stole a pair of trousers from him; how he complained to the king of Spain about the theft, and how the king laughed at him. From 9 to 11 he held forth, so that no one else could say anything. This almost displeased me.

Berlin, 27 March 1828

Humboldt is on the agenda. All large cities are alike. Fashion rules heart and mind. None of the hundreds of ladies who attend H.['s] lectures would miss even an hour for anything in the world, and yet there are perhaps not fifty among them with any interest in the subject matter itself. My good Herz especially, who hardly has the best head on her shoulders, and indeed, understands nothing which thanks its existence to the nineteenth century. But still, I believe, she would rather admit to her 64 years than confess that she derives no pleasure at all from her H.['s] lectures. I was there yesterday as she spoke with a very elderly lady about [Herder's] *Origin of the Human Race*, as well as about Steffens' and Humboldt's opinions on the work. Herz was for Steffens, the lady for Humboldt. I bit my tongue. It was a scene worthy of Molière. God only knows for which of my sins I always seem to find myself amongst old women.

Paris, 12 October 1830

The statesman, who is to be hired in Berlin, is not Stein, but rather Herr von Humboldt, brother of the traveler. The latter is presently here. "He is a genuine chatterbox," I heard a Frenchman say of him. Thus did I become acquainted with Humboldt in Berlin. He is an unbearable windbag to me. No one can interject a single word whenever he is in the room.

Chapter 13

CHARLES DARWIN
Letters
1831–1834

To W. D. Fox, April 1831

At present I talk, think, and dream of a scheme I have almost hatched of going to the Canary Islands. I have long had a wish of seeing tropical scenery and vegetation, and, according to Humboldt, Teneriffe is a pretty specimen.

To Henslow, 27 July 1831

I hope you continue to fan your Canary ardour. I read and re-read Humboldt; do you do the same? I am sure nothing will prevent us seeing the Great Dragon Tree.

To W. D. Fox, 17 Spring Gardens, 19 September 1831

And if I live to see years in after life, how grand must such recollections be! Do you know Humboldt? (If you don't, do so directly.) With what intense pleasure he appears always to look back on the days spent in the tropical countries.

To R. W. Darwin, Bahia, or San Salvador, Brazil, 1 March 1832

If you really want to have [an idea] of tropical countries, study Humboldt. Skip the scientific parts, and commence after leaving Teneriffe. My feelings amount to admiration the more I read him. […]

Charles Darwin, *The Life and Letters of Charles Darwin, Including an Autobiographical Chapter*, ed. Francis Darwin, vol. 1 (London: John Murray, 1887), 190, 212–213, 231–232, 233–234, 237, 255.

Tell Eyton as far as my experience goes let him study Spanish, French, drawing, and Humboldt.

To W. D. Fox, Botofogo Bay, near Rio de Janeiro, May 1832

But Geology carries the day: it is like the pleasure of gambling. Speculating, on first arriving, what the rocks may be, I often mentally cry out 3 to 1 tertiary against primitive; but the latter have hitherto won all the bets. So much for the grand end of my voyage; in other respects things are equally flourishing. My life, when at sea, is so quiet, that to a person who can employ himself, nothing can be pleasanter; the beauty of the sky and brilliancy of the ocean together make a picture. But when on shore, and wandering in the sublime forests, surrounded by views more gorgeous than even Claude ever imagined, I enjoy a delight which none but those who have experienced it can understand. If it is to be done, it must be by studying Humboldt. At our ancient snug breakfasts, at Cambridge, I little thought that the wide Atlantic would ever separate us; but it is a rare privilege that with the body, the feelings and memory are not divided. On the contrary, the pleasantest scenes in my life, many of which have been in Cambridge, rise from the contrast of the present, the more vividly in my imagination. Do you think any diamond beetle will ever give me so much pleasure as our old friend *crux major*? … It is one of my most constant amusements to draw pictures of the past; and in them I often see you and poor little Fran. Oh, Lord, and then old Dash, poor thing! Do you recollect how you all tormented me about his beautiful tail?

To J. S. Henslow, Rio de Janeiro, 18 May 1832

I never experienced such intense delight. I formerly admired Humboldt, I now almost adore him; he alone gives any notion of the feelings which are raised in the mind on first entering the Tropics.

To C. Whitley, Valparaiso, 23 July 1834

We have seen much fine scenery; that of the Tropics in its glory and luxuriance exceeds even the language of Humboldt to describe. A Persian writer could alone do justice to it, and if he succeeded he would in England be called the 'Grandfather of all liars.'

Chapter 14

CHARLES DARWIN
"Beagle" Diary
1832

St. Jago, 16 January 1832

Before returning to our boat, we walked across the town & came to a deep valley. — Here I first saw the glory of tropical vegetation. Tamarinds, Bananas & Palms were flourishing at my feet. — I expected a good deal, for I had read Humboldt's descriptions & I was afraid of disappointments: how utterly vain such fear is, none can tell but those who have experienced what I to day have. — It is not only the gracefulness of their forms or the novel richness of their colours, it is the numberless & confusing associations that rush together on the mind, & produce the effect. — I returned to the shore, treading on Volcanic rocks, hearing the notes of unknown birds, & seeing new insects fluttering about still newer flowers. — It has been for me a glorious day, like giving to a blind man eyes. — he is overwhelmed with what he sees & cannot justly comprehend it. — Such are my feelings, & such may they remain. —

Bahia, 28 February 1832

About 9 o'clock we were near to the coast of Brazil; we saw a considerable extent of it, the whole line is rather low & irregular, & from the profusion of wood & verdure of a bright green colour. — About 11 o'clock we entered the bay of All Saints, on the Northern Side of which is situated the town of Bahia or St. Salvador. It would be difficult [to] imagine, before seeing the view, anything so magnificent. — It requires, however, the reality of nature to make it so. — if faithfully represented in a picture, a feeling of distrust would be raised

Charles Darwin, *Charles Darwin's Diary of the Voyage of H.M.S. "Beagle,"* ed. Nora Barlow (Cambridge, MA: Cambridge University Press, 1933), 24–25, 39.

in the mind, as I think is the case in some of Martin's views. — The town is fairly embosomed in a luxuriant wood & situated on a steep bank overlooks the calm waters of the great bay of All Saints. The houses are white & lofty & from the windows being narrow & long have a very light & elegant appearance. Convents, Porticos & public buildings vary the uniformity of the houses: the bay is scattered over with large ships; in short the view is one of the finest in the Brazils. — But their beauties are as nothing compared to the Vegetation; I believe from what I have seen Humboldt's glorious descriptions are & will for ever be unparalleled: but even he with his dark blue skies & the rare union of poetry with science which he so strongly displays when writing on tropical scenery, with all this falls far short of the truth. The delight one experiences in such times bewilders the mind. — if the eye attempts to follow the flight of a gaudy butter-fly, it is arrested by some strange tree or fruit; if watching an insect one forgets it in the stranger flower it is crawling over. — if turning to admire the splendour of the scenery, the individual character of the foreground fixes the attention. The mind is a chaos of delight, out of which a world of future & more quiet pleasure will arise. — I am at present fit only to read Humboldt; he like another Sun illumines everything I behold. —

Chapter 15

Ralph Waldo Emerson
On the Relation of Man to the Globe
1833

Let a man keep his presence of mind, and there is scarcely any danger so desperate from which he cannot deliver himself. For there is a very wide interval betwixt danger and destruction which men in peaceful pursuits seldom consider. A man in his parlor in this civil town, thinks that to meet a lion in the desert, or to stumble over an alligator in wading knee deep through a savannah, is certain destruction. But the Fellatahs of Africa, or the Caribee Indians think no such thing. Their habitual acquaintance with these delicate circumstances, has taught them to see a wide distance betwixt danger and death, and in that discrimination their safety lies. Mungo Park rode slowly by a red lion, expecting every moment the fatal spring. Humboldt, having left his boat on the river Orinoco, to examine some natural objects on the bank, suddenly found himself near a large jaguar, and "though extremely frightened, he retained sufficient self command to follow the advice which the Indians had so often given, and continued to walk without moving his arms, making a large circuit towards the edge of the water." The tiger did not move from the spot. An Indian girl at Urituco being seized by a crocodile—she immediately felt for his eyes and thrust her fingers into them and thus compelled the animal to let her go, though with the loss of an arm.

The Early Lectures of Ralph Waldo Emerson: Volume I, 1833–1836, eds. Stephen E. Whicher and Robert E. Spiller (Cambridge, MA: The Belknap Press of Harvard University Press, 1959), 38–39. Copyright © 1959 by the President and Fellows of Harvard College. Reprinted by permission of the publisher.

Chapter 16

HONORÉ DE BALZAC

Administrative Adventures of a Wonderful Idea

1834

Whimsical Introduction

After midnight, in a salon in Paris, at the moment when the line of tea drinkers has lightened up, when those who show up to be seen have disappeared, a couple of people came together whose ideas joined in unison and vibrated nicely. There ensued one of those dynamic conversations, full of matters both taunting and polite at the same time, as is at times still to be heard in this city, which is as truly profound as it is crazy.

Have you ever in the winter studied from a bridge the bizarre movement of ice on a large river? The ice floes drift, come together, pile up, deviate from their route, go to the right, go to the left; then at one instant, you don't know why, all at once they mesh together, coalesce, the figures in the fluvial contra-dance come to a standstill, and a majestic surface forms over which a little kid audaciously skips barefoot and crosses from one side to the other. So it is with the harmony of the minds or the spirits in the salons of Paris just like this meshing of the ice. Men and women have seen and irritated each other, have come and have greeted each other yesterday, and they have not at all understood one another; today, nobody knows why, this evening, in front of the fireplace, they have found themselves connected in the same wave of ideas, enjoying together the charms of a unique moment, without ramifications in the future, without ties to the past. Is it the cold? Is it the heat? What tone has brought together the swarm of these thoughts? What shock has dispersed them? No answer to these questions. You will wish to know where is the in-

Translation by Rex Clark and Oliver Lubrich, from Honoré de Balzac, "Aventures administratives D'une Idée heureuse," *Causeries du monde* (10 March 1834), 97–101, 107–111.

solent kid who naively traces the bottom of his feet on this ice that has been moving and is now still? Read on.

"Do you believe, sir," said the lady of the house to a certain Prussian savant known for the unfailing fluidity of his speech, "do you believe in these miraculous powers of the human will, in the life of ideas, in their procreation? In short, do you believe, just as Monsieur …"

The lady turned toward a young man, pale and with long hair, named Louis Lambert.

"Do you believe," she repeated, "just as the gentleman claims, that ideas are the organized beings that occur outside of man, that act, that … ? My word, I'm getting lost in these concepts. You've listened to the gentleman, what do you say to his system?"

"But my lady," the Prussian responded smiling, "is it a system? I wouldn't be so bold as to affirm or deny it. On the other side of the Rhine, several men have elevated themselves in the ethereal regions, and have bumped their heads against the stars. Some authors, known by names ending with *org, ohm, oehm,* have found, it is said, in these stars sublime thoughts that some people grasp, who are nearly crazy, according to our weak and common opinions. We have many Germans, Saxons, and Swedes who have seen ideas; but we have an infinitely greater number, who have not seen them. Nevertheless I can give you some information on this subject that is taken for truth, but that I report without guaranteeing for it; if you permit me to apply this journalistic formulation full of charlatanism, in a salon where the charlatanism belongs exclusively to the women. A young Hanoverian, just arrived in London, complained several times about a bizarre theft. A gentleman had taken from him, he said, his brain, his ideas, and kept them in a jar. In Paris, no one would have been surprised at such thefts; here one takes just like that the ideas of the people who have ideas; only one doesn't put them in a jar, one puts them in a newspaper, in a book, into enterprises. In London, the people of society behaved as those in Paris behave; they made fun of my poor Hanoverian, but earnestly, in the English manner. This young man remained as a result of this robbery in a state of imbecility, of idleness, of boredom, of irritation that gave much distress to his friends. Then his complaints were remedied. He was put into Bedlam asylum. He stayed there almost two months. One day one of the best known doctors of London said to one of the doctors in Bedlam that he had just seen that morning one of their colleagues, half-crazy probably, who indulged in chemical operations on some masses of ideas taken from different individuals and stored in nicely-labeled jars.—'Good God!'

Notice that I do not say 'goddam!'" exclaimed the Prussian interrupting himself—"'Good God! let's go see if the brain of a poor lucid Hanoverian who followed the course of his ideas and whom I am treating at my hospice, is not perhaps, by any chance, in the jar that he tells me about.' The two doctors hastened to their colleague and found there the ideas of the German, which respectably filled a phial; they were blue. The two doctors naturally forced the alchemist of minds to deliver the spirit of the Hanoverian. When the prison was broken, they returned to the hospital where the young man declared to his guardians that he had recovered his ideas and he was transported with joy resembling that which a blind man might feel on seeing light again. This fact could, if it were scientifically proven, corroborate the theory that Monsieur Lambert has just exposed to us about the life and the iconography of ideas, a system that, by virtue of being German, I respect, as any good German should respect a system. …"

"It is not a system, sir, it is a brilliant truth," said a voice which seemed to come from a jar and which alarmed the group.

"Ha! You gave me a fright, sir," said the lady of the house on seeing a figure emerging from the recess of a distant window.

Although the lady began to smile, her smile appeared, to those who observed it, to have been produced by a convulsion the cause of which was exterior. Then, convinced that this violent action was caused by the unknown person, everybody turned around abruptly towards him. It was not without a prodigious interest, though we do not want to accuse the distinguished personages of which the assembly was composed of being easily frightened, that each one perceived the originator of that powerful exorcism.

~

When Monsieur de Lessones had risen to his feet and no longer wobbled, there was a grand silence.

"Sir," he said to the pale and frail young man, "do you call yourself Monsieur Lambert? Oh! blessed be this name! you have dedicated yourself to a truth, as the martyrs dedicated themselves to Christ! …"

The faces were frozen. Louis Lambert, who, for the only time in his life had dared to talk about his system, and who saw it delivered to the pitiless Parisian ridicules, broke out in a sweat of suffering; he would have wept, if he had dared, to see his chaste concept stripped naked, whipped, and polluted by the profane.

"Yes, gentlemen, the ideas are beings," the old man resumed, who grew larger, became animated and whose voice rang like a bell. "Just as you see me, I am under the power of an idea. I have become entirely idea: true demon, incubus and succubus; in turn the scorned and the scorner; active and patient; now victim, now torturer—Oh!" he said turning to Louis Lambert, the young man of the pure face, a face sealed against misfortune, characterized by genius, marked by the red mark put on trees to be cut down, "I will go further than you have just now, when you perceived ideas, that you paraphrased the principle of a science to come! … But I will go further than you have because I have less to lose. My current form will die, but my true nature, the idea! . . . the idea will remain! I will exist forever."

"Where is that fellow's jar?" said the Prussian in a low voice to the lady of the house.

Nobody was in the mood for humor, looking at the emaciated hand that the orator lifted toward Louis Lambert. An alert young woman said with some terror:

"Oh! my God, he is going to take him away from us!"

"There are in the moral world," continued Monsieur de Lessones, "small creatures, lame and clumsy, pockmarked, outdated, these are the ideas of what you call the men of letters. They live on the walls as yellow wallflowers do, they perfume the air for a day, disappear and drop. In these families of ephemeral beings, a few, similar to brilliant chemical efflorescences, emerge, reflect thousand colors, shine and persist; but they fall a little later like the preceding ones; finally, Dorat, Marmontel, these small green flowers, the 'Forty Immortals' … Others rise slowly, with grace, grow by extending with majesty the immense foliage of their branches, cover an époque with their shade, populate the cities like these alleyways with platane and linden trees under which five to six generations walk. These are the good works resulting from some brains, whose lively ideas reign for two or three centuries. The ideas of Luther have generated Calvin, who generated Bayle, who generated Voltaire, who generated the constitutional opposition, and finally the spirit of discussion and examination. They conceive one from the others, like plants, daughters of the same seed; like men, lineage of a first woman. The ideas of Luther were those of the Vaudois sect; the Vaudois beliefs descended from old and primitive heresies of the first Church; then these heresies, with their microcosms of ideas, started again the theosophies of the plains of Asia. Let's let them rest. To each climate its intellectual flowers, whose perfumes and colors harmonize with the conditions of the sun, with the mist of the atmosphere, with the snows of the mountains: so it is with ideas. The ideas in each country put on the garment of the nations. In Asia its tigers, its roses, its consuming fires, its poetry soaked with sun, its perfumed ideas. In Europe its plants humid, its animals less hot-blooded; but in Europe the instinct, its concise poetry, its analytical works, reason, discussions. If there is air and blue sky with Eastern writers, there is rain, lakes, moonbeams, painful happiness with the writers of Europe. Asia is pleasure; Europe is ridicule. In Europe, the ideas bark, laugh, frolic, as all that is terrestrial; but, in the East, they are voluptuous, celestial, elevated, symbolic. Dante alone welded together these two types of ideas. His poem is a bold bridge thrown between Asia and Europe, a Poulh-Sherro on which the generations of the two worlds march by with the slowness of shapes which we dream under the rule of a nightmare. Hence this majestic horror, this holy fear which takes hold during the reading of this work where the moral world whirls. But there are ideas whose system acts more directly on the men who seize them. These ideas torment them, make them go, come, fade, dry up. These are ideas, better materialized, which deal with the material world more vigorously. There are gigantic ones, monumental ones, which keep to the mineral world. They descend at the called for hour, rise up and drop down on the head of nations or of an individual, like a hammer on the anvil, and they forge centuries by preparing revolutions. They are the territorial ideas so to speak, the ideas which are born from the geographical configuration of a country; ideas which hammer from century to century the political brains: they rose slowly like pyramids, and you see them straight in front of you 'The Rhine must be ours!' says France. 'Let us swallow the Russians!' Napoleon said. Napoleon was a grand idea which still governs France. And, well, I am, in a less broad sphere, an idea of this type and of which I will tell you the marvelous, incredible, adventures; birth, life, misfortunes, but not death. *Calypso, in her pain, was not comforted to be immortal*, should be the epigraph of my account, because the ideas suffer and do not die. When they are too tortured, they take to wing like the swallows. There are many European ideas that have transmigrated from Europe to America, and which were acclimatized there. But listen. Give me two hours of attention, give due with some patience to a pauper who has millions in income. You will see if the writers, mounted on the horses of Doubt and Scorn; if Byron, Voltaire, Swift, Cervantes, Rabelais were wrong to leave the print of the hoofs of their chargers, as pale as that of the Apocalypse, on the head of the centuries plowed by their steeds. Shame on men! shame on the bureaucracy especially! because, you see, it is the organized mediocrity. ... My idea and I are victims of the base intrigues of the court of Louis XIV, of the reign of Louis XV, of the Convention, of the Empire and of the Restoration. You will have in few moments a sketch of these five grand operas, from behind the scenes. ... This is my preface from the editor."

"Before devoting our eyes, our ears and our attention to Monsieur the Count, don't we want to take a little tea?" asked the lady of the house to all the people who had sat in circle in front of the chimney.

"Gladly," said the Prussian baron, "but we shouldn't take too much of it, the tea puts you to sleep. ..."

Chapter 17

Hans Christian Andersen

Diaries

1834

Berlin, 1 June 1834

Uneasy sleep, had toothache, dreamed a lot of the King of Bavaria, a very strange dream, he told me the number 121, which I should play in the lottery in order to win, and I said: "Oh, that is just like the tale of 'Lumpazivagabundus.'" We departed at a quarter after five. It was a beautiful day, the region became lovelier, tall and beautiful oaks, we crossed the Alz and the Traun rivers. In Stein there were ruins of an old knight's castle, still standing—the region became more scenic, we saw Tachinger lake, which stretches out between spruce covered hills, about three hours in length and over half an hour in width. The mountains came into view, they stood covered in snow in broken wavy lines before us. The officer talked about the tree: aras or alas (Humboldt's Travels) that is an excellent subject for a poem.

Translation by Cathrine Blom, from *Dagbøger 1825–1875*, vol. 1, *1825–1834*, ed. Helga Vang Lauridsen (Copenhagen: G. E. C. Gad, 1971), 440. Every effort has been made to trace the copyright holder and to obtain permission for the use and translation of this excerpt.

Chapter 18

CHARLES DARWIN

Voyage of the Beagle

1836

It is argued that self-interest will prevent excessive cruelty; as if self-interest protected our domestic animals, which are far less likely than degraded slaves, to stir up the rage of their savage masters. It is an argument long since protested against with noble feeling, and strikingly exemplified, by the ever illustrious Humboldt. It is often attempted to palliate slavery by comparing the state of slaves with our poorer countrymen: if the misery of our poor be caused not by the laws of nature, but by our institutions, great is our sin; but how this bears on slavery, I cannot see; as well might the use of the thumb-screw be defended in one land, by showing that men in another land suffered from some dreadful disease. Those who look tenderly at the slave-owner, and with a cold heart at the slave, never seem to put themselves into the position of the latter;—what a cheerless prospect, with not even a hope of change! picture to yourself the chance, ever hanging over you, of your wife and your little children—those objects which nature urges even the slave to call his own—being torn from you and sold like beasts to the first bidder! And these deeds are done and palliated by men, who profess to love their neighbours as themselves, who believe in God, and pray that his Will be done on earth! It makes one's blood boil, yet heart tremble, to think that we Englishmen and our American descendants, with their boastful cry of liberty, have been and are so guilty: but it is a consolation to reflect, that we at least have made a greater sacrifice, than ever made by any nation, to expiate our sin.

On the last day of August [1836] we anchored for the second time at Porto Praya in the Cape de Verd archipelago; thence we proceeded to the Azores, where we staid six days. On the 2nd of October we made the shores of Eng-

Charles Darwin, *Journal of Researches Into the Natural History and Geology of the Countries Visited During the Voyage of H. M. S. Beagle Round the World, Under the Command of Capt. Fitz Roy, R. N.*, vol. 3, 2nd ed. (London: John Murray, 1845), 500–506.

land; and at Falmouth I left the Beagle, having lived on board the good little vessel nearly five years.

Our Voyage having come to an end, I will take a short retrospect of the advantages and disadvantages, the pains and pleasures, of our circumnavigation of the world. [...]

The pleasure derived from beholding the scenery and the general aspect of the various countries we have visited, has decidedly been the most constant and highest source of enjoyment. It is probable that the picturesque beauty of many parts of Europe exceeds anything which we beheld. But there is a growing pleasure in comparing the character of the scenery in different countries, which to a certain degree is distinct from merely admiring its beauty. It depends chiefly on an acquaintance with the individual parts of each view: I am strongly induced to believe that, as in music, the person who understands every note will, if he also possesses a proper taste, more thoroughly enjoy the whole, so he who examines each part of a fine view, may also thoroughly comprehend the full and combined effect. Hence, a traveller should be a botanist, for in all views plants form the chief embellishment. Group masses of naked rock even in the wildest forms, and they may for a time afford a sublime spectacle, but they will soon grow monotonous. Paint them with bright and varied colours, as in Northern Chile, they will become fantastic; clothe them with vegetation, they must form a decent, if not a beautiful picture.

When I say that the scenery of parts of Europe is probably superior to anything which we beheld, I except, as a class by itself, that of the intertropical zones. The two classes cannot be compared together; but I have already often enlarged on the grandeur of those regions. As the force of impressions generally depends on preconceived ideas, I may add, that mine were taken from the vivid descriptions in the *Personal Narrative* of Humboldt, which far exceed in merit anything else which I have read. Yet with these high-wrought ideas, my feelings were far from partaking of a tinge of disappointment on my first and final landing on the shores of Brazil.

Among the scenes which are deeply impressed on my mind, none exceed in sublimity the primeval forests undefaced by the hand of man; whether those of Brazil, where the powers of Life are predominant, or those of Tierra del Fuego, where Death and Decay prevail. Both are temples filled with the varied productions of the God of Nature: —no one can stand in these solitudes unmoved, and not feel that there is more in man than the mere breath of his body. In calling up images of the past, I find that the plains of Patagonia frequently cross before my eyes; yet these plains are pronounced by all wretched and useless. They can be described only by negative characters; without habitations, without water, without trees, without mountains, they support merely a few dwarf plants. Why then, and the case is not peculiar to myself, have these arid wastes taken so firm a hold on my memory? Why have not the still more level, the greener and more fertile Pampas, which are serviceable to mankind, produced an equal impression? I can scarcely analyze these feelings: but it must be partly owing to the free scope given to the imagination. The plains of Patagonia are boundless, for they are scarcely passable, and hence unknown: they bear the stamp of having lasted, as they are now, for ages, and there appears no limit to their duration through future time. If, as the ancients supposed, the flat earth was surrounded by an impassable breadth of water, or by deserts heated to an intolerable excess, who would not look at these last boundaries to man's knowledge with deep but ill-defined sensations?

Lastly, of natural scenery, the views from lofty mountains, though certainly in one sense not beautiful, are very memorable. When looking down from the highest crest of the Cordillera, the mind, undisturbed by minute details, was filled with the stupendous dimensions of the surrounding masses.

Of individual objects, perhaps nothing is more certain to create astonishment than the first sight in his native haunt of a barbarian,—of man in his lowest and most savage state. One's mind hurries back over past centuries, and then asks, could our progenitors have been men like these? —men, whose very signs and expressions are less intelligible to us than those of the domesticated animals; men, who do not possess the instinct of those animals, nor yet appear to boast of human reason, or at least of arts consequent on that reason. I do not believe it is possible to describe or paint the difference between savage and civilized man. It is the difference between a wild and tame animal: and part of the interest in beholding a savage, is the same which would lead every one to desire to see the lion in his desert, the tiger tearing his prey in the jungle, or the rhinoceros wandering over the wild plains of Africa.

Among the other most remarkable spectacles which we have beheld, may be ranked the Southern Cross, the cloud of Magellan, and the other constellations of the southern hemisphere—the water-spout—the glacier leading its blue stream of ice, overhanging the sea in a bold precipice—a lagoon-island raised by the reef-building corals—an active volcano—and the overwhelming effects of a violent earthquake. These latter phenomena, perhaps, possess for me a peculiar interest, from their intimate connexion with the geological structure of the world. The earthquake, however, must be to every one a most impressive event: the earth, considered from our earliest childhood as the type of solidity, has oscillated like a thin crust beneath our feet; and in seeing the laboured works of man in a moment overthrown, we feel the insignificance of his boasted power.

It has been said, that the love of the chase is an inherent delight in man—a relic of an instinctive passion. If so, I am sure the pleasure of living in the open air, with the sky for a roof and the ground for a table, is part of the same feeling; it is the savage returning to his wild and native habits. I always look back to our boat cruises, and my land journeys, when through unfrequented countries, with an extreme delight, which no scenes of civilization could have created. I do not doubt that every traveller must remember the glowing sense of happiness which he experienced, when he first breathed in a foreign clime, where the civilized man had seldom or never trod.

There are several other sources of enjoyment in a long voyage, which are of a more reasonable nature. The map of the world ceases to be a blank; it becomes a picture full of the most varied and animated figures. Each part assumes its proper dimensions: continents are not looked at in the light of islands, or islands considered as mere specks, which are, in truth, larger than many kingdoms of Europe. Africa, or North and South America, are well-sounding names, and easily pronounced; but it is not until having sailed for weeks along small portions of their shores, that one is thoroughly convinced what vast spaces on our immense world these names imply.

From seeing the present state, it is impossible not to look forward with high expectations to the future progress of nearly an entire hemisphere. [...]

In conclusion, it appears to me that nothing can be more improving to a young naturalist, than a journey in distant countries. It both sharpens, and partly allays that want and craving, which, as Sir J. Herschel remarks, a man experiences although every corporeal sense be fully satisfied. The excitement from the novelty of objects, and the chance of success, stimulate him to increased activity. Moreover, as a number of isolated facts soon become uninteresting, the habit of comparison leads to generalization. On the other hand, as the traveller stays but a short time in each place, his descriptions must generally consist of mere sketches, instead of detailed observations. Hence arises, as I have found to my cost, a constant tendency to fill up the wide gaps of knowledge, by inaccurate and superficial hypotheses.

But I have too deeply enjoyed the voyage, not to recommend any naturalist, although he must not expect to be so fortunate in his companions as I have been, to take all chances, and to start, on travels by land if possible, if otherwise on a long voyage. He may feel assured, he will meet with no difficulties or dangers, excepting in rare cases, nearly so bad as he beforehand anticipates. In a moral point of view, the effect ought to be, to teach him good-humoured patience, freedom from selfishness, the habit of acting for himself, and of making the best of every occurrence. In short, he ought to partake of the characteristic qualities of most sailors. Travelling ought also to teach him distrust; but at the same time he will discover, how many truly kind-hearted people there are, with whom he never before had, or ever again will have any further communication, who yet are ready to offer him the most disinterested assistance.

Chapter 19

José María Heredia
Journey to the Mountain of Toluca
1837

"Whoever wishes to see something new under the sun should climb to the peak of a real mountain," says a modern writer. Several years have passed since I wished to submit myself to the experience of such a statement; but occasional obstacles, and above all the feebleness of a weak constitution and a long period of sedentary life, had frustrated my designs.

On 1 October 1837, Soonkins, an English artist, invited me to accompany him on his next expedition to Nevado de Toluca, and an obliging friend at once resolved the difficulties that my idleness advanced.

At four in the afternoon we left for the estate of Veladero, situated on the eastern slope of the volcano, and five leagues distant from Toluca. There we passed the night and owed the great attentions shown us to its administrator, José Iniesta, to whom José Franco was kind enough to recommend us.

On 2 October at six in the morning and accompanied by Iniesta and three or four servants, we left. The ascent is at first gentle, but much later becomes rough and inclined, prolonging its twists and uprisings in a seemingly endless wood of gigantic pines. After about two hours of traveling we left behind and to our right the craggy peaks and perpendicularities of the hill called Tepehuirco, and from an altitude equal to or higher than that of the mountain range dividing the valleys of Mexico and Toluca, we already discerned between the trees—when the unevenness of the trail allowed us to look eastward—the snow-capped and majestic peaks of Popocatépetl and Iztaccíhuatl. The gaze rested close above the southeast part of the Tolucan valley, unfolded suddenly at our feet like a lovely panorama with its numerous populations and richly sown fields and the beautiful lake of Atenco, gilt by a cloudless sun.

Translation by Richard John Ascárate, from José María Heredia, "Viage al Nevado de Toluca," in *Calendario de las Señoritas Megicanas para el año de 1838*, ed. Mariano Galván [Rivera] (Mexico: Mariano Galván Rivera, [1837]), 241–254.

A little later one began to feel the woods thinning along with a progressive diminution in the height of the pines, until they hardly reached to our heads. Then we could enjoy in all its grandeur the vast perspective that the central valley of Toluca offered, as well as the sublime aspect of the highest, denuded pines that crowned the volcanic crater. Sketched upon the profound blue of the sky, they appeared to us—because of the extraordinary transparency of the air—almost terrifying in their proximity.

The diminution of the pines continued rapidly as we rose, until the last were hardly half a *vara* in height, presenting the singular spectacle of a miniature forest. In the end they disappeared, the vegetation being reduced to a waning and withered herb, among which frequently jutted the thorny stalks of a species of *Dipsacus*—commonly called "thistle"—gigantic and perhaps peculiar to that elevated region, which had been observed nowhere else. I noted also there for the first time a small, creeping plant of the *Castilleja* family (paintbrush) [flor de muis] whose spathaceous leaves ended in attractive, odorless flowers, some red, some yellow, some tinged with both colors. I afterwards returned to find this same flowering plant at the base of the crater and between the sands that lead to the most elevated peaks.

At ten, after some wandering, we scale the east rim of the crater which, being much lower than the rest of the circumference of that immense funnel and free of the enormous rocks defending the other sides, is more accessible. There we dismounted, warning the servants to wait for us together with the horses by the lakes lying at the base of the crater. We then begin to climb on foot up to the more elevated basaltic peak towards the south, at times passing over crystallized snow. This leg of the journey was very laborious because of the very rapid incline of the heights and the treacherousness of the loose sand covering the path. Perhaps there was also some danger; I was occasionally terrified by the inescapable conviction that the falling sand, rushing to replace that which our feet dislodged, would unbalance and hurl on top of us some of the enormous rocks that seemed to hang above our heads. After ten minutes, great fatigue had already set in. Fortunately, however, I recalled that the celebrated Boussingault had successfully attained the summit of Chimborazo without unduly tiring himself by taking the precaution of stopping for a moment every half minute. Thus did I and arrived rested at the peak at eleven in the morning.

I continued to climb to the cusp of the remote peak that dominates it there, but very soon I had to abandon the undertaking. Furthermore, I noticed that, because of the difficulty in climbing and jumping amongst the basaltic peaks and near vertical walls that they form, with every effort of mine the basalt pealed abundantly beneath my feet and hands. Such a situation was neither very secure nor agreeable for one such as I, who saw on either side only immense depths and chasms. I sat down on the easternmost corner that forms the base of the peak and lost myself in contemplation of a marvelous spectacle.

The sky above our heads, perfectly serene, was a beautiful dark blue peculiar to that region. The sun's light was as weak as if two thirds of its face had been eclipsed. Its heat was hardly noticeable. The moon, in its waning quarter, shone like silver, and to the naked eye, the dark spots of its demi-hemisphere were perfectly distinguishable. I do not doubt that I would have discerned Venus had this beautiful planet found itself somewhat more distant from the sun. The force of sounds had notably attenuated at that altitude. My blood circulated with greater velocity and I felt impulses as if I would launch myself into the skies.

I was suspended some 5,230 *varas* above the sea, and at more than 3,000 *varas* above Toluca, elevated beyond the limits of vegetation and life, seated on a crag that supported the weight of a human body probably for the first time. I found myself at the end of the large central plateau of the Anáhuac, which descended rapidly from this point to the south, where the sun reclaims its rights from the tropics and, from the eternal ices of a polar climate, has dominated with its gaze the temperate and torrid zones. The rim of a volcano was my seat. Everywhere I perceived in clear and tremendous signs the action of a smoldering fire throughout the immemorial course of century after century; and in the middle of that desolate scene, in the immense oven that in bygone days produced the Tartarus of Virgil and the Inferno of Milton, slept two most beautiful lakes beneath the golden light of the sun, lakes whose glacial waters exceeded in purity and loveliness by far what the imagination of any poet had dreamt.

To the north extended the rich valleys of Toluca and Ixtlahuaca, sprinkled with small, artificial lakes and numerous villages and farms. The great conical mountain of Jocotitlán dominated everything, and much farther distant a large series of peaks framed the region. To the east and up to the great valley of Mexico, beneath a sea of vapors, the snow-capped mountains of Popocatépetl and Iztaccíhuatl stood out majestically. Behind these brilliant and glorious peaks, idols of my fantasy, mountains towered behind mountains until the most distant ones—doubtless those of Veracruz—concealed their summits in a high zone of mists, distant offspring of the ocean. For this reason I failed to distinguish between the Orizaba and the Cofre de Perote, although the more distant and less gigantic summits of Oaxaca appeared very clearly to the southeast.

In this direction and toward the south the hot land declined rapidly, covered with rich vegetation, bristling with mountains and precipices, until at about forty or fifty leagues the gigantic ramparts of the Sierra Madre—enhanced in elevation by the depths of the ardent valleys that they dominate—bound the horizon. That admirable landscape, seen from my height, presented the image of a solidified sea, in which each wave was a mountain! In contemplating it, I felt myself irresistibly carried back to the dark era before the creation of man, in which the agency of internal fire raised those enormous incongruities on the surface of a globe not yet congealed. A little later, great masses of clouds that had formed in the southeast veiled that spectacle from us, gloriously illuminated by the sun and sailing majestically past some five hundred feet below us. In the intervals separating the diverse groups, we sometimes distinguished the settlements located on the slope of the volcano, Ocatelelco Lake, and the southern extreme of Fenancingo, whose major part covered an adjacent hill. Other smaller, sprightlier clouds covered us momentarily with their dispersing mists.

After solemn ideas inspired by such sublime images, grave and melancholy reflections followed at once. Oh, how the fugitive glories and desires of feeble mortality become dumbfounded before these indestructible monuments of time and nature! ... I had arrived for the first time at so stupendous an altitude and would not likely return to imbibe similar impressions in the interval separating me from the grave. My heart, which had been inflamed since childhood by a pure and noble love of humanity—and afflicted by cruel disillusionments and enduring injustices—senses the enthusiasm for more generous passions extinguishing, like that volcano whose crater has transformed the ages in a deposit of eternal snows.

Meanwhile, the clouds accumulate all around, and it was necessary that we should think of departing. We then hurled a few large, loose rocks to the base of the crater. But in observing them tumble down that slope from the snow to the sand, I almost repented having profaned the venerable repose in which they had rested for perhaps thirty or forty centuries.

Before descending, I threw a last look at the base of the crater, whose lagoons, reflecting along with the color of the sky the white, red, and black of the sands and basaltic peaks that rose all about, presented a truly magical spectacle.

We descend in eight or ten minutes to the bank of the greater lake, sliding over the sand on our heels, with a thrill of speed comparable only to that which skaters experience upon an inclined sheet of ice. The waters, agitated by a southeast wind, gathered in diminutive waves which, whispering as they broke upon the beach, left behind a soft line of foam. What memories, what images that faint semblance of the ocean sublime—delight of my childhood and near-cult object of my poetic youth—conjured in me after eleven years of absence!

We embark in a canoe carved from an enormous trunk and set there through Franco's ministrations, but fail to make the servants venture across the lake with us because of their crude anxiety of its unmeasurable depth, and because of a dangerous vortex in the center. We cross the lake at its widest part, describing an oblique line from the northern to the eastern bank, which bathes the rough base of a lava hill rising in the center of the crater dividing the two lagoons. The one we traverse extends, according to Velázquez, 344 *varas* along its major axis and 255 in the transverse direction. I believe these measurements to be slightly in error, for the length seems to be less than double the width. With the unaided eye, I would set the length at five hundred *varas*. Velázquez also asserts a maximum depth of about twelve *varas*; but this result hardly seems incontrovertible to me when one considers that the brief time Velázquez remained there could not have allowed him to sound all of the laguna, whose floor is probably as irregular as any volcanic formation. Along the line I traveled, I judge the depth to be no more than twenty *varas* in the center, for despite the complete transparency of the water, one sees blue rather than green, just as in the depths of the sea. In the area surrounding the aforementioned hill, a variety of enormous rocks, evidently hurled down from the heights, are distinguishable at the base.

From the center of the lake where this hill occludes the eastern horizon, one enjoys a unique and truly sublime spectacle. To the north and south and west rise, almost perpendicularly in a circle, elevations of 800 to 1,000 feet, covered by white, blue, black, or red sands and ashes—in whose slope distend huge lava fragments and ice floes—and whose summits crown inaccessible peaks sketched in the heavens. Beneath lay a prodigious lake whose deep, transparent waters reminded me of seascapes, although we were floating 15,000 feet above sea level.

The shores are covered with small fragments of pumice stone, porphyry, and lava mixed with sand, and among these we find certain insects belonging to the class of dragonflies—commonly called "little horses of the devil"—unique living beings that appeared to us in that silent, desolate region. As we relaxed at the base of the southern peak, some ravens passed alongside us, sending forth powerful caws.

Franco's wife and others who had visited these lakes before us found in their waters and shores recent signs of a superstitious cult. Divinity was ever sought in those sublime altars erected for it by nature, though at times ignorance may have conflated the temple with the great spirit presiding there. It is then not surprising that isolated natives in their primitive rusticity would have obeyed the instinct to worship in the heights, an instinct virtually contemporary with modern man. At one o'clock we undertook the return trip to Veladero, where we arrive at four.

Two days alone form an era in my memories by having become associated with grand and prodigious mysteries of nature. I had at last surmounted Nevado de Toluca; previously, I was immobile, taken aback, at the foot of the grand cataract of Niagara.

Illustration 19.1. Coffer of Perote.

Chapter 20

Frances Calderón de la Barca

Life in Mexico

1840–1841

Letter the Ninth

18 January 1840

I must tell you that I received a visit this morning from a very remarkable character, well known here by the name of La Güera (the fair) Rodríguez, said to have been many years ago celebrated by Humboldt as the most beautiful woman he had seen in the whole course of his travels. Considering the lapse of time which has passed since that distinguished traveller visited these parts, I was almost astonished when her card was sent up with a request for admission, and still more so to find that in spite of years and of the furrows which it pleases Time to plough in the loveliest faces, La Güera retains a profusion of fair curls without one gray hair, a set of beautiful white teeth, very fine eyes, and great vivacity. […]

I found La Güera very agreeable, and a perfect living chronicle. She is married to her third husband, and had three daughters, all celebrated beauties; the Countess de Regla, who died in New York, and was buried in the cathedral there; the Marquesa de Guadalupe, also dead, and the Marquesa de A——a, now a handsome widow. We spoke of Humboldt, and talking of herself as of a third person, she related to me all the particulars of his first visit, and his admiration of her; that she was then very young, though married, and the mother of two children, and that when he came to visit her mother, she was sitting sewing in a corner where the baron did not perceive her; until talking very earnestly on the subject of cochineal, he inquired if he could visit a certain district where there was a plantation of nopals. "To be sure," said La Güera from her corner;

Frances Calderón de la Barca, *Life in Mexico During a Residence of Two Years in That Country* (Boston: Charles C. Little and James Brown, 1843), 1:132, 133–134 (Letter 9), 192–196 (Letter 13); 2:97–98 (Letter 34), 156–158 (Letter 40), 343–345 (Letter 49).

"we can take M. de Humboldt there;" whereupon he first perceiving her, stood amazed, and at length exclaimed, "*Válgame Dios!* who is that girl?" Afterwards he was constantly with her, and more captivated, it is said, by her wit than by her beauty; considering her a sort of western Madame de Staël; all which leads me to suspect that the grave traveller was considerably under the influence of her fascinations, and that neither mines nor mountains, geography nor geology, petrified shells nor *alpenkalkstein*, had occupied him to the exclusion of a slight *stratum* of flirtation. It is a comfort to think that "sometimes even the great Humboldt nods."

Letter the Thirteenth

3 April 1840

To-day we have been visiting the Academy of painting and sculpture, called the Academy of Fine Arts, of which I unfortunately recollected having read Humboldt's brilliant account, in my forcibly prolonged studies on board the Jason, and that he mentions its having had the most favourable influence in forming the national taste. He tells us that every night, in these spacious halls, well illumined by Argand lamps, hundreds of young men were assembled, some sketching from the plaster-casts, or from life, and others copying designs of furniture, candelabras and other bronze ornaments; and that here all classes, colours, and races, were mingled together; the Indian beside the white boy, and the son of the poorest mechanic beside that of the richest lord. Teaching was gratis, and not limited to landscape and figures, one of the principal objects being to propagate amongst the artists a general taste for elegance and beauty of form, and to enliven the national industry. Plaster-casts, to the amount of forty thousand dollars, were sent out by the King of Spain, and as they possess in the academy various colossal statues of basalt and porphyry, with Aztec hieroglyphics, it would have been curious, as the same learned traveller remarks, to have collected these monuments in the courtyard of the Academy, and compared the remains of Mexican sculpture, monuments of a semi-barbarous people, with the graceful creations of Greece and Rome.

Let no one visit the Academy with these recollections or anticipations in his mind. ... That the simple and noble taste which distinguishes the Mexican buildings, their perfection in the cutting and working of their stones, the chaste ornaments of the capitals and relievos, are owing to the progress they made in this very Academy is no doubt the case. The remains of these beautiful but mutilated plaster-casts, the splendid engravings which still exist, would alone make it probable; but the present disorder, the abandoned state of the building, the non-existence of these excellent classes of sculpture and painting, and, above all, the low state of the fine arts in Mexico, at the present day, are amongst the sad proofs, if any were wanting, of the melancholy effects produced by years of civil war and unsettled government. ...

Letter the Thirty-Fourth

February 1841

We were not far from the ancient city of Cholula, lying on a great plain at a short distance from the mountains, and glittering in the sunbeams, as if it still were the city of predilection as in former days, when it was the sacred city, "the Rome of Anáhuac." It is still a large town, with a spacious square and many churches, and the ruins of its great pyramid still attest its former grandeur; but of the forty thousand houses and four hundred churches mentioned by Cortés, there are no traces. The base of this pyramid, which at a distance looks like a conical mountain, is said by Humboldt to be larger than that of any discovered in the old continent, being double that of Cheops. It is made of layers of bricks mixed with coats of clay and contains four stories. In the midst of the principal platform, where the Indians worshipped Quetzalcoatl, the god of the air (according to some the patriarch Noah, and according to others the apostle Saint Thomas! for *doctors differ,*) rises a church dedicated to the Virgin de los Remedios, surrounded by cypresses, from which there is one of the most beautiful views in the world. From this pyramid, and it is not the least interesting circumstance connected with it, Humboldt made many of his valuable astronomical observations.

The treachery of the people and priests of Cholula, who, after welcoming Cortés and the Spaniards, formed a plan for exterminating them all, which was discovered by Doña Marina, through the medium of a lady of the city, was visited by him with the most signal vengeance. The slaughter was dreadful; the streets were covered with dead bodies, and houses and temples were burnt to the ground. This great temple was afterwards purified by his orders, and the standard of the cross solemnly planted in the midst. Cholula, not being on the direct road to Puebla, is little visited, and as for us our time was now so limited, that we were obliged to content ourselves with a mere passing observation of the pyramid, and then to hurry forward to Puebla.

We entered that city to the number of eighteen persons, eighteen horses, and several mules, and passed some people near the gates who were carrying blue-eyed angels to the chosen city, and who nearly let them drop, in astonishment, on seeing such a cavalcade. We were very cold, and felt very tired as we rode into the courtyard of the hotel, yet rather chagrined to think that the remainder of our journey was now to be performed in a diligence. Having brought my story up to civilized life, and it being late, I conclude.

Letter the Fortieth

25 April 1841

You ask if the castes in Mexico are distinct. There are seven supposed to be so. 1st, the Gachupinos, or Spaniards born in Europe; 2nd, the Creoles, that is, whites of European family born in America; 3rd, the Mestizos; 4th, the Mulattoes, descendants of whites and negroes, of whom there are few; 5th, the Zambos, descendants of negroes and Indians, the ugliest race in Mexico; 6th, the Indians; and 7th, the remains of the African negroes.

Of pure Indians, Humboldt in his day calculated that there existed two millions and a half in New Spain (without counting mestizos), and they are, probably, very little altered from the inferior Indians, as Cortés found them. The principal families perished at the time of the conquest. The priests, sole depositaries of knowledge, were put to death; the manuscripts and hieroglyphical paintings were burnt, and the remaining Indians fell into that state of ignorance and degradation, from which they have never emerged. The rich Indian women preferred marrying their Spanish conquerors to allying themselves with the degraded remnant of their countrymen; poor artisans, workmen, porters, etc., of whom Cortés speaks as filling the streets of the great cities, and as being considered little better than beasts of burden; nearly naked in *tierra caliente,* dressed pretty much as they now are in the temperate parts of the country; and everywhere with nearly the same manners, and habits, and customs, as they now have, but especially in the more distant villages where they have little intercourse with the other classes. Even in their religion, Christianity, as I observed before, seems to be formed of the ruins of their mythology; and all these festivities of the church, these fireworks, and images, and gay dresses, harmonize completely with their childish love of show, and are, in fact, their greatest source of delight. To buy these they save up all their money, and when you give a penny to an Indian child, it trots off to buy crackers, as another would to buy candy. Attempts have been made by their curates to persuade them to omit the celebration of certain days, and to expend less in the ceremonies of others, but the indignation and discontent which such proposals have caused, have induced them to desist in their endeavours.

Under an appearance of stupid apathy they veil a great depth of cunning. They are grave and gentle and rather sad in their appearance, when not under the influence of pulque; but when they return to their villages in the evening, and have taken a drop of comfort, their white teeth light up their bronze countenances like lamps, and the girls especially make the air ring with their laughter, which is very musical. I think it is Humboldt who says that their smile is extremely gentle, and the expression of their eyes very severe. As they have no beard, if it were not for a little moustache, which they frequently wear on the upper lip, there would be scarcely any difference between the faces of men and women.

The Indians in and near the capital are, according to Humboldt, either the descendants of the former labourers, or are remains of noble Indian families, who, disdaining to intermarry with their Spanish conquerors, preferred themselves to till the ground which their vassals formerly cultivated for them. It is said that these Indians of noble race, though to the vulgar eye undistinguishable from their fellows, are held in great respect by their inferior countrymen. In Cholula, particularly, there are still caciques with long Indian names; also in Tlaxcala—and though barefoot and ragged, they are said to possess great hidden wealth. But it is neither in or near the capital that we can see the Indians to perfection in their original state. It is only by travelling through the provinces that we can accomplish this.

Letter the Forty-Ninth

31 November 1841

This place is so charming, we have determined to pitch our tent in it for a few days. Our intention was to proceed twenty leagues farther, to see the volcano of Jorullo; but as the road is described to us as being entirely devoid of shade, and the heat almost insupportable—with various other difficulties and drawbacks,—we have been induced, though with great regret, to abandon the undertaking, which it is as tantalizing to do, as it is to reflect that yesterday we were but a short distance from a hill which is but thirty leagues from the Pacific Ocean.

In 18[0]3, M. de Humboldt and M. Bonpland, ascended to the crater of this burning mountain, which was formed in September, 1759. Its birth was announced by earthquakes, which put to flight all the inhabitants of the neighbouring villages; and three months after, a terrible eruption burst forth, which filled all the inhabitants with astonishment and terror, and which Humboldt considers one of the most extraordinary physical revolutions that ever took place on the surface of the globe.

Flames issued from the earth for the space of more than a square league. Masses of burning rock were thrown to an immense height, and through a thick cloud of ashes, illuminated by the volcanic fire, the whitened crust of the earth was gradually seen swelling up. The ashes even covered the roofs of the houses at Querétaro, forty-eight leagues distance! and the rivers of San Andrés and Cuitumba sank into the burning masses. The flames were seen from Páscuaro; and from the hills of Agua-Zarca was beheld the birth of this volcanic mountain, the burning offspring of an earthquake, which bursting from the bosom of the earth, changed the whole face of the country for a considerable distance round.

> ——"And now, the glee
> Of the loud hills shakes with its mountain mirth,
> As if they did rejoice o'er a young earthquake's birth."

Here the earth returned the salutation, and shook, though it was with fearful mirth, at the birth of the young volcano.

In a letter written at the time of the event to the Bishop of Michoacán by the curate of the neighbouring village, he says, that the eruption finished by destroying the hacienda of Jorullo, and killing the trees, which were thrown down and buried in the sand and ashes vomited by the mountain. The fields and roads were, he says, covered with sand, the crops destroyed, and the flocks perishing for want of food; unable to drink the pestilential water of the mountains. The rivulet that ran past his village was swelled to a mighty river, that threatened to inundate it; and he adds, that the houses, churches, and hospitals are ready to fall down from the weight of the sand and the ashes—and that "the very people are so covered with the sand, that they seem to have come out of some sepulchre." The great eruptions of the volcano continued till the following year, but have gradually become rarer, and at present have ceased.

Chapter 21

HENRY DAVID THOREAU
A Walk to Wachusett
1842

Concord, 19 July 1842

The needles of the pine
All to the west incline.

Summer and winter our eyes had rested on the dim outline of the mountains
in our horizon, to which distance and indistinctness lent a grandeur not their
own, so that they served equally to interpret all the allusions of poets and travelers; whether with Homer, on a spring morning, we sat down on the many-
peaked Olympus, or, with Virgil, and his compeers, roamed the Etrurian and
Thessalian hills, or with Humboldt measured the more modern Andes and
Teneriffe. Thus we spoke our mind to them, standing on the Concord cliffs:—

With frontier strength ye stand your ground,
With grand content ye circle round,
Tumultuous silence for all sound,
Ye distant nursery of rills,
Monadnock, and the Peterboro' hills;
Like some vast fleet,
Sailing through rain and sleet,
Through winter's cold and summer's heat;
Still holding on, upon your high emprise,
Until ye find a shore amid the skies;
Not skulking close to land,
With cargo contraband,

For they who sent a venture out by ye
Have set the sun to see
Their honesty.
Ships of the line, each one,
Ye to the westward run,
Always before the gale,
Under a press of sail,
With weight of metal all untold.
I seem to feel ye, in my firm seat here,
Immeasurable depth of hold,
And breadth of beam, and length of running gear.

Chapter 22

Bettina von Arnim
This Book Belongs to the King
1843

There were once people—charburners who lived deep in the forest where blooming trees do not grow, only pines and firs perhaps. — The child of these poor people had never seen a cherry or a red apple. Nor did the rose bloom there. The secrets of nature which reveal its magic and delight had not reached into the lonesome wild. Yet one time the head of the family, traveling for miles, brought from the market just such a nature secret of the red delicious sort. With a very red cheek, the black core buds smiling playfully, and noble round-ness extending soft and smooth towards both poles, as the great Euler, New-ton, and Copernicus describe the world's globe. — Why shouldn't the apple imitate in its round curve that which is the object of each creature's becoming. — So did the child's heart, isolated from the world, by gazing at the apple with a longing of consuming fire, pay tribute to the ideal spirit of nature. — This brought the small earth dweller soon to the end of his journey. The inner ideal swelled the flood of his enthusiasm; nowhere in the desert did he find a gentle shore that could smooth it; it burst through to eternity with a double stroke of the pulse.

The innocent one stepped into heaven's chamber, the apple in hand, he did not let go of it in death, you take with you what you love, — his gaze did not fall on the emerald leaf-adorned gold and ruby fruits of paradise, painted by the sun in heaven's arched windows. — No! — When you love,—truly—a strange desire tugs not at the long-cherished desire of love. — The wonders of creation of the Almighty Father were invisible to the loving eye, and the songs of praise of everlasting echo that coursed through the heavens did not resound in his ear. — Only as creator of his apple did he perceive the Maker of all majesties and the lonely children of the desert. The white beard flowed like clouds of

Translation by Rex Clark and Oliver Lubrich, from Bettina von Arnim, *Dies Buch gehört dem König* (Berlin: E. H. Schröder, 1843), 1:V–VIII.

dawn around the godly image, likeness for humanity, softly separating God from the distraction-laden universe of heaven's treasure. No reflection of thousand-hued phantasy dared be mirrored in this beard's whiteness of shining solitude.

Here the stranger felt at home! — "Isn't the flowing over there like the smoke from the charcoal burner as it moves through the brush with a stiff morning breeze? And just like the ascending fog hangs in tufts on the firs and pines?" — No, it is the beard's fullness from which a godly, familiar human face shines on him. Then he hands his favorite to God as a present, as devout children will do.

God the Father took the gift without observing it. He knows by heart the products of his creation. Even though perhaps sometimes in the observing of them he reflects upon himself. He places the apple behind himself, on the mantelpiece, yet his gaze was turned to the innocent giver, who henceforth paid homage no longer to the apple but in loving contemplation to the creator of all beauty.

If only a well-formed roundness had lent *this* gift such desire, just as the favored apple had received it from nature, so there might have been hope for leniency from God the Father; and nothing would have been made of this apple, so there would not have been any fear that it would roll unnoticed down those stairs again, up which it had been carried in enthusiastic desire of giving; growing on the tree of knowledge which only carries alluring fruit, it had turned out twisted and crooked, Adam and Eve would have stood in the shadow of the tree free of sin for eternity, ere out of boredom they would bite the bad apple.

Ah, only with difficulty can boredom slip among the Horae who with flowered garlands wreath the ever-moving dance of the Muses on the steps of the throne of a king who loves them. Jealous Muses! — You make no room, — you sink not your head and slumber anon so that boredom might come with the apple covered with commas, question and exclamation marks like summer freckles. And the good Humboldt, the great, the wise, who also bows to a lesser, may he make the apple appetizing, arranging it with mild harmony and sense of spirit. Perhaps! — Yes, perhaps then surpassing you Muses.

Chapter 23

RALPH WALDO EMERSON
Journals
1845

Kosmos.
The wonderful Humboldt, with his extended centre and expanded wings, marches like an army, gathering all things as he goes. How he reaches from science to science, from law to law, tucking away moons and asteroids and solar systems in the clauses and parentheses of his encyclopaedical paragraphs!

The Journals and Miscellaneous Notebooks of Ralph Waldo Emerson: Volume IX, 1843–1847, ed. Ralph H. Orth and Alfred R. Ferguson (Cambridge, MA: The Belknap Press of Harvard University Press, 1971), 270. Copyright © 1971 by the President and Fellows of Harvard College. Reprinted by permission of the publisher.

Chapter 24

CHARLES DARWIN
Letters
1845–1854

Letter to J. D. Hooker

Down, 10 February 1845

I grieve to hear Humboldt is failing; one cannot help feeling, though unrightly, that such an end is humiliating: even when I saw him he talked beyond all reason. If you see him again, pray give him my most respectful and kind compliments, and say that I never forget that my whole course of life is due to having read and re-read as a youth his 'Personal Narrative.' How true and pleasing are all your remarks on his kindness; think how many opportunities you will have, in your new place, of being a Humboldt to others.

Letter to J. D. Hooker

Shrewsbury, September 1845

I write a line to say that Cosmos arrived quite safely (N.B. One sheet came loose in Part I), and to thank you for your nice note. I have just begun the introduction, and groan over the style, which in such parts is full half the battle. How true many of the remarks are (i.e. as far as I can understand the wretched English) on the scenery; it is an exact expression of one's own thoughts.

Charles Darwin, *The Life and Letters of Charles Darwin, Including an Autobiographical Chapter,* ed. Francis Darwin (London: John Murray, 1887), 1:336; 2:30, 43.

Letter to J. D. Hooker

Down, 26 March 1854

I shall be curious to hear what Humboldt will say: it will, I should think, delight him, and meet with more praise from him than any other book of Travels, for I cannot remember one, which has so many subjects in common with him. What a wonderful old fellow he is. ...

Chapter 25

Hans Christian Andersen
Diaries
1846

1 January 1846

Dinner with old professor Horkel, there I met both of the Grimm brothers, Wilhelm always teases me, Weiß and his wife. — Returning home in the evening I found a letter from Humboldt telling me that the King had told him to write me, that if it were convenient, in regard to my travels, for me to come to Potsdam, then he [the King] would receive me. I was pleased. Evening with Professor Bekker, who says nothing in seven languages. Here I met Countess Ahlefeldt, who couldn't speak Danish, Curtius was there.

3 January 1846

Headache. I visited Chamisso's children, the older one is called Ernst, the younger Max. Went to visit Tieck, who had tried to find me without success in the "Hotel Brandenburg" and he invited me out for dinner; he wanted to read to me "Yuletide Parlor." Frau Steffens also left an invitation for me. Went to Frau Savigny, in order to avoid an invitation to Prince Radziwill, since I so much wanted to see Shakespeare's "A Midsummer Night's Dream"; the Prince had a birthday, I met the Princess of Prussia, who gave me an invitation for tomorrow. At home I found a summons from the King, that he wanted to see me in Potsdam; ate with Simion, Geibel was there, traveled at seven o'clock by train to Potsdam, couldn't find my way into the palace, talked to the watch guards; the King and the Queen were very gracious, they sat on the sofa, Hum-

Translation by Cathrine Blom, from *Dagbøger 1825–1875*, vol. 3, 1845–1850, eds. Helga Vang Lauridsen and Tue Gad (Copenhagen: G. E. C. Gad, 1974), 38–39, 39–40. Every effort has been made to trace the copyright holder and to obtain permission for the use and translation of this excerpt.

boldt and I at the same table, two ladies in waiting and three gentlemen at another [table], drank tea, I read "The Fir Tree," "The Ugly Duckling," "The Top
and the Ball," and "The Swineherd"; I sat where Oehlenschläger had sat, the
King spoke of Denmark and of nature, was enthusiastic; Humboldt very much
so about my tales. After eleven o'clock I set out, went to the inn "Einsiedler"
and got a room.

Chapter 26

HONORÉ DE BALZAC

The Involuntary Comedians

1846

One of the Three Grand Coiffeurs of Paris

"Pray say no more, monsieur! I looked for better things from you. I mean to say that a hairdresser (I do not say a good hairdresser, for one is either a hairdresser or one is not), a hairdresser is not so easily found as—what shall I say?—as—I really hardly know—as a Minister—(sit still) no, that will not do, for you cannot judge of the value of a Minister, the streets are full of them. A Paganini?—no, that will not quite do. A hairdresser, monsieur, a man that can read your character and your habits, must have that in him which makes a philosopher. And for the women! But there, women appreciate us, they know our value; they know that their triumphs are due to us when they come to us to prepare them for conquest—which is to say that a hairdresser is—but no one knows what he is. I myself, for instance, you will scarcely find a—well, without boasting, people know what I am. Ah! well, no, I think there should be a better yet. Execution, that is the thing—! Ah, if women would but give me a free hand; if I could but carry out all the ideas that occur to me!—for I have a tremendous imagination, you see—but women will not cooperate with you, they have notions of their own, they will run their fingers or their combs through the exquisite creations that ought to be engraved and recorded, for our works only live for a few hours, you see, sir. Ah! a great hairdresser should be something like what Carême and Vestris are in their lines. (Your head this way, if you please, I am catching the expression. That will do.) Bunglers, incapable of understanding their epoch or their art, are the ruin of our profession. They deal in wigs, for instance, or hair-restorers, and think of nothing but sell-

Honoré de Balzac, *The Unconscious Mummers*, trans. Ellen Marriage, in *The Novels of Balzac: Seraphita and other Stories*, ed. George Saintsbury (Philadelphia, PA: The Gebbie Publishing Co., 1899), 28:377–379.

ing you a bottle of stuff, making a trade of the profession; it makes one sorry to see it. The wretches cut your hair and brush it anyhow. Now, when I came here from Toulouse, it was my ambition to succeed to the great Marius, to be a true Marius, and in my person to add such luster to the name as it had not known with the other four. "Victory or death!" said I to myself. (Sit up, I have nearly finished.) I was the first to aim at elegance. My salons excited curiosity. I scorn advertisements; I spend the cost of advertisements on comfort, monsieur, on improvements. Next year I shall have a quartette in a little salon; I shall have music, and the best music. Yes, one must beguile the tedium of the time spent in the dressing room. I do not shut my eyes to the unpleasant aspects of the operation. (Look at yourself.) A visit to the hairdresser is, perhaps, quite as tiring as sitting for a portrait. Monsieur knows the famous Monsieur de Humboldt? (I managed to make the most of the little hair that America spared to him, for science has this much in common with the savage—she is sure to scalp her man.) Well, the great man said, as monsieur perhaps knows, that if it was painful to go to be hanged, it was only less painful to sit for your portrait. I myself am of the opinion of a good many women, that a visit to the hairdresser is more trying than a visit to the studio. Well, monsieur, I want people to come here for pleasure. (You have a rebellious tuft of hair.) A Jew suggested Italian opera singers to pluck out the gray hairs of young fellows of forty in the intervals; but his signoras turned out to be young persons from the Conservatoire, or pianoforte teachers from the Rue Montmartre. Now, monsieur, your hair is worthy of a man of talent. Ossian!" (to the lackey in livery) "Brush this gentleman's coat, and go to the door with him. Who comes next?" he added majestically, glancing round a group of customers waiting for their turn.

Chapter 27

BERNHARD VON LEPEL

To Humboldt: An Ode

1847

The sun arose into the sign of the scales
During your birth:
Equilibrium and justice

You arrived to search, be it in the sky
Where orbiting matter
To matter is bound,

Be it in the deepest seclusion of the sea where
Through cellular moss atoms circle compulsively—
The research plunges deep, until the soul
Dives into the soul of the macrocosm

Through flaming clouds, there once thundered down
The voice of the Lord from the mount;
Down knelt man

And quaked, struck dumb by the sound of might:
He cast into bronze
The rigid *thou shalt.*

Yet there at the city's gates already lurked
The laughing Sphinx, she seized him with scorn:
Die, son of freedom, she called, or
Solve the riddle of the world: *Who are you?*

Translation by Steven Sidore, from Bernhard von Lepel, *An Humboldt. Ode* (Berlin: Alexander Duncker, 1847).

Wisdom kept watch there: soon on the Indus
Soon it meditated on the Nile;
Its fingers seized

The veil on the head of one dark deity—
Yet thicker still wove
The veil about the god.

Yet from afar, hearkening and prescient, Pythagoras
Heard the harmonic sound of the spheres;
A grand life, free in beauty
Undulated the quiet world of Plato.

It lightened, and from the crib
Up looked lovingly
The smiling God;

Yet once again the altar's smoke hid
With gloomy power
The divine countenance,

And dark night dimmed exploring vision.
Now spirits again rattled the iron bar—
And with brash voice the truth broke free
Behind the pledge of Galilei

With liberated verve now flew into space
The pondering mind:
Planets seized

And *swayed* Newton's mighty hand:
Discover he did the world's
Detaining power,

The binding force that bears and holds worlds.—
And look, man is again peaking the mount today;
A grand law in mind, he ascends
Today the peak of Chimborazo.

Up into the sky he sees hurled
The glowing stone
Through alien power;

Soon enough, though, the depths of the world
Rip it back down with elementary force,
Falling ever faster:

Anything moving to freedom is cut off imperially;
No matter where it lives, none may go free;
Demanding unity, strict and ferocious
The depths sacrifice everything to the grand altar!

Far behind the furthest star of Orion
There it shimmers in white
Like the fog of the night.

There mighty maelstroms spin around.
There a mixture fights
To find firm form,

In eternal conflict, energy is roused to energize
Seizing chaotically and then losing itself again,
Until finally there rolls forth from the fray
The power of unity, full of victor's pride.

Now the earthly ball floats in the freedom of space:
Yet greedily there arrives
A new force,

Escaping raw death, it revolves
Around its fiery grave,
The source of light;

Even if today the shielding forces hold it back,
Yet tomorrow a certain fall shall overtake it,
And all desire for sonorous change
Is ended by terrifying fate, annihilation.

Only the quiet balance of all forces
Checks it and preserves
Your fleeting being,

The world tumbling in the pull of the sun!
Its own force
Spreading out,

Your giant body grasps things that meander too close:
The flaming meteor you yank suddenly into the grave.
And you twirl about on a chain of mastery
Your gleaming satellite

Which incites the tides up to the edge,
Although back they are pulled
By the greater might.

Ha, sounds of the nearby struggle ring louder:
Keening departs
The elusive *wind,*

And saves itself in the blue, quiet distance;
Yet the earth's body greedily sucks it in again—
Nestled against its warm breast
In glowing spasm it quivers electric.

Down fall the trembling drops of the clouds;
From the high mountains
In a torrential fall

Down to the pit of the sea the *waters* rush,
And unto the land
The ocean floods.

On the wings of the storm it seizes about in wild haste,
And pulsates high in furious flood surges
Yet swells are always retrieved
Ripped down by the infinite, black depths.

Rigid in form shaped round the *earth* lies,
The force of mass
Presses down deep;

And denser and denser it becomes, and darker
From layer to layer,
Her nocturnal womb:

There it lies, carried to death's deepest dungeon,
Earlier fighting against him, the buried world;
Quietly rests its nothingness entombed in the dark
Under hardened veins of ore

Yet trapped deep in the seat of earthly riches
But never snuffed out,
To new violence

The blaze ever inciting, the *fire* lives:
Scornfully growing up
From its lurking repose.

High it arches up the plain to the towering mountain,
The giant wall broken open by the force of the blaze,
And in victory it cries out: I live!—
But it casts the world in ruins.

What do you prettify, threatened on all sides by eternal calamity
With fragrant dress
O Lily, thou!

On the silent cliff, why do you sway, grassy meadow,
In every blade
A burning impulse!

Wherefore do you wear the crown, majestic palm,
Why do you reach to the heavens, stubborn cedar-lings?—
Seeking your innumerable growing life
There lurks in the ground hidden destruction.

You who eternally thirst for freedom,
You spirits pushed down
With decrepit material,

Why do you look up in hope,
Why search ye the path
Over the grave,

Since in the universe's swirling tumult of battle
You see every existence crash and die.
And all around, the grand, dark parable
Prophesying your own obscured end!

To grandest triumph may man incite
His deep nature,
And then go into death

Love ablaze with eternity's breath,
Should he throw down the lure
Of his own dream

And sacrifice willingly his small, fleeting self,
And, as he sees the Savior's willing victim,
So only in death shall freedom be found
Shall the divine son find reconciliation.

Once—when in the final conquest of unity
The battle was *completed,*
And with joyful cries

A life in the victory glow of omnipotence
In full form
Emerged from the crypts,

Then in quiet *one* eternal, calm spirit flows up:
A quiet sea, crystalline and never clouded—
No drop shall be lost—all
Flow in the blessed realm of peace.—

Where day was never engulfed by the day,
Where never was separated
The pole from the pole;

Where in quiet contemplation in soft light
Love enjoys
The rewards of love;

Where under the vaults of eternal May green
Quiet rests the friendship, but the union of souls
Divides not you and I, where the yearning
Never dispatched to afar the sigh.

To you, though, on the altar of earnest wisdom,
Where the quiet sounds
Of your certain word

The mighty image of the universe unfurls,
They approach thee in fame's
Many voiced procession

The steps of poesy, fervently moved, O aged sir;
They roam in the orbit of your unveiled world
And rise up, just as your intuition,
Above the limits of the grand enigma.

It may well flee to the sun's glow,
It may well sink itself down
Into the sea, the spirit—

Reassuringly from your word flows insight
And full gratification
Toward the seeker.

Serenely he sees the giant whole emerging,
Sees deep in the reflecting image of the whole his own self,
And wafting through the earnest drama
He feels the refreshing breeze of beauty.

Chapter 28

Franz Grillparzer

Journals

1847

Met with Alexander Humboldt in Berlin. He said nothing but fine and sensible things. But the intellectual atmosphere was lacking. One doesn't sense the presence of an eminent man.

It is remarkable the facility with which A. Humboldt (*Kosmos,* Volume II) acquires and appropriates the opinions and sentiments of our current times which are so opposite to those of his age. This indicates a great vigor of the spirit, or a great shallowness.

Translation by Richard John Ascárate, from Franz Grillparzer, *Sämtliche Werke. Historisch-kritische Gesamtausgabe,* ed. August Sauer, vol. 11, *Tagebücher und literarische Skizzenhefte V, vom Frühjahr 1842 bis gegen Ende 1856* (Vienna: Kunstverlag Anton Schroll & Co., 1924), 173, 175.

Chapter 29

Edgar Allen Poe
Eureka: A Prose Poem
1848

With Very Profound Respect,
This Work is Dedicated
To
Alexander von Humboldt.

Preface

To the few who love me and whom I love—to those who feel rather than to those who think—to the dreamers and those who put faith in dreams as in the only realities—I offer this Book of Truths, not in its character of Truth-Teller, but for the Beauty that abounds in its Truth; constituting it true. To these I present the composition as an Art-Product alone:—let us say as a Romance; or, if I be not urging too lofty a claim, as a Poem.

What I here propound is true:—therefore it cannot die:—or if by any means it be now trodden down so that it die, it will "rise again to the Life Everlasting."

Nevertheless it is as a Poem only that I wish this work to be judged after I am dead.

E. A. P.

Eureka: An Essay on the Material and Spiritual Universe

It is with humility really unassumed—it is with a sentiment even of awe—that I pen the opening sentence of this work: for of all conceivable subjects, I ap-

Edgar Allen Poe, *Eureka: A Prose Poem* (New York: Geo. P. Putnam, 1848), 3 (Dedication), 7–10.

proach the reader with the most solemn—the most comprehensive—the most difficult—the most august.

What terms shall I find sufficiently simple in their sublimity—sufficiently sublime in their simplicity—for the mere enunciation of my theme?

I design to speak of the *Physical, Metaphysical and Mathematical—of the Material and Spiritual Universe:—of its Essence, its Origin, its Creation, its Present Condition, and its Destiny.* I shall be so rash, moreover, as to challenge the conclusions, and thus, in effect, to question the sagacity, of many of the greatest and most justly reverenced of men.

In the beginning, let me as distinctly as possible announce—not the theorem which I hope to demonstrate—for, whatever the mathematicians may assert, there is, in this world at least, *no such thing* as demonstration—but the ruling idea which, throughout this volume, I shall be continually endeavoring to suggest.

My general proposition, then, is this:—*In the Original Unity of the First Thing lies the Secondary Cause of All Things, with the Germ of their Inevitable Annihilation.*

In illustration of this idea, I propose to take such a survey of the Universe that the mind may be able really to receive and to perceive an individual impression.

He who from the top of Ætna casts his eyes leisurely around, is affected chiefly by the *extent* and *diversity* of the scene. Only by a rapid whirling on his heel could he hope to comprehend the panorama in the sublimity of its *oneness*. But as, on the summit of Ætna, *no* man has thought of whirling on his heel, so no man has ever taken into his brain the full uniqueness of the prospect; and so, again, whatever considerations lie involved in this uniqueness have as yet no practical existence for mankind.

I do not know a treatise in which a survey of the *Universe*—using the word in its most comprehensive and only legitimate acceptation—is taken at all:—and it may be as well here to mention that by the term "Universe," wherever employed without qualification in this essay, I mean, in most cases, to designate *the utmost conceivable expanse of space, with all things, spiritual and material, that can be imagined to exist within the compass of that expanse.* In speaking of what is *ordinarily* implied by the expression "Universe," I shall take a phrase of limitation—"the Universe of stars." Why this distinction is considered necessary, will be seen in the sequel.

But even of treatises on the really limited, although always assumed as the *un*limited, Universe of *stars,* I know none in which a survey, even of this limited Universe, is so taken as to warrant deductions from its *individuality.* The nearest approach to such a work is made in the "Cosmos" of Alexander Von Humboldt. He presents the subject, however, *not* in its individuality but in its generality. His theme, in its last result, is the law of *each* portion of the merely physical Universe, as this law is related to the laws of *every other* portion of this merely physical Universe. His design is simply syncæretical. In a word, he discusses the universality of material relation, and discloses to the eye of Philosophy whatever inferences have hitherto lain hidden *behind* this universality. But however admirable be the succinctness with which he has treated each particular point of his topic, the mere multiplicity of these points occasions, necessarily, an amount of detail, and thus an involution of idea, which preclude all *individuality* of impression.

It seems to me that, in aiming at this latter effect, and, through it, at the consequences—the conclusions—the suggestions—the speculations—or, if nothing better offer itself, the mere guesses which may result from it—we require something like a mental gyration on the heel. We need so rapid a revolution of all things about the central point of sight that, while the minutiæ vanish altogether, even the more conspicuous objects become blended into one. Among the vanishing minutiæ, in a survey of this kind, would be all exclusively terrestrial matters. The Earth would be considered in its planetary relations alone. A man, in this view, becomes mankind; mankind a member of the cosmical family of Intelligences.

Chapter 30

KARL GUTZKOW

Knights of the Spirit

1850–1851

And what of the spirit? said Pauline. You forget the declaration of contradiction, in which the inner circles are entangled regarding that matter.

My dear lady, said Schlurck, the spirit is a chameleon or one of those delicate fishes of antiquity, which was supposedly found in Italian lakes and of whose flavor I can no more speak than I can of the most felicitous manner of its preparation. This fish, however, so much I do know, my dearest, had the curious characteristic that when pinched and martyred it affected a hundred colors. About the stomach, about the heart, there is agreement; it is well known that dining and loving, or, to express myself more properly, to be loved, in this regard guarantee the most satisfying enjoyments, but what concerns the spirit—its sustenance, its gratification—about this the guardians of the spirit, the great minds, knock their heads bloody in disagreement. What spirit was in the middle ages, one knew full well then: religion and scholasticism. What spirit was in the Reformation, that was also known, it was biblical exegesis and parsing of Hebrew words. What spirit was in the last century, that was known under the name of *esprit,* Voltaire, Hume. But what spirit is today, dear lady, what should now appear to one deep and to another superficial, about that more anarchy reigns than in legislation about exceptions and prescriptions. Do not be surprised if, upon this question, the inner circles maintain that it is more spiritual to grant victory to the community than to the exchequer.

For more spiritual? repeated Pauline, laughing. I am too weak-minded to grasp that. More romantic, you say!

My dearest, Schlurck continued, who had often noticed in Pauline that she allowed herself be instructed; you see, that is something that can be felt more than described. Let me give you an analogy. When I eat caviar, which I love

Translation by Richard John Ascárate, from Karl Gutzkow, *Die Ritter vom Geiste. Roman in neun Büchern,* vol. 3 (Leipzig: Brockhaus, 1850), 41–44; vol. 5 (Leipzig: Brockhaus, 1851), 79–80.

very much, especially when it arrives in the tavern fresh and nicely granular … when I eat caviar and the green wine glass filled with Riesling stands before me and one begins to argue about which is truer, the saying of a wise man or that of a fool, I like the fool better. I often hear authors with a refined style pronounce judgments, and because they were corrupt and my caviar and Riesling are giving me a nice tingle, I loudly proclaim: Corrupt here, corrupt there! First, write as they do! Serve me up your virtues in a style as radiant as that in which their vices are written, and then I would immediately like to throw into my library and at the heads of such babblers the entire collection of twelve or twenty magnificently bound works of these detested rakes! I love wit, evil, and striking antitheses in writing, others love the inflated, the magnificent, the intoxicating, the substantial, others on the other hand the harmless, the modest, the pious, the flowery, the precious. But. …

Yes, you describe our critical anarchy, justice councilor! Pauline broke in.

I describe our entire confusion of spirit. It is everywhere found, in all areas. The miraculous appears wonderful to the people. The exception is the rule for them. Even the outlandish is supposed to be a commonplace to them. Conviction! I do not care to hear about this, for the appetite for it becomes well-nigh uncomfortable. But these high-minded sensitive people label conviction as unattractive. Why? It stirs emotions! It bespeaks much! It compels camaraderie! It walks! It runs! It dreams when it should speak of a bicameral system, not about Humboldt's *Kosmos,* not about Goethe's *Morphology of Plants,* not about Dante's *Paradise* and *Inferno.* … How can one be so spiritless and speak of the time, of tendencies, of conviction? Do you understand? …

Oh, I'm realizing something about the "inner circles," Pauline said smiling.

⌒

And your own principle, inquired Egon urgently, who had almost been frightened by the confidence of this tone amidst the great uncertainty about what should now be accepted as Truth.

I almost confess, said Stromer, that I am altogether against this demand of a principle. One should no longer ask, What is truth? One should take a person singularly and derive the individual truth for each one alone. My God, this abundance of appearances is so fascinating! How lovely is the drive toward beauty, how heavenly, how divine to wallow in the outer form, in the harmony of parts, to listen in on celebratory moments of nature! On the other hand, I take notice of, I honor, the lonesome thinker who by lamplight with green visor o'er dulled eye seeks knowledge from parchment writings—a second Faust! Every joy in the world of appearances, even when it fills me completely, when its charms overwhelm me, how long does it last? Then come the Humboldts and ruin for me all the myths of the creation story; then the Liebigs dismantle everything certain and majestic into illusion and minor deception. And the

mechanical, is it not truly a yet-to-be-slaughtered giant, one who with the terrible cudgel of his mathematical laws demolishes everything and who has almost unhinged the world from its previous conceptions of its own abilities?
Yes, Your Highness, what is truth? Man is the only truth that we can grasp;
man in his desires, needs, man in his hate and in his love, man in his greatness
and in his impotence, and if the writer now has a profession, it is to teach truth
to aesthetics, that is, feeling and sensitivity, trembling and shouting for joy,
despair and triumph of the thinking Ego. Aesthetic world perspective, Your
Highness, this will lead us to a mediation of the extremes. In this regard, I
hope, if the pen does not fail me in service, to exert beneficial influence.

Egon, who held strictly to the principles of Cato, indeed, who retained
something Stoic in his convictions, was almost frightened by this vague, glim-
mering explanation, even though he was then not in a position to recognize
the danger that could arise for the character and purity of all struggles over
opinion from such an exuberantly rampant pliability of the spirit.

Chapter 31

KARL GUTZKOW
A Girl of the People
1852

"After two years a trip to Germany was spoken of. Ernestine could not be spared the return to the homeland, for these strong-willed people would not accept a refusal to go back. Thus did the most conciliatory coincidence enable me to see her again. It happened when I entered upon the princess just as a soft voice read from Humboldt's *Kosmos,* though my eye did not immediately fall upon the reader dressed in white. The voice of the one reading faltered as I was announced. But the princess compelled her once again to share with him, the newcomer introduced to the circle by her grandchildren, some passages about which she desired immediately to begin a conversation with me. I recognized then neither the delicate features of the reader nor her voice, shaking and struggling for composure. Only as she was allowed to be silent, to softly retire, only then was it as if in my memory I was hearing traces of an old melody, as if something spirit-like, strange, and yet so familiar was traversing the room. I ventured to ask a question—already sensing the truth—about the pale young woman who spoke so surely the most difficult words and enunciated so perfectly. Then, from the blind princess I heard the name, Ernestine Waldmann.

I dared not venture to the upper floors to visit her," continued Oswald, "but two days afterward, by the same fireplace, illuminated in the same way, I extended my trembling hand to Ernestine in greeting. The princess did not notice the speechless attentions between the two whom fate had destined for one another. Yet the princess asked, 'What is the matter?'—in French—when Ernestine failed to respond to one of her queries. Ernestine knew that in these surroundings both her suffering and her joy would be inconsequential. She overcame her feelings and replied in that same language that she was not well.—'You have overstrained yourself,' said the princess. 'You know, Herr Os-

---

Translation by Richard John Ascárate, from Karl Gutzkow, *Ein Mädchen aus dem Volke,* in: *Unterhaltungen am häuslichen Herd* (Leipzig: Brockhaus, 1853), vol. 1, no. 7:108–109.

wald,' she continued, turning to her visitor, 'this young lady is fanatical about education. Now I have to hear that she is studying Greek!'—Ernestine smiled and said in a tone full of allusion, 'For Russia not inappropriate.' This reminder of the priests propitiated the enlightened, firmly Protestant princess. 'Yes, yes! Why should I not disclose it,' she continued. 'I became acquainted with Fräulein Waldmann as a young lady who did not dare read *Kosmos* for fear of making a false step over the difficult expressions therein. She then studied the nights through and stumbles over them no more. But,' the princess went on, with feeling, 'I hear that also her cheeks are paler than is becoming for one of her youth and, as I hear, of her beauty. Not from others do I hear that you are beautiful, Ernestine; one hears in the voice who is graceful. We blind see with all of the organs which you use merely to hear and feel.' And then the princess again turned within herself."—

Oswald related that as these words were spoken he held Ernestine's quivering hand in his own, and covered it with kisses and tears. Thereupon a visit was announced and the evening transitioned in that form of self-mastery, which spread a new allure, a new magic over this reencounter.

Chapter 32

FRANZ GRILLPARZER

Journals

1852

There can be no starker opposites than the Humboldt brothers. Wilhelm, the most dreadful pedant; Alexander, on the other hand, the nimblest nature, ever prepared to relinquish long-cherished opinions for new (and, of course, grounded) perspectives. The latter can be a great spiritual strength, but also a superficial regard for that which is called conviction. One usually holds fast to something one has bound to his inner being. Wilhelm first became disgusting to me through his correspondence with Schiller as well as through his clumsy speculations in matters of art and aesthetics. His correspondence with a woman, which is indeed excellent, seems to contradict this pedantry. I believe, however, his own barrenness shocked him. He then wished to apply a sentimental dressing and thereby chose a woman at random with whom he could practice under fire. He finally became mired in speculative grammar, and in this sandy ground his potatoes thrived.

Translation by Richard John Ascárate, from Franz Grillparzer, *Sämtliche Werke. Historisch-kritische Gesamtausgabe,* ed. August Sauer, vol. 11, *Tagebücher und literarische Skizzenhefte V, vom Frühjahr 1842 bis gegen Ende 1856* (Vienna: Kunstverlag Anton Schroll & Co., 1924), 232.

Chapter 33

FREDERIC EDWIN CHURCH
Letters
1853

Bogotá, 7 July 1853

My dear Mother,
about a week ago I was overjoyed to receive two letters from home, the first that I have received, which is accounted for by the bad mail arrangements. [...] We intend to start tomorrow for Quito and have engaged a capital servant and his son, a boy of fifteen whom Mr. Field has offered to take to New York and bring up. The boy is as efficient as the majority of grown persons here. Our cavalcade will consist of Mr. F., myself, Tomás the servant, his son, a peon or guide and six mules. Mr. Field and myself each send home a trunk containing such clothing, etc. as we can manage to dispense with and such curiosities as we have been enabled to obtain.

I have been twice to the Salto or falls of Tequendama which is a most wonderful cataract. The river Bogotá after a long, torturous and tranquil course through the plains suddenly breaks through a gap in the mountains and falls in one unbroken sheet into a terrific chasm of 670 feet and then descends in a series of waterfalls and cascades about as much more. At the top of the fall you are in what is called the cold country with the trees, plants and fruits of temperate climates: at the bottom grow palms, oranges, etc. The clouds formed by evaporation from the falls sometimes cover the mountains for miles and entirely prevent a view of the falls. The descent to the foot is very difficult but Mr. Gooding, an American gentleman here, and myself undertook it and a native gentleman Señor Udinato procured seven peons or guides for us and accompanied us himself. First we descended into the warm country and then traced the stream up, the peons with their machetas (or long heavy knives)

Courtesy of The Winterthur Library: Joseph Downs Collection of Manuscripts and Printed Ephemera.

and axes cutting away the matted branches, roots, vines, etc. which entangle themselves so obstinately in a tropical country. Our course was a crooked one owing to the necessity of being obliged to climb up the sides of mountains to avoid precipices but in spite of all the difficulties we went along very readily and arrived at the foot of the falls. At some little distance I made a sketch in pencil and also one as near as the spray would allow me to see. Near the cataract below a perpetual and heavy rain falls which causes a number of rivulets,

Illustration 33.1. Fall of the Tequendama.

which run among the rocks into the main river. Owing to the tremendous evaporation the river below is not more than *half* as large as above. We all took dinner near the falls and I carried a small French machine and made a cup of tea for Mr. Gooding and myself close to the cataract. [...] Huge and gaudy macaws and other birds of brilliant plumage were sailing in the air and bright rainbows in the mist served to enliven the scene.

⁓

The late hour makes it necessary for me to retire as I shall be obliged to get up early to prepare for our journey. I send love to all.

Your affectionate son,
Frederic E. Church

Chapter 34

HEINRICH HEINE
Lutezia
1854

Hardhearted are the rich, that is true. They are so even against their onetime colleagues who have fallen a little in fortunes. I recently met poor August Leo, and my heart bled at the sight of the man who once was so intimately bound with the heads of the exchange, with the aristocracy of speculators, and was himself even something of a banker. But tell me, you highly privileged gentlemen, what did poor Leo do to you, that you thrust him so disdainfully from the congregation?—I don't mean from the Jews, I mean from the financial congregation. Yes, this man—of all men the most to be pitied—has enjoyed for some time the disfavor of his comrades to such a high degree that he is barred from all gainful employments (that is, from all employments, whereby he might gain anything) like a diseased outcast. Nor had anything been allowed to trickle down to him from the last loan, and he must completely abstain from participation in new railroad enterprises, since he suffered such a miserable setback in the Versailles Railroad on the *rive gauche,* and his people calculated such terrible losses. No one any longer wants to know anything about him, everyone pushes him away, and even his own friend (who, by the way, could never stand him), even his Jonathan, the stockjobber Läusedorf, left him and now assiduously follows Baron Meklenburg, all but crawling between his coat-tails.—I likewise mention in passing that said Baron Meklenburg, one of our most fervent stock brokers and industrialists, is not, as is commonly believed, in any way an Israelite, either because he is confused with Abraham Meklenburg or because he is always seen among the powerful of Israel, among the Cherethites and Pelethites of the exchange, where they gather around him; for they love him very much. These people are not religious fanatics, as is manifest, and their resentment towards poor Leo is therefore not to be ascribed to any

Translation by Richard John Ascárate, from Heinrich Heine, *Lutezia. Berichte über Politik, Kunst und Volksleben,* in *Vermischte Schriften* (Hamburg: Hoffmann und Campe, 1854), 3:120–125.

intolerant origin. They resent him not because of his apostasy from the beautiful Jewish religion, and they shrugged only in pity about the shabby religious conversion-business of poor Leo, who now performs the office of a churchwarden in the Protestant prayer house of *rue des Billettes*—certainly a significant position of honor, but a man like August Leo would have risen to great distinction in the synagogue with time. At a circumcision ceremony, his hands would have perhaps been entrusted with the child from whom the foreskin was to be cut or with the little knife, with which such a deed is done, or one would have lavished the most expensive honors of the day upon him for reading the *Torah*. Yes, because he is very musical and possesses such an abundant sensitivity for church music, he would perhaps have been given a part blowing the shofar, the holy horn, in Jewish New Year's celebrations. No, he is not a sacrificial lamb of religious or moral indignation on the part of pigheaded Pharisees, nor are failures of the heart imputed to poor Leo, but rather errors of calculation, and not even a Christian forgives lost millions. But take pity finally on the poor fallen, on the descended great, take him up again in mercy, let him once more take part in a good transaction, allow him once again a small profit, whereby his broken heart may be refreshed, *date obolum Belisario*—give an obolus to Belisarius, who was, it is true, no great commander but was blind and never in his life gave an obolus to one in need!

There are also patriotic reasons that make the preservation of poor Leo worthwhile. I hear that a hurt ego and the large losses require the once so prosperous man to leave costly Paris and retire to the country, where he dines—like Cincinnatus—on cabbage sown with his own hand or grazes—like some Nebuchadnezzar—on his own grass. That would be a great loss to the German community. Because every second- and third-class German traveler who came here to Paris found in Herr Leo's house a warm reception, and some who felt ill at ease in the frosty French world could flee here with their German hearts and could feel at home again with those of similar dispositions. On cold winter evenings they found warm tea, somewhat homeopathically prepared, but not entirely without sugar. They saw Herr von Humboldt here, actually in effigy, hanging on the wall as decoy. Here they saw Nasenstern in his natural element. A German countess could be found here as well. The most distinguished diplomats from gossipville also made an appearance, beside their ravenish and angular wives. Here one occasionally heard outstanding pianists and violinists, fresh virtuosos who were recommended to Leo's house by traders in souls and who allowed themselves to be musically exploited at his soirées. There the lovely sounds of the mother tongue, even of the grandmother tongue, greeted the Germans. Here was spoken most purely the dialect of the Hamburg Dreckwall district, and whosoever heard these classical sounds was encouraged, as if smelling again the alleys of Mönkedamm. Yet when the "Adelaide" of Beethoven was sung, how the most sentimental tears flowed! Yes, that house was an oasis, a very carrion-like oasis of German good nature in the sandy desert of French intellectual life. It was a summerhouse of the saddest cancans, where one banded together as along the banks of the Main, where one mingled as in the heart of the sacred city of Cologne, where sometimes the small talk of the fatherland was also accompanied by refreshment with a small glass of beer—German heart, what more do you need? What a dreadful shame it would be, were this den of gossip to close.

Chapter 35

ADALBERT STIFTER

Indian Summer

1857

At the ring of the bell a man came towards me from behind the garden bushes. As he stood before me on the inner side of the fence I saw that it was a man with snow-white hair which he didn't cover. Otherwise he was unremarkable and was wearing a kind of housecoat or whatever the thing should be called that fit tight all over and reached almost to his knees. He looked at me for a moment when he approached me and then said: "What do you want, dear sir?"

"A storm is approaching," I answered, "and it will soon pass over this area. I am a wanderer, as you can see by my pack, and therefore ask that I be given shelter in this house until the rain, or at least the worst of it, is over."

"The storm won't break," said the man.

"It won't be an hour, before it comes," I countered, "I am well acquainted with these mountains and I know a little about the clouds and storms in them."

"If the storm should not come," I said, "then I have no reason really to stop here; since it was only on account of the approaching storm that I departed from the road and climbed up to this house. But forgive me if I bring up the question again. I am practically somewhat of a natural scientist and I have concerned myself for several years with things of nature, with observations, and in particular with these mountains, and my experience says to me, that today a storm will pass over this area and this house."

"Now you should really by all means turn in here," he said, "now the issue is that we wait together and see which of us is right. I am not a natural scientist and can't really say that I have concerned myself with the sciences, but I

Translation by Richard John Ascárate and Rex Clark, from Adalbert Stifter, *Der Nachsommer* (Pesth: Gustav Heckenast, 1857), 1:66–67, 69–70, 74, 78–79, 91, 110–111, 116–118.

have read something about these matters, have tried during my life to observe things, and to think about what I've read and seen."

⁓

And now I was sitting in the white house, to which I had climbed, in order to await the storm.

⁓

After I had sat for quite a while and the sitting began to no longer provide me such comfort as in the beginning, I stood up and went on tip toes in order to protect the floor over to the bookcase in order to look at the books. There were however almost all literary authors. I found volumes of Herder, Lessing, Goethe, Schiller, translations of Shakespeare by Schlegel and Tieck, a Greek Odyssey, but then also some of Ritter's *Geography,* some of Johannes Müller's *History of Humanity* and some of Alexander and Wilhelm Humboldt. I put the literary writers aside and took Alexander Humboldt's *Travels in the Equinoctial Regions,* which I was familiar with, but always read again with pleasure. With my book I went back to my seat.

After not reading for very long, my host stepped in.

⁓

After some time my companion said, "Your journey doesn't have a purpose that would be disrupted by a stay of several hours or a day or several days."

"It is as you say," I answered, "my purpose is, as long as my strength lasts, to follow scientific pursuits and along the way to enjoy the out-of-doors life which I also do not feel is unimportant."

⁓

"I shall now leave you alone. In the anteroom today you were reading from Humboldt's *Travels.* I have left the book in this room. If you would like another book now or for the evening, just name it so that I may see whether it is to be found among my collection."

I declined the offer and said that I was satisfied with the present volume and that if I wanted to occupy myself with any other words besides Humboldt's, I had reserves in my little satchel: a pencil with which to write something and material written earlier to read through and polish, which occupation I often take up in the evenings while on my wanderings.

⁓

I closed the door behind him, took off my coat, and loosened my scarf, because, though the hour was already late, the peaceful night still bore considerable heat and humidity. I walked several times back and forth in my room, went to the window, leaned out, and observed the sky. Insofar as the darkness and the still bright, illuminating lightning allowed one to tell, the shapes of things appeared the same as they had this evening before the meal. Cloud fragments lay about in the heavens, while the stars revealed empty spaces between them. At times a lightning bolt charged forth from them over the hills of grain and the tops of the motionless trees, the thunder rolling along afterwards.

After I had enjoyed the fresh air for a while, I closed the one window, then the other as well, and gave myself over to rest.

Then, having read some time in bed, as was my custom, and during which I had even written some lines in my papers with the pencil, I extinguished the light and prepared myself for sleep.

Before slumber had fully overcome my senses, I still heard how a wind arose outside and set the tops of the trees to rustling strongly. I no longer had, however, enough strength to rouse myself, but just then drifted into sleep.

I slept very peacefully and fast.

As I awoke, the first thing I did was to observe whether it had rained. I leaped from the bed and tore open the window. The sun was coming up, the entire heaven was brilliant, no breeze stirred, from the garden sounded the chatter of birds, the roses emitted their fragrance, and the earth beneath my feet was completely dry. Only the sand had been swept somewhat against the green of the bordering grass, and a man was busy leveling it again to bring the whole into a proper balance.

Thus, my opponent had been right, and I was eager to learn upon what grounds he had been so certain, had argued so confidently against me, and how he had discovered and researched these causes.

Chapter 36

EUGEN HERMANN [VON DEDENROTH]

A Son of Alexander von Humboldt

1858

Some years ago, back when there were still censors in Berlin and the privy councilors had not yet moved into the exclusive quarter beyond the Potsdam and Anhalt Gates, but rather pursued their noiseless existence in all streets of the royal city, back when there were still the green Gendarmes and smoking on the streets cost two thaler, when the noble race to the peaks of periodic literature was run by Auntie Voß and Uncle Spener, that is, a very, very long time ago: the works of art at the painting exhibit of the Berliner Academy drew high praise, and not just because the expressing of reproval could lead the reviewer to be cast down into the despised class of the unpopular, but rather because the art in this case had borne extraordinary fruits on the market. Because however live examples of the beauties painted there in oil and watercolors were also to be found at the Academy, I made my way there more frequently than the draw of the images themselves alone could have justified.

For some time now I had noticed that there was a man who stood before the new image of the famous nature researcher Alexander von Humboldt, a man who appeared to have come to the Academy solely because of that painting, since he planted himself before it, regarded it, paced back and forth several times, returned again to the painting and only left the exhibit when it closed, to return again for more of the same amusement on the next day. In the beginning I thought him a disciple of the sciences, who studies the features of the worthy man, to deduce character from his expressions, as one might do from his writings, but after more extensive observation it was impossible to

Translation by Steven Sidore, from Eugen Hermann [von Dedenroth], *Ein Sohn Alexander's von Humboldt oder der Indianer von Maypures*, in *Gesammelte Novellen und Skizzen* (Leipzig: Rollmann; Philadelphia: John Weik, 1858), 3–4, 4–12, 16–18, 19, 20–22, 53, 126, 128–129, 129–138.

mistake this tall, broad-shouldered man for an industrious academic. He was too changeable, too agile to have lived at the lectern of science, too muscular to have worked alone with the quill; the reddish-brown face would have made a sea captain proud, the dark, fiery, dynamic eyes could follow the flight of an eagle, outsmart a fox, but not search for learned morsels in the pages of a folio.

"What business does this man have before the portrait of Alexander von Humboldt?" I asked myself involuntarily, and my curiosity grew with each day. The learned man appeared to be neither a buccaneer nor a hunter, between himself and the viewer of the painting there could be so little relationship as between a Lord and the Swiss guide who once showed his eminence the way.

"A very accurate portrait!" I murmured so loud that the stranger could hear it, as I positioned myself next to him and cast a glance at the reddish-brown man that indicated to him that he was welcome to reply to this commentary.

The stranger looked down on me from above in a manner akin to a rich planter looking down on a cheeky Negro, and turned his back to me with such phlegmatic coarseness that I was convinced that I was seeing either a son of Albion or a seller of lumber before me, as he was too well fed to be a pre-revolutionary postal clerk.

I touched him lightly on the arm and commented both briefly and brusquely that he was standing in my light and had viewed the portrait long enough, and that other people should be afforded the pleasure as well.

What I had expected came to be. Course people thaw when treated coarsely, and cold-blooded fish feel at home only in cold water.

The stranger gave me a second glance, this time expressing surprise and curiosity; he appeared not to be accustomed to having anyone touch his Herculean extremities.

"Goddam, what you want?" he asked in broken German, with that nasal tone which so perfectly characterized John Bull, while taking a half step backward.

I right away squared myself up so broadly that he also had to retract his other leg as well, and responded to him with the most indifferent and gentlemanly of demeanor:

"I wish to see the picture, the gentleman is an acquaintance of mine."

My statement was somewhat bold, but since I was in the fourth grade of school, Alexander von Humboldt was no longer a stranger to me, and since I had, what is more, even read his shorter texts, I could more justifiably count myself among his acquaintances just as Herr Mayor R ... who, having received a missive about the poor cobblestones in the city of X ... in a cabinet memorandum with the sovereign's personal signature, boasted of being known to His Majesty.

My words were hardly uttered before I regretted them, as the stranger appeared to grasp them in their entire momentousness.

"What is this man called, your acquaintance, Humbug, isn't it?"

"No," I said, smiling over the haste with which the stranger was speaking, "His name is Alexander von Humboldt."

"Umboldt, right, that's the one name, Humbug is the other."

"You're mistaken, Herr von Humboldt has nothing to do with Humbug," I responded.

The stranger appeared not to heed my objection; perhaps he didn't even hear it at all, as he appeared to be considering something else.

"This man is alive?" he asked me suddenly.

"Certainly."

"Does she live in province?"

"Yes, in Berlin no less."

"I want to talk to him. Show me his house."

The stranger appeared to expect that I would leave the Academy with him and immediately bring him to Humboldt as if to a barber or a rarity cabinet where no more than a few pennies was required as admission; and he appeared to interpret the astounded look with which I regarded him in a most peculiar way, for seeing me stop short he added: "I will pay for the trip."

"Most friendly," I laughed at this truly trans-oceanic fantasy that holds all things to be for sale, "I am no wage servant, but rather a gentleman; and as un-flattering as your offering is to my person, I would gladly proffer you the favor if it were to have any chance of fruition. Herr von Humboldt will not admit you."

"What? And why not? Is Master Humbug ill?"

"No, but Herr Humboldt considers his time very precious and receives only men of science, dignitaries, chamberlains and under exceptional cases per-haps a rare monstrosity, but under no circumstances a stranger whose name he doesn't even know."

"Me he'll let in," the reddish-brown man answered without showing the slightest sensitivity to my dismissal, with the self-confidence of a Yankee, "I'll tell him that I come from Orinoco, the great water."

"From Orinoco!" I exclaimed, now regarding the stranger with interest. "Truly, that is a different matter. Herr von Humboldt has a fondness for the Orinoco, and as widely as he has travelled around the world, the memory of the virgin forests of that river is dearest to him. But," I added doubtfully, "are you so well known there that it would be of interest to Herr von Humboldt to speak with you about that majestic area?"

"I am born there, at Maypures on the great waterfall," the stranger said in a tone so indifferent that he might as well have been saying his homeland was in nearby Teltow or Jüterbog.

"What!" I cried, "Are you an Indian?" and the reddish-brown forehead of the stranger appeared to glow before me with the heat of the tropics and thou-sands of romantic images from the American library that I had read in my youth crowded against my soul; I thought to see the last Inca before me who, in desperation over the fate of the Children of the Sun, had left the Cordillera and put on a European tailcoat. Never in my life did the fantastical dress of Paris appear so prosaic on the body of a man as that tailcoat appeared on what was in any case the sensuously tattooed body of my Indian.

"I am child of the white man who came to blue mountains," the American answered.

"What," I cried, practically breathless from taut interest and curiosity. "You don't mean to say—you're surely not—"

"What?" the Indian asked, as I dared to bring across my lips the question already decorating my fantasy.

"A son of Humboldt!" I exclaimed.

"I—I am Humbug or Umboldt, as you name the man. That is painting of my father."

With that he pointed to the portrait of Alexander von Humboldt.

I shook with surprise and joy. One glance was enough to satisfy me that no one had overheard us. I was in possession of a secret for which every writer would have paid me the Indian's weight in gold, had he possessed that many coins. This redskin was a treasure trove. How much the man could tell and how much he could add on in lies without anyone doubting him! I could write down his story and publish a novel without copying from a guidebook or plundering from a half-dozen forgotten writers. America was as foreign to me as history was to Louise Mühlbach, and I could write American novels like she could historical ones without a dozen gaffes on each page. And not to mention the material! A son of Humboldt! I was quivering at the thought of sending my manuscript to a publisher, where Frau Birch-Pfeif[f]er might happen to see it and make a comedy of it before I even had the galley proofs in my hand.

Nothing is more dangerous than an idea, than literary material; no cabinet of Arnheim is in a position to protect such treasures from thieves; books and people are plundered like the Christmas trees, empty long before the New Year's Eve of their oblivion, the best thoughts—the sweets—wander into the hungry belly of the aesthetes, and how they are digested there, that is something the audience of the lending library knows and that can be seen in the books sitting prominently with their gilt edgings in the display windows of the courtly bookstore of the book-'knights.'

But my joy was soon to be quenched. I had taken the arm of my Indian, this exquisite treasure from the topics, and to ensure that he was mine alone, I promised him that I would arrange for him to see Humboldt that very day, and to speak with him no later than tomorrow.

~

"So," I asked, "have you previously seen Humboldt's picture?"

"Yes, indeed," he answered, "how else would I have known him again? But it was a young man and now it is an old man."

"But how do you know then that he is your father?"

"Because it's his portrait and the name Humbug."

"But," I objected, "the original of the painting is named Humboldt, not Humbug."

"That doesn't matter at all," he answered with his characteristic obstinacy, "I know that it was him, he was in Maypures."

The answer was given in a tone that did not allow me to further insist on my doubts. I therefore changed the topic and hurried to come to the point which interested me most actively.

"Your life story must be extremely interesting," I said.

"Yes," he answered, "I have experienced much and seen much."

"In your place," I continued, "I would not hold back such a rich and instructive history from the world, and would either publish my memoirs on my own or entrust them to the expert hand of an author."

"That I will not do," the Indian replied quickly, "because what I say is only truth—and people love lies. If I wanted printed my diaries, they would not think it was truth, because there is much in it different than in the books about America, which are lies."

"What," I cried, "You've kept a diary!"

"Certainly; since I have learned writing and have gotten education I have recorded my experiences."

"I hope," I said with anxious energy, "that you find me worthy of at least learning the contours of your interesting life. I myself am a writer and therefore know how books are fabricated. It would be my most closely held desire just once to hear something not exaggerated about America."

"If I wanted to be explaining my story to everyone who wants to hear it," replied my reddish-brown friend, "then I would have to chatter very much and would very become tired. But since you are a writer, I will give you my diary. You do understand English language?"

"Certainly," I cried, although I could barely decipher it. "While I cannot speak English, I can read it well."

"Good. Then read this book and tell me your judgment whether I am right to believe that the famous Herr Humbug will be satisfied with his son. I do not want that my father is ashamed of me, I'd rather go back to Maypures, because I am also a proud man."

He stepped over to a suitcase made of palisander wood which, wrapped with gleaming brass bands, had the appearance of a footlocker and took from it a manuscript which he handed me.

～

I […] left him then, both to satisfy my curiosity and to provide him no time to set limits on the use of the manuscript he had entrusted to me, for I had made the decision to thoroughly plunder it, since the author had not intended it to be printed.

Let all be herewith warned against recounting your life story or giving your diaries to an author; it will be indiscriminately sent into the public realm, even if it should offer no more than the outlines of a comic figure. The diary of the American was written in good and, what was rather amenable to me, in legible English; I will share the content before I continue with the rest of my experiences with the adventurous son of Humboldt. Should the style be deficient and a gap or weak spot appear here or there, then I beg the reader to remember that this is a translation from English, and I am not so lucky as to have enjoyed Mr. Jacobi's written or Mr. Selig's oral Universal Instruction in this language.

*

The Story of the Indian

My home land is the most beautiful country in the world. The iron-black cliff masses arise like ruins and fortresses from the mile-long, foaming surface of the Orinoco—thick fog wisps across the blue mirror of the water and the green tips of high palms penetrate through the steaming clouds of foam. The beams of the glowing sun break apart in the moist air, and thousands of colored arches gleam like visual magic across the majestic scene. The melastoma, drosera, the little silver-leafed mimosas and splendid ferns adorn the bleak stone like flower beds. In the blue distance the eye rests on the mountain chain of the Cunavami, whose coned peaks abut the azure horizon and which, illuminated by the setting sun, glow like glaciers in reddish fire. There a palm bush breaks forth from the frothing surface of the water, and on the high rock nests the golden yellow Barbary Partridge with its resplendent feather crown—the loveliest bird of the tropical world. Here the cliffs stare out into the blue current and its moist walls are clad with luminescent byssus. The thunder of the waterfall numbs the ear. There, out across the western shore, the gaze rests on the immeasurable grassy meadow of the Meta. The fragrant steppe laughs back colorful and verdant. The weed-like mimosa raises its drowsing leaves to the sun, like the bird's early song greeting the light. Out in the high, tall-reaching grasses the beautifully spotted jaguar lurks. On the horizon the Uniana Mountain looms like a threateningly towered mass of clouds. When the sun disappears—the shadows of vultures and the cawing nightjar flitter across the dull cliff walls, and then the lunar disk, surrounded by colored rings, stands high in the zenith. It illuminates the fringe of the fog covering the water's foaming surface like clouds with sharp borders. Countless insects pour their phosphor-like light over the weed-covered earth, the ground glows with living fire, as if the star-filled firmament had sunk down onto the grassy meadow. Tendriled bignonias, fragrant vanilla and yellow-blooming banisteriopsis adorn the entry to the caves where man can lay his head to rest.

The rapids in the current appear like a countless collection of little cascades formed by small islands in the 8000 foot-wide river. Just a short way away lies Maypures, my birthplace, in a large and wild area of nature. The air is filled with countless flamingos and other water birds, set off from the blue heavens like a dark cloud with a fine, constantly shifting border. The edge of the forest, stretching out across the broad surface, is bounded by a low hedge; behind it arises the almost impenetrable wall of giant-sized trunks. There are openings in the hedges, made by the animals of the forest to allow access to the river. As evening falls the forest comes to life. The crocodiles approach shore, one hears the snorting of the dolphins. The multihued herons, the proudly strutting peacock pheasant turn to the river to drink and bathe. Wild animal calls tumble through the forest. One can distinguish between the monotonous moaning wail of the howler apes, the whimpering, fine fluting tones of the sapajou, the scratching grumble of the owl monkeys, the scream of the tiger, of the cougar, of the sloth and of the parrot. "The animals are celebrating the full moon," the Indian says.*

*Note: It can be seen that the Indian had read and made use of the "Views of Nature."

~

[In the following part of his narrative, the Indian gives an account of his birth and biography. Tibeima, his mother, was seduced by "a white man," "whom his fellows referred to as 'Humbug' whenever he spoke." He was part of a group of four strangers who traversed his native country as "envoys of the great Spirit," using mysterious instruments and "measuring everything." Before she died, she asked her son to find his "white father." As the young man grows up he is hired to work for a Dutch landowner, Van Heeren. Among black slaves, the mestizo is in the company of the foreman Wilkins and the monk Rosalba. He secretly falls in love with Van Heeren's daughter, Maria, when the following tragedy occurs:]

A neighboring plantation owner came over to Van Heeren's in order to conclude an agreement; he was a rather young man, was considered very rich and on first sight his appearance was pleasing. I noticed very soon that Herr Van Holk followed Maria with his gaze which expressed clearly enough, that he would have liked to make another agreement with Van Heeren, and Maria, instead, as I wished in secret, of punishing the lusting gazes of Herr Van Holk with indifference, busied herself so much with him and smiled so seductively and encouragingly, that I bit into my lips out of anger.

~

A piercing scream of pain and a muffled thud—Van Holk had killed his spouse.

Taken with rage, I knocked the miserable figure to the ground with a blow from the butt of my pistol, instructed Wilkins to bind him up, and jumped to Maria's aid; but she was lost, no further sound came to her lips, the bullet had pierced her heart.

Van Holk's Negros stormed up the stairs upon hearing the shot, but when they saw the corpse they shuddered and a wave from me was enough for them to drop their rifles and fetch the plantation's doctor.—

I will briefly relate this dreadful episode. Van Holk, who guessed that I intended to hand him over to the authorities, hung himself in the night; I handed over his children to Rosalba's care, who in turn procured them a proper nanny and served as a tenant for the plantation. Wilkins assumed my duties and three weeks later I climbed onto my ship to sail across the ocean.—

The ocean—London!

~

I have seen the market of London, the market of the world market. How millions work to fill one market, and London is the trading post for those markets the world over: The production, actions, and thoughts of millions are needed before the stroke of the hammer is heard sounding endlessly in the secretive workshops of nature; and what the sciences catch a glimpse of, here and there, quiet and loud, at the Earth's pole, in the tropics or on the glaciers, that is carried forth from people to people by the intellectuals, and the great trading post of ideas from all academies of the world is—an old man—

All academies of the world report to one man—and not just those of the sciences, for poetry and the arts subject themselves to this judge as well—uniquely, as never before, as never one head has worn the crown of all genius, Alexander von Humboldt stands at the peak of mankind as it wrestles toward the truth.

The indifferent achievements of the masses are hence not in vain, as flat and hollow as it may appear; but the achievements of millions also provide the eye of the wise one with but a kernel of truth, and this he places down like the cornerstone of a foundation—as the Persians use millions of roses to create but a few drops of precious oil, so it takes countless human ideas in order to create one whose scent is unfading, like the breath of perpetually creating nature.

Here the manuscript broke off.

*

How Mr. Humbug came upon the idea that he was truly the flesh-and-blood son of a man whose grandness was not unknown to him was not clear from the manuscript, as the naive confessions of the beautiful Tibeima demonstrated quite clearly enough that her heart had been lost to one of the porters of the traveling party, whose rodomontades laughingly criticized Herr von Humboldt and Bonpland with the characteristic word "Humbug." The more the manuscript won me over to the author, the more inexplicable it became to me, that an otherwise so practical man could not long ago have perceived the mistake of his red-brown mama, and wanted by all means to impose himself upon Herr von Humboldt as his son. Since the time was quite ripe for the theater, I carefully repacked the manuscript and moved on to my interesting friend.

Mr. Humbug was already waiting for me.

"Have you read all?" he asked in his broken German, without so much as a trace of that shameful curiosity which marks our authors as they await the first critiques of their friends.

I began to speak of the tremendous level of interest his story held for me, but he broke me off short.

"Now," he asked, "what do you think. Do I have the right to be the son of the great man?"

"Herr Humbug," I answered him candidly, "Herr von Humboldt could not wish himself a better and more worthy son; but you yourself will perceive that he was likely the one who arranged for the measurements, and did not carry the box with instruments.—"

"My mother could have been mistaken," he replied, not angered in the slightest by my unflattering objection. "I however am convinced that he is my father, for he is dear to me and his portrait has made an impression on me. I will ask him myself."

With that the discussion was dropped and we went into the theater.

The old opera house had already burned down by that time and the new one had been inaugurated and opened, but it was no more militarily organized than the darkened theater house. Herr von Hülsen was still a quite young lieutenant at that time and took up the study of theater only in secret. The critics still had respectable seats, pretty faces could be seen on the stage, and the smiles on them did not die into fearful grins when the director entered into his box—the people were still people in the theater, the public was not so well educated as now, it cried, clapped and whistled with neither order nor decorum, and there were still playwrights who wrote plays that were in fact even performed, as Madame Birch-Pfeiffer was still much younger than today and very many novels hadn't yet been written which today have already been exploited. Shakespeare had not yet been set to music, still we were already thinking about new operas like "Hegel's System—The Constitution of 1848—Statutes of the Moderation Club—The Potsdam Language Losers" and other material which would have been very well suited for use as opera lyrics, because a person must have something new after digesting the prophet. Comparing the current stage personnel with the earlier one, it's possible to say: "The dread is there, but no improvement."

Herr Humbug was filled with indignation at being forced to remove his hat despite the draft, and to hide his legs in such a manner that he himself no longer knew where they were. "I go take a spot up there," he said in rising, pointing to the Royal Box. I indicated to him that those seats were not for sale.

"Then I will going out," he grumbled, "I love freedom and do not want to sit like in a cage in a menagerie."

The curtain had already been raised up however, and no one stirred to make space for him, and the people sitting behind us began making clear pantomimes that he should sit down. He turned neither to them nor to the siren song on the stage but instead forced his way out, trampling several dozen feet in the process.

"What is that!" he cried, coming to a sudden stop and pointing to the royal box. "He looks like my father."

I had no time to answer him, however, for a police officer had already taken my American friend by the arm and politely invited him to a private discussion.

"Do not touch me or I will box you out!" Humbug thundered at the servant of the law. The audience laughed, the policeman became even more crimson red than the collar of his uniform.

"That is a constable!" I whispered into Humbug's ear, "We have to go with him."

"Goddam, if he'll make room that's fine with me."

I barely need mention that the officer was hardly of a mind to clear a path for Mr. Humbug, but rather began actively inquiring about his personal details and endorsed his intention to not return to the theatre.

We left the house; I swore silently never again to play tourist guide and was pleased that we escaped the situation without the prospect of a court case.

"You have very odd customs," Humbug said suddenly to begin the conversation.

"How so?" I asked in bewilderment.

"You give the great learned one a poor uniform, I am astounded that my father finds it necessary to wear a gaudy dress coat. I will tell him that."

"Herr Humbug," I replied hastily, for his attack on the chamberlain uniform could have ill consequences, "it is considered an honor to be chamberlain to the king."

The American looked at me as if he doubted the earnestness of my words.

"Is Humboldt no longer like a king?" he asked, "Is it not an honor for the city that he lives here?"

"Certainly," I objected, "he is beyond any decoration that he could be awarded, but potentates wear orders and uniforms, and he does so as well; furthermore he is a subject of Prussia, and as such he very much prizes every sign of benevolence from his king. He does not seek decorations, but he accepts them."

The American shrugged his shoulders. "I did not believe," he said, "that a great intellect can have pleasures in such things which are bait for vain men." He then came to speak his piece about decorations, and I do not wish to repeat his purely American view of that, as it might wound the sensibilities of some readers. Perhaps that reader possesses a medal, without being able to explain sufficiently—why—he strives for one perhaps in the most innocent naiveté, or he possesses the mark of a true service, and Mr. President bears the higher class of his order without being able to excuse himself for this in the slightest, in short—I wish no insult to anyone, then there are many who wear medals, and there are even more of those who envy them, and the number of those who earn a medal are few and—and—and—I could add a thousand sentences to this but I do not want to do so, for if through an odd caprice of fate I were to receive a medal myself tomorrow, I would wear it on twice as long a band as humility would dictate before I would blush at the recognition of a medal-worthy deed.

Humbug visited Alexander von Humboldt the next day. How he managed to pry his way in I do not know; I am obligated to give credence to the account he himself provided of his visit.

Herr Seifert, the castellan, guardian, servant, and custodian of the famous old man in all matters of the world not related to nature, led him through the room with birds and through the library into the learned man's famous, simply furnished study, made so popular through Hildebrandt's excellent engraving that a description of it would be superfluous.

Humboldt had just finished responding to a number of missives from town councilmen, magistrates and elderly spinsters; for the learned man was bedeviled by all people through esteem, stupidity, and obeisance, yet is too human, too kind, makes too much allowance for the vanity of man to respond to one single inanity in a befitting manner. Where he finds the time to be polite to millions of people is an enigma, but it is clear that no one can claim to have ever turned to Humboldt in vain, that there is no one whose greeting was not returned amicably by Humboldt; yet instead of honoring this humanity, it was universally exploited, with the exception of those who honor him because he must be honored. The scholar shies away from disturbing him; but one clever lady even managed to ask him whether he didn't also believe that the comets were large animals—and Alexander von Humboldt nevertheless has avoided any misanthropy or reclusiveness—he writes the *Kosmos* and answers with one of his great virtues, friendliness, to the piteous follies of his—fellow human beings. (?)

Humbug's visit with the great man was brief. Humboldt spoke with him about the waterfalls at Atures, of the Orinoco—and his memories were fresh, like that of a young man.

A holy awe restrained the Indian from asking questions; when Humboldt asked after his place of birth, he said only: "I was born in Maypures, my father, Tibeima is my mother's name."

Humboldt went on speaking—had he not heard the word "my father," or had he held it to be an Indian way of addressing an elderly man?—

"My father, farewell, I return to America," Humbug said, deeply moved by the dignity, the freshness and the quality of the elderly man, and Humboldt offered him his hand.

"May luck be with you on your travels, my son—were I young like you, then I would like to see the snow-covered cone mountains again, rising from the luscious vegetation of the tropics."

Humbug left Berlin the next day. The visit to Humboldt had made him into a different person—the American had found someone who had impressed him.

With a smile he left his manuscript behind with me as a souvenir—perhaps he sensed the purpose for which I would use it, but he himself doubted that he was the son of that singular man.

"But," one of my friends asked upon hearing of the encounter, "is Humboldt supposed never to have loved? The story of the Indian brings me to quite personal thoughts. Humboldt stands there too pure, too isolate, too little human—why is it that no one knows anything of the life of his heart?"

"The life of his intellect towered over all else," was my answer.

"And yet he has a heart, like that of a child."

"Probably," I smiled, "because he never loved. He had no time for love, and for that reason his heart remained young."

"Actually I consider it improper to publish the story of the American," I continued in quiet doubt, "it looks like a plagiarism."

"No," the friend smiled, "but you are riding on the coattails of a great name."

"We all do that; my passport even contains the name of the King—and the name of Humboldt should be the passport for this story that I want to smuggle into the world."

"And your direction is?" asked my friend.

"The direction?"—I considered for a while—finally I found the answer.

"My direction," I said, "should be the question as to whether Alexander von Humboldt has never loved—in Maypures it appears that only his porter lost his heart."

"Loved—pah—everyone has been in love once in his life—" said my friend, "you just don't know about it for some."

"It wouldn't be interesting for everyone—but what I'd like to know," I called, "is what kind of woman it was that made Alexander von Humboldt feel like he was a youth and not always a learned man!—"

Chapter 37

Friedrich Adolf Maercker

Poems

1858

To Alexander v. Humboldt

Genius, lift me to the light from Earth's surging mists,
You who in hand carries the torch of knowledge to us,
Bright so as to light the path, which Mankind laboriously seeks,
Spellbound fast by night and by pathetic darkness circumscribed,
Deep within its own Soul: she, who struggles futilely to break,
Ah, the diamantine shackles, chained to her by fate.
Show me the way, oh, Spirit, who creating worlds guides the suns
Into eternal channels and who with the fire's glow
Surges through all and sundry that live, while those who strive you changeless
Govern, never mislead, according to your resolute laws.

Listen, from the Indus Valley and from the Ganges hear I a call.
Better to direct my steps for here the path of the soul itself manifests,
As the soul from darkness and night upward swings and
Unites herself finally with joyful desire, as in eternal richness
Creatively she lives within her, an immortal Being in the Universe.

Cheerful spirit-choirs about me floated, divine songs
They sang to the Primeval Spirit and escorted me higher and higher
Into the mountains, 'til finally I onward pressed to the highest of the peaks,
Which stared forth from an icy chasm, a wonder to behold.
Suddenly the choirs fell silent: a sacred stillness

Translation by Richard John Ascárate, from Friedrich Adolf Maercker, "An Alexander v. Humboldt," in *Gedichte*, 2nd ed. (Berlin: Verlag der Königlichen Geheimen Ober-Hofbuchdruckerei R. Decker, 1858), 1:13–15; "An Alexander von Humboldt," 2: 157.

'Round the cliffs prevailed, only the vultures' screeching
Did I from afar fading hear, which hovered above my head.
Praying, uplifted I my hands to implore Heaven above:

World-Soul and Universal Spirit, who called them forth from the Primordial
    Being,
Hear my passionate prayer, oh, allow me to look upon the mystery
Of your immortal construction, grant that I explore the depths
Of every organism: How you hide the path to the Eternal Light from us!

The mountain deeps sounded thunderously while beneath me
The ground shook, so that my knees trembled in unsteady steps.
Clouds enshrouded the view, clouds suddenly rising from
The steaming cliff side caverns, flowing onward to the looming peak
Veiling both pinnacle and me, along the abyss lightning flashed.
Lo, a figure illumines the clouds with a scarlet sheen,
As ne'er 'fore by human eye beheld,
Marvelous, divine creation, her head by snakes entwined;
Though in surrounding mists I perceived it like the Spirit Choirs,
Approaching to serve the Lord, to announce His appearance.
Astonished, my sight dazzled, I called loudly to the Sublime Figure:
    Do I gaze into the Indras? Oh, speak: Are you Siva? Look I upon Brahma?
    Dormant and self-absorbed, the Sublime One with nary a word responded,
But merely motioned and from the choir, like the Magic of Love in spring,
Steps forth a figure—with shy steps approaching him—
Radiating beauty, fashioned the heavenly beings themselves to charm.

Be thou Prophetess to the Inquirer, spake thus the God to the Grace,
Show him the dances of men, who deep into the Divine Sources
Shall enter, by thirst for knowledge and wisdom compelled,
Which only the explorer sees, who within a generative soul may
Again in himself the world fashion after the Spirit's design,
And unites every strength and form to the image
Of the glorious All, to the All, as the Divinity planned.

With inward-turned gaze saw I now appear the Sages
All, bowing to the God, yearnful longing
Him fully to view, though only to address Wisdom were they granted.
A miracle, what then transpired: To the Prophetess saw I the Old Men
Step with conviction, while she with lofty voice loudly proclaimed:

Dignity of Elders, I give to you the power to embrace in spirit
One and All, to you also the Art, to produce it anew,
Divine Image of Beauty, that reflects itself again in the Universe.
As I built it, so will the Sages unveil it to Mankind.

Thus She spake and the contemplating God, who only within Himself does
    move,
Applauded; again raised themselves the choirs of
Countless spirits; still heard I their moans: then from before me vanished the
    vision.
All alone stood I amongst the wide mountains, by emptiness surrounded;
But while homeward bound I was filled with the image of the cosmos
That you created, Master, you, the Hero of Sages, Alexander.

To Alexander von Humboldt

One is the All, nothing lost from the Whole,
One is the Origin with the final Goal,
And he, who has given birth to Differences all,
Surrendered them not to whate'er may befall:
Necessity with Band of brass entwines
The Formation of Being in Time.

Thus spake the Greek: yet piercing the All
Your Explorer's Gaze first the Unity reveals;
Of Art, of Tongues, Nature trusting,
Combining all, World's Fate you teach

And what the adage of ancient wisdom asunder splits:
The Creation of Being through the free Spirit.

Chapter 38

RALPH WALDO EMERSON
The Conduct of Life
1860

So the men of the mine, telegraph, mill, map, and survey, —the monomaniacs, who talk up their project in marts, and offices, and entreat men to subscribe: — how did our factories get built? how did North America get netted with iron rails, except by the importunity of these orators, who dragged all the prudent men in? Is party the madness of many for the gain of a few? This *speculative* genius is the madness of few for the gain of the world. The projectors are sacrificed, but the public is the gainer. Each of these idealists, working after his thought, would make it tyrannical, if he could. He is met and antagonized by other speculators, as hot as he. The equilibrium is preserved by these counter-actions, as one tree keeps down another in the forest, that it may not absorb all the sap in the ground. And the supply in nature of railroad presidents, copper-miners, grand-junctioners, smoke-burners, fire-annihilators, &c., is limited by the same law which keeps the proportion in the supply of carbon, of alum, and of hydrogen.

To be rich is to have a ticket of admission to the master-works and chief men of each race. It is to have the sea, by voyaging; to visit the mountains, Niagara, the Nile, the desert, Rome, Paris, Constantinople; to see galleries, libraries, arsenals, manufactories. The reader of Humboldt's "Cosmos" follows the marches of a man whose eyes, ears, and mind are armed by all the science, arts, and implements which mankind have anywhere accumulated, and who is using these to add to the stock. So is it with Denon, Beckford, Belzoni, Wilkinson, Layard, Kane, Lepsius, and Livingston. "The rich man," says Saadi, "is everywhere expected and at home." The rich take up something more of the world into man's life. They include the country as well as the town, the ocean-side, the White Hills, the Far West, and the old European homesteads

Ralph Waldo Emerson, *The Conduct of Life* (Boston: Ticknor and Fields, 1860), 80–83.

of man, in their notion of available material. The world is his, who has money to go over it. He arrives at the sea-shore, and a sumptuous ship has floored and carpeted for him the stormy Atlantic, and made it a luxurious hotel, amid the horrors of tempests. The Persians say, "'Tis the same to him who wears a shoe, as if the whole earth were covered with leather."

Kings are said to have long arms, but every man should have long arms, and should pluck his living, his instruments, his power, and his knowing, from the sun, moon, and stars. Is not then the demand to be rich legitimate? Yet, I have never seen a rich man. I have never seen a man as rich as all men ought to be, or, with an adequate command of nature. The pulpit and the press have many commonplaces denouncing the thirst for wealth; but if men should take these moralists at their word, and leave off aiming to be rich, the moralists would rush to rekindle at all hazards this love of power in the people, lest civilization should be undone. Men are urged by their ideas to acquire the command over nature. Ages derive a culture from the wealth of Roman Caesars, Leo Tenths, magnificent Kings of France, Grand Dukes of Tuscany, Dukes of Devonshire, Townleys, Vernons, and Peels, in England; or whatever great proprietors. It is the interest of all men, that there should be Vaticans and Louvres full of noble works of art; British Museums, and French Gardens of Plants, Philadelphia Academies of Natural History, Bodleian, Ambrosian, Royal, Congressional Libraries. It is the interest of all that there should be Exploring Expeditions; Captain Cooks to voyage round the world, Rosses, Franklins, Richardsons, and Kanes, to find the magnetic and the geographic poles. We are all richer for the measurement of a degree of latitude on the earth's surface. Our navigation is safer for the chart. How intimately our knowledge of the system of the Universe rests on that!

Chapter 39

WALT WHITMAN

Leaves of Grass

1860

Kosmos
Who includes diversity, and is Nature,
Who is the amplitude of the earth, and the coarseness
    and sexuality of the earth, and the great charity
    of the earth, and the equilibrium also,
Who has not looked forth from the windows, the eyes,
    for nothing, or whose brain held audience with
    messengers for nothing;
Who contains believers and disbelievers—Who is the
    most majestic lover;
Who holds duly his or her triune proportion of realism,
    spiritualism, and of the æsthetic, or intellectual,
Who, having considered the body, finds all its organs
    and parts good;
Who, out of the theory of the earth, and of his or her
    body, understands by subtle analogies, the theory
    of a city, a poem, and of the large politics of
    These States;
Who believes not only in our globe, with its sun and
    moon, but in other globes, with their suns and
    moons;
Who, constructing the house of himself or herself, not
    for a day, but for all time, sees races, eras, dates,
    generations,
The past, the future, dwelling there, like space, inseparable
    together.

Walt Whitman, "Kosmos," in *Leaves of Grass* (Boston: Thayer and Eldridge, 1860/1861), 414–415.

Chapter 40

FRIEDRICH ADOLF MAERCKER

Poems

1862

Alexander von Humboldt among the Citizen Voters in the 170th Berlin Electoral District, 12 November 1858

My fatherland, your name holy and sweet,
Enthused you raise to me anew the breast!
From dismal night you arise with confidence,
Freedom sprouts, and law from tender seed.

In all hearts blazes high the flame
Of love, which happ'ly fills the citizen.
Hail, Germany, you need not look upon
The waning power of Friedrich's heroic lineage!

The Prussian masses gather for the election campaign,
Newly do courage, honor their spirits command,
Oh, fatherland, within their hearts your call did burn!!

The right of freedom to protect, here comes an old man,
Full of reverence everyone stands,
Because it was Humboldt, who stood on the urn.

Translation by Richard John Ascárate, from Friedrich Adolf Maercker, *Erinnerungen. Gesammelte Gedichte* (Berlin: Verlag der Königlichen Geheimen Ober-Hofbuchdruckerei R. Decker, 1862), 74–75.

On Alexander von Humboldt's Deathbed, 6 May 1859

I saw him dying! Tears, lament only o'er the year
Flows and bitter sorrow forebodes!
Toward the light winds Humboldt's ghost,
And a world in mourning trails the bier.

That God his life preserve, oh, we prayed,
Orphaned, our leader we seek, our friend!
But all for naught: the soul's tether rent,
She flies, to gather round the blissful choir.

'Twas the sixth of May, one of spring's sunny days,
I heard him, ah! draw his ultimate breath;
Then did sleep eternal softly 'pon him descend.

The spirit rustled his feathers, stillness all 'round then,
He led Humboldt forth toward the valley of death;
But heroic legend of humanity exalts him.

Chapter 41

THEODOR FONTANE

Travels through the Mark of Brandenburg

1862

Tegel

Hope—
It is not buried with the old man.

Down the Havel from Oranienburg, quite close to Spandau, lies the village of *Tegel,* twice blessed through its charming location and its historical memory. Everyone knows that this is the estate of the *Humboldt* family. The famous pair of brothers should lend for centuries this speck of the Mark's sand its importance and make it into a pilgrimage site for thousands. They rest there united at the foot of a granite pillar, from whose apex the figure of "Hope" looks down on their graves.

We leave the house and its picture-lined rows of rooms. Our steps lead us toward perhaps the most remarkable and enthralling spot in an estate already rich in peculiarities and anomalies—the *gravesite.* The taste of the Humboldtian family, and perhaps something even grander than that, has distained wanting to outlast death as it were and withhold the ashes from the earth in long rows of oaken caskets. Secure in the afterlife of their spirits, their motto rightly was: "Dust to dust." No mausoleum, no church crypt receives the earthly remains here; a grove of silver firs encloses the gravesite, and there in the sandy soil of Tegel rest the members of a family that is almost unmatched in the fame and respect it has brought to that sand.

Translation by Steven Sidore, from Theodor Fontane, *Wanderungen durch die Mark Brandenburg,* vol. 1, *Die Grafschaft Ruppin, Der Barnim, Der Teltow* (Berlin: Hertz, 1862), 189, 203–205.

Two paths lead from the castle down to this graveyard set amidst a hilly slope. We choose the linden avenue, which runs straight through the park before finally bending lightly up into the stand of firs. Unnoticed, the path's trees have led us uphill, and before we can even wonder about whether and where we shall find the graveyard, we are already in the middle of its enclosure, below thick, wall-like firs that rise above us on all four sides. The entire scene touches us with the same quiet magic that we sense when we suddenly step from the dark of a wood onto a forest meadow above which the shadows and lights of heaven draw past in turns. The mountain wall, which hems the space to the north and east, protects it from the wind and produces its rarely broken silence. The entire area takes an oblong shape, some thirty or forty paces long and half as wide. The overall space is divided into two halves, a garden area and the graveyard proper. The latter consists of a fenced-in square upon whose outermost end a thirty-foot high granite pillar rises upon rectangular steps. From atop the pillar's ionic capital, the marble statue of "Hope" looks down upon the graves. Flower beds enclose the iron fencing.

The number of graves, if I've counted them correctly, runs to twelve, with little room left for newcomers. The gravestones closest to the pillar, including those of Wilhelm von Humboldt, his wife, and his oldest daughter Caroline, bear no inscription. The names and birth and death years of the dearly departed are inscribed into the pedestals of the cubic block. The mounds that lie more toward the other end of the fence offer small marble plaques that simply bear names and dates and, in their plainness, remind of the little sticks that gardeners put in the earth in the autumn to mark where they have planted grains for the spring. The graves are all thickly overgrown with ivy; only one, the closest to the fence gate and to the observer, does not yet bear that fresh, dark green gown. Sickly fir branches cover the site, but the branches bear laurel and oak wreaths and readily disclose who lies beneath them.

If I am to describe my impression upon parting from this gravesite, it would be that of having encountered a decisive genteelness. All things speak with a smile and a resigned testimony: We know not what lies ahead, and we must— await it. Meaningfully the figure of Hope gazes down upon the graves. In the heart of the one who carved out this graveyard, there was a certain tentative hope alive, but no definitive conviction of assured victory. A spirit of love and humanity floats over it all, but nowhere a hint of the cross, nowhere an expression of unshakeable faith. These are not intended to be the words of a hypocritical judge, even less words of accusation; they would not suit him, he who lives even more in hope than in belief. But one point cannot remain untouched and unnamed by me, which makes this castle and this graveyard a unicum among all of the noble manors of the Mark. The castles of the Mark, if not exclusively bastions of old Lutheran confession, have seen an ebb and flow of belief and non-belief in their walls; strict piety and lax freethinking have each had their turns within. Only Tegel castle has harbored a third element, that spirit, which is just as far removed from orthodoxy as frivolity, which in the midst of classical antiquity slowly but surely develops itself, and, smiling at the struggles and feuds between the two extremes, enjoys this world and preserves, for the enigmatic hereafter, hope.

Chapter 42

Jules Verne

Voyage to the Interior of the Earth

1864

If the grotto of Guachara, in Colombia [Guácharo grotto in Venezuela], visited by Humboldt, had not given up the whole of the secret of its depth to the
philosopher, who investigated it to the depth of 2,500 feet, it probably did not
extend much farther. The immense mammoth cave in Kentucky is of gigantic
proportions, since its vaulted roof rises five hundred feet above the level of an
unfathomable lake and travellers have explored its ramifications to the extent
of forty miles. But what were these cavities compared to that in which I stood
with wonder and admiration, with its sky of luminous vapours, its bursts of
electric light, and a vast sea filling its bed? My imagination fell powerless before such immensity.

Jules Verne, *A Journey into the Interior of the Earth,* trans. Frederick Amadeus Malleson (London:
Ward, Lock and Hall, 1877), chap. XXX.

Chapter 43

JULES VERNE

Adventures of Captain Hatteras: The Desert of Ice

1865

"My friend," answered the doctor, "the upshot of it all is that we are well off where we are, and need not want to go elsewhere."

"You said just now," resumed Altamont, "that perhaps it would be worth while to make a journey to the centre of the world; has such an undertaking ever been thought of?"

"Yes, and this is all I'm going to say about the Pole. There is no point in the world which has given rise to more chimeras and hypotheses. The ancients, in their ignorance, placed the garden of the Hesperides there. In the Middle Ages it was supposed that the earth was upheld on axles placed at the poles, on which it revolved; but when comets were seen moving freely, that idea had to be given up. Later, there was a French astronomer, Bailly, who said that the lost people mentioned by Plato, the Atlantides, lived here. Finally, it has been asserted in our own time that there was an immense opening at the poles, from which came the Northern Lights, and through which one could reach the inside of the earth; since in the hollow sphere two planets, Pluto and Proserpine, were said to move, and the air was luminous in consequence of the strong pressure it felt."

"That has been maintained?" asked Altamont.

"Yes, it has been written about seriously. Captain Symmes, a countryman of ours, proposed to Sir Humphry Davy, Humboldt, and Arago, to undertake the voyage! But they declined."

"And they did well."

Jules Verne, *The Voyages and Adventures of Captain Hatteras,* part II, *The Desert of Ice* (Boston: J. R. Osgood, 1876), chap. XXIV, 419–420.

"I think so. Whatever it may be, you see, my friends, that the imagination has busied itself about the Pole, and that sooner or later we must come to the reality."

"At any rate, we shall see for ourselves," said Johnson, who clung to his idea.

"Then, to-morrow we'll start," said the doctor, smiling at seeing the old sailor but half convinced; "and if there is any opening to the centre of the earth, we shall go there together."

Chapter 44

JULES VERNE

The Children of Captain Grant

1865–1867

Meantime the yacht, favoured by the currents from the north of Africa, was making rapid progress toward the equator. On the 30th of August they sighted the Madeira group of islands, and Glenarvan, true to his promise, offered to put in there, and land his new guest.

But Paganel said—

"My dear Lord, I won't stand on ceremony with you. Tell me, did you intend to stop at Madeira before I came on board?"

"No," replied Glenarvan.

"Well, then, allow me to profit by my unlucky mistake. Madeira is an island too well known to be of much interest now to a geographer. Every thing about this group has been said and written already. Besides, it is completely going down as far as wine growing is concerned. Just imagine no vines to speak of being in Madeira! In 1813, 22,000 pipes of wine were made there, and in 1845 the number fell to 2669. It is a grievous spectacle! If it is all the same to you, we might go on to the Canary Isles instead."

"Certainly. It will not the least interfere with our route."

"I know it will not, my dear Lord. In the Canary Islands, you see, there are three groups to study, besides the Peak of Teneriffe, which I always wished to visit. This is an opportunity, and I should like to avail myself of it, and make the ascent of the famous mountain while I am waiting for a ship to take me back to Europe."

"As you please, my dear Paganel," said Lord Glenarvan, though he could not help smiling; and no wonder, for these islands are scarcely 250 miles from Madeira, a trifling distance for such a quick sailer as the *Duncan*.

Jules Verne, *A Voyage Round the World*, vol. 1, *South America* (London/New York: Routledge, 1876), chap. VIII, 73–77.

Next day, about 2 p.m., John Mangles and Paganel were walking on the poop deck. The Frenchman was assailing his companion with all sorts of questions about Chili, when all at once the captain interrupted him, and pointing toward the southern horizon, said—

"Monsieur Paganel?"

"Yes, my dear captain."

"Be so good as to look in this direction. Don't you see anything?"

"Nothing."

"You're not looking in the right place. It is not on the horizon, but above it in the clouds."

"In the clouds? I might well not see."

"There, there, by the upper end of the bow-sprit!"

"I see nothing."

"Then you don't want to see. Anyway, though we are forty miles off yet, I tell you the Peak of Teneriffe is quite visible yonder above the horizon."

But whether Paganel could not or would not see it then, two hours later he was forced to yield to ocular evidence, or own himself blind.

"You do see it at last, then," said John Mangles.

"Yes, yes, distinctly," replied Paganel, adding in a disdainful tone, "and that's what they call the Peak of Teneriffe!"

"That's the Peak!"

"It doesn't look much of a height."

"It is 11,000 feet, though, above the level of the sea."

"That is not equal to Mont Blanc."

"Likely enough, but when you come to ascend it, probably you'll think it high enough."

"Oh, ascend it! Ascend it, my dear captain! What would be the good after Humboldt and Bonpland! That Humboldt was a great genius. He made the ascent of this mountain, and has given a description of it, which leaves nothing unsaid. He tells us that it comprises five different zones—the zone of the vines, the zone of the laurels, the zone of the pines, the zone of Alpine heaths; and, lastly, the zone of sterility. He set his foot on the very summit, and found that there was not even room enough to sit down. The view from the summit was very extensive, stretching over an area equal to Spain. Then he went right down into the volcano, and examined the extinct crater. What could I do, I should like you to tell me, after that great man?"

"Well, certainly, there isn't much left to glean. That is vexing, too, for you would find it dull work waiting for a vessel in the Peak of Teneriffe."

"But, I say, Mangles, my dear fellow, are there no ports in the Cape Verde Islands that we might touch at?"

"Oh, yes, nothing would be easier than putting you off at Villa Praya."

"And then I should have one advantage, which is by no means inconsiderable; I should find fellow-countrymen at Senegal, and that is not far away from those islands. I am quite aware that the group is said to be devoid of much interest, and wild, and unhealthy, but everything is curious in the eyes of a geographer. Seeing is a science. There are people who do not know how to use their eyes, and who travel about with as much intelligence as a shell-fish. But that's not in my line, I assure you."

"Please yourself, Monsieur Paganel. I have no doubt geographical science will be a gainer by your sojourn in the Cape Verde Islands. We must go in there anyhow for coal, so your disembarkation will not occasion the least delay."

The captain gave immediate orders for the yacht to continue her route, steering to the west of the Canary group, and leaving Teneriffe on her larboard. She made rapid progress, and passed the Tropic of Cancer on the 2nd of September at 5 a.m.

Chapter 45

WILHELM RAABE
Abu Telfan
1868

It was merely a rumour that the great traveller, natural philosopher, and chamberlain of his majesty, King Frederic William the Fourth, had one day visited the tailor's inn of our Residence, in order to look up another great traveller, leaving his calling card with folded edge when he did not find the person he sought for. It was merely a rumour, but for all that, this rumour kept alive with strange pertinacity, in all the circles of the "Turks' Quarter," who had made the acquaintance of the celebrated man, by means of the popular illustrated papers of the day; and whom else could the great Alexander von Humboldt have honoured with his visit, if not Mr. Felix Zölestin Täubrich, who also could show his journeyman's book, and who was known and appreciated far beyond the boundaries of the Turks' quarter by the name of "Täubrich Pasha"?

His father had been a sweep, a sooty but honest man, who hardly knew how he came by such a son. His mother, formerly a dainty milliner, considered all this climbing, creeping, and scraping in other people's chimneys very vulgar, and not at all compatible with personal cleanliness and the higher aspirations of the soul; and the forming of the character in question, may chiefly be attributed to her influence.

Täubrich Pasha believed in Alexander von Humboldt's visit as firmly as he believed in his own existence; but how much he did believe in the latter, can only be ascertained by a prolonged and more intimate intercourse with him.

He first beheld the light of this world as a very small, white, little creature, greeting it with a shrill little voice. The black father and his grimy workmen looked at him with wonder and amazement, calling him an odd fish. Contrary to all expectations, he throve very well under the careful nursing of his mother;

Wilhelm Raabe, *Abu Telfan: or, The Return From the Mountains of the Moon*, trans. Sofie Delffs (London: Chapman and Hall, 1882), 2:27–40.

and nature likewise took very good care of him in giving him a very irritable, nervous system, a very scanty growth of reddish hair, and a great quantity of freckles; at the same time withholding the chief pride of man—a beard, which, as a born ladies' tailor, he did not at all require.

So he became a ladies' tailor, in opposition to the grumblings of his father. Growling and crumbling, the old man, who had long become over fat for his profession, climbed up his own chimney, stuck fast there, and after having been searched for in vain for some time, he was only discovered when a fire was lighted for preparing the evening meal, as he prevented the smoke from escaping. He was pulled down by the feet, without saying as much as "thank you." A fit of apoplexy had carried him off, and delivered him quickly from all earthly troubles. His widow maintained herself still a few years, as the well-read proprietress of a small but select circulating library, when she, too, died in rather reduced circumstances.

After this, Felix Zölestin wandered out into the world, brimful of fine and romantic sentiments, and, like our friend Hagebucher, he got far beyond Constantinople, and was likewise counted among the lost for a considerable time.

Like Leonhard Hagebucher, he also came back, with woefully torn shoes, in which he had come all the way from Jerusalem.

As, but a few days ago, he gave a full account of his home journey to the man from Abu Telfan, we take pleasure in substituting his narrative to ours.

"Oh, Jerusalem is a beautiful place," cried he with enthusiasm. "To be sure, Adrianople, Constantinople, Smyrna, and Jaffa, have also their agreeable sides, but for a man of feeling Jerusalem surpasses all these. There they keep Crispin's holiday all the year round, Jews as well as Christians, heathens and Turks, and the latter hold the ruling power. You have not been in Jerusalem, *Sidi*, else you might also speak about it. Oh, dear, dear! There I worked two years with a tailor from Böblingen in Württemberg, and, I am sorry to say, only as a man's tailor; for with regard to the fair sex, I had to relinquish their custom, to my greatest regret, already at Adrianople. I must say that I was quite well off with my master from Böblingen, until Easter in the year '59, when we fell out, for such is the custom there. At holy Easter-time, every man falls out with his neighbour, in Jerusalem, and already a week beforehand, the Moslem, the governor as well as the Turkish garrison, exercise handling the whip, all for the benefit of the pious pilgrims. So it is. One must always first become acquainted with the customs of the country, not to give offence; and when on Holy Thursday my master began to grow quarrelsome, and in a state of pious contrition called me a confounded fool and a good-for-nothing vagabond, I thought, 'Täubrich, restrain yourself, and do not begin a row in these holy places, especially on the eve of such a great church festival.' *Bon*, the next year I knew the customs of the place, and when my Suabian called me a north-German braggart, I followed the lead, and there began a fight and a noise in the workshop, such as one may witness at the gate of the holy Sepulchre, and, *naturellement,* I am turned out of the house, and my little knapsack is sent flying after me; and then I should have fared ill if it had not been for a good friend. This friend was a monk from the convent of Mar-Saba, situated in the valley of Kidron, near the Dead Sea; and he found me with my head bandaged, sitting on a stone between a dead ass and a drunken pilgrim, and he—meaning the monk—took me with him to his monastery, there to work for my board and lodging. So I had to mend the entire wardrobe of the saints; and there was plenty of work to do, though not of a pleasant kind, but the table was good. So I maintained myself in this pious solitude of the desert quite as well by my profession as I might have done in Hanau or Offenburg, until this pleasant time came again to an end by help of the stick. And this is the most curious thing about the Orient, that nobody is safe from a whipping at any hour, and if this were not so, it would be all too beautiful. So, one day there comes a man from Nebi Musa to our abbot, stating that he knew of a treasure buried in Wadi-en-Naar, the fire-valley, which joins the valley of Kidron; and it is incredible how the entire brotherhood pricked their ears at this tale. 'Where and how? How and where?' was eagerly asked by one after another, and the Bedouin had an answer ready for every one. A Christian was said to have buried the treasure, and only a Christian could lift it; and the following night would be the right time, because Dshinn, the evil spirit keeping watch over it, was then absent on a spree to Bahr Sut in the Dead Sea, with others of the same sort, where they had a great banquet near Ain Djidi, the salt pillar.

In Offenburg or Frankfurt on the Main nobody would have believed this, but at Mar-Saba it was greedily swallowed, and on the following night we set out to lift the treasure. One half of the monks, headed by the abbot, and under the Bedouin's guidance, went out to the fire-valley—a ravine which is at least a thousand feet deep. And when we had reached the bottom, and there was not the possibility of an escape, the joke began, and it was as if the spirit of the Christian had smelt a rat, and had quickly returned to look after his rights. First there comes a shower of stones from above, and then a shower of blows from all sides. To our horror and amazement, human beings started up from behind every bush and stone, for from a circuit of twenty miles, from Mird, from Nebi Musa, from Khan Hudrur, yes, even from Gilgal and Dshebel al Fureidis, the inhabitants had been summoned to witness and heighten the fun by their presence. Every man who could carry a stick had been lying in ambush since sunset, patiently waiting for our arrival.

In vain the abbot first called unto the saints, and then to the governor, for help, and the last thing which I beheld in this moonlight night, was a well-known colleague of mine, who, from envy and professional jealousy, had tied up a pebble as big as a fist in his turban, with which he hit me right on the head, so that every thing became as black before my eyes as his own soul, and

I dropped down unconscious beside those of my spiritual friends who were already lying along the brook of Kidron. This was a most romantic adventure, *Sidi;* but it was a much greater marvel when I awoke from my stupor, to find myself not in Wadi-en-Naar or in the monastery, nor in a hospital at Jerusalem, but here in my native place; here in the Turks' quarter; here at the very entrance of the Kesselstrasse!"

"What!" exclaimed the man from Tumurkieland, who had also met with many a wonderful adventure, when the tailor arrived at the point of his narrative; but Täubrich Pasha had coolly added—

"Yes, it is a wonder, but you need only ask the people downstairs whether it is not as I have told you; or, better still, here is my passport, Mr. Hagebucher, and there you will find it written down how it all happened."

And sure enough, there it was written, and in English—

We, the undersigned, prophets and teachers of the Word, as it is written in the Book of Mormon, *elders of the Church of Jesus Christ of Latter-day Saints,* have gone out to the land from which came Lehi, the father of the people who will be the Lord's own Elect, and we came from the holy city of Jerusalem to the river Jordan, there to fetch water wherewith to baptize the children of the golden book. And there we filled each a small tun, holding fifty quarts, and then we followed the course of the river to the *mare mortuum, seu salsum,* to behold the sign of God's wrath; and then we rode along the brook called Kidron, with our brethren and our followers. And it happened that we came to a place called Wadi-en-Naar, "the valley of fire," where we found the owner of this passport, and seeing that there was yet life in him, we put him on a donkey's back, and took him with us to Jerusalem. There we left him.

J. T. Johnstaff,

J. W. Smithfield,

Both messengers and saints of the latter days.

"To be sure they left me there," continued Täubrich Pasha; "but others have sped me on, for the fun of the thing I suppose, and all have written their names in my journeyman's book. And here, a Viennese doctor at Jaffa has written down that I was a very curious case—all right on my legs, but confused in my head. There, you see, is my ticket from Beiroot; and so I was transported to Trieste; always on and on, so that I could not have lost my way, even if I had wished to do so. Look here, *Sidi,* there is no stamp, and no police signature which is wanting, and therewith I can give a full account of myself before every magistrate, though I only awoke in the Kesselstrasse when the last police-officer let go his hold of my collar. What do you think of that?"

"Wonderful! most wonderful!" Mr. Leonhard Hagebucher had said; but it was no wonder that he felt a very strong sympathy for this strange wanderer, especially as the reception which the latter had met with, after his return from the Promised Land, bore a striking resemblance to his own reception at Nippenburg and Bumsdorf.

The days of amazement and wonder had likewise been followed by a time of indifference and contempt. The mad tailor got out of fashion, in spite of the great Alexander von Humboldt; and since the peace of Villafranca, he had become so well accustomed to slow starvation, that he hardly minded it any longer, and was able to consider a plentiful meal as a most abnormal state of things.

His art had also been outstript by fashion, and so he led a miserable life, half as a tailor, that is, mender of old clothes, and half as a much-teazed and tormented messenger and hired servant. If his colleague from Mird had had the faintest notion what magic there was in the pebble from the brook of Kidron, he would either have dealt a still harder blow, or he would not have lifted his hand at all; and it might be wished that many a respectable, sensible, and worthy man should receive from his best friend a blow similar to that which Mr. Felix Cölestin Täubrich, called Täubrich Pasha, had received.

Chapter 46

Emil Rittershaus

For the Humboldt Festival in America

1869

Ten years ago, exulting loud, we kept a solemn festival!
From North and South, from East and West, we Germans were united all
In *one* great spirit; far as beats the German heart with vigour—aye—
As far as sounds the German tongue, we all were one on Schiller's Day!
Hail Schiller! Hear the deafening shout like thunder now reverberate;
'Twas he who "Tell," and "Wallenstein," "Posa," "the Robbers" did create.
In every heart he sat enthroned, in burgher's house, in prince's hall,
We felt with conscious pride we were one Nation's children, each and all!
'Twas not the Poet's noble art, tho' sure this too all honor worth,
'Twas not that a propitious Muse had smiled with rapture on his birth,
'Twas this alone: he was High priest at th'altar of Eternal Truth,
The Prophet of a Better Time—its "John the Baptist," he, in sooth!
'Twas therefore that the freeman sung, in country free, his praise's strains,
And angrily the bondsman shook his fist in thrall and iron chains!
The farmer in the far far West, in warm and ruddy ingle-nook;
At evening-tide takes out the old, much used and well-beloved book;
Into the fire then he throws the crackling logs; the blaze starts bright,
He reads and feels with pride he is Germania's son once more to-night!
He gaily strokes his rugged beard; his heart and mind are moved and stirred!—
Again united see our race, by Schiller and his flaming word!

*

Again behold a festival! Again a German's honors rise!
From North and South, from East and West, his name ascends up to the skies!
Where ferns and palms luxuriant grow, where the gazelle bounds shy away,

Emil Rittershaus, *Fest-Gedicht für die Humboldt-Feier in Amerika am 14. September 1869*, trans. Kate Kroeker-Freiligrath (New York: L. W. Schmidt, 1869), 3, 5, 7.

Where floating icebergs close the sea, 't is *Humboldt's* name is heard to-day!
In Brandenburg, whose sands enclose the body of the illustrious Dead,
Or at the Rhine, where on its stem the grape doth blush a deeper red,
Or here in the New World—behold! the eager crowds that press to hear—
In every heart doth *Humboldt's* name fall like a sunbeam warm and clear!

*

Yes! Ours he is, and of our land, and proud we are of his high place,
But what his Genius has conceived, belongs to all the Human Race!
And as the name of Schiller doth each German bosom fast unite,
So let this day on History's Page, with burning letters, proudly write:
"Again are joined East and West, by one great spirit strong and good,
This Humboldt-Festival doth prove the Nations' Day of Brotherhood."

*

A nobleminded man thus wrote: "Those of my kith and kin, I ween,
More than myself I love, but more than these I love my country e'en;
And dearer than my fatherland, shall be to me all human kind!"
Oh, etch these words into each soul, fix them forever in each mind!
If Germany has brought him forth, Champion of Science, vast and free,
A citizen of all the World, he has declared himself to be!
In every realm he was at home, in mountain-shaft, in solar space,
He passed thro' storm and blustering seas, his was no idle dreamy chase!
With open eyes he gazed around, and darkness fled from his bright lore,
And he has raised a World for us, as ne'er Explorer built before!—
But lo! The Ever Wise approach, with frosty and disdainful smile,
Accompanied by Folly's wit, and Priestcraft's cunning treach'rous guile;
They utter slow reluctant praise, his knowledge to commend are fain:
"Yet many others equal him, if not surpass him—that is plain!"
Oh long we know that Meanness thus its needle-thrusts delights to pass,
What should it know of Humboldt's mind, that shewed the world as in a glass?
'Twas the same Spirit, kindling now in Schiller's brain the pith of thought,
Which he to Song and Picture bold, to Word and Rhyme has deftly wrought;
It pierced thro' fog and darkness thick! It was the same wild daring cast!
"Art" was the fiery sword of one, "Science" the rapier of the last!
The Sage passed on from tribe to tribe, restless he roved from land to land,
Into a giant-picture wove these thousand scenes his master-hand;
His note-book on his knees, he wrote what he had seen upon the earth;
The Poet bade his Phantasy for him around the world go forth;
The Poet with his nation walked, his heart-blood thro' his Song doth gush;
The Sage has listened to the bent of Nature's heart with awe-struck hush:
The olden Times—how wondrous are they wakened by the Poet's call!

What was, before Man did exist, the Sage, far-sighted shewed it all!
And while the First on Pegasus winged forth his sunward flight on high,
The latter, in earth's entrails deep, mused over mould and relics dry.
Thus one on high, and one below! The poet from the hand of Jove
Doth fearless snatch his thunderbolts! Meanwhile the other one doth prove
What Fraud, (time-sanctioned tho' it be!),—what Bad, what Good,—what
    False, what True!
And equal honors they divide.—*One* Spirit's children are the Two!

*

This Spirit we adore to-day; its breath sweeps over land and sea!
Oh, may our glasses thus ring in its resurrection glad and free!
With Bays the world hath crowned the bust of Schiller: he, its high-priest great!
And as its "Marshall Vorwärts" fought, He, whom to-day we celebrate!
Humboldt we therefore glorify!—Beneath his bust you all may read:
"What mostly vexes them is this, that ever onward we proceed!"
Aye, onward then! Away with bonds that shackle us, or here or there,
Fraternity the watchword be! Let Liberty the banner bear!
All Nations one, in Spirit free! Oh, hearken World, to this our cry:
"Only in Freedom's holy glance, can fortune thrive and multiply!"
Old World! Dash off thy fetters bold, and hold communion with the Free!
Renew thyself, Old World, and thrive a New World, with the New to be!
And thou, New World, we would exhort, from this thy City, Ocean's Bride
Set free the Spirit everywhere, so that thy Freedom may abide!
Then shall the Palm of Peace wave high, from Cape to Cape, from Bay to Bay!
Oh, Destiny, be this the fruit, the blessing of our *Humboldt Day*!

Chapter 47

OLIVER WENDELL HOLMES

Humboldt's Birthday

1869

Bonaparte, Aug. 15th, 1769—Humboldt, Sept. 14th, 1769

Ere yet the warning chimes of midnight sound,
    Set back the flaming index of the year,
Track the swift-shifting seasons in their round
    Through five score circles of the swinging sphere!

Lo, in yon islet of the midland sea
    That cleaves the storm-cloud with its snowy crest,
The embryo-heir of empires yet to be,
    A month-old babe upon his mother's breast.

Those little hands that soon shall grow so strong
    In their rude grasp great thrones shall rock and fall,
Press her soft bosom, while a nursery song
    Holds the world's master in its slender thrall.

Look! a new crescent bends its silver bow;
    A new-lit star has fired the eastern sky;
Hark! by the river where the lindens blow
    A waiting household hears an infant's cry.

This, too, a conqueror! His the vast domain,
    Wider than widest sceptre-shadowed lands;

Oliver Wendell Holmes, "Bonaparte, Aug. 15th, 1769—Humboldt, Sept. 14th, 1769," in Louis Agassiz, *Address Delivered on the Centennial Anniversary of the Birth of Alexander von Humboldt. Under the Auspices of the Boston Society of Natural History; with an Account of the Evening Reception* (Boston: Boston Society of Natural History, 1869), 86–88.

Earth and the weltering kingdom of the main
    Laid their broad charters in his royal hands.

His was no taper lit in cloistered cage,
    Its glimmer borrowed from the grove or porch;
He read the record of the planet's page
    By Etna's glare and Cotopaxi's torch.

He heard the voices of the pathless woods;
    On the salt steppes he saw the starlight shine;
He scaled the mountain's windy solitudes,
    And trod the galleries of the breathless mine.

For him no fingering of the love-strung lyre,
    No problem vague, by torturing schoolmen vexed;
He fed no broken altar's dying fire,
    Nor skulked and scowled behind a Rabbi's text.

For God's new truth he claimed the kingly robe
    That priestly shoulders counted all their own,
Unrolled the gospel of the storied globe
    And led young Science to her empty throne.

While the round planet on its axle spins
    One fruitful year shall boast its double birth,
And show the cradles of its mighty twins,
    Master and Servant of the sons of earth.

Which wears the garland that shall never fade,
    Sweet with fair memories that can never die?
Ask not the marbles where their bones are laid,
    But bow thine ear to hear thy brothers' cry:—

"Tear up the despot's laurels by the root,
    Like mandrakes, shrieking as they quit the soil!
Feed us no more upon the blood-red fruit
    That sucks its crimson from the heart of Toil!

We claim the food that fixed our mortal fate,—
    Bend to our reach the long-forbidden tree!
The angel frowned at Eden's eastern gate,—
    Its western portal is forever free!

Bring the white blossoms of the waning year,
    Heap with full hands the peaceful conqueror's shrine
Whose bloodless triumphs cost no sufferer's tear!
    Hero of knowledge, be our tribute thine!"

Chapter 48

WILLIAM MCJIMSEY

The Memory of Humboldt

1869

The Progress of Genius and Science

Part I

1. *Humboldt*! is a great and honored Name,
Of wide and celebrated Fame.
Berlin's Honor and Germania's Joy,
Where long he did his Genius well employ.

2. Science did raise him as their favorite son,
Whose name has well high admiration won;
A Century has passed away,
Since first he saw the brilliant light of day.

3. From early life for Science he did good,
And in the world its noble Champion stood;
He saw from Nature's Laws Creation's God,
Whose voice did speak the Universe abroad!

4. He analysed the Laws of Nature bright,
And all his Lessons gave the Soul delight;
Both in the Globe and Heavens above,
He saw the signs of Wisdom, Power and Love!

William McJimsey, *The Memory of Humboldt*. *Born in Berlin, Germany, September 14th, 1769, Finished His Work Entitled* Cosmos, or the World, *September 14th, 1858. Died in Berlin, Prussia, May 6, 1859. A Poem On the occasion of the unveiling of the Statue of Alexander von Humboldt, on the Celebration of his Centennial Birth-day in the Central Park, City of New York, September 14, 1869* (New York: [n.p.], 1869).

5. When on the Earth, he loved Humanity,
And, like the Eagle, did his spirit see
The great and noble, useful, good and wise
With power that raises Spirits to the Skies.

6. He taught the Beauty of Creation fair,
As seen in colors of the Earth and Air;
And Wisdom's Lessons fixed upon the mind,
For the improvement of all mankind!

7. He rose with strength to Mountain's prospects high,
To see the Beauty of Earth, Sea and Sky;
He also sought the Valleys deep and low,
Where Flowers rise and Rivers onward flow!

8. With Telescope his eyes did see afar,
The Solar System and each shining star;
He saw the Planets blaze and did rehearse,
The glory of the expansive Universe!

Illustration 48.1. Statue of Alexander von Humboldt by
Gustav Blaeser, dedicated 1869, Central Park, New York City.

The Voice of Fame

Part II

9. In Fame's high Temple shines his honored Name,
And millions here his virtues did proclaim;
Admiring Friendship early felt his worth,
Before he rose to eminence on earth!

10. Long will abide his Memory and Name,
Inscribed clear upon the Roll of Fame;
Where Busts are found upon the spacious Globe,
May light surround them as a splendid Robe!

11. The name of *Humboldt* is well known on Earth,
As in the land that gave the Scholar Birth;
America respects his Worth and Name,
With honor, glory, joy, esteem and fame.

12. The Powers of Thought made knowledge all his own,
His Soul has gone to Orbs and Worlds unknown;
He lives in Regions here far out of sight,
In scenes of joy and of Everlasting Light!

13. His Fame is known in Cities and in Town,
For deeds of Genius, Virtue and Renown;
Let sculptured Brass and Marble still proclaim,
The merits of Illustrious Humboldt's Name!

14. He studied Nature's Objects, Works and Laws,
He wrote and spoke for Freedom's onward cause;
To do good was the high and noble Aim,
That gave to him Celebrity and Fame!

15. In *Central Park,* as record to his Name;
Is reared a Statue to extend his Fame;
Let History tell his usefulness and worth
To future Ages of the admiring Earth!

16. *Science* advances Hope and Happiness,
And with its impulse gives to Mind success;
Its Light imparts great Cheerfulness and Joy,
And applies Talents to sublime employ.

Chapter 49

Ralph Waldo Emerson
Journals
1869

Humboldt [was] one of those wonders of the world, like Aristotle, like Crichton, like Newton, appearing now & then as if to show us the possibilities of the Genus Homo, the Powers of the eye, the range of the faculties; whose eyes are natural telescopes & microscopes & whose faculties are so symmetrically joined that they have perpetual presence of mind, & can read nature by bringing instantly their insight & their momentary observation together; whilst men ordinarily are, as it were, astonished by the new object, & do not on the instant bring their knowledge to bear on it. Other men have memory which they can ransack, but Humboldt's memory was wide awake to assist his observation. Our faculties are a committee that slowly, one at a time, give their attention & opinion,—but his, all united by electric chain,—so that a whole French Academy travelled on his shoes. You could not put him on any sea or shore, but his instant recollection of the past history of every other sea & shore illuminated this, & he saw in this confirmation or key of the old fact. You could not lose him. He was the man of the world, if ever there was one. You could not lose him; you could not detain him; you could not disappoint him. The tardy Spaniards were months in getting their expedition ready & it was a year that he waited; but Spain or Africa or Asia were all harvest fields to this armed eye, to this Lyncaeus who could see through the earth, & through the ocean, who knew how mountains were built, & seas drained.

Humboldt with great propriety named his sketch of the results of Science Cosmos.

His words are the mnemonies of science, "volcanic paps," "magnetic storms," &c.

The Journals and Miscellaneous Notebooks of Ralph Waldo Emerson: Volume XVI, 1866–1882, eds. Ronald A. Bosco and Glen M. Johnson (Cambridge, MA: The Belknap Press of Harvard University Press), 160–161. Copyright © 1982 by the President and Fellows of Harvard College. Reprinted by permission of the publisher.

Chapter 50

JULES VERNE

Twenty Thousand Leagues Under the Seas

1869–1870

Captain Nemo stood up. I followed him. Contrived at the rear of the dining room, a double door opened, and I entered a room whose dimensions equaled the one I had just left.

It was a library. Tall, black-rosewood bookcases, inlaid with copperwork, held on their wide shelves a large number of uniformly bound books. These furnishings followed the contours of the room, their lower parts leading to huge couches upholstered in maroon leather and curved for maximum comfort. Light, movable reading stands, which could be pushed away or pulled near as desired, allowed books to be positioned on them for easy study. In the center stood a huge table covered with pamphlets, among which some newspapers, long out of date, were visible. Electric light flooded this whole harmonious totality, falling from four frosted half globes set in the scrollwork of the ceiling. I stared in genuine wonderment at this room so ingeniously laid out, and I couldn't believe my eyes.

"Captain Nemo," I told my host, who had just stretched out on a couch, "this is a library that would do credit to more than one continental palace, and I truly marvel to think it can go with you into the deepest seas."

"Where could one find greater silence or solitude, professor?" Captain Nemo replied. "Did your study at the museum afford you such a perfect retreat?"

"No, sir, and I might add that it's quite a humble one next to yours. You own 6,000 or 7,000 volumes here. ..."

"12,000, Professor Aronnax. They're my sole remaining ties with dry land. But I was done with the shore the day my *Nautilus* submerged for the first time under the waters. That day I purchased my last volumes, my last pamphlets, my last newspapers, and ever since I've chosen to believe that humanity no

Jules Verne, *Twenty Thousand Leagues Under the Seas,* trans. Louis Mercier (London: Sampson Low Marston Low & Searle, 1872), chap. XI.

longer thinks or writes. In any event, professor, these books are at your disposal, and you may use them freely."

I thanked Captain Nemo and approached the shelves of this library. Written in every language, books on science, ethics, and literature were there in abundance, but I didn't see a single work on economics—they seemed to be strictly banned on board. One odd detail: all these books were shelved indiscriminately without regard to the language in which they were written, and this jumble proved that the *Nautilus*'s captain could read fluently whatever volumes he chanced to pick up.

Among these books I noted masterpieces by the greats of ancient and modern times, in other words, all of humanity's finest achievements in history, poetry, fiction, and science, from Homer to Victor Hugo, from Xenophon to Michelet, from Rabelais to Madame [George] Sand. But science, in particular, represented the major investment of this library: books on mechanics, ballistics, hydrography, meteorology, geography, geology, etc., held a place there no less important than works on natural history, and I realized that they made up the captain's chief reading. There I saw the complete works of Humboldt, the complete Arago, as well as works by Foucault, Henri Sainte-Claire Deville, Chasles, Milne-Edwards, Quatrefages, John Tyndall, Faraday, Berthelot, Father Secchi, Petermann, Commander Maury, Louis Agassiz, etc., plus the transactions of France's Academy of Sciences, bulletins from the various geographical societies, etc., and in a prime location, those two volumes on the great ocean depths that had perhaps earned me this comparatively charitable welcome from Captain Nemo. Among the works of Joseph Bertrand, his book entitled *The Founders of Astronomy* even gave me a definite date; and since I knew it had appeared in the course of 1865, I concluded that the fitting out of the *Nautilus* hadn't taken place before then. Accordingly, three years ago at the most, Captain Nemo had begun his underwater existence. Moreover, I hoped some books even more recent would permit me to pinpoint the date precisely; but I had plenty of time to look for them, and I didn't want to put off any longer our stroll through the wonders of the *Nautilus*.

"Sir," I told the captain, "thank you for placing this library at my disposal. There are scientific treasures here, and I'll take advantage of them."

Chapter 51

Heinrich Laube

Memoirs

1875

Among others, we became acquainted with the Princess Pückler-Muskau, a relationship which over the course of our life has become a valuable blessing. She was the daughter of the late Chancellor of State von Hardenberg, a native of Hanover who embodied the better virtues of the northern German nobility. For the most part, this Hanoverian nobility has been extensively criticized—perhaps justifiably—for it is the paragon of Junker haughtiness and otherwise objectionable qualities. Nevertheless in the German lowlands, from along the Elbe north to Schleswig, there was always one family which had honorably strived after truly noble principles. Who does not recall with gratitude the Holstein Count Schimmelmann, who without being asked provided our Schiller with monetary support? In this regard, the distinguished University of Göttingen, the intellectual center for the northern German nobility, has rendered an excellent service. Through great scholars, this institution has provided the substance and higher, inner laws toward refinement. The Prince Hardenberg—who was granted his title by Prussia, as Bismarck is now—had kept this Göttingen tradition of the sciences and arts until the end of his life, a tradition soundly conferred to his daughter, the Princess Pückler. She considered it her duty to call on and gather people of intellect and talent with accommodating friendliness, and thus to sustain the same liberal traditions of her father. Although not explicitly politicized, these liberal traditions were presumed and quietly suggested in opposition to the prevailing ways of governing. Her husband, the Prince Pückler-Muskau, was then in the Orient, and the curiosities he found there presented occasions to gather parties of notable personages at Pariser Platz. There, near the Brandenburg Gate, she lived in an charmingly decorated ground-floor apartment.

Translation by Joshua Clemente Bonilla, from Heinrich Laube, *Gesammelte Schriften*, vol. 1, *Erinnerungen 1810–1840* (Vienna: Braumüller, 1875–1882), 329–334.

Among these notables, Alexander von Humboldt was one of the most important. In such society, he played a most unusual role. From the moment of his entrance, every single man and woman would fall silent, and he alone would speak. Even when he did not hold a formal lecture, which would happen on occasion, he continuously held the floor. For him it was a necessity, and for the society it was a necessity that they continuously listen to this extraordinary man. And it would have been no different, had the society felt no compulsion to do so.

I remember in detail such a formal lecture hosted by the Princess. Humboldt appeared at the appointed hour, received by the Princess at the door like a great ambassador. Moderately tall, if not a small figure, dressed in a worn, black suit with an already silver-gray head of hair, his head was tilted a little to the side, and from a ruddy countenance his small eyes darted here and there while he glanced around. Discreetly gliding over the floor, slightly bowing, left, then right, he spoke right from his entry in an uninterrupted flow of words to the Princess. He did not speak loudly, yet his words were comprehensible, in well constructed sentences. Whenever the Princess managed to slip a polite word in edgewise between his sentences, this single word would spark in him an entirely new string of thoughts, which expanded in every direction.

Generally speaking, one imagines a wise person as relatively quiet, attentively watching and listening, speaking only briefly and topically. Humboldt was not of this sort at all; rather, he was one of the workers who never rest. During the few hours that I saw and heard him, he always struck me as if he were the steward of an immensely great dominion, who reckons all accounts by night, and by day hastens from one administrative post to another, everywhere prescribing the next line of action, everywhere addressing some lofty goal. Meanwhile, he spoke with the utmost authority on every possible subject and with everyone he met. At the same time he made obligatory visits to the sovereign lords and their circles thereby garnering a formal yet natural cordiality which allowed him to introduce his observations seamlessly into conversation. These observations grew into scientific expositions; for the ruler and the ruling knew that he possessed an immeasurable depth of knowledge and understanding. They would casually sample a portion of this knowledge; and because they were lords, they would stop up the gushing source as soon as they felt full. However Humboldt would go on and make his regular visits in the vicinity and would pour out his cup of wisdom from place to place. On his way from one visit to another, he continued to mull these themes through silent monologues, which were constantly on his mind, then return for a short time to his apartment, filled with its walls of books and with people seeking audience from all five continents. He spoke to them all and listened to their most essential details—only the most essential details, by which I mean to say, those which were yet unknown to him of their world. Through his long residence in France, he had become accustomed to their fine way of living, answering every inquirer, therefore also the hundreds of letters that he received. He would do this on the smallest scrap of paper, for too much free space might elicit the complaint of undue brevity. His writing was slanted, and he sat with his body half-turned to his work, the other half moving on to something else, or he sometimes wrote on his knee. Eating and drinking were only secondary matters; but this by no means benefited those seeking help. His old servant had to keep an exact list, and inquiries about the worthiness of the help seekers were constantly in progress. I have often asked myself: how does sleep manage to find even a moment with Alexander von Humboldt? It found only very modest accommodation, and would often encounter him still in his chair.

Moreover, I often asked Varnhagen, how a man of such intellectual capacity and prowess could endure taking part in so many empty courtly affairs and live within a system of government which he can no longer endorse?

"He does not endorse it," came his answer, "however in order to at least be able to work against it, he must first obtain entrance, and to do this he has to be present and participate in all the ceremony."

At that time and without a doubt later it became clear to me that Humboldt, amidst all the great scientific questions which concerned him, and amidst all the superficial courtly obligations which occupied him, unwaveringly adhered in his standards to a liberal system of governance. In addition it cannot be said that he shyly held back: he would express dissent against every illiberal measure. Often he did it sarcastically and ironically and would not ask afterwards if and how ungraciously his claims were understood. From his position of scientific renown he remained immune.

His brother Wilhelm was Prussian minister during a season of liberal aspirations after the War of Liberation, but by this time he was already dead. Unhappy with the subsequent political progress, he had withdrawn himself and died a short while afterwards. Both brothers came from Tegel, a family manor not far from Berlin, and both are rightfully the pride of the Mark [Brandenburg]. Wilhelm as well was guided by grand, boundless goals.

And yet if I should maintain the respects owed to him, I must not have seen this great Alexander of Science for a long while. The admiration for his work, for his knowledge and surely for his character cannot be enough. In fact, the respect for his personal being always diminished whenever I was in his presence. For example, that evening at the Princess Pückler's, he lectured on rich, often high and dignified matters. From an aesthetic perspective, these lectures were thoroughly ornate, yet only because in all his abundance he knew to observe nothing of an aesthetic economy. With admiration I saw this small man end his speech and raise himself from his chair. Now however, he spoke on, drifting from room to room, momentarily pausing to stand in each doorway, and only the servant, who closed the last door behind him, made the final point in the unending speech. A vision emerged thus: here was not a man, but an overcharged instrument, and this instrument would continue to pour itself out on the street.

On a single occasion four years later, I spoke to him in his apartment, at that time he was somewhat different—to my disadvantage. Then he posed questions, and I knew nothing. I had been in Algiers and I was to give an account. I began the description from my point of view which, I freely admit, was a very limited perspective compared to his. But it was obviously trivial stuff for him, and right away he broke his rare, short silence and proceeded to give me an exam. Question upon question gushed out at me, about earth layers and rock, about air and water, and there remained hardly any place for me to expose myself in my ignorance. At the end, I laughed and he smiled along, and then answered for me admirably.

Was he vain? I shouldn't think so. He had hardly any place or time for it. His goals were too numerous for personal, ulterior motives. Yet when ignorance became too pervasive in his company, he would spring out from his plain, elusive form and express himself angrily—positively angrily. For example, when the séance was so much in favor. To one of such reason, to have to see people for decades believe in such garbage! Although he would otherwise put up with this or that "influenza" which spoils a healthy mind, this seemed much more base than what he could tolerate.

Indeed he remained an astonishing presence among us humans. People would often complain of him: "Too much! Too much!"— one says of him, with his *Kosmos* as well, when one approaches him with aesthetic pretenses. But how seldom is there such a person who gives so much and still gives so much of value!

Chapter 52

Karl Gutzkow

Looking Back on my Life

1875

After the performance of my theatrical first born began a run in Berlin as well—and not without success—I visited my hometown shortly before the death of Friedrich Wilhelm III. The atmosphere was unusually stifling. The king had not appeared in public for a long time. As he did so for the last time, the signs of his imminent passing were manifest. Schönlein had been summoned. There was talk of how this resolute man thwarted authoritative personalities in the medical field. *Alexander von Humboldt,* whom I met in the home of Meyerbeer's mother, predicted the direst outcome.

The famous natural explorer could well say: Berlin was proud to celebrate him! Berlin takes a fancy for a while to every personality that steps into the foreground. It truly loves the effect, and nothing makes more of an effect than momentary favor. On the other hand, whomsoever the sunshine of success does not quite illumine, whoever wishes to be advanced because of his merit from yesterday and the day before, such a man cannot be accommodated. As a rule, title and rank are helpful. With Humboldt, it was for the one, who stood in devotion before him, like the unmediated courtly relationship with the king; for the other, more the scientific immortality. Humboldt's coming and going were as if accompanied by the blasts of trumpets. Shakespearean kings thus take the stage. In Berlin I had the place of honor at his side and I remember that the son of the "pivot between two centuries," for fully as such Humboldt was looked upon, had little favorable to say about the academic world of Berlin. He excepted from his radical judgment only August Boeckh. Among the learned of Berlin he missed "more and more the universal education and humanity in the Herderian spirit." Surely, each was a fully competent researcher in his own field, thereby neglecting in his education, however, the

Translation by Richard John Ascárate, from Karl Gutzkow, *Rückblicke auf mein Leben* (Berlin: A. Hofmann & Co., 1875), 242–244.

general, the philosophical, the literary. Indeed, one no longer even encounters among the professors receptiveness for such. To linger upon such an interesting theme wasn't possible. I would have liked to reply that the cause for such retraction of the finer sensitivities lay only with political atmosphere; everyone quietly plows and tends to his own field. But Humboldt leapt from one matter to another. The table guests numbered about twenty, and the benevolent man—like the princes—was inclined to bring to life, if only for a moment, everyone at the table. He essentially spoke alone. The others allowed themselves only a quiet whisper with their neighbors. Had one the boldness to do this and then listened again to the lecturing star, so might one be astounded at how the themes changed. Just now the latest discovery of a fossil skull was touched upon. "Would you please pass the salt?" The neighbor to the left passes it. After this small distraction, one listens again. But already the discussion turns to the cuneiform writing of the ancient Assyrians. Only with the salad and various desserts did the spontaneity of the guests develop enough for them to use the pauses somewhat more freely. Once the company took coffee beneath the trees of the Tiergarten park they could breath easy. The great man was up and away to Potsdam. In service to the court he neglected nothing. His tenet: I besiege the sovereign, take care to maintain his friendliness to me, will not trip up on the so highly polished parquet, perform chamberlain service like every other Uckermarkian grandee, who right then has his day in the sun; only thus do I attain what I need for science! Only thus does boredom sometimes ask me: What's new, Humboldt? Only thus can I say: Ah, there's a traveler who wants to go to Asia, or a scholar who has found a codex to publish, artists who want to make the most of their portfolios! In brief, whoever desires to obtain something by means of the great must possess and hold them in a free moment! These are almost Humboldt's own words that I repeat here. Concerning the place of my name in literature, he was only aware of it, it seems, through the transcribed proceedings of parliament.

Chapter 53

KAROLINE BAUER

My Life on the Stage
1876

I saw many interesting and famous people glide on past me at Rahel's salon, although I did not approach all of them personally. So too have many of these personalities faded in my memory to shadows, as the Laterna Magica casts them, motley and flickering, upon the wall in a darkened room.

Alexander von Humboldt, tall and thin, elegant and nimble like a Frenchman, would often surface suddenly—like lighting—an entrancing will-o'-the-wisp at Rahel's tea table, nibbling a few roasted chestnuts or biscuits, uttering the sweetest flatteries in passing to Rahel, Henriette Herz and Bettina, sprinkling the most delicate and savory news from the court and the city into the clinking of the teacups as if he were a fountain of Cologne water, chatting with Herr von Varnhagen for two more minutes in the window alcove—material for the diaries—and then disappearing again like a will-o'-the-wisp.

The famous scholar and traveler held lectures on the topic of "Physical Description of the Earth and World" at the Berlin Singakademie during the winter of 1827–28—before a very diverse public. Ladies were the most numerous and, at the request of my mother, who felt I could never learn enough, I too went there whenever I was not busy at the theater. I gleaned only a pitiful amount from these learned matters, struggle as I might with my poor head. For relief and recuperation I occasionally took a peek at the faces of the other female listeners. They didn't look like they got any more than I did. And that was truly a small saving grace—that Humboldt didn't expect or demand particularly much from his female listeners is clear from one of his many well-known sarcastic remarks which quickly began circulating in Berlin.

Translation by Steven Sidore, from Karoline Bauer, *Aus meinem Bühnenleben. Erinnerungen*, ed. Arnold Wellmer (Berlin: R. v. Decker, 1876–1877), 1:272–274.

Prince August asked him whether he believed that the so numerously represented female listeners were in a position to follow his learned lectures productively?

And Humboldt answered with a smile: "But that's not at all necessary; by merely coming they've already done all that is possible!"

Humboldt, the Paris-ified man of the salon, had no love of his home city of Berlin and had a low opinion of the Berliners. He found Berlin "boring and oppressive, an intellectually blighted, small, unliterary and as such overly gloating city where one can natter thoughtlessly for months on end on a self-created caricature of flat imagination!"

My dear old Berlin!

The man of learning found his royal chamberlain uniform to be a "laughable outfit" and his court appointment the most boring, most intolerable. ... Why then did he wear both for more than a half-century? Surely not because of the 5,000 thaler chamberlain's salary? Or out of courtly vanity? Either would be equally pitiful for our great world scholar.

Humboldt's sharpest and cleverest opponent at the court was Friedrich von Ancillon, the former tutor of the Crown Prince and later the Minister of State. He gave the omniscient and lithesome chamberlain a funny moniker: the Encyclopedic Cat!

It made for quite a sensation when Humboldt held a magnificent tea party for ladies at the large Conference for Nature Researchers in Berlin's Schauspielhaus. From a balcony I was able to cast a gaze over the colorfully undulating, gaily noisy scene. Humboldt was indeed in his element there: he flitted about the hall at a seemingly enchanted pace, now here, now there surfacing at one tea table, with fleeting small talk, a compliment, a joke—and whoosh! whoosh! onward!

Humboldt's oldest friend at Rahel's salon was the Lady Hofrat Herz—once the most esteemed and famous beauty in Berlin. By the time I saw her she was already over sixty years old—but retained a graceful, regal appearance with silver-grey curls, the loveliest triumphant dark eyes and charming smile. At the same time mild and reserved in conversation; a sharp contrast to the effervescent Rahel and the clownish wren Bettina. Yet the things Henriette Herz said had character, intellect and clarity and were always genial. After I had seen her only once, I understood immediately the deep long-lasting friendship between Schleiermacher and the lovely Jewess. The smallish pastor of the Trinity Church, with his soulful eyes and warm-hearted mouth, the confessor to my mother and myself and our mild guide of conscience for difficult worldly problems, that man loved Henriette Herz not for her intoxicating beauty—only the beautiful, clear, grand person whom he could not help but address with the familiar "Du" form. I also understood how seventeen year old Ludwig Börne could fall so unhappily in love with Henriette Herz, fully twenty-two years his elder, to the point of madness—yes to the planned rat poison, and that Minister of State Count Dohna-Schlobitten could ignore all societal and courtly prejudices and offered the widow of the Jewish doctor Markus Herz his hand and name in marriage. But she thanked him warmly for both and—remained Henriette Herz, the intellectual friend of Schleiermacher. Alexander and Wilhelm von Humboldt never forgot that Henriette Herz was the first radiantly beautiful and noble feminine ideal of their youthful years. The most charming lady in Berlin taught them to write in Hebrew, and corresponded in that language with the young sons of "Castle Boredom" (Tegel by Berlin), as well as practicing and dancing the newfangled *Menuet à la Reine* with them. Both famous Humboldts remained true to their aging friend with tender tributes.

Chapter 54

José Martí

A Voyage to Venezuela

1881

To travel to *Caracas*, the most important city of the Republic, the Jerusalem of the South Americans, the cradle of the free continent, where Andrés Bello, a Virgil, studied, where Bolívar, a Jupiter, was born, where both the myrtle of the poet and the laurel of the warrior flourish, where all that is grand has been thought and all that is terrible has been suffered, where Liberty—how hard she fought there!—is cloaked in a mantle stained with her blood, one must plunge into the lap of the mountain colossus, edge along cliffs, ride on ridges, perch on the peaks, and greet the clouds up close. At the beginning of the trip, when in La Guaira one takes the post carriage, the coach used for the journey, you want to dispense with all clothes, so dreadful is the heat; half way along the route you are looking for clothes from the neighbor, since you do not have enough of your own: the cold begins. What a beautiful route! It is a path along the precipice: during the trip one breathes a fresh air—the savory air of danger. One shouldn't look down: vertigo takes hold. With feverous rapidity, as in fairy tales, which honors the intelligence and activity of the country, a winding and audacious train track is presently being built, which will pierce, like a toy out of steel, this heap of mountains. Like the handle of a Chinese fan, the diverse rail lines, already planned and designed, will merge and diverge like pointed arrows, splitting sluggish forests, waking sleepy cities, in all regions of the land.

Venezuela is a rich country within natural boundaries. The mountains have veins of gold, silver, and iron. With the slightest look of love, the earth, like a young girl, awakens. The *Société Agricole de France* recently published a book, wherein it was shown, that no other country in the world was so well endowed for establishing all types of agriculture. Potatoes can be planted here, and tobacco, tea, cocoa and coffee beans; the oak grows alongside the palm tree. In

Translation by Rex Clark and Oliver Lubrich, from José Martí, "Un Voyage à Venezuela," in *Obras completas*, vol. 55, *Viajes 1* (Havana: Editorial Trópico, 1944), 180–182, 193–194.

the same bouquet is found the Malabar jasmine and the Malmaison rose, and in the same basket the pear and the banana. Every climate, every elevation, all types of waters; ocean coasts, river banks, lowlands, mountains; the cold zone, the temperate zone, the hot zone. The rivers are grand like the Mississippi; the soil fertile like the slopes of a volcano. [...]

The city of Caracas is beautiful. Spacious one-story houses are continuously being built and in their courtyards between large pots with rare flowers a jet of water shoots up and falls into an elegant basin just as in Seville. Beautiful rivers, their high banks carpeted with fragrant greenery, wind through the streets that are everywhere continued with solid bridges. A nice theater and a beautiful church are now being erected. Humboldt had something to say regarding this church. "When will you return?" he was asked as he was leaving the city: "when this church is finished," he said smiling. And indeed, it was not until ninety years after his departure that the work was finished. Branches covered with blossoms still caress the ruined walls of the house where Humboldt lived—Humboldt who would never forget the "cultivated, hospitable, and intelligent Caracas." In a plaza where the trees in the summer are crowned with large red blossoms as if they had suddenly caught fire, a sundial built by Humboldt can still be seen. And if, using one of the light carriages that are found throughout the city, one takes an outing in the environs of Caracas, inhabited by coffee plantations, scattered in the friendly shadow of the red and tall *bucare,* a portal can be found, above which in letters sketched by the hand of a wise man the name can be read of the charming place that "once was a delightful place of leisure": *Sans Souci.* The city, circled by mountains, was built in a calm and serene valley that is irrigated by a large and tranquil river, the noble Guaire, a river of the nymphs; there is also another river, twisting and full, loud and unruly, the Catuche; and yet another, peaceful like its name, the gentle Arauco, that brings to mind a garland of flowers. From the bridge built over the Guaire, one of the favorite promenades of the people of Caracas, one sees a harmonious plain, full of pleasant sounds, sprinkled with common plants, colored in subtly nuanced tones, magnificently calm. The palm trees, like sentinels, rise from corn-fields. Pastures border the murmuring river. In the distance the mountains, as if wrapped in a veil of magic, change their soft colors under the powerful influence of the sun: they become now red, now yellow, now gray, now blue. The cows low, the deer leap, the shepherds carry in amphora fired from red clay the milk that was skimmed in a remote hut. A coach awakes us and reminds us that we are by the city. It is a great charm to have them so close to each other—the city, that eats away at life, and the country, that restores it. It feels good in the mysterious dawn to merge the tired spirit into the universal spirit.

Chapter 55

JULES VERNE

The Giant Raft: Eight Hundred Leagues on the Amazon

1881

From its commencement the Amazon is recognizable as destined to become a magnificent stream. There are neither rapids nor obstacles of any sort until it reaches a defile where its course is slightly narrowed between two picturesque and unequal precipices. No falls are met with until this point is reached, where it curves to the eastward, and passes through the intermediary chain of the Andes. Hereabouts are a few waterfalls, were it not for which the river would be navigable from its mouth to its source. As it is, however, according to Humboldt, the Amazon is free for five-sixths of its length.

And how can we say that the hydrographical system of the Amazon is not known?

In the sixteenth century Orellana, the lieutenant of one of the brothers Pizarro, descended the Río Negro, arrived on the main river in 1540, ventured without a guide across the unknown district, and, after eighteen months of a navigation of which his record is most marvelous, reached the mouth.

In 1636 and 1637 the Portuguese Pedro Texeira ascended the Amazon to Napo, with a fleet of forty-seven pirogues.

In 1743 La Condamine, after having measured an arc of the meridian at the equator, left his companions Bouguer and Godin des Odonais, embarked on the Chinchipe, descended it to its junction with the Marañón, reached the mouth at Napo on the 31st of July, just in time to observe an emersion of the

Jules Verne, *The Giant Raft: (Part I) Eight Hundred Leagues on the Amazon. (Part II) The Cryptogram*, trans. W. J. Gordon, 2 vols. (New York: Scribner's, 1881–1882), 1: chap. V, 56, 59–60; chap. VII, 86–87; chap. XIV, 168–169.

first satellite of Jupiter—which allowed this "Humboldt of the eighteenth century" to accurately determine the latitude and longitude of the spot—visited the villages on both banks, and on the 6th of September arrived in front of the fort of Para. This immense journey had important results—not only was the course of the Amazon made out in scientific fashion, but it seemed almost certain that it communicated with the Orinoco.

Fifty-five years later Humboldt and Bonpland completed the valuable work of La Condamine, and drew up the map of the Marañón as far as Napo.

Since this period the Amazon itself and all its principal tributaries have been frequently visited.

~

A large break now appeared. There, in the more open air, which is as necessary to it as the light of the sun, the tree of the tropics, *par excellence,* which, according to Humboldt, "accompanies man in the infancy of his civilization," the great provider of the inhabitant of the torrid zones, a banana-tree, was standing alone. The long festoon of the liana curled round its higher branches, moving away to the other side of the clearing, and disappeared again into the forest.

"Shall we stop soon?" asked Manoel.

"No; a thousand times no!" cried Benito, "not without having reached the end of it!"

~

The coloration of these waters is a very curious phenomenon. It is peculiar to a certain number of these tributaries of the Amazon, which differ greatly in importance.

Manoel remarked how thick the cloudiness was, for it could be clearly seen on the surface of the whitish waters of the river.

"They have tried to explain this coloring in many ways," said he, "but I do not think the most learned have yet arrived at a satisfactory explanation."

"The waters are really black with a magnificent reflection of gold," replied Minha, showing a light, reddish-brown cloth, which was floating level with the jangada.

"Yes," said Manoel, "and Humboldt has already observed the curious reflection that you have; but on looking at it attentively you will see that it is rather the color of sepia which pervades the whole."

"Good!" exclaimed Benito. "Another phenomenon on which the *savants* are not agreed."

"Perhaps," said Fragoso, "they might ask the opinion of the caymans, dolphins, and manatees, for they certainly prefer the black waters to the others to enjoy themselves in."

Chapter 56

CHARLES DARWIN

Letters

1881

Letter to J. D. Hooker

Down, 6 August 1881

I believe that you are fully right in calling Humboldt the greatest scientific traveller who ever lived. I have lately read two or three volumes again. His *Geology* is funny stuff; but that merely means that he was not in advance of his age. I should say he was wonderful, more for his near approach to omniscience than for originality. Whether or not his position as a scientific man is as eminent as we think, you might truly call him the parent of a grand progeny of scientific travellers, who, taken together, have done much for science.

Charles Darwin, *The Life and Letters of Charles Darwin, Including an Autobiographical Chapter,* ed. Francis Darwin (London: John Murray, 1887), 3:247.

Chapter 57

Joaquim de Sousândrade

O Guesa

1884

Humboldt (*Vue des Cordillères*) more scientifically writes the story thus:

The beginning of each *indiction* was marked by a sacrifice, the barbarous ceremonies of which, from the little we know, appear all of them to have a connexion with astrological ideas. The human victim was called *guesa*, wandering, houseless, and *quihica*, door, because his death announced as it were the opening of a new cycle of a hundred and eighty-five moons. This denomination reminds us of the Janus of the Romans, placed at the *gates* of Heaven, and to whom Numa dedicated the first month of the year, *tanquam bicipitis dei mensem*. The *guesa* was a child torn from the paternal home. He must necessarily be taken from a certain village, situated in the plains called at the present day the *Llanos de San Juan*, which extend from the eastern slope of the Cordilleras to the banks of the Guaviare. It was from this same country of the *east* that *Bochica*, the emblem of the *Sun*, came, when he made his first appearance among the Muyscas. The *guesa* was most carefully educated in the temple of the Sun at Sogamozo, till the age of *ten* years; he was then made to go out to walk in the paths, which Bochica had trodden, at the period when, in his instructions to the people, he had consecrated those spots by his miracles. At the age of *fifteen* years, when the victim had attained a number of *sunas* equal to that contained in the indiction of the Muysca cycle, he was sacrificed in one of those circular places in the centre of which was an elevated column.

At the time of the celebration of the sacrifice, which marked the opening of a new indiction, or of a cycle of fifteen years, the victim, *guesa*, was led in procession by the *suna*, which gave its name to the lunar month, toward the column that appears to have served to measure the solstitial or equinoxial shadows, and the passages of the Sun through the zenith. The priests, *xeques*,

Translation by Odile Cisneros, from Joaquim de Sousândrade, *O Guesa* (London: Cooke & Halsted/ Moorfields Press, n.d. [1884]), 1–2, 320 (Canto XII).

in masks like the Egyptian priests, followed the victim. Some represented Bochica, who is the Osiris, or the Mithras, of Bogota, and to whom were attributed three heads, because, like the *Trimurti* of the Hindoos, he contained three persons, who formed only one divinity; others bore the emblems of *Chia,* the wife of Bochica, Isis, or the Moon; others were covered with masks resembling frogs, in allusion to the first sign of the year, *ata*; finally others represented the monster *Fomagata,* the symbol of evil, figured with one eye, four ears, and a long tail. This Fomagata, whose name in the Chibcha language signifies fire, or *melted matter in a state of ebullition,* was considered as an evil spirit. He travelled through the air, between Tunja and Sogamozo, and transformed men into serpents, lizards, and tigers. According to other traditions. Fomagata was originally a cruel prince, whom, to secure the succession to his brother Tusatua, Bochica caused to be treated on the night of his nuptials, as Uranus had been by Saturn.

We are ignorant what constellation bears the name of this phantom; but Mr. Duquesne thinks, that the Indians attach to it the confused remembrance of the appearance of a comet. When the procession, which reminds us of the *astrological processions* of the Chinese, and that of the feast of Isis, had reached the extremity of the *suna,* the victim was tied to the column we have already mentioned, a cloud of arrows covered him, and his heart was torn out, to be offered to the *King Sun,* Bochica. The blood of the *guesa* was received into sacred vases.

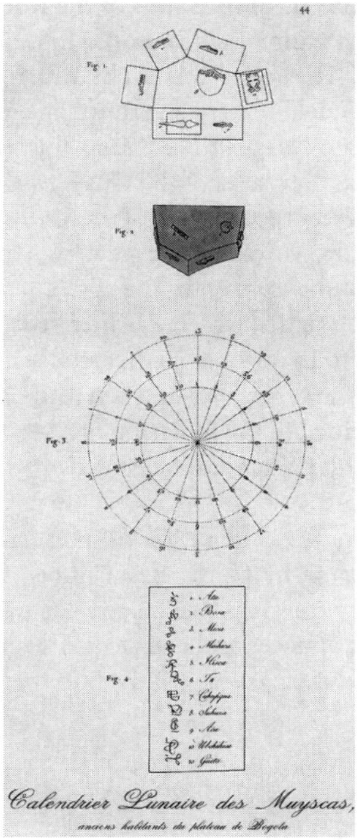

Illustration 57.1. Calendar of the Muysca Indians, the ancient inhabitants of the plain of Bogotá.

Canto XII

Let us climb higher—higher, the immortal
   Spirit rises above the horizon
   When the West burnishes the roses
   Of limitless ice—infinite mountains!
The perilous range adorns itself
   With the melancholy roses that evening lights up
   Heavens! The Andes, like our celestial soul,
   The more the sun declines, the more they rise and shine.
A lonesome glory on a severe brow
   Humboldt's gray hairs; the lovely ethereal light
   The soul brandished in its august solitude
   As if it were sounding on the crystal of the spheres.
Feelings. And such snow exists
   As much in the solitude of Andean heights
   As in the heights of human life: you rose?
   You die or rather you breathe in a light divine!

However, at the fatal human touch,
   Oh, even the Andes diminish, God!
   In the distance … Roam mysterious ghosts
   Nearby … other heavens we command.
And the man who climbed may share
   In the calm nature of heights,
   Which rises from them, magnificent;
   And vanish from the surface strange
Differences, of the ones that now confound,
   Breathe as one; before, measured themselves.
   —Heavens of the Andes! may they not change into clouds
   So many of your glories illuminating me.

Chapter 58

JULIUS STINDE

The Buchholz Family

1884

Summer Retreat

When all is said and done, there is no art in showing off by traveling some-where aboard an inexpensive train just to be able to say later: "We were in Switzerland or Zoppot or in some other distant, foreign lands." But to pass time modestly in the vicinity of Berlin so that wife and children may enjoy a change of air and the man of the house emerges on Sundays and enjoys himself as well—that, in my opinion, is no simple task. It requires one to lay aside the crown of pride so as to don the smock of virtue.

For that reason, we decided to make an excursion to Tegel, as much because of the apartment and surroundings—which pleased us very much—as well as because of my Karl.

My husband's business is doing just fine, in spite of the protective tariff. So, I believe, if it were not for that, within two years he would be part of the upper crust and for that reason can't simply leave off business for weeks at a time. Should he then just completely avoid me and the children? No, at least once a week he must see the grateful faces of those for whom he works himself to death. And Tegel serves that purpose quite nicely.

Furthermore the Tegel Castle and its park are not far removed from the village of Tegel. And in the park Alexander von Humboldt lies at rest, that extraordinary scholar who also invented the globe, which now belongs among the most beloved decorations of a room, although its blue color doesn't al-ways harmonize with the upholstery. When so close to such an historical back-ground, one feels the presence of genius upon the footpaths and is happily conscious of being among the learned as well.

Translation by Richard John Ascárate, from Julius Stinde, *Die Familie Buchholz. Aus dem Leben der Hauptstadt* (Berlin: Freund & Jeckel, 1884), 138–141.

[…] This is a lovely place to stay. The same large linden and elm trees, which provide shade to the small church, keep the sunlight from the windows of our front rooms, and if we sit outside the front door, we have before us the old churchyard with its monuments, hanging ash trees, and flowering shrubberies. […]

Two small rooms with a garden view as well as the kitchen are located in the back. The other half of the little house is similarly built, and the people who rent the house reside there, but they are too far below us to associate with because they—although born in Tegel—haven't the slightest idea about Humboldt and his significance.

We decided flat out not to become friendly with the locals and we thereby did wisely, because one would only be misunderstood. They called us the "ghost family" out of revenge. Thereby hangs a tale.

There are, you see, in and around Tegel frighteningly many mosquitoes, which the lake breeds. As Betti and I took our first evening stroll on the banks of the lake, we both returned home pretty mangled. These scourges of the human race had an eye for my neck, so that I looked as if I had a goiter. And while I confess that my neck is a bit fat, I must also say that my Karl nevertheless finds it very pretty, and so there's no reason for me to let it be ruined. For that reason, we rubbed ourselves before the next stroll with laurel tree oil, which is supposed to work against mosquito bites, although the stuff smells so abominable that it completely spoils one's enjoyment of nature's soothing power. I therefore wrote Emmi that she should bring us both of the muslin ball gowns. From these we manufactured two Egyptian veiled robes to protect our upper bodies and arms. When we sit on the edge of the forest and revel in the sight of nature, we decorate the robes with wild flowers and bedeck the sunshades with large leaves. The Tegel locals take this poetical activity for insane and because of the white veils they call us the "ghost family." Just to vex them even more we walk with our costumes and decorated shades steadfastly through the village, so as to show that we are far above such laughable prejudices.

~

Our life very quickly fell into a pattern. Mornings were for swimming in the lake and Betti soon swam excellently. Then we had breakfast and Betti cared for the rabbit, while I put the apartment in order. Then came the woman who performed the more strenuous chores, I cooked and we had lunch. Then we took a couple winks of sleep and prepared ourselves for a walk.

Naturally we were also provided with reading material; Uncle Fritz had to get hold of a copy of Humboldt's *Kosmos*. He said as he brought it: "Wilhelmine, this book will be far above your head." My, how he compliments a lady! I replied:

"Unfortunately, I've often enough experienced how you underestimate the abilities of women, because you are a free thinker. But that's a long way from saying that I don't understand what you can't grasp!"

Whereupon he smiled maliciously and said: "Good luck with *Kosmos*. Send it back soon, so that I can return it to the library."

It was now my foremost duty to read *Kosmos*. We took the book and the rabbit, which we called Muck, into the forest, and Betti read aloud to me about the mountain ranges of Mexico and the rock strata lying atop them. The first time, unfortunately, I fell asleep because of the heat; the second time, because we'd had beans for lunch, which made both of us tired. The third time, Betti read very badly because Muck was always hopping away and she had to grab him. We will notwithstanding read *Kosmos* in peace and quiet during the winter, for it would be laughable not to be able to understand a printed book. That is a presumption on the part of Uncle Fritz.

Chapter 59

CHARLES DARWIN
Autobiography
1887

Cambridge 1828–1831

During my last year at Cambridge, I read with care and profound interest Humboldt's 'Personal Narrative.' This work, and Sir J. Herschel's 'Introduction to the Study of Natural Philosophy,' stirred up in me a burning zeal to add even the most humble contribution to the noble structure of Natural Science. No one or a dozen other books influenced me nearly so much as these two. I copied out from Humboldt long passages about Teneriffe, and read them aloud on one of the [...] excursions, to (I think) Henslow, Ramsay, and Dawes, for on a previous occasion I had talked about the glories of Teneriffe, and some of the party declared they would endeavour to go there; but I think that they were only half in earnest. I was, however, quite in earnest, and got an introduction to a merchant in London to enquire about ships; but the scheme was, of course, knocked on the head by the voyage of the *Beagle*.

From my marriage, 29 January 1839, and residence in Upper Gower Street, to our leaving London and settling at Down, 14 September 1842

I once met at breakfast at Sir R. Murchison's house the illustrious Humboldt, who honoured me by expressing a wish to see me. I was a little disappointed with the great man, but my anticipations probably were too high. I can remember nothing distinctly about our interview, except that Humboldt was very cheerful and talked much.

Charles Darwin, *The Life and Letters of Charles Darwin, Including an Autobiographical Chapter*, ed. Francis Darwin (London: John Murray, 1887), 1:55–56, 74.

Chapter 60

JULES VERNE

The Mighty Orinoco

1898

Despite Sergeant Martial's consternation, the three colleagues from the *Maripare* were obliged to share these quarters with him and his nephew, because no other hut dwellers had offered their hospitality. M. Miguel, even more than his associates, was very considerate of the two Frenchmen. So Jean de Kermor had a chance to become better acquainted with his fellow travelers—while keeping his distance, of course, as his uncle's scowling looks warned. From the outset, Jean was captivated by the little Indian girl, who seemed attracted by his friendliness.

So they chatted away while the storm howled outside. Their conversation was frequently interrupted. The peals of thunder echoed so noisily that they could not hear their own voices. Neither the little Indian girl nor her mother seemed at all alarmed, not even when thunder clapped and lightning flashed at the same instant. And more than once, as they would verify the following day, bolts of lightning shattered trees near the hut, making the appalling racket they had heard.

Such storms are commonplace along the Orinoco, so the Indians were used to them and did not feel the fear that even animals experience. They remained perfectly calm throughout this physical and emotional disturbance. Not so with Jean—like any strong-minded person, he had no deep-seated dread of thunder, but it still made him jumpy.

Inside the Indian hut, they continued to talk until midnight, and Sergeant Martial would have been a more active participant if his Spanish had been as proficient as that of his nephew. At the suggestion of MM. Miguel, Felipe, and Varinas, the conversation focused on the egg hunting that had taken place

Jules Verne, *The Mighty Orinoco,* trans. Stanford L. Luce, eds. Arthur B. Evans and Walter James Miller (Middletown, Conn.: Wesleyan University Press, 2002), 76–79, 91–101. Translation © 2002 by Stanford L. Luce and reprinted with permission of Wesleyan University Press.

three months earlier, an activity that draws many hundreds of natives each year to this part of the river.

To be sure, turtles frequent other parts of the Orinoco, but nowhere in such huge numbers as on the sandbars between the Cabuliare River and the town of La Urbana. Their Indian host, wise in the ways of these reptiles and an expert at their hunting and fishing, which is essentially the same thing, explained to them that these turtles start showing up as early as the month of February by the hundreds of thousands.

It goes without saying that this Indian would know nothing about biological classifications and could not name the species of these turtles that multiply so prolifically on the Orinoco mud flats. He was happy just to prey on them along with the Guahibos, Otomacos, and others, plus the half-breeds from the nearby plains. They gathered up the eggs during nesting season and distilled their oil by a very simple process that is as easy as extracting olive oil. For a basin you merely use a dinghy you have hauled up onto the bank. You put your baskets of eggs in the dinghy, crack them open with a little club, let their contents dribble into the bottom of the boat, then pour in water. Within an hour the oil rises to the surface; you add heat and the water evaporates, leaving pure oil. That is all there is to it.

"And this oil is supposed to be excellent," said Jean, who got this verdict from his beloved guidebook.

"Truly excellent," added M. Felipe.

"What kind of turtles are they?" the lad asked.

"They belong to the species *Cinosternon scorpioides*," M. Miguel replied. "These creatures have shells nearly a yard long, and they weigh around sixty or seventy pounds."

And since M. Varinas had not yet shown off his specialized knowledge of the order Chelonia, he then jumped in to explain that the true scientific name of his friend Miguel's turtle was actually *Podocnemis dumeriliana*, an appellation which meant very little to their Indian host.

Then Jean de Kermor said to M. Miguel: "One basic question—"

"You're talking too much, nephew," Sergeant Martial muttered, chewing on his mustache.

"Sergeant," M. Miguel said with a smile, "why keep your nephew from improving his mind?"

"Because ... because he has no business knowing more than his uncle!"

"That much is understood, my dear Mentor," the young man replied. "Anyhow, here's my question—are those animals dangerous?"

"In large numbers they can be," M. Miguel answered. "If you get in their way, you'll be in great danger because they'll be coming at you by the hundreds of thousands!"

"Hundreds of thousands!"

"Every bit that many, M. Jean. At least fifty million eggs are gathered each year, furnishing enough oil to fill ten thousand demijohns. Now then, since a single turtle lays an annual average of a hundred eggs, since predators polish off a substantial number of these, and since enough eggs are still left over to perpetuate the race, I calculate that right in this part of the Orinoco, around these Manteca sandbars, there'll be a good million turtles."

M. Miguel was definitely not overstating the case. Lured by some sort of mysterious attraction, these creatures gather by the hundreds of thousands; as Professor Élisée Reclus has put it, a living tidal wave, slow but relentless, overwhelming everything in its path like a flood or an avalanche.

True, human beings destroy far too many of them, and the species could disappear someday. To the Indians' great loss, some of these mud flats were already deserted, including the shores by Cariben, just below the mouth of the Meta.

Their Indian host then supplied some fascinating details on the behavior of these turtles during nesting season. Over a three-week period from mid-March on, their shells can be seen plowing furrows across the vast tracts of sand, where the creatures dig holes some two feet deep, lay their eggs, then carefully cover up the holes with sand. Soon after, the eggs start hatching.

In addition to extracting oil from the eggs, the natives also try to catch the turtles themselves for food, because their meat is held in high regard. To catch them underwater is nearly impossible. But if you see one alone on a sandbar, you can capture it simply by thrusting a stick under its shell and flipping it over—a difficult position for a turtle, because it cannot right itself unaided.

"Some people are like that too," M. Varinas commented. "When a bit of bad luck turns their world upside down, they never get back on their feet!"

This unexpected footnote wrapped up their conversation on Orinoco turtles.

Then M. Miguel asked the Indian the following question: "Around Buena Vista, have you seen the two French explorers who came upriver four or five weeks ago?"

～

"And," continued Jean, "do you know what part of the territory they were preparing to visit?"

"From what I know of their plans," explained M. Marchal, "they must have headed toward the Sierra Matapey, to the east of the Orinoco, a little-known area frequented only by the Yaruros or the Mapoyos. Your two compatriots and the leader of the escort were on horseback; the other Indians, numbering some half-dozen, accompanied them on foot, carrying packs."

"Is the land to the east of the Orinoco subject to flooding?" asked Jean de Kermor.

"No," replied M. Miguel, "and the surface of its plains is considerably above sea level."

"True enough, M. Miguel," added the head official, "but it is subject to earthquakes, and you know they are not rare in Venezuela."

"At all times?" asked the lad.

"No," declared M. Marchal, "at certain times of the year. Over the last month we have felt rather violent tremors as far as the Tigra ranch."

It is common knowledge that the Venezuelan soil is often troubled by volcanic tremors, although its mountains do not have active craters. Humboldt even called it "the country of earthquakes par excellence." That title seems justified by the destruction of the city of Cumaná in the sixteenth century, which was struck again 150 years later when the region "trembled" for fifteen months. Another city in the Andean territory, Mesida, also found itself devastated by those dreadful commotions. And, in 1812, twelve thousand inhabitants were crushed under the ruins of Caracas. These disasters, which have had thousands of victims, are still to be feared in the Hispano-American provinces, and it was true that, for some time now, they had been feeling the ground tremble in the eastern area of the mid-Orinoco.

When all questions were asked and answered about the two Frenchmen, M. Marchal then turned his attention to Sergeant Martial and his nephew.

"We now know," he said, "why MM. Miguel, Varinas, and Felipe undertook their journey on the Orinoco. No doubt your trip does not have the same goal."

Sergeant Martial made a sweeping gesture of denial; but on a sign from Jean, he had to refrain from further expressing his disdain for these geographic questions which, in his mind, would interest only publishers of textbooks and atlases.

The lad then told his story, what motives had brought him to leave France, what filial sentiment he was obeying in going up the Orinoco, and his hope of finding some new information in San Fernando, where the last letter from his father was sent.

Old M. Marchal could not disguise the emotion this response caused him. He seized Jean's hands, drew him into his arms, kissed him on the forehead—which made the Sergeant grumble under his breath. It was like a blessing that he gave him, along with the warmest wishes for the success of his project.

"But neither you, M. Marchal, nor you, monsieur the official, you haven't heard of the Colonel de Kermor?" asked the lad.

They both shook their heads.

"Perhaps," answered the official, "the colonel did not stop in La Urbana? That would surprise me, though, for it is rare that a boat doesn't stop here to stock up. It was in 1879, you say?"

"Yes, sir," replied Jean. "Were you already living in this town?"

"Certainly, and I never heard that the Colonel de Kermor had come through here."

Again that incognito with which the colonel had sought to cover himself since his departure.

"Don't worry, my dear lad," affirmed M. Miguel, "it is impossible that your father didn't leave some trace of his stay in San Fernando, and there you will no doubt obtain information which will assure the success of your search."

The discussion continued until ten o'clock, when the guests of the head official, after taking leave of this hospitable family, returned on board their boats, which were to cast off the next day at dawn.

Jean went to lie down on his cot in the passenger quarters, and, once his usual mosquito hunt was completed, Sergeant Martial stretched out on his own.

Both fell asleep, but not for long.

Toward two o'clock they were aroused by a distant rumbling, continuously growing.

It was like a dull murmuring which they could not mistake for thunder, even distant. The river waters, unusually agitated, began rocking the *Gallinetta*.

Sergeant Martial and the lad got up, left their quarters, and stood at the foot of the mast.

The skipper Valdez and his crew, standing in the bow of the falca, were searching the horizon.

"What's happening, Valdez?" asked Jean.

"I don't know."

"Is it a storm approaching?"

"No. The sky has no clouds. The wind is from the east, and it's very weak."

"Where's this disturbance coming from?"

"I don't know. ... I just don't know," repeated Valdez.

Indeed, it was inexplicable, unless it was being produced, upstream or downstream from the village, by a sort of tidal bore caused by the sudden rise of the river. Anything could be expected from the capricious Orinoco.

On board the *Maripare*, the passengers and crew showed the same surprise. M. Miguel and his two friends, outside their quarters, were seeking in vain to determine the cause of this phenomenon.

Remarks exchanged between the two boats gave no plausible explanation. Further, if this movement of the water was being felt in both boats, the ground along the riverside was also not exempt from it. Almost at the same instant, the inhabitants of La Urbana, abandoning their huts, came down toward the riverbank. M. Marchal and the head official rapidly joined them. A growing alarm was beginning to overtake the town's population.

It was then four-thirty in the morning, and day was about to break.

The passengers in both ships disembarked and went at once to the head official.

"What's going on?" asked M. Miguel.

"No doubt it is an earthquake in the Sierra Matapey," he answered, "and the shocks are extending as far as the riverbed."

M. Miguel was of the same opinion. There was no doubt that the region was undergoing shocks due to seismic disturbance, quite frequent in the land of the plains.

"But … there is something else," observed M. Miguel. "Do you hear that sort of hum that's coming from the east?" And, by listening intently, one could hear a sort of snoring, a continuous low sound, the origin of which was unknown.

"Let's wait," said M. Marchal. "I don't believe that La Urbana has anything to fear."

"That's also my opinion," declared the official, "and there is no danger in returning to our homes."

That was probable, yet only a minority of the inhabitants took the advice. Besides, the day was brightening and perhaps eyes would find an explanation of a phenomenon that ears could not provide.

For three hours the distant murmur kept increasing in a strange way. There seemed to be a kind of gliding sound, creating a powerful vibration on the surface of the entire region. Heavy and cadenced, this vibration was transmitted all the way to the right bank of the river, as though the soil had been made of peat. That the trembling could be attributed to an earthquake whose center was located in the Sierra Matapey sounded logical, and it was not the first time that the town had to contend with such a phenomenon. As for that rolling sound, like what might be produced by the matériel of an army on the march, no one could yet understand its real cause.

The official and M. Marchal, accompanied by the passengers of the falcas, walked toward the first rise of the Urbana hill, in order to observe a larger radius of the surrounding countryside.

The sun rose into a pure sky like an enormous balloon swollen with luminous gas that the breeze had pushed toward the shores of the Orinoco. Not a cloud on the horizon, no indication that the day would be stormy. When the observers had climbed up some thirty meters, they cast their eyes toward the east.

The immense prairie appeared before them, the vast and verdant plain, that "sea of silent grasses," following the poetic metaphor of Élisée Reclus. The surface of this sea was not calm. It must have been troubled in its depths, for, some five kilometers away, the plains were crowned with sandy swirls.

"That," said M. Marchal, "is a heavy dust cloud; the dust of the soil is being thrown up."

"Even so, it cannot be the wind that is raising it," affirmed M. Miguel.

"Indeed, since it is barely blowing," responded M. Marchal. "Could it be from small whirlwinds? No, that explanation doesn't hold up."

"And besides," added the official, "there's that continuous noise, which seems to come from heavy steps."

"What is it then?" exclaimed M. Felipe.

And, at that moment, like a response addressed to him, a detonation was heard—the discharge of a firearm, echoing across the hill of Urbana. It was followed by others.

"Gunfire!" declared Sergeant Martial. "Those are gunshots, or I don't know what one is!"

"They must be hunters, hunting on the plain," observed Jean.

"Hunters, my dear lad?" responded M. Marchal. "They wouldn't raise such a cloud of dust, unless they are an entire legion."

There was no doubt, however, that the detonations heard came from firearms, revolvers or carbines. And one could even discern a whitish vapor, which stood out against the yellow tint of the dust cloud. More gunshots burst out. Although still distant, the sounds were easily carried to the town by the light breeze.

"To my way of thinking, gentlemen," said M. Miguel, "we should go check out what's going on out there!"

"And bring some assistance to those, perhaps, who have a dire need of it!" added M. Varinas.

"Who knows," said Jean, looking at M. Marchal, "they may be my compatriots."

"Then they must be fighting an army," said the elderly man, "since it would take thousands of men to raise so much dust! You're right, M. Miguel, let's go down onto the plain to investigate."

"And go well armed!" added M. Miguel.

This measure of prudence was indeed warranted. If Jean de Kermor's premonition were correct, it could well be the two Frenchmen that the Indians of the area were attacking and who were defending themselves with their guns. In a few moments, everyone had regained his hut or boat. The official and a few villagers, the three geographers, Jean, and Sergeant Martial, a revolver tucked in his belt, the carbine on his shoulder, headed toward the plains, walking around the foot of the Urbana hill.

M. Marchal had wanted to join them as well; he was very impatient to find out what this was all about.

The little troop moved off at a good pace, and since the cloud remained in front of them the three or four kilometers which separated them would not take long to cover. Even at that distance, it would have been possible to distinguish human forms if the clouds of dust had not been so thick. The flashes accompanying the detonations, which were continuing, could be clearly seen and now became increasingly perceptible to the ear.

The heavy, rhythmic sound became ever louder as they approached the low, creeping mass which was still hidden from their view.

One kilometer from that spot, M. Miguel, who was walking at the head with the official, their carbines ready to be shouldered, suddenly stopped. An exclamation of extreme surprise rang out.

Truly, if ever a mortal had the chance to see his curiosity satisfied, if ever man was proven wrong in his disbelief, that man was Sergeant Martial. Ah! the old soldier had not believed in those thousands of chelonians which, during the mating season, invaded the beaches of the Orinoco between the mouth of the Arauca and the sandbars of Cariben.

"Turtles! They're turtles!" exclaimed M. Miguel, and he was not mistaken.

Indeed! Turtles, a hundred thousand or perhaps more, were advancing toward the right bank of the river! And why this abnormal exodus that was contrary to their habits, since it was no longer laying time?

M. Marchal responded to that question which was on everyone's mind.

"I think these beasts were frightened by the shocks of the earthquake. No doubt chased out of the waters of the Tortuga or the Suapure when their beds were shaken, they've come to search for shelter in the Orinoco, or even beyond, pushed along by the irresistible instinct of self-preservation."

That was a very natural explanation and the only admissible one. The Sierra Matapey and its environs must have been profoundly changed by this earthquake. In similar conditions, other such invasions had already taken place outside the regular months of March and April, and there was no reason for the riverbank dwellers to be surprised. However, to a certain extent, they had reason to be somewhat worried.

And now, with the exodus of the turtles explained, where did the rifle shots come from? Who were defending themselves against the chelonians? And what could bullets do against their impenetrable shells in any case?

They soon discovered the answer through occasional rifts in the thick cloud.

Indeed, these thousands of tortoises were advancing in a compact mass, pressed against each other. Together, they resembled one immense surface of shells, covering several square kilometers and slowly moving ahead.

Before this shifting mass of shells, a number of struggling animals could be seen. To avoid being crushed, they were seeking refuge. Among them, surprised by this invasion across the plains, was a group of howler monkeys who were running and leaping and who seemed "to find it funny," to use an expression of Sergeant Martial. Then they noticed several pairs of wild animals indigenous to the vast Venezuelan plains—jaguars, pumas, tigers, and ocelots—just as fearsome as if they had been running freely through the forest or plain.

And it was against these savage beasts that two men were defending themselves, with rifle and revolver shots.

Already a few bodies were lying on the backs of the turtles, whose undulating movement could only hinder the human beings who could not get their footing, while the quadrupeds and monkeys paid no mind to it.

Who were these two men? Neither M. Marchal nor the head official was able to recognize them because of the distance. In any case, by their dress, it seemed safe to say that they were not Yaruros nor Mapoyos, nor any of the other Indian tribes frequenting the territories of the middle-Orinoco.

Were they the two Frenchmen who had ventured out on the eastern plains, and whose return had been awaited for so long? This thought had occurred to Jean de Kermor—was he going to have the joy of meeting his countrymen?

MM. Marchal, Miguel, Felipe, and Varinas, the local official, and those among the inhabitants who accompanied him had stopped. Was it possible to continue going forward? No, absolutely not. Stopped by the first row of turtles, obliged to retreat, they would be unable to join the two men who were surrounded on all sides by wild animals.

Jean insisted that they rush to their rescue, never doubting that these two men were the explorer and the French naturalist.

"It's impossible," said M. Marchal, "and it's useless. You'd put yourself in danger without helping them. It's better just to let the turtles reach the river. When they get there, their mass will begin to break up."

"Undoubtedly," said the official, "but we are threatened by a serious danger!"

"What?"

"If these thousands of turtles pass through La Urbana on their way, if their march does not break upon reaching the river, our village will be destroyed!"

Unfortunately, nothing could be done to prevent this catastrophe. After circling the base of the hill, the slow and irresistible chelonian avalanche approached La Urbana, some two hundred meters away. Everything within the village would be flattened, crushed, obliterated! As the saying goes, "the grass no longer grows where the Turks have passed"; well, not one hut, not a single shanty, neither tree nor shrub would remain where this mass of turtles would have passed!

"Fire ... fire!" shouted M. Marchal.

Fire—that was the only barrier that could stop the invaders.

As the danger approached, the inhabitants of the village, both women and children, were seized with panic, crying out with shouts of despair.

M. Marchal had been understood by his companions. The passengers of the boats and their crews all immediately set to work.

Before the village, there were broad prairies that were covered with thick grasses which two days of hot sun had dried up, and in which some guavas and other trees stretched out their branches laden with fruit.

There could be no hesitation in sacrificing these plantations, nor was there any.

In ten or twelve spots, some hundred paces from La Urbana, the grasses were simultaneously set on fire. Flames shot up as though they were leaping from the very entrails of the earth. An intense smoke mixed with the dust cloud that descended toward the river.

Yet the mass of turtles was still advancing, and it would continue to advance, no doubt, until the first row was touched by the fire. But, perhaps, the last rows would keep pushing the first right into the flames, which might then be extinguished?

In that case, the peril would not have been averted, and La Urbana, crushed and destroyed, would become but a heap of ruins.

Fortunately, things turned out otherwise, and the plan proposed by M. Marchal was destined to succeed.

First, the wild animals were greeted by gunfire from Sergeant Martial, M. Miguel and his two friends, and the armed villagers, while the two men on the backs of the turtles exhausted their last munitions on them as well.

Caught on both sides, some of the beasts fell under this hail of bullets. The others, frightened by the plumes of fire swirling skyward, tried to escape by turning eastward and following the monkeys, who preceded them, filling the air with their howls.

At that instant, one could see the two men rushing toward the barrier of fire before it reached the first row of turtles who were still advancing slowly.

A minute later, Jacques Helloch and Germain Paterne—for it was indeed they—found safety in the hill near M. Marchal.

Soon after, the mass of chelonians, turning away from this curtain of flame that stretched for half a kilometer before them, suddenly turned to the left of the village, descended the riverbank, and disappeared into the waters of the Orinoco.

Chapter 61

WINSTON CHURCHILL

The Crisis

1901

From the stairs Stephen saw Mr. Lincoln threading his way through the crowd below, laughing at one, pausing to lay his hand on the shoulder of another, and replying to a rough sally of a third to make the place a tumult of guffaws. But none had the temerity to follow him. When Stephen caught up with him in the little country street, he was talking earnestly to Mr. Hill, the young reporter of the *Press and Tribune*. And what do you think was the subject? The red comet in the sky that night. Stephen kept pace in silence with Mr. Lincoln's strides, another shock in store for him. This rail-splitter, this postmaster, this flat-boatman, whom he had not credited with a knowledge of the New Code, was talking Astronomy. And strange to say, Mr. Brice was *learning*.

"Bob," said Mr. Lincoln, "can you élucidate the problem of the three bodies?"

To Stephen's surprise, Mr. Hill élucidated.

The talk then fell upon novels and stories, a few of which Mr. Lincoln seemed to have read. He spoke, among others, of the "Gold Bug." "The story is grand," said he, "but it might as well have been written of Robinson Crusoe's island. What a fellow wants in a book is to *know where he is*. There are not many novels, or ancient works for that matter, that put you down anywhere."

"There is that genuine fragment which Cicero has preserved from a last work of Aristotle," said Mr. Hill, slyly. "'If there were beings who lived in the depths of the earth, and could emerge through the open fissures, and could suddenly behold the earth, the sea, and the vault of heaven—'"

"But you—you impostor," cried Mr. Lincoln, interrupting, "you're giving us Humboldt's Cosmos."

Mr. Hill owned up, laughing.

Winston Churchill, *The Crisis* (New York: Macmillan, 1901), 137–138.

Chapter 62

AUGUST STRINDBERG

Conquering Hero and Fool

1903

It was on the evening of a spring day in 1880 (a day which will never be forgotten in Sweden, because it is the day of commemoration of a national event), when an old couple, simple country people, were standing on the headland at the entrance to the harbour of Stockholm, looking at the dark watercourse under the dim stars, and watching a man who was busy with a dark, undefinable object on the landing bridge. They stood there for a long, long time, now gazing at the dark watercourse, now looking at the brilliant lights of the town.

At last a light appeared on the fjord, then another, then many lights. The old man seized the woman's hand and pressed it, and in silence, under the stars, they thanked God for having safely brought home their son whom they had mourned as dead for a whole year.

It is true, he had not been the leader of the expedition, but he had been one of the crew. And now he was to dine with the king, receive an order, and, in addition to a sum of money from the nation, which Parliament had voted for the purpose, an appointment which would mean bread and butter for the rest of his life.

The lights grew in size as they approached; a small steamer was towing a big dark craft, which, seen close by, looked as plain and simple as most great things do.

And now the man on the bridge, who had been very busy about the dark object, struck a match.

"Whatever is it?" said the old man, much puzzled. "It looks like huge wax candles."

They went nearer to examine it more closely.

August Strindberg, "Conquering Hero and Fool," in *In Midsummer Days, and Other Tales*, trans. Ellie Schleussner (London: H. Latimer, 1913), 79–89.

"It looks like a frame for drying fishes," said the old woman, who had been born on the coast.

Ratsh! It-sh! Si-si-si-si! it said, and the old people were instantly surrounded by fire and flames.

Great fiery globes rose up to the skies and, bursting, lit up the night with a shower of stars; an astronomer, observing the heavens with a telescope, might have come to the conclusion that new stars had been born. And he would not have been altogether wrong, for in the year 1880 new thoughts were kindled in new hearts, and new light and new discoveries vouchsafed to mankind. Doubtless, there were weeds, too, growing up together with the splendid wheat; but weeds have their uses, also; shade and moisture depend on their presence, and they will be separated from the wheat at harvest time. But there must be weeds, they are as inseparable from wheat as chaff is from corn.

What had puzzled the old couple, however, was a rocket frame, and when all the smoke had cleared away—for there is no fire without smoke—not a trace of all the magnificence was left.

"It would have been jolly to have been in town with them to-night," said the old woman.

"Oh, no!" replied the man. "We should have been in the way, poor people like we ought never to push themselves to the front. And there's plenty of time to-morrow for seeing the boy, after he has left his sweetheart, who is dearer to him than we are."

It was a very sensible speech for the old man to make; but who in the world is to have sense, if old people have not?

And then they continued their way to the town.

*

Now, let us see what happened to the son.

He was the leadsman, that is to say, it was his business to sound the depths of the sea; he had plumbed the profound abysses of the ocean, calculated the elevation of the land and the apparent motion of the sky; he knew the exact time by looking at the sun, and he could tell from the stars how far they had travelled. He was a man of importance; he believed that he held heaven and earth in his hand, measured time and regulated the clock of eternity. And after he had been the king's guest and received a medal to wear on his breast, he fancied that he was made of finer stuff than most men; he was not exactly haughty when he met his poor parents and his sweetheart, but, although they said nothing, they felt that he thought himself their superior. Possibly he was a little stiff, he was built that way.

Well, the official ceremonies were over, but the students also had decided to pay homage to the heroes, who had returned home after a prolonged absence. And they went to the capital in full force.

Students are queer people, who read books and study under Dr. Know-all; consequently they imagine that they know more than other people. They are also young, and therefore they are thoughtless and cruel.

The respectful and sensible speeches which the old professors had been making all the afternoon in honour of the explorers had come to an end, and the procession of the students had started.

The leadsman and his sweetheart were sitting on a balcony in the company of the other great men. The ringing of the church bells and the booming of the guns mingled with the sound of the bugles and the rolling of the drums; flags were waving and fluttering in the breeze. And then the procession marched by.

It was headed by a ship, with sailors and everything else belonging to it; next walruses came and polar bears, and all the rest of it; then students in disguise, representing the heroes; the Great Man himself was represented in his fur coat and goggles. It wasn't quite respectful, of course; it wasn't a very great honour to be impersonated in this way; but there it was! It was well meant, no doubt. And gradually every member of the expedition passed by, one after the other, all represented by the students.

Last of all came the leadsman. It was true, nobody could ever have dreamt of calling him handsome, but there is no need for a man to be handsome, as long as he is an able leadsman, or anything else able. The students had chosen a hideous old grumbler to impersonate him. That alone would not have mattered; but nature had made one of his arms shorter than the other, and his representative had made a feature of this defect. And that was too bad; for a defect is something for which one ought not to be blamed.

But when the fool who played the leadsman approached the balcony, he said a few words with a provincial accent, intended to cast ridicule on the leadsman, who was born in one of the provinces. It was a silly thing to do, for every man speaks the dialect which his mother has taught him; and it is nothing at all to be ashamed of.

Everybody laughed, more from politeness than anything else, for the entertainment was gratuitous, but the girl was hurt, for she hated to see her future husband laughed at. The leadsman frowned and grew silent. He no longer enjoyed the festivities. But he carefully hid his real feelings, for otherwise he would have been laughed at for a fool unable to appreciate a joke. But still worse things happened, for his impersonator danced and cut all sorts of ridiculous antics, in the endeavour to act the leadsman's name in dumb charade; first his surname, which he had inherited from his father, and then his Christian name, which his mother had chosen for him at his baptism. These names were sacred to him, and although there may have been a little boastful sound about them, he had always scorned to change them.

He wanted to rise from his chair and leave, but his sweetheart caught hold of his hand, and he stayed where he was.

When the procession was over and everybody who had been sitting on the balcony had risen, the great man laid a friendly hand on the girl's shoulder, and said, with his kindly smile:—

"They have a strange way here of celebrating their heroes, one mustn't mind it!"

In the evening there was a garden party and the leadsman was present, but his pleasure was gone; he had been laughed at, and he had grown small in his own estimation, smaller than the fool, who had made quite a hit as a jester. Therefore he was despondent, felt uneasy at the thought of the future and doubtful of his own capability. And wherever he went he met the fool who was caricaturing him. He saw his faults enlarged, especially his pride and his boastfulness; all his secret thoughts and weaknesses were made public.

For three painful hours he examined the account book of his conscience; what no man had dared to tell him before, the fool had told him. Perfect knowledge of oneself is a splendid thing, Socrates calls it the highest of all goods. Towards the end of the evening the leadsman had conquered himself, admitted his faults, and resolved to turn over a new leaf.

As he was passing a group of people he heard a voice behind a hedge saying: —

"It's extraordinary, how the leadsman has improved. He's really quite a delightful fellow!"

These words did him good; but what pleased him more than anything else were a few whispered words from his sweetheart.

"You are so nice to-night," she said, "that you look quite handsome."

He handsome? It must have been a miracle then, and miracles don't happen nowadays. Yet he had to believe in a miracle, for he knew himself to be a very plain man.

Finally the Great Man touched his glass with his knife, and immediately there was silence, for everybody wanted to hear what he had to say.

"When a Roman conqueror was granted a triumphal procession," he began, "a slave always stood behind him in the chariot and incessantly called out, 'Remember that you are but a man!' while senate and people paid him homage. And at the side of the triumphal car, which was drawn by four horses, walked a fool, whose business it was to dim the splendour of his triumph by shouting insults, and casting suspicion on the hero's character by singing libellous songs. This was a good old custom, for there is nothing so fatal to a man than to believe that he is a god, and there is nothing the gods dislike so much as the pride of men. My dear young friends! The success which we, who have just returned home, have achieved, has perhaps been overrated, our triumph went to our heads, and therefore it was good for us to watch your antics to-day! I don't envy the jester his part—far from it; but I thank you for the somewhat strange homage which you have done us. It has taught me that I have still a good deal to learn, and whenever my head is in danger of being turned by flattery, it will remind me that I am nothing but an ordinary man!"

"Hear! Hear!" exclaimed the leadsman, and the festivities continued, undisturbed even by the fool, who had felt a little ashamed of himself and had quietly withdrawn from the scene.

So much for the Great Man and the leadsman. Now let us see what happened to the fool.

As he was standing close to the table during the Great Man's speech, he received a glance from the leadsman, which, like a small fiery arrow, was capable of setting a fortress aflame. And as he went out into the night, he felt beside himself, like a man who is clothed in sheets of fire. He was not a nice man. True, fools and jailers are human beings, like the rest of us, but they are not the very nicest specimen. Like everybody else he had many faults and weaknesses, but he knew how to cloak them. Now something extraordinary happened. Through having mimicked the leadsman all day long, and also, perhaps, owing to all the drink he had consumed, he had become so much the part which he had played that he was unable to shake it off; and since he had brought into prominence the faults and weaknesses of the leadsman, he had, as it were, acquired them, and that flash from the leadsman's eye had rammed them down to the very bottom of his soul, just as a ramrod pushes the powder into the barrel of a gun. He was charged with the leadsman, so to speak, and therefore, as he stepped out into the street he at once began to shout and boast. But this time luck was against him. A policeman ordered him to be quiet. The fool said something funny, imitating the leadsman's provincial accent. But the policeman, who happened to be a native of the same province, was annoyed and wanted to arrest the fool. Now it is just as difficult for a fool to take a thing seriously as it is for a policeman to understand a joke; therefore the fool resisted and created such a disturbance that the policeman struck him with his truncheon.

He received a sound beating, and then the policeman let him go.

You would think that he had had enough trouble now—far from it!

The chastisement which he had received had only embittered him, and he went on the warpath, like a red Indian, to see on whom he might avenge his wrongs.

Accident, or some other power, guided his footsteps to a locality mainly frequented by peasants and labourers. He entered a brewery and found a number of millers and farmer's labourers sitting round a table, drinking the health of the explorers. When they saw the fool they took him for the leadsman, and were highly delighted when he condescended to take a glass in their company.

Now the demon of pride entered into the soul of the fool. He boasted of his great achievements; he told them that it was he who had led the expedition, for would they not have foundered if he had not sounded the depth of the sea? Would they ever have returned home if he had not read the stars?

Smack! an egg hit him between the eyebrows.

"Leadsman, you're a braggart!" said the miller. "We've known that for a long time; we knew it when you wrote to the paper saying the Great Man was another Humboldt!"

Now another of the leadsman's weaknesses gained the upper hand.

"The Great Man is a humbug!" he exclaimed, which was not true.

This was too much for the assembly. They rose from their seats like one man, seized the fool, and with a leather strap bound him to a sack of flour. They covered him with flour until he was white from top to toe, and blackened his face with the wick from one of the lanterns. The millers' apprentice sewed him to the sack; they lifted him, sack and lantern, on to the cart, and amid shouting and laughter proceeded to the market-place.

There he was exhibited to the passers-by, and everybody laughed at him.

When they let him go at last, he went and sat on some stone stairs and cried. The big fellow sobbed like a little child; one might almost have felt sorry for him.

Chapter 63

Theodore Roosevelt
Through the Brazilian Wilderness
1914

The Work of the Field Zoologist and Field Geographer in South America

Roughly, the travellers who now visit (like those who for the past century have visited) South America come in three categories—although, of course, these categories are not divided by hard-and-fast lines.

First, there are the travellers who skirt the continent in comfortable steamers, going from one great seaport to another, and occasionally taking a short railway journey to some big interior city not too far from the coast. This is a trip well worth taking by all intelligent men and women who can afford it; and it is being taken by such men and women with increasing frequency. It entails no more difficulty than a similar trip to the Mediterranean—than such a trip which to a learned and broad-minded observer offers the same chance for acquiring knowledge and, if he is himself gifted with wisdom, the same chance of imparting his knowledge to others that is offered by a trip of similar length through the larger cities of Europe or the United States. Probably the best instance of the excellent use to which such an observer can put his experience is afforded by the volume of Mr. Bryce. Of course, such a trip represents travelling of essentially the same kind as travelling by railroad from Atlanta to Calgary or from Madrid to Moscow.

Next there are the travellers who visit the long-settled districts and colonial cities of the interior, travelling over land or river highways which have been traversed for centuries but which are still primitive as regards the inns and the modes of conveyance. Such travelling is difficult in the sense that travelling in parts of Spain or southern Italy or the Balkan states is difficult. Men and women who have a taste for travel in out-of-way places and who, therefore, do

Theodore Roosevelt, *Through the Brazilian Wilderness* (New York: Charles Scribner's Sons, 1914), 343–346.

not mind slight discomforts and inconveniences have the chance themselves to enjoy, and to make others profit by, travels of this kind in South America. In economic, social, and political matters the studies and observations of these travellers are essential in order to supplement, and sometimes to correct, those of travellers of the first category; for it is not safe to generalize overmuch about any country merely from a visit to its capital or its chief seaport. These travellers of the second category can give us most interesting and valuable information about quaint little belated cities; about backward country folk, kindly or the reverse, who show a mixture of the ideas of savagery with the ideas of an ancient peasantry; and about rough old highways of travel which in comfort do not differ much from those of mediaeval Europe. The travellers who go up or down the highway rivers that have been travelled for from one to four hundred years—rivers like the Paraguay and Paraná, the Amazon, the Tapajos, the Madeira, the lower Orinoco—come in this category. They can add little to our geographical knowledge; but if they are competent zoologists or archaeologists, especially if they live or sojourn long in a locality, their work may be invaluable from the scientific standpoint. The work of the archaeologists among the immeasurably ancient ruins of the low-land forests and the Andean plateaux is of this kind. What Agassiz did for the fishes of the Amazon and what Hudson did for the birds of the Argentine are other instances of the work that can thus be done. Burton's writings on the interior of Brazil offer an excellent instance of the value of a sojourn or trip of this type, even without any especial scientific object.

Of course travellers of this kind need to remember that their experiences in themselves do not qualify them to speak as wilderness explorers. Exactly as a good archaeologist may not be competent to speak of current social or political problems, so a man who has done capital work as a tourist observer in little-visited cities and along remote highways must beware of regarding himself as being thereby rendered fit for genuine wilderness work or competent to pass judgment on the men who do such work. To cross the Andes on muleback along the regular routes is a feat comparable to the feats of the energetic tourists who by thousands traverse the mule trails in out-of-the-way nooks of Switzerland. An ordinary trip on the highway portions of the Amazon, Paraguay, or Orinoco in itself no more qualifies a man to speak of or to take part in exploring unknown South American rivers than a trip on the lower Saint Lawrence qualifies a man to regard himself as an expert in a canoe voyage across Labrador or the Barren Grounds west of Hudson Bay.

A hundred years ago, even seventy or eighty years ago, before the age of steamboats and railroads, it was more difficult than at present to define the limits between this class and the next; and, moreover, in defining these limits I emphatically disclaim any intention of thereby attempting to establish a single standard of value for books of travel. Darwin's "Voyage of the Beagle" is to me the best book of the kind ever written; it is one of those classics which decline to go into artificial categories, and which stand by themselves; and yet Darwin, with his usual modesty, spoke of it as in effect a yachting voyage. Humboldt's work had a profound effect on the thought of the civilized world; his trip was one of adventure and danger; and yet it can hardly be called exploration proper. He visited places which had been settled and inhabited for centuries and traversed places which had been travelled by civilized men for years before he followed in their footsteps. But these places were in Spanish colonies, and access to them had been forbidden by the mischievous and intolerant tyranny—ecclesiastical, political, and economic—which then rendered Spain the most backward of European nations; and Humboldt was the first scientific man of intellectual independence who had permission to visit them. To this day many of his scientific observations are of real value. Bates came to the Amazon just before the era of Amazonian steamboats. He never went off the native routes of ordinary travel. But he was a devoted and able naturalist. He lived an exceedingly isolated, primitive, and laborious life for eleven years. Now, half a century after it was written, his "Naturalist on the Amazon" is as interesting and valuable as it ever was, and no book since written has in any way supplanted it.

Travel of the third category includes the work of the true wilderness explorers who add to our sum of geographical knowledge and of the scientific men who, following their several bents, also work in the untrodden wilds. [...]

An immense amount of this true wilderness work, geographical and zoological, remains to be done in South America.

Chapter 64

MÁRIO DE ANDRADE

Macunaíma

1928

Epilogue

This story is over and its glory has faded away.

There is no longer anyone left. Sorcery and bad luck have finished off the scions of the Tapanhuma tribe, one by one. The places they knew—those spacious savannas, those clefts and gullies, those balata bleeders' trails, those abrupt ravines, those mysterious forests—they are all now as solitary as a desert. An immense silence slumbers over the river Uraricoera.

No one on this earth knows how to speak the language of this vanished tribe, nor how to recount its flamboyant adventures. Who can know anything of the hero? His brothers, transformed into a leprous ghostly shadow, have become the second head of the Father of the King-Vultures; and Macunaíma became the constellation of the Great Bear. No one can learn any more the fascinating history and the speech of the extinct Tapanhumas. An immense silence slumbers over the riverbanks of the Uraricoera.

One day a man went there. It was before dawn, and Vei, the Sun, had sent her daughters to drive the stars away. The vast deserted forest had stifled the fish and the songbirds with terror, and nature itself swooned and lay abandoned over all. The silence was so immense that it extended into space like the trees of the illimitable forest. Suddenly a voice from the foliage jarred the aching senses of the man: "Curr-pac, papac! Curr-pac, papac!"

This squawking turned the man's insides cold with fright. Then he noticed the fluttering of a hummingbird that hovered at his lips—"Whisht, whisht, whisht. ... There! A magic charm"—and flew quickly up into the trees. The man craned his neck to follow the flight of the hummingbird overhead.

"Pull the leaves aside, beefy one!" laughed the hummingbird, and fled.

There in the foliage the man discovered a green parrot with a golden beak looking at him. He said, "Come down, parrot, come down!"

The parrot came down and perched on the man's head, and the two went along together. The parrot started to talk in a gentle tongue, something new, completely new! Some of it was song, some like cassiri sweetened with wild honey, some of it had the lovely fickle flavor of unknown forest fruits.

The vanished tribe, the family turned into ghosts, the tumble-down hut undermined by termites, Macunaíma's ascent to heaven, how the parrots and macaws formed a canopy in the far-off times when the hero was the Great Emperor, Macunaíma: in the silence of the Uraricoera only the parrot had rescued from oblivion those happenings and the language which had disappeared. Only the parrot had preserved in that vast silence the words and the deeds of the hero.

All this he related to the man, then spread his wings and set his course for Lisbon. And that man, dear reader, was myself, and I stayed on in order to tell you this story. That is why I came here. I crouched in the shelter of the leaves, picked off my ticks, struck a few chords on my little fiddle, and with a sweeping touch started the mouth of the world singing in vulgar speech the deeds and words of Macunaíma, the hero of our people.

There's no more.

Chapter 65

Jordan Herbert Stabler

Bolívar

1930

Bolívar in Memoriam

December 1830–December 1930

The Spirit of Chimborazo speaks.
Snow-clad, majestic, hoary Chimborazo raised
    This ancient head,
Looked Northward toward the Carib Sea, across the
    vallies far outspread;
Northward and saw four Nations rise from one,
    through war, strife and turmoil:
Colors of Iris tint their flags, fruits of the
    Liberator's toil.
Looked South, where stretched the Inca's Lands, past
    Illimani's snowy crest;
Two other Nations owe their all to that great
    Patriot's bequest.

*

Then Chimborazo's deep, rough voice was heard,
Clearing his frozen throat to speak a word;
That great deep voice, only for once released
To praise a friend, these hundred years deceased.
"What memories I have! How moved the Hand of God!
Since up the Humboldt trail he trod

Jordan Herbert Stabler, *Bolívar. December 1830 – December 1930. In Memoriam. The Spirit of Chimborazo Speaks* (Caracas: Vargas, 1930), 7–8, 17–20.

And reached my crest.
A burning flame, fire and steel,
    From all ideals and truths,
      He took the best.
I came to him as ancient Father Time,
I pointed out to him those things sublime
    He wrote in ecstasy;—
'Delirium' he called that which he heard from me—
'Delirium' some call it—but
      Bolívar set a New World free!

*

We like to think that the Divine Fire
Grows brighter with the Ages and mounts higher
    And never dies,
Passed on by God's discerning hand,
    Enters the heart and soul
    Of some great man,
Brave, noble, extra wise.
Such was Bolívar, such fire his soul did fill,
In Rome when he paced on the Sacred Hill;
    And thus he spake;
      'I shall not rest, O Liberty,
      Until I set my country free.'
Gone was wild youth, gone gambler and rake,
Steadfast, full of zeal, with soul awake,
Westward he turned his flaming eyes
Westward to Glory's enterprise!

◝◞

Five years had passed since he had started forth
He found alas! great changes in the North—
His work of Federation seemed undone
Unrest in Venezuela had begun.
He took command and forced again his will,
His strength of purpose dominated still.
Once more he stood on Venezuelan soil,
Forced Páez once more to heel, began to toil
To save his country from that civil strife
Which threatened to exterminate its life,
While here came news of Bustemente's vile revolt,
Santander's attacks came like a thunder bolt,

Bolívar, leaving Páez in charge returned
To Cartagena, for his ire burned.

*

He cried: 'And is our country really free
Or have we only ploughed the sea?'

*

September found him once more re-installed
In Bogotá—once more was he recalled
By Congress, which begged him to resume
The Presidency and to assume
Extraordinary powers. This was done
But evidence of good faith, there was none.
Green eyed, ignoble Jealousy appeared
To plant a seed of discord far and wide,
East, West and South—Bolívar feared
The spark Liberty had died,
Died down, blown out by Jealousy and Spite,
He paced his quinta floor both day and night.

Beset by cares and having just escaped
Assassination at the hands of one time friends,
Worn out with battles, Destiny then shaped
His Future on the narrow path which ends
Sometimes in greatest *Triumph,* whiles one lives,
Sometimes, disdainful of the *All* one gives.

*

Heartsick, weary and ill, overburdened with pain
　　　and care,
Bolívar dreamed of a quiet place, of a quiet
　　　shelter, where
He could go for a little time, for a little
　　　while to rest;
And he dreamed of the Palms on the shore, on the
　　　shore of the Isles of the Blest.
He wished to forget why his Heart so bled, bled for
　　　Illusions, now no more,
Ideals or Illusions, he could not tell, wounded he was
　　　to his own Heart's core:
So he summoned his failing strength, strength, which
　　　was waning, he knew,

And one last gesture he made, gesture brave, noble
        and true.
His Fire Divine was dying, and only a Spark remained,
Gone was his greatest Hour, Glory, which he had attained.
So he summoned the Congress, addressed his last words,
        while in pain;
Resigned once more as their Leader, returned them his
        Power again.
He then left, reduced to half of the man he was and
        never would be again,
Wearily down the River, stream that he wrested
        from Spain.
Painfully reached a resting place, on the shore
        and under the Trees,
Could he rest, could he forget, could he find
        a little ease?"

                              *

A quiet fell, no more the Voice
        was heard;
A Condor wheeled on High, gigantic
        Bird;
Clouds veiled the glistening Heights,
        descending slow;
No sound disturbed that great
        expanse of Snow.

                              *

As in pain and with an
        effort great,
Again the Voice of Chimborazo spoke;
"No mortal ease for those, who
        soon or late
Attain their Goal; no rest
For those Great Beings, who provoke
The envy of the Human Kind;
Each would command, each would be King,
For each one has this in his mind
Resentful, if another's praise they sing!
No, no, Bolívar is not dead!
He lives, lives in the hearts
        of all true Men;

I sometimes feel his feet upon
  my Head.
As he mounts up the Humboldt path
  again.
His soul, at Santa Marta left
  this human Coil,
His Spirit sees the Fruits of
  all his Toil!
Before his God he kneels, a time
  and prays;
Content that all his work
  of Independence Days
Has justified his Quest.
Now he has found great Peace and
  all his Labours blest!
High! o're the World he made,
  Bolívar lifts his Sword;
Re-born, he finds his Handiwork
  accepted by Our Lord!"

Chapter 66

Ernst Bloch

Astonishment at the Rhine Falls

1933

No beautiful or large-scale attraction ceases to have an effect, even when it is thickly covered in the spoilage of renown. Even when it cannot be considered innocent of this renown, but tries to meet fame halfway, from one side. New views wash away this varnish of banality, as well as the attitude of disdainful rejection that sets no value in all-too-familiar things. Words can go stale; what incited them does not.

Often the spectator finds something other than what he expected. The thing itself stands next to its customary image, being for the most part occupied only with itself. This is the effect of the Blue Grotto in Capri and of the Rhine Valley (in spite of Stolzenfels and the Lorelei), and not least of the Rhine Falls at Schaffhausen, even though its simulacrum sits on everybody's knickknack shelf. Of course, whoever views it from the train, or in general from the front, has only the decor of the picture postcard. A power plant on the left, castle-kitsch on the right, and in the middle a framed panorama after the style of the nineteenth century. This is ersatz Niagara, a kind of cut-rate Tivolian cascade, a "natural" ornamental waterworks, so to speak. When Goethe prophesied in 1797 that "This natural phenomenon will often be painted and described," he did not know what sort of touristic paint job awaited the Rhine Falls. The souvenirs collected in the Walter Scott castle, at the entrance to this "phenomenon," include musical beer tankards, barometers, carved cuckoo clocks, and bulls' horns: the leftovers of a bygone era, and also the magical mementos of that era. Yet as Goethe went on to say in his letter to Schiller concerning the phenomenon itself: "Nobody can fix its meaning, much less exhaust it." Our need for such inexhaustible phenomena is growing today, and is more than just holiday relaxation, more than mere "disinterested contemplation." Precisely what is interested and non-restful has increased to the same extent that life has become ever more gray and hollow, with nature serving as a new refuge and likewise as a new source of astonishment. As a new mediation between humanity, its inner self, and the unconquered new world that presses urgently upon its natural horizon.

One has to walk alongside the immense picture of the falls, and at the same height. One has to remain still, living alongside the phenomenon, so to speak, until one's eyes and ears are completely united with the undisturbed being of the falls. A pulpit has been constructed at the water's edge, as well as a kind of nautical bridge over which the water spews ceaselessly. Although no sermon issues from the pulpit, visitors can stop in this small area and stand before the power of the falls. The noise, heavy with foam, is deafening as an African drum. A very deep, uniform sound underlies it: the pedal-note of the roaring rock. Rising up over this, and varying according to the optical height, are the overtones of the rushing water itself: the hissing water snake. These acoustical and optical manifestations as a whole do not overlap. The acoustical part lacks multiplicity, openness, and (obviously) human intervention—the happiness of the blind differs from the richness of vision. The view from the pulpit gives an encyclopedic overview of all the possibilities of water, that remarkable element, which is brought to dance by means of gravity. Looking upward, one sees, five meters above one's eyes, the Rhine coming down in a broad curve shaped like an ocean wave. At eye level, this changes into a glacier field of such unvarying, victorious whiteness that it seems to rest atop the plunging waters; little gates of rock rise up from the snowy roam at the edge. If the gaze is cast downward, however, the water becomes full of contradictions, running from a hundredfold to a thousandfold, collides against the rocks, then launches high arrows and needles, long tongues and shards of glitter, swirling out lush agitations of chrysanthemums, blowing Venetian glass. A baroque carving in active motion, and over this, a veil of vapors: the water spirit, as a woman called it, the distillation of a spirit guarding its treasures, expressive and empty, garrulous and secretive. Also beautiful is the rainbow in the mist, not a fragment, but a veritable bridge completely constructed from start to finish, from the end that touches upon the shore, to the other end that reaches a crag amid the flow. This quiet apparition, which usually links the far horizons, here shines ten meters below the onlooker; while the unquiet spray shoots beneath, driving the mists high, the emanations of a wild, watery sun that mirrors the other, fiery one. The water is no rivulet of dust, and is comparable neither to the soul nor to the fare of humanity; rather, even in its familiar running, it exists beyond our existence. Only a *crossing* of images becomes palpable, not only as a series of substitutions, from here up to the great Niagara; an interplay of bell-creation and headlong dive, of outflow and downfall, until the water, at the foot of ecstasy, very rapidly attains a state of rest. The whirlpool turns into peacefulness and milk, and the extravagant falls change back into a river, reflecting the human shore. Only then does the onlooker become aware of the banal background against which, all this time, the phenomenon had been situated. Civilized hills, a restaurant, villas, a few old houses surround this uncanny, self-animating aquarium in an all-too-familiar fashion. An old church spire, at least, relates to the *genius loci* as the sign of another great power, not just as decoration. The cults that celebrated the river god here are still present, but only as gaps in the memory. The cults have dried up, but the X that they marked has not.

As the saying goes, those who are disgusted by filth are always disgusted by themselves. However, awe in the face of the beautiful or meaningful is an experience that transcends those who experience it. For such an experience indicates not only internal states, but at the same time expresses something—however cryptic—about the natural occasion that called it forth. Today, natural curiosities such as grottoes and waterfalls especially arouse feelings of awe, and for good reason: the rupture that has developed within the subject and traditional society corresponds to the one within the traditional context of nature. There is something here like groundwater, like a water clock that measures both ancient and not yet elapsed time. Waves, above all, have provided an age-old image for raging emptiness, and for the misery of undisciplined life; thus, the old nature cults imagined the most miserable souls as swirling in torrential waters. But from Tauler to Böhme, waves have also signified the steed which the subject rides toward a breakthrough beyond conventional rigidity. The roaring cataracts, here within nature itself, constitute the elements of the journey. Also, to the extent that these kinds of archetypes are awakened by a sense of awe, the phenomena that contain them, as Goethe says, cannot be so easily "fixed, much less exhausted." The awe aroused by a self-transcending delight in water phenomena is largely archaic, yet it extends likewise into the "hollow" of natural being, and into the unknown being that—beyond hydroelectric power—still brews in nature. The Rhine Falls are just a small, middle-European attraction; there are similar, but much more important, points of interest in other countries. Yet even sublimity does not always require quantity, in order to be recognized as such. A line of fracture requires it even less.

In short, one no longer visits such wonders for the sake of pleasure alone. Something has changed—the reception of natural wonders is not simply contemplative, but awe-inspired. Along with this, the feeling of responsibility has also greatly increased. In the midst of awe, there is a striving for objective clarity about the observer's relation to the thing observed; there is an effort to move beyond the receptivity produced by the "rupture" in our social order, as well as beyond the thereby signified "hollow space." So that, in comparison to the nineteenth century, a true experience of the landscape can no longer remain subjective. Here, too, the nineteenth century practiced double book-keeping, keeping its subjective feeling for nature cleanly—but dishonestly—separate from its objective idea of nature. Both stood side by side: the color and freshness of summer (for relaxation, rewarding views, souvenirs to bring home) and total mechanics (as the only truth that counted). The incompat-ibility is vast: here, merry revelry, subjectively abandoning mechanized society for the bosom of nature; there, nature made into a skeleton, objectively reflect-ing a mechanized industrial mode, a world emptied of qualities. After this, nothing could remain of the experience of astonishment at the Rhine Falls but illusion, at best a "world of feeling," corresponding to nothing but the displace-ment of water molecules in the "world of reason." Today, of course, undiluted repudiations of this mechanized picture of nature have been brought forward, imbued with qualitative, even morphological, conscience. Undoubtedly this too was able to be misused and violated by fascism, which opposes not just the mechanical, but every form of reason. Yet such an eventuality came to pass unhindered only because the experience of astonishment at the Rhine Falls, indeed, everything that might correspond objectively to qualitative wonder-ment, has long been excluded from progressive teachings. In this respect, the socialist relation to nature has remained a bourgeois-mechanistic one, uphold-ing nature-friends and nature-murderers side by side: Goethe and Karl Eugen Dühring. All the more urgently, the qualitatively defined landscape has come into prominence once again, with an admonitory reminder of the Goethean relation to nature, and not only as an aesthetic, but equally as a philosophical problem. Obviously, empathetic feeling—like the sadness of a somber autumn evening, the happiness of a spring meadow, of a blossoming cherry tree under a cloudless sky, the sublimity of storm and thunder, even of a waterfall—is by no means present as such within phenomena. But just as obviously, whatever *calls forth* affects like these cannot be entirely missing from the landscape; oth-erwise the significance of phenomena like smoke and fire would not be so sim-ilar, so inevitable, for people at all times and places. And furthermore (to go beyond merely affective responses), it's not without reason that geographically distinct "landscape types," each characterized by a distinct "nimbus," are objec-tively studied and exploited beginning with a thoroughly qualitative "overall impression." So that, in consideration of the shaping forces, even the "physi-ognomy" of landscapes has been discussed—by none other than Alexander von Humboldt. In his book *Views of Nature*, he declares quite unreservedly that "The primeval force of organization, notwithstanding a certain indepen-dence in the abnormal development of individual parts, binds all animal and vegetable structures" (of a landscape) "to fixed, ever-recurring types. For as in some individual organic beings we recognize a definite physiognomy ... so also there is a certain natural physiognomy peculiar to every region of the earth." And Humboldt does not limit this only to mineralogically produced forms, where the same kinds of rocks everywhere generate the same kinds of mountainous shapes; instead, even the "expression" (Humboldt describes "smoothly rounded hilltops," "grotesque masses of rock," even a "landscape of friendly pastures") must be objectively anchored. So much here, on the occasion of the Rhine Falls, about feeling without the necessity of deception, about understanding without the necessity of becoming soulless. The non-subjective content of the experience of awe relevant here is still often imprecise, sometimes even fantastically imprecise; yet it is certainly never empty, never meaningless. On the contrary, when this specific imprecision is sharply focused, it allows something still fermenting within the impressed to become objectively recognizable. Here, something goes with us into its own meaning, into a content that itself has not yet been determinately brought out. And which, in any case, has not yet been exhausted by mechanical-quantitative determinations, not even (probably least of all) in the realm of "dead" nature. Already, the relatively modest Rhine Falls lead us toward something in regard to which it may be said: not constructed for us, but pertaining to us in the end. In all such natural "places of interest," something mysteriously looks back at us, which is not at all articulated in the cities.

Chapter 67

ALDOUS HUXLEY

Beyond the Mexique Bay
1934

Cholula

I did not bother to count the churches visible from the top of the great pyramid. But one did not have to invoke the aid of arithmetic to perceive that the town at one's feet was fairly bubbling with round domes, that all the plain for miles around was strewn with the fossil remains of ecclesiastical life. The religious emotions rank, with sunlight, hunger, and falling water, as one of the great natural sources of energy. Harness this Niagara, and at once millions of horse-power are at your disposal. There are enough bricks in the Cholula pyramid to cover an area twice as large as the Place de la Concorde to a depth equal to twice the height of the Louvre. And when Quetzalcoatl had gone, the missionaries re-canalized the old energies in the imported name of Jesus; the towers of the new *mezquitas* sprouted everywhere like mushrooms on an autumn morning. It was the decay of faith that made it necessary to invent the steam engine.

Humboldt, in his *Essai Politique sur la Nouvelle Espagne,* makes a remark which every enthusiastic pyramid-climber should strictly meditate. "If," he says, "we analyze the mechanism of the Peruvian theocracy, generally so much over-praised in Europe, we observe that, wherever nations are divided into castes, and wherever men do not enjoy the right to private property and work solely for the profit of the community, we shall find canals, roads, aqueducts, pyramids, huge constructions of every kind. But we shall also find that these people, though for thousands of years they may preserve the air of external prosperity, will make practically no advance in moral culture, which is the result of individual liberty."

Pyramids on the one hand; personal liberty on the other. We have an ever increasing number of pyramids, or their modern equivalents; an ever diminishing amount of personal liberty. Is this merely a historical accident? Or are these two goods essentially incompatible? If they turn out to be essentially incompatible, then, one day, we shall have to ask ourselves very seriously which is better worth having—pyramids and a perfectly efficient, perfectly stable community; or personal liberty with instability, but the possibility, at least, of a progress, measurable in terms of spiritual values.

Descending from Quetzalcoatl's mountain of petrified energy, we set out to explore the Christian monuments.

Illustration 67.1. Detached mass of the pyramid of Cholula.

Chapter 68

EGON ERWIN KISCH

Dialogue with a Nazi

1944

On the 14th September 1944, for the 175th Birthday
of Alexander von Humboldt

To commemorate Mexico's grateful love towards Humboldt, Emperor Wilhelm II gave the Mexicans a marble statue, which stands in front of the National Library on Uruguay Street. At the unveiling on September 13, 1910, the president of the republic was handed a commemorative document. It was written in German and thus neither the president nor likely any other Mexican read it. Had any of them read it, there would have been no small scandal.

For in this collection there appears an article—"Humboldt and the Politico-Economical and Ethnological Development of Mexico"—by one O. Peust, who calls himself Departmental Director in the Ministry of Public Works. This same Mexican state official of German nationality was an early herald of the Nazis, a future bulwark of racist mania with ambitions of comporting himself scientifically. With a complete lack of shame he describes the Caucasian (nowadays, Aryan) race as superior to all others and the Mexicans expressly as inferior and indolent. But to do this, a new "refutation" of Humboldt was demanded, which he provided in a coarse and tactless way right under the new statue, and saw to it that this load of rubbish was handed over to the president of the republic.

When the findings of Humboldt's ethnological studies are compared word-for-word with the objections of the Nazis, it results in this fundamental controversy regarding the race problem:

Translation by Richard John Ascárate, from Egon Erwin Kisch, "Zwiegespräch mit einem Nazi," in: *Gesammelte Werke in Einzelausgaben,* eds. Bodo Uhse and Gisela Kisch, Fritz Hofmann and Josef Polácek, vol. 10, *Läuse auf dem Markt. Vermischte Prosa* (Berlin/Weimar [GDR]: Aufbau, 1985), 273–277. Copyright © Aufbau Verlag GmbH & Co. KG, Berlin 1985.

HUMBOLDT: The general picture of nature which I have endeavoured to de-
lineate, would be incomplete, if I did not venture to trace a few of the most
marked features of *the* human race, considered with reference to physical
gradations—to the geographical distribution of contemporaneous types. ...
[*Cosmos*, 1:360]

PEUST: There are no simultaneously existing types, as Humboldt falsely believes. The distinct characteristics are determined by the racial predisposi-
tions of each people.

HUMBOLDT: ... in a few strokes. The investigation of this problem will
impart a nobler and, if I may so express myself, more purely human interest to [...] my work. [*Cosmos*, 1:361] Our era, fortunately enlightened by
science. ...

PEUST: Representations—such as Humboldt's book on Mexico—that restrict
themselves to the time in question, are worthless for defining the special
character of a period. Among the writers of Humboldt's era, not a single
one recognized the growing importance of the races, in which lethargic individuals predominate.

HUMBOLDT: As long as attention was directed solely to the extremes in varieties of colour and of form, and to the vividness of the first impression of
the senses, the observer was naturally disposed to regard "races" rather as
originally *different* species than as mere varieties. [*Cosmos*, 1:361] In my
opinion, however, more powerful reasons can be advanced in *support* of
the theory of the unity of the human race, as, for instance, in the many in-
termediate gradations in the colour of the skin and in the form of the skull,
which have been made known to us in recent times by the rapid progress
of geographical knowledge—the analogies presented by the varieties in the
species of many wild and domesticated animals—and the more correct observations collected regarding the limits of fecundity in hybrids. [*Cosmos*,
1:361–362] The different races of mankind are forms of one sole species, by
the union of two of whose members descendants are propagated. They are
not different species of a genus, since in that case their hybrid descendants
would remain unfruitful. [*Cosmos*, 1:364]

PEUST: There are three races independent from each other: the first encom-
passes the nations of the Caucasian race, which created the capitalistic in-
dustrial system. To the second race belong Japanese, Chinese, etc., which
are capable of imitating the capitalist system. While the third group of these
races, which is composed of, for example, the American Indians, lacks the
requisite willpower for the implementation of this system.

HUMBOLDT: Accustomed to a long slavery, as well under the domination
of their own sovereigns as under that of the first conquerors, the natives of
Mexico patiently suffer the vexations to which they are frequently exposed
from the whites. [*Political Essay on the Kingdom of New Spain*, 1:127] As the

Indians, almost all of them, belong to the class of peasantry and low people, it is not so easy to judge of their aptitude for the arts which embellish life. [...] When an Indian attains a certain degree of civilization, he displays a great facility of apprehension, a judicious mind, a natural logic, and a particular disposition to subtilize or seize the finest differences in the comparison of objects. [*Political Essay*, 1:128]

PEUST: Despite differences of one hundred percent and more between the work-capacity of various Indian tribes, the American Indians are nevertheless an inferior race. In the time of Alexander von Humboldt the race question did not exist. This explains Humboldt's opinion when he maintains that it is possible in a short time to uplift and improve the most essential intellectual characteristics which are nowadays recognized as unchangeable.

HUMBOLDT: Oppression produces everywhere the same effects, it everywhere corrupts the morals. [*Political Essay*, 1:127]

PEUST: Humboldt did not treat the topic with systematic thoroughness. In general, in and of themselves, social characteristics mean absolutely nothing. Humboldt was thereby in no position to specify the characteristics that he found suitable for the natives of Mexico.

HUMBOLDT: The population will grow and arrive at a higher moral level in the fertile and temperate zones only through great changes of state or when aided by other events. All branches of mankind are capable of this. Whilst we maintain the unity of the human species, we at the same time repel the depressing assumption of superior and inferior races of men. There are nations more susceptible of cultivation, more highly civilized, more ennobled by mental cultivation than others—but none in themselves nobler than others. [*Cosmos*, 1:368]

PEUST: Those are not economical definitions, not sociological categories. The racial group of American Indians, etc., is unfit for utilization of the capitalistic system of industry.

HUMBOLDT: All are in like degree designed for freedom. ... [*Cosmos*, 1:368] ["]If we would indicate an idea which throughout the whole course of history has ever more and more widely extended its empire—or which more than any other, testifies to the much contested and still more decidedly misunderstood perfectibility of the whole human race—it is that of establishing our common humanity—of striving to remove the barriers which prejudice and limited views of every kind have erected amongst men, and to treat all mankind without reference to religion, nation, or colour, as one fraternity, one great community, fitted for the attainment of one object, the unrestrained development of the physical powers. [...] Thus deeply rooted in the innermost nature of man, and even enjoined upon him by his highest tendencies—the recognition of the bond of humanity becomes one of the noblest leading principles in the history of mankind.["] [*Cosmos*, 1:368–369, quoting Wilhelm von Humboldt, *Ueber die Kawi-Sprache*, 3:426]

In these beliefs are revealed the opposition between the petty bourgeois, who can be proud of nothing but his "race," and the German citizen of the world, Humboldt. Who is right? What is certain is that in the years of the Hitler regime the Humboldt Societies of Latin America would have excluded Alexander von Humboldt from their ranks, if he had belonged to them.

Illustration 68.1. Alexander von Humboldt's statue in the garden of the Biblioteca Nacional in Mexico City, Uruguay Street.

Chapter 69

ARTEMIO DE VALLE-ARIZPE

The Fair Rodríguez

1949

From the Humanity of Science to the Divinity of Love

On the 22nd day of the month of March in the year 1803, the famous German traveler, Friedrich Heinrich Alexander Baron von Humboldt, arrived in the land of Mexico. He entered New Spain at the Port of Acapulco, where shortly before a noisy festival had been celebrated on the occasion of the longed-for arrival of the galleon from Manila, the *Nao of China*, which always carried within its fabulous hold dazzling cargos of silk and other colorful fabrics, porcelain, lacquered pieces, ivories, odoriferous spices. The baron came accompanied by his lively and courageous French collaborator, Aimé Bonpland. Both gentlemen sailed from Guayaquil in the frigate *Orúe,* which arrived dismasted and thoroughly battered from a tumultuous passage, all the winds having conspired against it. Submerged a thousand times beneath the waves, the vessel righted its prow during a tranquil time near Acapulco where, on the above-mentioned date, the men arrived at port and upon the desired shore.

Humboldt gazed as if enchanted upon Acapulco, whose imposing beauty and majesty enamored his vision. Its spell held him fast while maddening his intellect. His entranced imagination could not accommodate such prodigious loveliness. One never wearied of looking all about, and wherever one directed enraptured eyes they never failed to encounter something that captivated. The sight surpassed all admiration. With the memory of Acapulco still vivid, he wrote in the *Essai politique sur le royaume de la Nouvelle-Espagne* (*Political Essay on the Kingdom of New Spain*): "the most beautiful port of all encountered along the Pacific coast"; "immense basin carved within mountains of granite"; "site of unparalleled savage aspect but at the same time gloomy and romantic,

Translation by Richard John Ascárate, from *Obras,* 2 vols. (Mexico: Fondo de Cultura Económica, 2000), 1:165–177. Copyright D.R. © 2000 Fondo de Cultura Económica.

with enormous masses of rock whose form brings to mind the jagged crests of Montserrat in Catalonia, and with rocky coasts so sheer that a man-of-war can pass by, brushing against them without running the slightest risk because everywhere the depth extends ten or twelve fathoms."

This wandering globetrotter of whom we speak was not very tall, as are almost all Teutons, nor of stunted stature, but he found himself somewhat between these two extremes; limbs slender yet tough, strong muscles, fair brow, and about his white countenance, blasted and darkened by the harsh American days, a long and wispy lock of blonde hair falling in fixed and perpetual disheveledness from his thick scalp. He had blue expressive eyes, possessed of a deep gaze, inquisitive and withdrawn, mouth small and lip smooth; hands, large.

His clothing was in the French fashion of the *Directoire,* meticulous, ever sparkling clean; buttoned white trousers, jacket with long tails and high collar reaching halfway up the back of his head; white trouser cuffs with gold buttons, white as well the shirt cuffs and criss-crossing vest; long, encircling tie fastened with a variety of knots from which the tips hardly projected—stiffened by starch—beyond the shirt; boots of lustrous, turned-out leather, of the kind that were called *Federicas.*

Humboldt arrived in Mexico City on the tenth of October in the aforementioned year of 1803, and there they lodged him amidst all comfort and cleanliness in the old mansion bearing the number 3 on San Agustín Street. There he was maintained with great pleasure and very well treated. Not only did they entertain him with magnificent meals in the houses of rich gentlemen, but even the Viceroy Don José de Iturrigaray himself offered Humboldt the seat of honor at his table. He went with him to visit the important and interminable drainage works in Huehuetoca that were to prevent forevermore the inundations that the city frequently endured. Every day they sent to the feted baron dishes with rich and succulent Mexican stews, their flavors marvelous, or laden with magnificent varieties of sweets, or with the fragrant fruits of those climates, redolent of glory.

On one particular evening he paid his respects to Doña María Ignacia Osorio y Bello Pereyra, and from the podium, after lecture upon lecture—on the journeys of the wandering baron around the world, the surprising beauties of this realm of the sun, by which the city astonished through the beneficent mildness of its climate, on its surroundings with attractive pastoral and mountainous landscapes, all Mexico being a place of admirable palaces—he concluded with a certain place of interest nearby where they told him there was a thick cactus patch within which the purple cochineal developed.

From the far end of the room emerged the limpid cadence of a voice, which arrived upon listeners' ears in successive and delicious waves, saying: "Sir, we will be able to convey you in the coach from the house to the place you desire so that you may become acquainted with that miniscule animal, who cleans its body by completely converting itself into a flammable substance."

As if through cajoling and refined music, Humboldt was astonished by this unexpected find. The baron was beside himself with admiration. He inquired about the identity of the speaker with so agreeable an accent, whose delicious harmonics caressed the ears. Señora de Osorio answered him with the affectionate smile of a contented mother that this was her daughter, María Ignacia. And if Humboldt admired the charm of the voice, the beauty of the woman suddenly standing before him mesmerized him even more. It was as if a lightning bolt had dazzled his eyes. Several days passed before he was able to compose himself, so blinded was he by the abrupt illumination.

From that very afternoon, Baron von Humboldt and the most gentle Doña María Ignacia Rodríguez de Velasco remained good friends. Learned aridity socialized intimately with this gracious passion, one which warmed even the incorporeal coldness of an algebraic equation. Constant sparks of vivacity and mischief fastened Humboldt to that acute wit. The Fair One was then twenty-five years old.

Friedrich Heinrich Alexander, Baron von Humboldt, was fairly caustic and dry, like the class of studies to which he had dedicated his life with eager determination: studying rare plants, immersing himself in strange minerals and rocks, determining coordinates and parallels, making astronomical and thermobaric observations, taking the geographic coordinates of the places he visited, longitude and latitude, and other such things besides. He cast off his German severity to travel the terrestrial and aquatic globe, enjoying other sights, other lands, and discovering novelties. He was an attentive observer of the world. He was very full of natural sciences and desiccated mathematics, and, for that reason, the torpid idiom of carnal delights was foreign to his ears. Matters of the flesh were tedious to him.

But the rather devilish and fair Rodríguez had magnificent, superlative resources with which to calmly waylay a man from his set path and to lull the most perceptive. And whatever caused him to change direction was appealing. Thus it is that when the grave and conceited Don Friedrich Heinrich Alexander consented, he already enjoyed intimate friendship with Doña María Ignacia, a force of nature. She was a siren who sang to him, and he allowed himself to be lost in contentment, without binding himself to any mast like that wise, historical Ulysses.

With astuteness, enchantments, and skills, she began to call upon and entice the serious baron when he least suspected, I repeat, he already walked with the Fair Rodríguez in very elegant distractions of sweet savor. He had no enduring resolve against the graces of that creature of passions. She deployed her most skillful resources against any who denied her love. Two out of three times she left her object submissive and beyond hope. She laid sophisticated traps beneath the feet of him whom she attempted to catch, nor had the man yet been born who could escape her. She possessed ingenuity and facility for seduction; with a single breath she felled the virtuous and within the soul of a child induced calm.

Humboldt, after climbing and descending from the highest hills, moving about winding and elevated slopes, walking laborious paths through uninhabited mountains; along caustic paths of goats and pointy, parasitic mushrooms; after long hikes through hidden, remote terrains, savage and unformed; wandering through deserted places without rails to direct the soul, ever curious and insatiable in the study of rocks, and of the trees, shrubs, and barbed flowers growing among the crags; after performing long, complicated algebraic calculations, taking levels, observing the various altitudes of stars and distant moons; attending the exams of the Royal College of Mining; studying the great books, robust and copious tomes, whose singular perspective instilled respectful awe; rummaging about disorganized archives among selections of huge, dusty, moth-eaten volumes, after this constant hustle and bustle of body and spirit, Humboldt prepared his extensive writings and works, among them *Las tablas geográfico-políticas de México (The Geographic-Political Tables of Mexico)*, out of which later evolved the famous *Political Essay on the Kingdom of New Spain*, "which has been the source of all of the errors and all of the certainties. This book was the inspiration for Mora and Alamán, for Zavala and Dr. Mier. Its pages stimulated Jackson's agents in their freebooting plans. Humboldt's work inspired magnificent portents within the foolish obsessions of Napoleon III."

He wrote the *Geographic-Political Tables* in a Spanish as perfect as the other works he composed in German—his native language—or in French. He was compelled to write a diary, following the Latin precept that many of us take as a rule: *Nulla dies sine linea*, never a day without writing a line.

Although he was a great hiker and great student, flesh and bones did become weary, as well as concentration, and drawing near to the very pleasing Fair One—she of playful grace who always had a thousand kindnesses for him strewn upon a luscious mouth—offered tender and gentle repose from his labors. She was a sensation of fresh wind to his weariness.

After so many rough and uneven paths, sweet rest at the side of Doña María Ignacia pleased Humboldt, because briefly, in the words of our Savior, she cast off his wearisome burdens and even offered him freedom in the delight that bears love along. Whereas before the stiff baron had preoccupied himself with rough stones and flora, with long, cold rows of numbers, algebraic formulae, and complicated astronomical and geometrical calculations, content now occupied him, while an abundant pleasure broke forth from him in the effervescent and sighing verses of the poets from mist-enshrouded German lands. Thus did his soul regale itself day after day and seemed to him as though it had surmounted the sun's very sphere.

The Fair One and the baron walked together and alone all about the city; they were seen strolling intimately arm-in-arm, carrying on animated conversations, or in small, slow boats which they rowed through the broad canal of Orilla, or in the theater box of the Coliseum, very close, often hand-in-hand. Their mutual fascination nearly prevented them from attending to what the persons of the comedy were floridly speaking. He, when he did not have those long meals whereby he was obliged to attend upon inescapable Mexican courtesy, was seated alone at the table in the house of the Fair One, who availed herself of every means to delight, and succeeded much to his liking. She laid before him as gifts magnificent courses seasoned in the local style with long-practiced skill, expressing the taste and wealth of their owner. Oh, one served them well in the French fashion, which Humboldt loved so much, and always with good, aromatic Spanish wines of vintage also pleasing to the learned Teuton.

Another exquisite pleasure was attached to these lavish banquets, that of music. The Fair One played magnificent melodies on the clavichord, very rational ones, the hearing of which placated and eased the most grueling indigestion. She also accompanied herself on the guitar to pretty songs, "with special grace," like Cervantes's Gitanilla, in a very attractive voice, whose tenderness entertained the baron and provided soothing relief from his labors. "She played so as to make the guitar speak and knew how to transform it into a cage of songbirds." When they had no appetite for music, they passed the time delightfully in weaving conversations.

The Fair Rodríguez also very much enjoyed going to Humboldt's house to continue agreeable discussion and so that she might satisfy some of her curiosity and overcome some of her ignorance. The baron showed her his books, his flowers and dried plants, some still exuding the gentle fragrances they possessed in the country, his multicolored collection of butterflies, his sparkling minerals, small animals that appeared exactly as in life, birds of variegated plumage, innumerable shells of red, blue, and green, vivid sunflowers of every shade, all of them collected with incomparable patience during four years of arduous expeditions through South America.

The Fair One listened attentively to the simple, precise explanations that the baron gave, relishing them as if he were telling her sweet nothings, compliments, and sacred words. She never found his lessons tedious nor complicated nor obscure, but rather very clear and transparent. The difficult became easy and lucid in passing through the wise lips of the baron, for he explained things masterfully. He demonstrated throughout the excellence of his knowledge.

Equally well pleasing to Doña María Ignacia were her doctor friend's lessons about his scientific apparatuses. He would offer her detailed explanations particular to each one regarding its function and handling. The lady was as delighted by those peculiar mechanisms as if she had seen beautiful jewels or delicate laces or sensuous fabrics for her wardrobe. And she received from him lucid instruction for every one. There were sextants, standards of every size with their restless bubbles, numerous reflecting circles, theodolites, chronometers, eyeglasses, graphometers, compasses, magnetometers, hygrometers, cyanometers, thermometers and thermometric probes, squares and surveying lines, anemometers, metric standards of crystal and brass to verify the measures of longitude, pantographs, triangles to take and measure angles.

On the ninth day of December in the year 1803, with great solemnity and fanfare, the equestrian statue of King Don Carlos IV was unveiled in the Plaza Mayor, supreme work of Don Manuel Tolsá, "the Valencian Phidias," as he was called in his glory days. The shamelessness of Viceroy Branciforte was such that he had the sycophantic idea to erect the monument to that patient sovereign. Tolsá, on the other hand, was dedicated to the dishonorable task of chiseling and polishing, which lasted fourteen long months after the smelting and left the statue not at all clean and smooth. The work was provisionally placed on a beautiful pedestal, a piece of wood and golden stucco to commemorate the birthday of the queen, Doña María Luisa.

Seven years after its splendorous finish, the statue was about to be inaugurated on the date I have given *ut supra*. A broad, red veil covered the work, which stood in the center of a commodious plot, encompassed by a high stone balustrade containing four lofty iron doors of exquisite craftsmanship, masterpiece of metalworker Luis Rodríguez de Alconedo. The plaza filled from sea to sea, an enormous, turbulent, restless crowd. A pin could not be inserted between any two of the spectators. Windows, balconies, and terraced roofs overflowed with the curious, who immersed themselves in conversation.

There was a multitude of ladies and gentlemen of the noblest houses in Mexico—ostentatiously adorned—in the windows and spacious balconies of the Royal Palace, from which undulated tapestries and velvet pendants. His Excellency, the Viceroy Iturrigaray, stood out upon the principal balcony, along with the Viceregenta, Doña María Inés de Jáuregui, both surrounded by dignitaries of the court, judges, leading ladies and gentlemen of lineage, bejeweled silks, laces, military insignias, perfumes, multicolored plumes, and precious gems expelling a thousand rays of polychromatic light.

Baron von Humboldt found satisfaction there with Doña María Ignacia Rodríguez de Velasco, replete as she was with the lively sparkle of jewels and squandering the favor of her good words. The florid crowd, loud and palpitating, burning with the fever of impatience, enchanted both of them. At a sign from the Viceroy and as if actuated by a precision spring, the red veil that covered the statue ripped in two, which scattered reflections in the midst of the blue morning full of sun. All eyes were focused upon it. The crowd was transfixed in silent amazement. The forced roar of applause abruptly broke forth. A long wave of ovations extended into the distance. From windows, balconies, and rooftops white handkerchiefs agitated in the wind.

The smoky thunder of ten artillery pieces unanimously discharging broke the crystalline-limpid atmosphere. Then an uproar from the dense jungles of the regiments of New Spain, of the Dragoons, and of the Crown. And as finale to this grand noise to the heavens, from the robust city rose the shrill clamor of bugles and the hearty roar of drums and the deafening festive peal of bells, which the city enwrapped expansively in music and returned fully resonant.

The four broad doors of the ellipse were opened and the human wave poured through them like restrained, tumultuous water for which the floodgates had been raised to allow free flow. A tawdry aroma of swollen, admiring commentaries filled the air. All in the wide plaza was chat and babble. A wave of rumors waxing.

Before unveiling the statue, great solemnity prevailed in the Cathedral of the Holy Church, the Archbishop Don Francisco de Lizana y Beaumont officiated the pontifical mass, and the cathedral choir sang a solemn *te deum* to the accompaniment of the vast polyphony of the organ. Not only the clergy, but a multitude of friars of all orders along with the viceroyal family and the most eminent citizens of the city attended that solemn function, filled with an infinite number of candles large and small, the altar decked with silver. All at once this colorful assembly removed to the Palace to place itself in windows and upon balconies, while the ample joy sounded of a peal taking flight, within which there was a trembling blast of brilliant trumpeting. Shortly thereafter that elegant nobility thundered from enthusiastic applause in a commotion of bejeweled hands.

The colorful flatterers formed a path—of color white, embellished with gold and by living flesh incarnadined—so that Their Excellencies the viceroys with their long entourage passed to scrutinize the magnificent monument, work created by a great Spanish artisan from Valencia. The Fair Rodríguez went happily arm-in-arm with Humboldt. The baron lauded the great merit and beauty of the statue. He did not fail to extol it with most amplified praises. He was entirely transformed into applause. He spoke afterwards, enchanting all those who heard him, of the grand equestrian statues that he had seen and admired in his travels throughout the world, none of them superior to this magnificent one of Carlos IV, though there were some of equal valor, such as the mercenary leader Bartolomeo Colleoni in floating Venice, modeled by Andrea Verrocchio; in Padua, that of Erasmo Gattamelata, work of Donatello; that of pious Marcus Aurelius, which stood in the Roman Capitol. The baron also praised the harmonious simplicity of the pedestal that supported the heroic bronze of King Carlos IV, attired—or better phrased, laid bare in the Roman style—and crowned, though not as he ever was in life, with long and pointed ornaments, thanks to the exquisite graces of his spirited wife. Instead, Tolsá had here placed upon him symbolic laurels. There are more laurel leaves on the royal head than an able cook would need to season a great number of beef stews.

But straight away the perspicuity of the Fair Rodríguez detected in the horse a terrible and fundamental defect where no one before had found either flaws or shortcomings. Very much to the contrary, all had judged the steed perfect in every detail and dimension. With uttermost grace she said that they were at the same height which men, horses, and other animals have at different levels. Her personal experience taught her this about gonads, something which the noted Valencian Tolsá did not correct.

At once, to properly complete the festivity, there was great kissing of hands in the Palace, with magnificent refreshment, exquisite libations from cloistered monks. And then banquets, public promenades in full-dress along the Alameda and Bucareli, pyrotechnics, bullfights, lovely comedies in the Coliseum. There was a subtle literary contest which—with the enticement of excellent prizes—loosened the tongue of the pompous and affected canon Don José Mariano Beristáin de Sousa. Many poets competed against him, bards of stingy muse with their unruly verses, heavy as lead. Not even Christ who created language would have understood such gibberish. Seven years before this grandiloquent Señor Beristáin, when Viceroy Branciforte described a model of the statue, he delivered a rather inflated sermon, ostentatiously embellished with the tremendous riches of his hyperbolic literary abilities. It was called the *Sermon of the Little Horse.*

Furthermore, the archbishop made a fine gift of a pound of silver and new clothes to two hundred poor children. The senior judge, Don Cosme de Mier and his wife, Doña María Iraeta, invited Don Manuel Tolsá and his wife, Doña Luisa Sáenz, to go with them by coach to the public procession where they were cheered, and in the evening they offered them a lavish banquet with innumerable courses, each of extraordinary succulence, and with persons of noble bearing to honor them at the side of such a distinguished artisan. The judge presented Tolsá with a great medallion of fifteen gold marks.

This long and colorful series of festivities did not lack—for what was there to lack?—the Fair Rodríguez in the good company of Baron Humboldt. And in the midst of all there was a precious and vital center, one that attracted the onlookers like a magnet whose mysterious and irresistible force none could evade.

Two of one will, Humboldt and Doña Ignacia almost did not separate. They were united in one body and one soul. Both experienced a sovereign sweetness in being together, and they bathed themselves in life's delights, swimming in the waters of their own pleasures. They walked alone following their joys and tastes, but everything passed as a flower, which does not endure. They had finished the chapter and closed the book on their contentment. Baron Friedrich Heinrich Alexander von Humboldt, who was like an epitome of the Renaissance, left Mexico, which was the ideal end to his willing and prolonged vicissitudes with the Fair Rodríguez. They threw their arms around one another and then disentangled themselves from that narrow embrace. The baron retreated with every step while she followed him with her eyes, never losing sight of him while he turned his head several times. This farewell, drawn from the souls, took their hearts as well.

The celebrated Scotswoman Frances (Fanny) Erskine Inglis, who later became the Marquise from Calderón de la Barca, writes that Baron von Humboldt was even more enamored of the talent than of the beauty of the Fair Rodríguez,

> considering her a sort of western Madame de Staël; all which leads me to suspect that the grave traveller was considerably under the influence of her fascinations, and that neither mines nor mountains, geography nor geology, petrified shells nor *alpenkalkstein,* had occupied him to the exclusion of a slight *stratum* of flirtation. It is a comfort to think that "sometimes even the great Humboldt nods."

The Fair Rodríguez was for him a singular, brief, and torrid flash who illuminated his days and also set them ablaze with ineffable delight. Elevated from the humanity of science to the divinity of love.

Chapter 70

ALEJO CARPENTIER
The Lost Steps
1953

Seventy years earlier, in a scientific report, a noted geographer had claimed to have caught a glimpse, in the vicinity of the Great Plateaux, of something resembling the fantastic city Urre had gazed upon one day. The Amazon women really existed: they were the women of the men slaughtered by the Caribs on their mysterious migration to the Kingdom of Corn. Out of the jungle of the Mayas there had emerged stairways, boat landings, monuments, temples decorated with unbelievable paintings representing the rites of the fish-priests, the shrimp-priests.

Huge heads suddenly came to light under fallen trees, looking at their discoverers with closed eyes more terrifying, because of their inner contemplation of Death, than if the pupils had been visible. In other places there were long facing Avenues of the Gods, side by side, whose names would remain for ever unknown, overthrown gods, dead gods, who for centuries and centuries had been the images of an immortality denied to man. On the shores of the Pacific gigantic designs had been discovered, so huge that people had walked over them without being aware of what they were treading upon, drawn on such a scale as though intended to be visible from another planet by peoples who had kept their records with knotted strings, and had punished with the maximum penalty any attempt to invent an alphabet. Every day new carvings turned up in the jungle; paintings of the feathered serpent were to be found on remote rock walls, and nobody had yet deciphered the thousands of petroglyphs that spoke a language of animal forms, astral symbols and mysterious designs along the banks of the Great Rivers.

Yesterday I had amused myself with the thought that we were conquistadors searching for Manoa. It suddenly came to me that there was no difference between this Mass and those Masses which the seekers for El Dorado had listened to in similar wildernesses. Time had been turned back four hundred years.

～

I now saw the breath-taking possibility of traveling in time, as others travel in space. ... *Ite misa est, Benedicamos Domino, Deo Gratias.* The Mass was ended, and with it the Middle Ages.

But dates were still losing figures. In headlong flight the years emptied, ran backwards, were erased, restoring calendars, moons, changing centuries numbered in three figures to those of single numbers. The gleam of the Grail has disappeared, the nails have fallen from the Cross, the moneychangers have returned to the temple, the Star of Bethlehem has faded, and it is the year 0, when the Angel of the Annunciation returned to Heaven. Now the dates on the other side of the year 0 are back—dates of two, three, five figures—until we are at the time when man, weary of wandering about the earth, invented agriculture, when he established his first villages alongside the rivers and, needing greater music, passed from the rhythm-stick to the drum, which was a wooden cylinder with burned ornamentation, invented the organ as he blew into a hollow reed, and mourned his dead by making a clay jar roar. We are in the Palæolithic Age.

～

Just as other cultures were branded with the sign of the horse or the bull, the Indian with his bird profile placed his culture under the sign of the bird. The flying god, the bird god, the plumed serpent were the nucleus of his mythologies, and everything beautiful was adorned with feathers. The tiaras of the emperors of Tenochtitlán were made of feathers, as were the decorations of the flutes, the toys, the festive and ritual vestments I had seen here.

Struck by the discovery that I was now living in the Lands of the Bird, I remarked somewhat superficially that it would probably be difficult to find in the cosmogonies of these peoples myths that paralleled ours. Fray Pedro inquired if I had read a book called the *Popol-Vuh*, of which I did not know even the name.

"In that sacred book of the Quichés," the friar told me, "with tragic intuition the myth of the robot is set down. I would even go so far as to say that it is the only cosmogony that has foreseen the threat of the machine and the tragedy of the Sorcerer's Apprentice." And in the language of the scholar, which must have been his before it became petrified in the forest, he told me how, in the first chapter of Creation, the objects and utensils invented by man, which he used with the help of fire, rose against him and killed him. The water jars, the stone griddles, the plates, the cooking-pots, the grinding-stones, the houses themselves, in a horrifying apocalypse, to the accompaniment of the barking of maddened dogs, had turned on him and wiped out the generation of man.

He was still telling me of this when I raised my eyes and found myself at the foot of the grey wall with the rock carvings attributed to the demiurge who, in a tradition that had reached the ears of the primitive inhabitants of the jungle below, triumphed over the Flood and repopulated the world. We were standing on the Mount Ararat of this vast world. This was where the ark had come to rest when the waters began to withdraw and the rat had returned with an ear of corn between its paws. We were where the demiurge threw the stones over his shoulder, like Deucalion, to call into being a new race of men. But neither Deucalion, nor Noah, nor the Chaldean Utnapishtim, nor the Chinese or Egyptian Noahs left their signature scrawled for the ages at the point of their arrival. Whereas here there were huge figures of insects, serpents, creatures of the air, beasts of the water and the land, designs of the moon, sun, and stars which *someone* had cut here with a Cyclopean chisel, employing a method we could not divine. Even today it would be impossible to rig up the gigantic scaffolding that would be needed to raise an army of stonecutters to a height at which they could attack the stone wall with their tools and leave it so clearly inscribed. ...

~

This added another subject for thought to the many already filling my mind. What had happened was that after days of absolute mental sloth, during which I had been the physical man, oblivious of all that was not sensation—sunning myself, taking my pleasure with Rosario, fishing, accustoming my palate to totally new taste sensations—my brain had begun to work at an impatient, headlong pace, as though this rest had been essential. There were days when I would wish to be a naturalist, a geologist, an ethnologist, a botanist, a historian, so that I could understand all this, set it down, explain it so far as possible.

One afternoon I learned with surprise that the Indians here preserved the memory of a confused epic, which Fray Pedro was reconstructing bit by bit. It was the account of a Carib migration moving northward, laying waste everything in its path, and filling its victorious march with prodigious feats. It told of mountains moved by the hand of fabulous heroes, of rivers deflected from their courses, of singular combats in which the planets intervened. The amazing unity of myths was borne out by these accounts, which dealt with the abduction of princesses, stratagems of war, memorable duels, animal allies. On nights when in a religious ceremony the Headman of the Indians intoxicated himself with a powder inhaled through a bird's bone, he became a bard, and from his lips came fragments of the epic poem, the saga, which the missionary took down. The poem lived in the memory of the generations of the jungle.

Chapter 71

Ezra Pound

The Cantos, Canto LXXXIX

1956

And in the time of Mr Randolph, Mr Benton, Mr Van Buren
     he, Andy Jackson
         POPULUM AEDIFICAVIT
which might end this canto, and rhyme with
         Sigismundo.
Commander Rogers observed that the sea was sprinkled with
     fragments of West India fruit
and followed that vestige.
     Giles talked and listened,
more listened, and did not read.
     Young Jessie did not forward dispatches
so Frémont proceeded toward the North West and
     we ultimately embraced Californy
The Collingwood manned 80 guns.
     "Those who wish to talk
May leave now" said Rossini,
     "Madame Bileau is going to play."
"Trade,
     trade,
        trade!"
     Sang Lanier.

Van Buren already in '37 unsmearing Talleyrand.
And the elderly Aida, then a girl of 16, in the '90s,
      visiting some very stiff friends in New England
giggled (and thereby provoked sour expressions)
      when some children crossed the front lawn with
a bottle of water strung on a string between them
      and chanting:
          "Martin
Van Buren, a bottle of urine".
          Sagetrieb, or the
oral tradition.
"Ten men", said Ubaldo, "who will charge a nest of machine guns
      for one who will put his name on chit."
"No dog, no goat."
        said Pumpelly.
     Said Bonaparte: Imagination.
220 riflemen and one piece of artillery
"To environ us" said Mr Dix.
      "The irish are devout, moral, industrious"
he even said: sober.
      Kit Carson sea-sick.
        Ciudad de los Angeles.
          That g sounded as h.
3 days with no food but rosebuds,
Che tolgo lo stato.
      Don Jesus broke his parole.
      Guadalupe ('48) Hidalgo
Out of von Humboldt: Agassiz, Del Mar and Frobenius
      The wrong way about it: despair.
      (I think that is in Benton)
Randolph of Roanoke: Charlotte Court House, '32,
Henry's passion: fiddling, dancing and pleasantry
      (Patrick Henry)
"We ought not to have turned you out."
     said some old crump to Van Buren
"Great blackguard from Tennessee, by name of Jackson."
"No auction of slaves here in the Capital."

Chapter 72

THEO PIANA AND HORST SCHÖNFELDER
Alexander von Humboldt
1959

Translation by Joshua Clemente Bonilla, from Theo Piana and Horst Schönfelder, *Alexander von Humboldt. Ein deutscher Weltreisender und Naturforscher* (Berlin [GDR]: Altberliner Verlag Lucie Groszer, 1959). Every effort has been made to trace the copyright holder and to obtain permission for the use and translation of this excerpt.

The great hall of the Berlin Choral Academy can hardly contain all who wish to hear Humboldt's speeches. In countless lectures he presents his findings, introducing an astonished audience to a seemingly unreal world. And yet, every word is grounded in the results of meticulous research. Humboldt calls to his listeners: "With knowledge comes thinking, and thinking imparts to the people earnestness and power."

However it pleases Humboldt when he is able to escape Berlin—a city which strikes him as an "unpopulated desert." During a journey of the court to Bohemia, Humboldt is again mistaken for a road worker, just as during earlier days on Lake Lucerne. The wife of the king has her servant slip a thaler into his bag while he inspects stones beside the way.

Some weeks later Humboldt, with a condescending smile, returns the thaler to the horrified Princess, who had not recognized him earlier on account of his simple clothing. The occasion is well chosen: Humboldt is leading an International Congress of Natural Sciences in the Berlin Theater—the most prestigious event of the year, with the entire court in attendance.

But once again the musty air of the Prussian capital drives the sixty-year old to far regions. For quite some time he has entertained the idea of an expedition to Asia. Now the time has come: an invitation from Russia has arrived. The horses, which will carry his entourage and equipment, already paw impatiently in front of his house.

The perilous crossing of the Daugava foreshadows the coming difficulties. During a heavy snowstorm, the ferry, transporting the two road coaches across the river, has to force its way through rushing drift ice.

To the German travelers Kazan seems like a fairy tale from the Thousand and One Nights. The inhabitants are strangely dressed. The architecture is curious as well, that of the Islamic Mosques is most striking.

They reach Petersburg by the end of April, 1829. Humboldt, overjoyed to have escaped the confines of Berlin, feels young again, as during his expedition in the Americas. In simple clothing, he visits the marketplace in order to eavesdrop on the foreign traders and to study their customs.

In the rushing gallop of a troika, according to the custom of the land, the group of travelers press forward to the east, outfitted by the government with fast teams. Leaving from picturesque Nizhny-Novgorod, they travel a comfortable stretch on a Volga steamer.

But he also discovers other things which sorely offend his liberal sensibilities. First of all, there are the police spies of the Tsar, who monitor his every step. Humboldt hates nothing more than the malicious system of informers, which cannot be reconciled with his understanding of democracy and human dignity.

Where personal freedoms are so abused as in tsarist Russia, there is no shortage of political prisoners. In long chain gangs, the wretched prisoners, shackled to one another like dangerous felons, are marched to Siberia by heartless guards. Thus Humboldt slowly becomes aware that he is not traveling as a free researcher, but is constantly under surveillance.

Soon he notices that in addition to the poor, those who foster progressive convictions are also oppressed. On the other hand, the estate owners in Ural live an extravagant life built on exploitation. They surround themselves with unimaginable splendor and wild revelry, while their subjects suffer from hunger.

Humboldt exchanges gifts and stimulating discussions with the sentry on the Russian-Chinese border near Naryn. He receives two precious, hand-written books from ancient China as a gift. In return, the polite border guard requests Humboldt's pencil. Such a writing tool is still completely unknown in China.

In the end, Humboldt is rewarded for the unusual difficulties of his hurried Asian expedition. "It is a highlight of my life to have seen with my own eyes the largest inland body of water in the world and to have collected its products." This is his enthusiastic pronouncement to a large crowd of people gathered in Astrakhan to bid Humboldt farewell after several weeks studying the Caspian Sea.

A festive reception at the Petersburg Academy of Sciences. People marvel at the man like a world-wonder, who in spite of his sixty years has covered a distance of over 15,000 Kilometers in barely six months. That he crossed rivers fifty-three times and needed to change 12,244 horses at 658 post stations bears witness to the speed and breadth of this truly Humboldtian research expedition. Once again it has brought him an exceptional yield of scientific knowledge.

Humboldt the "Jacobin" (as his detractors call him on account of his sympathies for the French Revolution) finds his departure from Tsar Nicholas I much less pleasing. Although the Tsar had financed the expedition, Humboldt cannot forgive him for the excessively brutal suppression of the Decembrist Revolt and for fashioning Russia into an unparalleled police state.

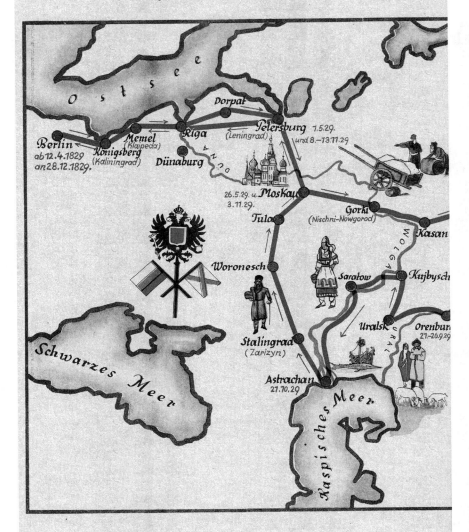

In 1831, just two years after beginning his Asia
Expedition, his book on the Urals and Siberia
appeared in Paris as the first fruits of his journey
through Central Asia. As did his travel writings from

America, Humboldt's account stirred excitement everywhere. The geologic formations and weather patterns of this little-explored area appear in a new light.

O B

B O

Bogoslawsk
6.7.29.

Nischni-Turinsk
7.7.29.

Perm

Newiansk
24.7.29. *Tobolsk*

Tomsk

Swerdlowsk
(Jekaterinburg)

Tara 27.7.29.

Slatoust

Miask
Humboldts 60. Geb.
14.9.29.

Omsk

Kainsk

Kolywan-See

Kolywan

Barnaul
1.8.29.

I R T Y S C H

Semipalatinsk

Ust-Kamenogorsk

Bachty
19.8.29.

Aral-See

Balkasch-See

I R T Y S C H

Chapter 73

REINALDO ARENAS

Hallucinations

1966

From the friar's diary

Have just come home from *salon* of Madame de Récamier. Nothing of import. La Récamier moved constantly among her guests, offering light jests and sallies of wit which provoked no great mirth though everyone laughed greatly at them. Then came Benjamin Constant (a man of weak frame and bitter character, with whom I have spoken on various occasions and from whom have had very little satisfaction), and the two went off toward the upstairs chambers. After an hour they reappeared hand in hand and Récamier smiling like a well-satisfied mare. ... The later the evening grew, the more bored I. On leaving, met a young man from Guanajuato—Lucas Alamán, who woke me from that *lethargie saloniste* when he spoke so feelingly of *his land,* which is mine also, and his great passion, which is likewise mine.

Paris, 1 August. ...
Have made a friend of young Alamán, who invited me to go and visit the famous *salon* of Fanny. There met another haughty young man, very proud, rebellious, and fiery—named Simón Bolívar (Fanny's lover, as he is of almost all the noble ladies who frequent these *salons*). Told me he'd been a student of Simón Rodríguez, which of course sufficed me to call him a friend as well. Spoke to me of Robinson, and told me that Robinson was currently in Vienna, though but for a few days. Knew not which way the restless Master would go next. ... Another personage who impressed me greatly was Madame de Staël

Reinaldo Arenas, *Hallucinations or, the Ill-Fated Peregrinations of Fray Servando,* trans. Andrew Hurley [1987] (New York: Penguin, 2002), 132–136, "Chapter XX", copyright © 1987 by Andrew Hurley. Original copyright © 1968 by Editions du Seuil. Used by permission of Penguin, a division of Penguin Group (USA) Inc.

(née Necker). Most attractive and above all stands out from other women (so mannered and haughty) by her small interest in standing out. Asked Alamán to present me to the lady, but at that moment Alexander von Humboldt entered the room. All call him *the Baron*. Humboldt was the *pièce de résistance* of the *salon*. He spoke in a most clear and fluent French about everything, and with great discernment and knowledge moreover, though without any show. He knows the New World better than most men born and bred there, and his political ideas are of the most *avant garde*. Many people shivered when he said, "Spanish America is ripe for its freedom, though still it lacks a great man to set it on the move." And young Bolívar, who at every moment had to be pushing Fanny away, for she tired him with her constant *kissy-wissy*, listened most attentively to him, seeming most exalted and inspired. At last, seeing that Fanny would no way let him pay any attention to the Baron's stirring words, he boxed her ears with a slap that sounded all across the room. So then Madame de Staël laughed, most contagiously in fact. And the Baron talked some more.

Paris, 16 August. …

Young Alamán introduced me to the other *formidable* young man, Humboldt. We talked all afternoon here in the chapel and then at dusk we walked out for a run in the Baron's coach. Return to America! It is as though I were there, speaking in the most natural way with the people in the street, my very own street. You can *touch* things. When the Baron forgets a detail, I recall it instantly. … We talked about the rivers, which he knows by rote, and even about the most insignificant creeks and *arroyos*. … And of the City of Mexico he has forgotten not one jot, not the name of a single street. He now has found out all the privations and hardships I have suffered. We leave the coach and walk through the streets, and at every moment a new detail springs to our minds. To talk over. To fill us again with that passion. And then we walk some more. It is rather cold, though hardly yet winter. The Baron invites me to his castle. … It is surrounded by thousands of plants brought from every part of the Americas. Crossing the garden we can hear the shrieks, cackles, caws, calls, whistles, and peeps of New World birds I had never hoped to hear again. … And now on one of the castle's many terraces, the Baron shows me his essay on New Spain, on which he is now at work. I give him what information I can. I fill him with new ideas and descriptions. I am carried away by my emotions. … In the early morning we take our leave of one another, though with the promise to meet soon again.

Paris, 30 September. …

At last have met Madame de Staël. Just as I thought, she is a *femme formidable*. … "You come from a place which very soon will begin to exist," she said to me when I was introduced. And then we commenced just as we are, with no show of thoughtful reticence or haughtiness of grandeur. ... Told her I detested Frenchwomen, who were all bigmouthed and rather terrible, made to the cut of a great frog. She responded that she loved American men, who all were so full of fire, a fire which had gone out long since in Europeans. Told her I could not understand why her house was always filled with such complaining contemptible people.

"What makes man most sociable is his weakness," she answered, quoting Rousseau, that new Bible. "And I am weak," she added in a tone mixing coquetry and confession.

"The truly happy being is solitary," I riposted, still quoting.

"Oh, only the good man remains alone," she added, and there we ended our catechism in Rousseau.

We passed into another hall and there sat down. She then took out a fine cigarette case on which was engraved the figure of Louis XVI, his body on the case and his head on the top, so that they were cut in two when the case was opened.

"It suits him, does it not?" She smiled at me. "It is to remind everyone who sees it that here once a king's head was cut off and that," and here she raised her voice a bit, as though in a fit of passion, "it could happen again at any moment."

"Are you doing something to bring us to that pass, madame?"

"At this moment," she said, as though it were the most natural thing in the world to be talking of, "I am investing all my capital in gunpowder ... to see whether we cannot blow this empire up, and blow up that pack of Bourbon rogues who are about to ascend to it."

"The unmentionable family," I added, quoting Constant this time.

"That whore," she said, referring to Constant—which led me to believe they had been lovers once.

From the first *salon* there came to us the music from the orchestra, but pretty far off, so it was not terribly hard to bear. Staël smoked awhile, and then she lay back upon the couch and did not speak. We were in perfect understanding.

"We have missed our great chance. Perhaps our only chance," she finally sighed. "A revolution is not accomplished in ten years, or in a century. It is a long accumulation of eras, of men. And we have now reached the end, and we are besmirching and besmearing it, bedaubing it with our own dirt, changing it, deforming it, and by doing so giving Humanity itself a slap in the face. Such disrespect for Man!" ... But then she said to me, "And yet, Servando ... what if we had respected those positions? what if everything had turned out as it ought to have done? would we, do you think, have achieved happiness? ... I put myself in that position, and I ask myself, 'Could you live without these *soirées*? without these unbearable people? without these walls to have them all in? without a sense of self-importance in the midst of all this pettiness and meanness, this contemptible and despicable social-climbing?' And above all, and this is what worries me most, Servando, would those others, those who hate and want to destroy us, would they be any less mean and petty and contemptible than we are? ..."

She slowly stirred, and lay the ashes of her cigarette to rest in an urn standing by on long silver legs, and then sat back again. She wept for a moment, making hardly a sound. When her tears were spent she took out a very fine linen napkin which she carried hidden about her in a spot I cannot remember, and patted her cheeks.

"There. Let us walk," she said finally, now once more cheerful and animated. "I have not shown you my apartment."

In Madame de Staël's apartments. She presented me with a red flag on which is written the words of the "Marseillaise." She showed me her edition of the collected works of Voltaire bound in gold. She reclined on her bed, wrinkling its silks and laces, which crackled painfully, and said to me, "Prove to me that my opinion of the American man is true." And called me a reactionary royalist when I explained to her that my religious vows forbade my performing certain acts which any other man would perform most gladly. She got up. Gave me her hand with very great courtesy and said, "It is of no import. It was only a gesture of hospitality which I extend to almost all my guests." And with her on my arm we went back to the first floor.

Constant and la Récamier were dancing without moving. Fanny and her "fiery" American disappeared behind a post. On the other side of the room, Humboldt and Alamán were very peacefully talking, the both seated in great armchairs turned toward the dining room. Most of the women were outdoing each other in flirtations and coquetries. Madame de Staël made a polite curtsy before l'Abbaye Grégoire, who took her by the hands and lifted her up and guided her into the crowd.

Paris, 21 November. ...

All day in the chapel. A while ago the Spanish Ambassador's private secretary arrived and tried to turn me to atheism with his arguments taken from a dreadfully bad book, just published. After I had reduced his arguments to powder, he begged five gold coins of me and left.

Not a soul in the chapel all day (save that hateful secretary). (Who on second thought probably lacks one.)

Paris, 11 December. ...

The Baron von Humboldt has departed for the New World. He came to bid me goodbye. We spoke very little, though at the end I said to him, "If you stay long there, surely we will see each other." "I have no doubt," he replied. And the moment was relieved with laughter. ... When I think of my America, it is of a place too beloved and too fervently desired to be real. Sometimes I ask myself whether it truly exists.

Chapter 74

ERNST JÜNGER

Seventy Drifted Away

1966

On board, 22 October 1966

Noon the next day the Canary Islands came into view. We had earlier encountered the *Impero,* a troop transport ship returning home from Africa. Exactly thirty years ago I traveled between Las Palmas and Tenerife, this time between Tenerife and Gran Canaria. In some spots the dull color of the Atlantic takes on a faint violet hue, reminding one of the Aegean.

Pico de Teide seemed at first asymmetric, then, however, as the adjoining crater was covered by the silhouette, in pure conical form. As in 1936, again this time a band of clouds divided it. Although we quickly receded from it, until nightfall the mountain raised itself above the background of the sky. The Teide affected one even more forcefully, lifting itself directly from the sea; the vision must have acted upon the first discoverer as a dream. It is reckoned among the wonders of the world, and once again I regretted my patchy knowledge of geography. I can't even say if anyone had seen the volcano active. By all means, the first thing I read after returning should be Humboldt's classical descriptions.

*

Two days later the first flying fish. Not a trace of the excitement I felt upon my earliest encounter with this phantasmagoric being. Still, I hope that's the result of familiarity rather than of indifference. Back then it was an initiation. Of course, I thought at sixteen that one had to travel before reaching twenty, otherwise the enchantment would be lost. Today, it rather seems to me that enjoyment grows with experience. These are old matters for dispute.

*

Translation by Richard John Ascárate, from Ernst Jünger, *Siebzig verweht,* vol. 1, *Siebzig verweht I* (Stuttgart: Klett-Cotta, 1980), 308–310. Copyright © 1982 by Ernst Klett, Stuttgart.

Completely new to me was the island of São Tomé, which is cut through by the equator. The night before we lay in the port; come morning I saw the tropical coast with a harbor fort, before which a double island, shaped like a bosom that dipped into the ocean surface. In the background modern barracks, then woods and, far to the left, emerging from the steamy verdure, pointed cylinders like sugar cones or steer horns. Frigate birds with fork-shaped tail feathers circled the ship.

We could walk about on land for a few hours in the morning. Revisiting the tropics has an archaic attraction, not in the sense of human history but rather in the history of the earth: half melancholy, half dreaming, as if one's homeland had once looked so. Vegetative pleasure is great wherever the cacao tree grows best. The banana leaf, strong and yet still almost yellow, must burst forth overnight. Musa paradisiaca. The hibiscus, larger than I had ever seen it; the red leaves unfold themselves into bowls. Same goes for the giant palm, bamboo, Indian lilies. Banana trees pull themselves up one atop another from the seething earth on the slopes. In front of the villas both of their relatives: the parrot-headed Strelitzia and, with its giant fan, the traveler's palm. Jehovah must have been in the best of moods with this "Let there be!"

In the front garden a tall mountain lily, which will probably be a favorite because of its stunning fragrance, further on a wealth of Malvaceae; the climate appears to be especially hospitable to the species. By the way, it recently occurred to me that although I have observed both in the garden at Wilflingen, the hibiscus must belong to the Malvaceae—because of the unusual sexual development alone: the female organ affixes itself to the masculine as outgrowth.

"Great is Diana of the Ephesians!" These words came to mind, not only upon seeing powerful hibiscus blooms with their sophisticated construction for cross-pollination, but upon seeing papaya trees as well, around whose stems drape heavy fruits like yellow flounces upon breasts.

For a moment over the lily stood, like a kite on a string, a yellow butterfly. A thought: Were I to take a flash photo now, the image would remind me of that moment; if I were to close my eyelids, I would grasp its content.

Chapter 75

PABLO NERUDA

Corollary Bird

1966

Minus Cothapa

From so much seeing and not seeing
the corollary bird
I learned that yes it knew,
I learned that no it doesn't fly,
I learned that it was on its branch,
perched on its parashade,
watching for the cyclones
that fall upon the Amazon:
its song's rumbling echo
is distributed equally
between the black Orinoco
and our torrential Acario.

Its song falls over the buzzing
of recalcitrant flies
the size of eggplants,
falls over the green vapor
that rises from the river,
over the explorers
who jot down the time,
the corollary bird's name,
the circumstances of its song.

And tumbling down the ravine
its raucous syllables grow louder,
until the bird burns out
so that Brazil can sleep.

Chapter 76

ERICH FRIED

The Guacharo

1969

The word means, "He mourns and cries"
The Indians in Venezuela
feared this cave-dwelling bird:
"Our dead are calling us
We will never return
from this cavern
If we follow the call
we must die"

The missionaries
called the cries of spirits
heathen superstition
and brought light into the cavern
There they found the Guacharo
It lives in darkness
and avoids the cave walls
by the echo of its cry

Its offspring are plump and round
The Indians, become fearless,
fill sacks with them
and boil the fat from their bodies
to cook with and
as oil for cave lanterns

Translation by Richard John Ascárate, from Erich Fried, "Der Guacharo," in *Die Beine der größeren Lügen. Einundfünfzig Gedichte* (Berlin: Klaus Wagenbach, 1969), 26. Copyright © 1969 Verlag Klaus Wagenback, Berlin.

so they may find more
Guacharo offspring to cook

Alexander von Humboldt
called the cave dweller
Oil bird
because its offspring nourish oil lamps
thanks to the glow of enlightenment
which the priests brought
into the darkness of the Guacharo
It is now dying out

Chapter 77

Ernst Jünger

Seventy Drifted Away

1970

Las Palmas, 7 June 1970
Reading: Adolf Meyer-Abich: *Alexander von Humboldt,* a biography. From there the following excerpts:

"Humboldt received as methodical principle from Goethe's *Morphology* the idea of a dynamic type to describe figures in their historically formed entirety. For example, such a dynamic primordial figure was Goethe's primordial plant, as a model which formed the basis not only for all existing plants as a common pattern, but according to whose plan of construction one could at will devise still more plants … "

"… which, even if they do not exist, nevertheless could exist and are not merely some artistic or poetic shadows or patterns but possess an inner truth and necessity. The same law will be applied to all other living things" (Letter of Goethe to Madame von Stein, 8 June 1787).

Wasn't aware of the passage until today; however, could have been active subliminally at the time I began to outline the figure of the Worker.

Translation by Richard John Ascárate, from Ernst Jünger, *Siebzig verweht,* vol. 1, *Siebzig verweht I* (Stuttgart: Klett-Cotta, 1980), 584–585. Copyright © 1982 by Ernst Klett, Stuttgart.

Chapter 78

TANKRED DORST

On the Chimborazo

1974

IRENE *remains standing, bends over:* Ooops—my shoe! *The others move on.*

DOROTHEA It's all overgrown here. You can't see anything at all! It's all over-grown here.

HEINRICH We're not all the way up yet.

DOROTHEA Of course we're up top!—If I'd have known that you couldn't see anything, I wouldn't have come.

HEINRICH No, we're not all the way up yet.

DOROTHEA For years I've wanted to get onto this mountain, and now I finally have both of my sons with me—they do indeed both have obligations and responsibilities in their positions, so different from the way it is for us old people!

DOROTHEA As I arrived down below in our new house and unpacked my books, your father started laughing. It was an entire series of books, we both had them, and my favorite book was *Walden,* and he had it too.

KLARA What was the book called?

DOROTHEA You don't know it. *Walden* by Thoreau.

HEINRICH *corrects her pronunciation, saying with an American accent:* Thoreau.

DOROTHEA *attempts to copy him:* Thoreau. We always said Thoreau—*said as a French name.*

Translation by Steven Sidore, from Tandred Dorst, *Auf dem Chimborazo. Eine Komödie* (Frankfurt: Suhrkamp, 1975), 9, 23, 26–27, 36–37, 49, 50, 55–56, 57, 60, 64. Copyright © 1975 Suhrkamp Verlag Frankfurt am Main.

HEINRICH *says it in English:* Thoreau.

DOROTHEA We also learned mötsch *(attempt at "much")* and bötter *(attempt at "better")*. But things were just different back then.

TILMAN It's true, we did have two copies of *Walden*.

HEINRICH *says it in English:* Thoreau.

DOROTHEA Your father marked many passages, and left comments on them as well, and he read to me from it, often and often, and I read aloud to him. Even later, when he was already on his deathbed. I had to sit at his bedside for days and read aloud to him.

KLARA I'm sorry that I don't know the book.

DOROTHEA That's how we wanted to live. Like in "Walden." We planned on it.

HEINRICH A man who goes into the wilderness and lives alone in the woods.

~

DOROTHEA There's something black in there, Klara! Little black dots, what are they then?

KLARA I'm eating my apple sauce.

DOROTHEA But there are—black things everywhere in there! Everywhere! Take a look, Heinrich!—Did *you* cook this?

Klara nods and continues eating.

DOROTHEA Give me the spoon!

Klara sticks the spoon in her mouth.

DOROTHEA *takes the jar away from here and looks at it closely:* Here, loads of little brown dots, here, everywhere!

Silence.

I have to put on my glasses.

HEINRICH Just leave the apple sauce alone.

KLARA If you'd like to have a try, Heinrich.

She pushes the jar over to Heinrich.

HEINRICH *takes the salami wrapper as a spoon and tries:* Tastes good, Klara.

DOROTHEA *now has her glasses on and takes the jar again, examining:* Lots of little brown dots! What are they?

TILMAN *leans in, excited:* Really! They're ants!

DOROTHEA Ants? How disgusting! Loads of dead ants!

TILMAN Yes, they really are ants! *He takes a pencil from his jacket pocket and fishes in the apple sauce.* Yes, how did these ants get into the apple sauce?

DOROTHEA Ten thousand ants! How disgusting!
TILMAN *laughs:* And so now Heinrich has just eaten a bunch of ants! *Shaking with laughter.* That is just weird, now the ants are crawling around inside you! *Laughs.*

～

DOROTHEA When I think of the poor people sitting over there in the East. They can see our beautiful mountain and it is unreachable for them.
TILMAN Chimborazo! *To Heinrich:* Do you still remember how as a child you were always saying "the Chimborazo." You read about it in a book of adventure stories.
HEINRICH Perhaps they don't all want to come over.

～

DOROTHEA *to Heinrich:* We've all come over!
KLARA *to Heinrich:* Of course, I am old, but for the young people in particular it's understandable.
DOROTHEA *to Heinrich:* The people want to be free! When I crossed over here to the West, I cried.
TILMAN *to Heinrich:* I will not keep letting things be constantly dictated to me. I want to make my own decisions.
HEINRICH You? About what?

～

DOROTHEA I want to participate too! You all are still in the prime of life, you are active! What are you doing?
HEINRICH Nothing!
DOROTHEA What do you mean, nothing?
HEINRICH Not a thing! Nothing!
DOROTHEA But that's no answer.
TILMAN *wants to stay out of it, he busies himself intensely with gathering branches for the fire. Finds a piece of newspaper:* If the newspaper isn't moist, we can burn it. *Lifts it up and tests it.* Dry.
DOROTHEA You can't just say: nothing, you are doing something at the university library.
HEINRICH Yes. In the cellar.
DOROTHEA What are you doing in the cellar?
HEINRICH I sort. Dissertations.
KLARA Well, that's certainly something very important.
HEINRICH Anyone who knows the alphabet can sort.

～

KLARA It's surely just a coincidence that your office is in the cellar.

DOROTHEA He's just saying that to rile me up! Of course you don't just sit around in the cellar all day long.

HEINRICH I'm upstairs in the afternoon.

DOROTHEA Well, there you go!

HEINRICH Afternoons I shred magazines.

DOROTHEA I'm not going to pay you any mind.

KLARA But Heinrich, why do you shred them? You don't really shred them, do you.

HEINRICH Sure I do. I tear the ads out of each volume, the last page too, and bind together a year's volume of issues.

KLARA *to Dorothea:* Well there you see, it is quite important, the volumes need to be bound together, of course.

HEINRICH It's all very important. I make a little black dot and write: T dash R, and then I make a red dot, and later I erase that all again, and then I write Hist. ped. or Eph. pol. or Art., and then put a cord around it, and then I give it to Mr. Zeth, who has a hole in the top of his skull.

KLARA The poor man has a hole in the top of his skull?

HEINRICH They all have a hole in the top of their skulls. One has a hole in his forehead, another has a piece of silver up on top of his head, and the third is blind.

KLARA But why?

HEINRICH War damaged. They're given work there.

～

HEINRICH What do you do at the Technical Inspection Agency?

DOROTHEA The TIA is a very important institution. They oversee every-thing—they make appraisals, they oversee all technical facilities, large in-dustrial firms, and everything.

HEINRICH What do you do there every day?

TILMAN I work in the information center.

HEINRICH They need a trained engineer for that?

TILMAN Well, it's just half-days you know.

DOROTHEA You need to know all of the specialist terms, of course, it's a highly complicated area, there are so many specialist terms. Technology is making such incredible advances, all over the world, there are always new inventions. You've really been too long in the ivory tower, Heinrich.

HEINRICH Why haven't you tried over the last ten years to work as an engineer?

DOROTHEA Come, he applied to Siemens back then. They absolutely wanted to have him for their research, what with his outstanding exams.

HEINRICH So why aren't you there?

TILMAN It's a very interesting field.

DOROTHEA He would have completely overexerted himself there.

TILMAN There were a lot of expectations there. You're not allowed to have any side interests.

DOROTHEA He has so terribly many interests, in all areas. And he just has no interest in money and formalities. He's a philosopher.

~

HEINRICH I know what the problem is! An incredible unscrupulousness is needed to write anything at all!—

Dorothea sits there stiffly and tears run down her face.

HEINRICH I don't want talent, and I don't need any talent either, and I don't have any talent too!—I'm afraid of words, and the fear's getting bigger and bigger. Each sentence is an assertion. And the next sentence is an assertion too. I go from assertion to assertion, and I get light-headed. "A man named Kupsch opens the door suddenly—" this sentence makes me light-headed!—I'd rather just sit in my cellar and shred magazines with my brain-damaged mates.

Chapter 79

SAUL BELLOW

Humboldt's Gift

1975

Waldemar was now saying, "What a dog's age since anybody visited. I've been forgot. Humboldt would never have stuck me in a dump like this. It was temporary. The chow is awful, and the help is rough. They say, 'Shut up, you're gaga.' They're all from the Caribbean. Everybody else is a kraut. Menasha and me are practically the only Americans. Humboldt once made a joke, 'Two is company, three is a kraut!'"

"But he did put you here," said Renata.

"Just till he could iron out some problems. The whole week before he died he was looking for an apartment for us both. Once we lived together for three months and that was heaven. Up in the morning like a real family, bacon and eggs, and then we'd talk baseball. I made a real fan of him, you know that? Fifty years ago I bought him a first-baseman's mitt. I taught him to field a grounder and throw a guy out. Football, too. I showed him how to toss a forward pass. My mother's railroad apartment had a long, long corridor where we played. When his dad took off it was a houseful of women and it was up to me to make an American boy out of him. Those women did plenty of damage. Look at the names they gave us—Waldemar! The kids called me Walla-Walla. And he had it rough, too. Humboldt! My goofy sister named him after a statue in Central Park."

Chapter 80

HANS MAGNUS ENZENSBERGER
A. v. H. (1769–1859)
1975

Outside, painted in oil and very blue, the faraway peaks, the palms,
the naked savages: inside, in the shade of the leafy hut,
the walls hung with skins and giant ferns, a gaudy macaw
perched on the pack-saddle, the companion in the background held a blossom
under the magnifier, orchids were strewn on the crates of books,
the table was covered with plantains, maps, and instruments:
the artificial horizon, the compass, the microscope, the theodolite,
and shiny brassy, the reflecting sextant with the silvery limbus;
bright in the middle, on his camp-chair, sat the celebrated geognost
in his laboratory, in the jungle, in oil, on the banks of the Orinoco.

The terra incognita melted like snow under his gazes.
He cast his net of curves and coordinates over the last glaciers,
the bleakest mountains. He measured the magnetic variation,
the sun's altitude, the salt content, and the blue of the sky. Incredulous,
the natives watched him. What *wonderful people* they are,
who traverse the world to seek plants and compare their hay
with other hay! Why do you let yourselves be devoured by mosquitoes,
merely to get the lay of land that doesn't even belong to you?
They're foreigners, heretics and fools. But as unwaveringly as the cleric
waves his censer, the voyager wields his Leyden jar.

Born in the blaze of Messier's Comet, he galvanized frogs,
put electrodes on himself and reported *Conjectures on*

Irritated Nervous and Muscular Fibers. Later, he chased after
electric storms on the Amazon and northern lights in Siberia: pirogues
carried him there, sleighs and steamers, hammocks and coaches.
He depicted *entire lands as a mine.* A vulcanist and vulcanologist,
he had a genuine mania for burning craters, which he passionately
climbed, surveyed, and examined. Isolated and anxious,
he recalled the youths he had liked. Most of them were gentle
and penniless. He helped them, however, and held his tongue. The agonizing
     nights
were devoted to writing. *Random Remarks on Basalt.*
On Quinquina Forests. A Memoir on Ocean Currents. On the Native Populations
of America and the Monuments they Left Behind.
Lectures on … Contributions to … Aphorisms from … and Views concerning …
Provisional Note on a Life-saving Bottle. On the Lower Borders
of Perpetual Snow. On the Temperature Occurring on the Ocean Surface
in Various Parts of the Torrid Zone. On Electrical Fish.
This man is a perfect walking academy. He mounted
to the highest layers of air, and, in an iron bell,
with a lunatic Briton named Brunel, he dived to the bottom of the Thames.

I always admired him: now I worship him. For he alone
offers a notion of the feelings aroused in the soul
when arriving in the Tropics. Later, however, after breakfast,
Darwin was *rather disappointed: I found him to be very cheerful,*
but he talked too much. In point of fact, the basis of his greatness
is not quite clear. He slept only three or four hours, he was vain,
enthusiastic, innocuous, *infinitely busy. An excellent dancer,*
from the minuet to the animalito.
Blue tails, gold buttons, the waistcoat
yellow, striped trousers, a white cravat, a black, worn-out hat:
his wardrobe had stopped in the days of the Directoire.

A celebrity back then: *Scarcely has any private gentleman*
ever provoked a greater sensation. Paris in suspense: the New Class still didn't
     trust
its own triumph. Deceptive, a classicistic innocence blossomed
after the Terror, before the bestial bellowing of brokers
filled the *Bourse* with frenzy, boom, crash, and *the open, shameless,*
direct, brutal exploitation raced over the entire globe. … A lucid moment
clean and homogenous. The Bourgeoisie acted exemplary and cool
like the primal meter. Even our noble hero contributed a mite
to determining it and, with his instruments, traveled the meridian

of Dunkirk-Barcelona. (As usual, he paid the expenses out of his own pocket.)

Then the reactionaries won. Back to German wretchedness. A gentleman-
in-waiting, a reader, i.e., flunky at Potsdam's court. He secluded himself in
    Berlin,
a *tiny, intellectually desolate, overly malevolent town.* In this heavily policed
sandy waste, he often thought about the Tropics. Why were they so bewitching?
Why had he endured it all: insects, lianas, downpours,
and *the sullen gazes of the Indians*? It wasn't the tin, the jute,
the rubber, the copper. A healthy man he, an unwitting carrier
of the disease, a selfless harbinger of plundering, a courier
who didn't realize he had come to announce the annihilation
of what he lovingly painted until ninety, in his *Views of Nature.*

Illustration 80.1. *Alexander von Humboldt and Aimé Bonpland in Jungle Hut.* Painting by
Eduard Ender.

Chapter 81

Peter Hacks

A Conversation in the House of Stein about the absent Herr von Goethe

1975

Goethe understood that he could not devise the design of the world according to his vision. It therefore follows that it fell to him to arrange himself, but to my surprise he never considered this for a second. He let the world be the world and remained who he was. He never learned to approve of the Creator. All that he ever learned was to remain silent about creation.

This is how his diverse states of being can be understood as being a single one, and how his famous transformations never took place.

During his loutish years he asserted the right to be uncouth from the fact that he was a poet.

I am not speaking in opposition to the writing profession; I too have received a nice endowment for it. I fully believe that women could easily do it equally well, and certainly less oafishly, if one would but leave them the time to do so. The money, I've seen it myself, flows quite dutifully into the pockets of authors, and if our poor Kochberg [estate] continues producing such small yields, then one day I too will know to compete with Goethe. But I digress. I protest against the underestimation of this proficiency, just as I have perpetually resisted the senselessly high opinion that Goethe held of it as well.

One day I had to inform him that he was held to be presumptuous. "That's what pill bugs would have said about the phoenix," he responded.

That is to say, we were the pill bugs, he the magic bird. He wanted to sing us into the golden age in one fell swoop, and it struck him as deeply inharmonious that we felt quite at ease with the unrefined alloy from which we had originally been poured.

Translation by Steven Sidore, from Peter Hacks, *Ein Gespräch im Hause Stein über den abwesenden Herrn von Goethe. Schauspiel* (München: Drei Masken, 1975), 12–14. Copyright © 2003 Eulenspiegel. Das Neue Berlin Verlagsgesellschaft mbH.

Thus it was just part of the same tune when he gave up writing poetry from one day to the next, postulating the maxim that it no longer applied to the current age and instead turned to one of the newest ways of asserting his mind: politics. Poeticizing was followed by ministerizing. Even if we were not worthy of his verse, so it went, nevertheless he retained some sympathy for us. He closed himself off to us, albeit without hate. He sacrificed himself for us whom he disdained; he was still always ready to save us, we who did not want to be saved.

Everyone now sees that he is long since tired of this other fancy. He tends to his business sluggishly and with a tortured look; how often does one still chance upon him in the halls of the council? Just as one had heard him fulminate against literature as if it were completely worthless, now he mutters against all courts and cabinets and distresses his friends with viewings of predatory protozoa related to polyps, by consulting Humboldt's tables about palm trees, and by smelling an actual elephant's skull. Science has finally united him with truth, without the arduous detour of dealing with the likes of us. He understands people and now loves skeletons.

Chapter 82

VOLKER BRAUN

Guevara, or the Republic of the Sun
1975

Guerilleros and soldiers in positions of death. Through a hole in the ceiling, which looks like a mine entrance, falls the bloody, half-burnt corpse of Guevara. [...]

Bumholdt scratches the ground with a spade. Bedray peers into the distance through field glasses. Both in civilian clothes.

BEDRAY I don't see anything.

BUMHOLDT *pauses, stares at the ground:* It must lie deeper. *Scratches.* The earth has covered it. Swallowed up. Our common fate. *Pauses.* Although one could say, we stand on average a meter to a meter-and-a-half above the level of the Incas. *Grins broadly, becomes serious again, extends a hand:* About this high—*adjusts the height* so high will humanity advance in the next five hundred years.

BEDRAY Hello, haven't you seen anyone?

Bumholdt looks unwillingly at him.

Didn't you see any guerilleros?

BUMHOLDT *takes a film from the camera bag, looks at the pictures:* I haven't seen anyone.

BEDRAY *attempts to climb up a large stone:* You have to be higher up. Help me.

BUMHOLDT *digs:* You can call me Hugo. Hugo Bumholdt.

BEDRAY Denis ... *slips* Bedray. *Holds himself up with his last bit of strength. Very calmly:* Are you going to help me or not?

BUMHOLDT To do what?

Translation by Richard John Ascárate, from Volker Braun, *Guevara oder Der Sonnenstaat*, in *Gesammelte Stücke* (Frankfurt: Suhrkamp, 1989), 1:161–164, 182–184, 202–204. Copyright © 1975 Suhrkamp Frankfurt am Main.

BEDRAY To climb up.

BUMHOLDT *looks at him:* But you're going down.

BEDRAY It just looks that way. Really, though, I'm trying to climb up.

BUMHOLDT I don't understand, Denis.

BEDRAY Place the spade under my foot.

BUMHOLDT Now? *He does so.*

BEDRAY Thanks, Hugo. That did the trick. *Looks through the field glasses.*

BUMHOLDT Somewhere near the sole of your foot the streets will wind, but still the streets of the Incas will remain an unexcelled achievement. The Spanish were rather astounded—*Looks up at Bedray:* What are you doing there?

BEDRAY I'm doing lookout.

BUMHOLDT Into the distance?

BEDRAY Do you know of any other way?

BUMHOLDT Not at the moment.

BEDRAY Look.

BUMHOLDT *irritated:* Look, look.

BEDRAY I don't see anything.

BUMHOLDT I, on the other hand, need my spade.

BEDRAY Please, please. Don't trouble yourself.

BUMHOLDT Thanks.

Takes the spade away. Bedray falls down.

The Spanish were rather astounded when they looked upon the two, solid military roads, along the Andean high plateau and the Pacific coastal strip from north to south—

BEDRAY What is it? Couldn't you let me know before you start something?

BUMHOLDT Yes. Would you be willing to take part in my excavations?

BEDRAY I think not. *Sits motionless:* I've hurt myself.

BUMHOLDT That's just the desire to be away from home. If only you'd stayed in Europe.

BEDRAY But that's still no reason to cast off all humanitarian responsibilities.

BUMHOLDT I'm not interested in living people.

BEDRAY *raises himself to his knees:* That's an interesting perspective. *Beaming:* Do you mind if I contradict it?

BUMHOLDT Go ahead. It doesn't interest me. Take it apart.

BEDRAY *disappointed:* You'll allow that?

BUMHOLDT Go ahead and shit on it, if you like. *Picks up a clump of earth.* Here we have something.

Bedray looks away scornfully. Bumholdt takes a spatula, cleans the clump.

Uniquely-formed lumps of stone, laid in the water pipe, ensured the favorable effect of irrigation of the irrigated—the irrigated—

Wipes sweat off himself. Bedray clambers up the stone.

The type of irrigated terraces indicating the remarkable expansion of arable lands, made possible only by state planning and the collective work of the masses, in that the Incas suppress cannibalism and the oppressed, instead of eating them ... instead of eating them—

BEDRAY *sitting above:* Which we would have done.

BUMHOLDT *examines the "clump":* Wrong said the hedgehog and climbed from the toilet brush. A Coca-Cola bottle.

Drinks the rest, spits. Bedray groans.

What are you groaning about? You haven't drunk anything.

BEDRAY The sun blinds me.

BUMHOLDT The Incas worshipped the sun as a god. They prayed to it.

BEDRAY I don't feel quite right. *Covers his eyes.*

BUMHOLDT It's not important. Can you see me?

BEDRAY I can't see anything.

BUMHOLDT It's not important. *Takes from Bedray's briefcase a variety of provisions. Starts gorging himself.* The Republic of the Sun ... no slaves, no debts, no differences. ... After the Inca ... even on state holidays ... had taken spade in hand ... first, by forced communal labor, the Land of the Sun was cultivated, then ... the fields of the poor and the sick, the widows ... and orphans as well as the army. And then each was allowed ... his own field. ... And then finally the voluntary assignment in the Inca potato fields.

BEDRAY You talk so strangely, Hugo, as though your mouth were full.

BUMHOLDT It's not important. *Goes to Bedray.* I'm still here.

Wipes his hands and mouth on Bedray's pants.

BEDRAY Hand my bag up to me. I'll stay on the lookout.

BUMHOLDT *irritated:* Look well, look well!

BEDRAY I'm waiting for the fighters. An interview will come of it.

BUMHOLDT *sneeringly:* At sunset.

BEDRAY *fishing about in his bag:* My provisions have been stolen.

BUMHOLDT Unbelievable. These black savages.

BEDRAY *shaking with wrath:* Bombs should be dropped.

BUMHOLDT *alarmed:* Now just a minute. Not blindly into the crowd. Allow sublime nature to shame you.

BEDRAY Away with nature. Onwards to humanity.

BUMHOLDT Downwards. Downwards to humanity.

BEDRAY *highly-pitched:* Onwards, Hugo.

BUMHOLDT Downwards, where it's buried. *Digs:* It must be deeper.

BEDRAY *stands on the stone, looks through the field glasses, loses balance, and almost falls off:* I'll see it soon enough.

～

Bumholdt stands in a hole up to his midsection, excavating. Bedray hangs on the face of a very high cliff, ties himself fast.

BEDRAY A beautiful day.

Bumholdt looks up as though tortured, wipes away sweat.

They must be underway.

Bumholdt bends down in the hole, tosses out a thermos bottle and brassiere.

Hey, Hugo, did anyone happen?

BUMHOLDT *stares into the hole, irritated:* Did *something* happen. Denis, we say—*looks up:* What was supposed to happen?

BEDRAY Why happened?

BUMHOLDT You ask if something—

BEDRAY Why what? Who!

BUMHOLDT Why who?

BEDRAY *resigned:* Absolutely nothing is happening.

BUMHOLDT I've stumbled upon gravel.

BEDRAY "A good play requires many shallow parts, impenetrable places, a lot of gravel, and an astounding amount of nonsense. And it must be alive before it can be anything else."—Bertolt Brecht.

BUMHOLDT Gravel signifies something. It suggests burial grounds. *Draws a rifle from the hole, examines it distractedly.* Some bodies were buried in mass graves, others under the resistant gravel bed—

BEDRAY What do you have there in your hand, Hugo?

BUMHOLDT Strange. *Listens at the gun barrel.* I'm not deep enough. *Aims at Bedray.* The dead packed together in a hunched position—

BEDRAY *trembling:* Could you change the subject, Hugo?

BUMHOLDT … hunched and sewn up in mats and tied—

BEDRAY It's me: Denis!

BUMHOLDT Who calls? *Bellows:* Silence!

BEDRAY *with growing fear:* At least no one should get upset without cause. The danger lies in our having to approach and master a virtually revolutionary, but actually critical situation with ideological systems, methods of action and, in certain ways, inherited reflexes from earlier, surmounted phases. "We've made a revolution that's bigger than ourselves," said Fidel one day under different circumstances.

BUMHOLDT *simultaneously:* … sewn fast and tied up in animal hides and mats. These balls were then further wrapped in blankets, thus producing larger mummy-balls, which one affectionately tried to shape like an Indian sitting beneath his poncho. For that reason one often set atop the ball a false head made of pillows.

Laughs broadly, slings the rifle. Bedray lets the field glasses drop.

BEDRAY A false head?

BUMHOLDT Finders keepers. *Slings the field glasses.* Once I'm deeper I'll need them.

BEDRAY Now you're showing your true colors.

BUMHOLDT Look for your savior. For your idol.

BEDRAY I will. You're dead to me, just like your mummies. *Climbs higher, until his head can no longer be seen.*

BUMHOLDT At least they have not been eaten. In this legendary Incan republic only the prominent from newly-won regions were still sacrificed. These highly cultivated—

BEDRAY Hey, my head.

BUMHOLDT And a child or woman was slaughtered only on very special occasions.

Bares his teeth. Bedray's head falls off.

BEDRAY Give me my head.

BUMHOLDT *surprised:* What do you need it for?

BEDRAY I've got my eyes in my head.

BUMHOLDT "I've got eyes in my head." That's just empty talk. Look.

BEDRAY What a dirty trick!

BUMHOLDT Tell me, Denis, what are you speaking with?

BEDRAY *ashamed:* Pardon me. My accent sounds a bit unclear.

BUMHOLDT I mean, out of which hole are you speaking?

BEDRAY *hurt:* Still from my throat, of course.

BUMHOLDT As you wish. I won't write any instructions for you. *Picks up the spatula, cleans the head.* A handsome head. As if from plaster of the Académie Française. You could have been a philosopher, Denis.

BEDRAY I'll punch you in your bourgeois puss. I'll send you back to the Stone Age. *Throws down a lump that crushes the head.*

BUMHOLDT You've broken your own head. *Laughs.* Denis, you've lost your mind.

BEDRAY I give up. You'll never change.

BUMHOLDT I don't see why I should. *Bares his teeth.* I feel fine. *Puts Bedray's head in the camera bag.* Look.

BEDRAY Don't worry about me.

BUMHOLDT *picks up the spade, excavates:* Now, however, to the good stuff.

⌒

Bumholdt, up to the neck in his hole, looks up grumpily. Bedray can still be heard but not seen.

BEDRAY *sings:*
"It was as if Heaven
Had silently kissed the Earth,
Who in the blossoms' glimmer
Needs dream only of him."

BUMHOLDT: Denis, control yourself.

BEDRAY *sneezes, sings:*
"The wind blew through the fields,
Softly waved the grain,
The woods airily rustled,
So crystalline was the night."

BUMHOLDT Since he lost his head, he can only sing. He needs to be taken
to an opera house.

BEDRAY
"And my soul spread
Wide its wings
Flew through the quiet lands
As if flying home."
[Joseph von Eichendorff]
Ha, ha, ha!

BUMHOLDT Eh?

BEDRAY Ha.

BUMHOLDT Poor Denis. That's Eurocentrism for you.

BEDRAY Lalala, lalala.

BUMHOLDT He's gone too far astray. *Strenuously excavating.* Down, down
into the matter, into history, into tradition. Always remaining human. *Un-
slings the rifle, releases the safety, lays it on the edge of the hole.* Denis?

BEDRAY Hurrah, hurrah, hurrah!

BUMHOLDT But he still can't renounce his honest soul. *Looks up through the
field glasses.* He built himself a platform high in a cedar and gazes headless
upon the heights. Better to look down into the depths. *Excavates in the hole
without being seen.*

BEDRAY Okay, okay, okay, okay, okay.

BUMHOLDT *muffled:* I feel *hungry. Digs wildly.* In Mexico 20,000 people
were said to have been sacrificed in one single ceremonial act, and surely
a good portion of them were eaten. The land was overpopulated. Tributes
of food were needed from neighbors and thus the need to conduct wars.
Hence the pretext for not sending the prisoners of war home, which was
stripped of supplies anyway, or putting them to work, in which case they'd
have to be fed, so the conquerors ate them. After all, because of the sorry
state of agriculture, meat was scarce. Human flesh was so highly valued that
the conquistadors anonymously made cannibalism in Mexico into a *casus*

belli. The priests even concocted an ideology for it. *Pauses.* Denis. *Louder:*
Denis. *Hollers:* Denis!
BEDRAY *sings:*
    Arise, arise
    Wretched of the earth.
    The day approaches—
BUMHOLDT: He won't listen. Those who don't listen—
BEDRAY *sings:*
    Day—
    Day—
BUMHOLDT I can't take it anymore. *Grabs the rifle.* Denis, report. Denis,
    you're it. Denis, if you're not it, I can no longer make allowances. *Listens.*
    It's nothing to him. I think way too much. *Wavering:* Hello, Denis? *With*
    determination: That's morbid of me. Well, attention, Denis!

Shoots several times. Bedray squeaks, then his corpse falls down into Bumholdt's
hole.

    There he is. All right.

Sounds of cracking bones. With a full mouth:

    A tender fellow. ... Everything that's proper. He had a beautiful voice. ...
    Ah, Denis. *Eats noisily, throws the bones out of the hole, finally begins to dig*
    again. So, onward.

Chapter 83

Claus Hammel

Humboldt and Bolívar, or The New Continent

1979

Scene One

From the beginning to the end of the piece the scene is theatrical; abundant, spacious, and far from an imitation of nature. If at all something remotely natural, it might remind one of the area around a volcanic crater. [...]

BONPLAND As we set out on our grand voyage—I, a Frenchman, and he, a German—the striking of the pickaxes that demolished the Bastille yet lingered in our hearts.

As this line is spoken, six figures [...] come forth from the crater. Another seven follow them. They transform their pennants into biers. They place the dead upon the biers, as well as the condemned whom they cut from the cross. They throw away the tablet with the name upon it. The last figure shoulders the cross and the biers are lifted. The procession gets underway—walking off slowly in a long row to the left, the cross following. Montúfar, who, exhausted from carrying the heavy trunks, has rested some distance from Humboldt and Bonpland, honors the dead and takes up the tablet.

HUMBOLDT (*above*) We met many inhabitants of Caracas the first time we went to the Venezuelan capital. They argued about the uprising over the liberation of the land that had just occurred. José España ended up on the scaffold; his wife languished in prison for having given refuge to her husband

Translation by Richard John Ascárate, from Claus Hammel, *Humboldt und Bolívar oder Der neue Contintent. Schauspiel* (Berlin [GDR]: Aufbau, 1980), 9, 11–12, 13, 18, 22–24, 39–43, 64–66, 71–72, 77, 78–84, 108–110, 117, 118–121, 122, 131–136. Used by permission of henschel SCHAUSPIEL Theaterverlag Berlin.

rather than turning him in to the government. The stirred-up feelings, the bitterness with which questions were debated, questions which should never cause disagreement among fellow countrymen, struck us immensely.

BONPLAND As we returned home from our grand voyage, the air was filled with the triumphant songs of the bourgeoisie, who trampled upon the graves of the revolutionaries with the stomping of their dances.

Scene Two

The bells of Notre-Dame strike midnight. [...]

Bolívar with two whores—one very young; the other, older.

BOLÍVAR There she is! Take a look at her, the revolution! A hag without shelter! A discarded whore! [...]

ALL (*above*) An anecdote! An anecdote!

HUMBOLDT In Cajamarca, amongst the pathetic architectural remains of old, waning grandeur, live the descendants of Atahualpa. The son of the cacique, a friendly young man of seventeen who accompanied me through the ruins of his homeland and the old palace, charged his imagination with images. ...

BOLÍVAR Who is that?

RODRÍGUEZ Humboldt. He's just come from our country.

HUMBOLDT ... with images of subterranean glory and golden treasures underneath the rubble heaps over which we strolled. He related how one of his ancestors once bound the eyes of his wife and led her down to the underground garden of the Incas. There she saw, artfully rendered in the purest gold, trees full of leaves and fruits, birds sitting on the branches, and the much coveted golden palanquin of Atahualpa. The man commanded his wife not to touch anything of this magical work. The long prophesied time had not yet arrived. Whosoever takes from the treasure before then must die the same night.

BOLÍVAR Stories! Fairy tales!

RODRÍGUEZ He has them from us, Simón. He was there.

HUMBOLDT The boy's morbid confidence made a deep but gloomy impression upon me. Fantasies and illusions serve here as consolation for great deprivation and earthly sufferings.

BOLÍVAR He was there.

HUMBOLDT "Do you feel," I asked the boy, "certain as you are that these gardens exist, a desire amidst your poverty to unearth these treasures so close?" The boy's answer fully expressed quiet resignation, which characterizes the race of natives inhabiting this land: "We don't feel such a craving.

The padre says that would be sinful. If we did have the golden branches and golden fruit the white neighbors would hate us and harm us."
BOLÍVAR I'm becoming a politician.

Scene Five

Humboldt, Bonpland, and the physicist Gay-Lussac before the many assembled members of the French Academy. Isabey the artist is also present, capturing the event in his sketchbook. [...] Offstage, Bolívar and Rodríguez listen.

GAY-LUSSAC Gentlemen! I open the afternoon session of the Academy! Baron Humboldt will continue with his description of earthquakes! Baron, if you please.
HUMBOLDT I thank my honorable friend and colleague, Monsieur Gay-Lussac. Now then: The earthquake of November 4, the first I had ever experienced, made such a strong impression on me because it was accompanied by remarkable meteoric events. It was also a true upheaval from below upwards, not an undulating tremor. I didn't believe then, that after long stays in the highlands of Quito and on the Peruvian coast, I would become so accustomed to rather strong movements of the earth, the way we're used to storms in Europe. In Quito we no longer thought of getting out of bed, when at night subterranean thunder heralded a tremor. The carefree attitude of the natives, who know their city hasn't been destroyed in three hundred years, soon seeps into the fearful stranger. Worry about danger doesn't usually upset one when first exposed to a slight tremor. Rather, it's the characteristic sensation.

From our childhood certain contrasts impress themselves upon our imagination. We regard water as a moving element and the earth as a stationary, inert mass. These concepts are a product of our daily experience and they correspond to all of our sense impressions. But let the ground shake and the earth wobble in foundations that we assumed were immoveable. A long-held illusion thus collapses in a moment. It is as if one were awakening, though hardly in a pleasant manner. One feels that the provisional peace of Nature was only an appearance. Afterwards, one listens carefully to the faintest sound and for the first time mistrusts the floor upon which one has so long and confidently set one's foot. Should the quakes recur, should they befall several days one after another, then this fearful hesitation soon ends. In 1784 the inhabitants of Mexico were as accustomed to hearing thunder beneath their feet as we are to hearing thunder in the air. People quickly regain confidence. Along the Peruvian coasts one finally becomes accustomed to the undulations of the ground, just as the mariner does to the waves that pound his craft. ...

BOLÍVAR No!

Silence. The audience forms a passage with Humboldt at the upstage end, Bolívar at the downstage one.

It's not true that one becomes accustomed to it!

HUMBOLDT I am happy to be set right. Before you present your argument to me, however, I would like to ask you if "becoming accustomed" in our case is not a desirable condition for man? Should he flinch at every expression of Nature and prepare himself for the end of the world? Does not a beneficial resilience obtain and preside there, one that allows man to direct his thoughts toward more important things than the continuous fear of something that he can't escape anyway if it should happen?

Scattered applause.

BOLÍVAR And the habituation to injustice and lawlessness?

HUMBOLDT Has nothing to do with the discussion here.

BOLÍVAR But should you not also have spoken of these after such a journey? Did you not also encounter them as well?

GAY-LUSSAC Usher!

The usher approaches Bolívar and Rodríguez.

RODRÍGUEZ Please, because of his extreme youth, pardon the comments of my student!

Wants to pull Bolívar away.

HUMBOLDT I'm a naturalist and a guest of France. I haven't had the honor of becoming acquainted with either you or your protégé. But I'm sure I do not err in assuming that you enjoy the hospitality of this incomparable city as well.

BOLÍVAR Should that hinder us from indicting facts that turn an entire part of the world into a living hell, one that draws its hope from what transpires here?

GAY-LUSSAC Usher!

HUMBOLDT Whoever rescues himself from life's stormy waves follows me gladly into the thickets of forests, through immeasurable steppes, and onto the high ridges of the Andean chain. To him speaks the world-directing choir: "Freedom stands atop the mountains, where the specter of death / dares not exhale its foul breath; / in the world does perfection reign, / wherever man carries not his pain."

BOLÍVAR "As long as a people is compelled to obey, and obeys, it does well; as soon as it can shake off the yoke, and shakes it off, it does still better; for, regaining its liberty by the same right as took it away, either it is justified in resuming it, or there was no justification for those who took it away."

HUMBOLDT Gentlemen, you've wandered into the wrong academy.

BOLÍVAR You have the nerve to banish the great Jean Jacques Rousseau from the Paris Academy?

HUMBOLDT You misconstrue terribly, my dear boy!

BOLÍVAR Alexander von Humboldt, the Second Discoverer of America—a tourist! He's a tourist!

Scene Ten

Bolívar and Rodríguez by the Seine.

BOLÍVAR I'm going to the German.

RODRÍGUEZ Don Pedro has frightened you.

BOLÍVAR He makes me ill.

RODRÍGUEZ The Brotherhood is one way. Faith alone is impotent. Look at me: I can do nothing but live out my faith, which has no instruments. The Brotherhood can be an instrument. Don't go to the German.

BOLÍVAR Do you fear him?

RODRÍGUEZ I fear the openness of your feelings. Anyone might now come along with some arbitrary opinion and, if he's credible enough, you would worship him. I doubt whether you truly know what would be good for us. Yesterday all of your thoughts centered upon a young lady—today you assume the pose of a liberator. You've never engaged yourself with your country. It gave birth to you, but what did it give you?

BOLÍVAR What did you give me?

RODRÍGUEZ A few sayings about how humanity should be practiced. Or so I flatter myself. A handful of suggestions about how to rise above a vulgar, swinish, low-life existence.

BOLÍVAR Please, Rodríguez—my parents were not swine.

RODRÍGUEZ No. And were they still alive you would probably see no reason for changes. Your life would have followed a well-trodden path. At some point you would have brought me—one who does not think about master and servants as the others do—before a tribunal as your enemy, and as the enemy of the ruling powers at that. You would have fought me. That you now in all innocence announce the rebellion is the consequence of your rootlessness. I'm for the rebellion, but who am I?

The bells of Notre-Dame strike midnight.

BOLÍVAR The German is objective. The German is independent. He bore the expense of his travels from his private resources. He is obliged to no one. Nor is he Napoleon's lackey.

RODRÍGUEZ He will be grateful to Spain for the visa. His letters of safe-conduct were addressed to advocates of Spanish interests.

BOLÍVAR He attacked Spain in his reports. He has independent judgment. And: Is an earthquake to him truly an earthquake? Does he not conceal behind appearances an essence of a completely different nature? And does "to become accustomed" perhaps not mean the pride of the unflappable, who for three hundred years have coped with every disturbance, in that they have pushed it back into the earth by virtue of their magnificence? Does the "shaking of the earth" perhaps not mean the perpetual threat from the depths of the ancient people? Those closest to the earth who will destroy the foundations of what was believed to be of permanence up above? This awakening, Rodríguez, this disquiet of which he speaks, this attentiveness to the slightest sound, this mistrust of the ground "upon which one had so long and confidently set one's foot"—was all this perhaps not said on my behalf?

RODRÍGUEZ You hear familiar texts and then proceed like an agent of the censor. Don't go to the German. He will ask you why you're here and not there. He will ask you why you lie here in Paris upon costly beds instead of. ...

Humboldt strides over.

BOLÍVAR Humboldt!

QUASIMODO (*with fishing pole and storm lantern*) He has been granted an audience.

RODRÍGUEZ At night?

QUASIMODO He wants to be the first. (*off*)

RODRÍGUEZ Don't go to him.

Shining light above. Napoleon in magnificent regalia, golden seed capsules on his watch chain. Count Ségur, master of ceremonies. Rustam. Then Humboldt.

SÉGUR Alexander Baron von Humboldt, member of the Prussian Royal Academy of Science in Berlin, member of the Royal Göttingen Society of Science, member of the American Philosophical Society in Philadelphia, member of the National Institute of France in Paris, member of the Society of Physics and Natural History in Geneva. ...

NAPOLEON (*after he has looked over Humboldt for a while*) Do you know what I had intended? I wanted to ask if you pursued botany. And before you could have answered, I would have said: My wife does a little bit of that, too. It will remain a rumor. (*off*)

SÉGUR The audience has ended!

Dark. Only Bolívar remains, below. And Rodríguez.

BOLÍVAR For one glance from the eyes of a basilisk he knuckled under! Curse him! To Fanny!

RODRÍGUEZ To Miranda! Francisco Miranda won't refuse us. You'll like Miranda. A man whose heart is in the right place. He was in Russia. Even in Mecklenburg. He's fearless.

BOLÍVAR To Fanny, Rodríguez! Why do you still try it with me? It doesn't depend upon me! Miranda may win the glory, Don Pedro may redeem America, you may thresh empty straw—I will enjoy the lover! Tulips, corn, and gladiolas should sprout from her womb! Pepper pods and agave! The New Empire will be founded upon the sofa, beneath groans, whispers, and caresses!

RODRÍGUEZ And oppression, brutality, and murder will continue in the name of the Holy Trinity and the Virgin! And our brothers of a different skin color will continue to carry the white man over impassable mountain paths upon all fours, a feat the pack animals themselves refuse to do! And disease and dejection will further decimate the creations of sun and rain! And our shame will wax from day to day, our shame in being what we are and in never having tried to become anything else!

BOLÍVAR Oh, I have tried! And on your side! Just leave me alone!

Scene Twelve

The circle in Fanny's salon has broken up. Humboldt lingers in the background, Fanny in the foreground. [...]

Bolívar goes up to Humboldt.

BOLÍVAR Do I disturb you?

HUMBOLDT Not for the first time.

BOLÍVAR Forgive me. And I'll forget that you were with the Emperor.

HUMBOLDT Your cockiness has something impressive about it.

BOLÍVAR You were in my fatherland, Baron. How did you find it?

HUMBOLDT It was the first country upon whose coast my foot touched American soil. For this reason alone I shall always retain the most vivid memory.

BOLÍVAR What do you remember best?

HUMBOLDT The mosquitoes, to be honest.

BOLÍVAR You must have a considerable fortune to undertake so long a journey for so little gain.

HUMBOLDT I nevertheless believe that the money was not wasted.

BOLÍVAR You live the sciences. I, on the other hand, am interested in mankind.

HUMBOLDT I occupy myself with nature, of which man is a part. Therefore, I too am interested in mankind.

BOLÍVAR With savages, no? Europeans do have a weakness for savages. Their desire to rediscover the lost paradise never diminishes. But they will fail. The old paradise is irrecoverable. One must found a new one.

HUMBOLDT In Paris?

BOLÍVAR You consider Prussia more suitable? I hardly know your homeland, monsieur, but based upon everything I've heard, I believe the French have more talent than either the Prussians or the Russians to construct a paradise. You yourself—you'll forgive me—seem to lack the requisite faith in your countrymen's aptitude for paradise. Why else did you travel to Venezuela?

HUMBOLDT It just happened that way. Whoever wishes to see the world today cannot choose the region.

BOLÍVAR I am grateful to chance that you were led to Venezuela. I am burning to hear the latest news.

HUMBOLDT My information is of no value to you.

BOLÍVAR Your gratitude toward the Spanish crown forbids you from being outspoken. Or is it because of Napoleon?

HUMBOLDT Outspoken about what? And what has the Spanish crown to do with it? Or Napoleon? By the way, I dearly hope you agree with me that it would be folly to strike the hand that opens for me a book with seven seals.

BOLÍVAR Only force may undo the seven seals. But we don't mean the same ones. That is all. I demand too much of you.

HUMBOLDT You demand too little of yourself.

BOLÍVAR But isn't it conceivable that the young man whom you happen not to love would want to satisfy his blood with the breath of revolution, a revolution which, despite everything, had not stopped disturbing humanity? And where would the atmosphere for such a notion be more favorable than in Paris?

HUMBOLDT Assuming that you really mean Paris and not its salons.

BOLÍVAR You've been too long amongst the vapors of the tropical forest, monsieur. The spirit of revolution has retreated from the streets. It now prefers to have a roof over its head. It surrounds itself with culture. And with beautiful women. Until its day comes.

HUMBOLDT The word "revolution" acquires a certain caché in the mouth of an aristocrat. You were still half a child when you left Caracas. How do you now conclude that the day must come?

BOLÍVAR (quoting) "That populous mercantile cities, that fertile lands tilled by free hands, take the place of impenetrable forests." Tilled by free hands. You said that. In your lecture. Yesterday. Who will free those hands?

HUMBOLDT One waxes perhaps a bit too enthusiastically.

BOLÍVAR For whom was that spoken?

HUMBOLDT A common phrase. Very common, my dear Monsieur Bolívar.

BOLÍVAR Your eye is sharp; the integrity of your judgment about rocks, plants, and insects, highly regarded. But I doubt that you have insight into man. You're beguiled by your experiences of the foreign. You've unraveled secrets—a couple of connections of the developed. You've been a guest in regions where others continue to live even after you've departed. You return to the freedom of your habits. You enjoy the thrill of having escaped emergencies which fate would have forced upon you had you stayed in place. No, you're unacquainted with discontent. It doesn't lie exposed like a shell tossed up on the sand. Pride has concealed you—pride, Monsieur Baron: the pride that decrees my brothers shall not initiate the fleeing guest into the pain they suffer. What service could they expect from you? Assistance? In what way? Sympathy? There's nothing so debilitating to a proud people than the avowal of a passerby who says he sympathizes with them. What is this avowal worth when one is not prepared to share the pain and to take up the struggle?

HUMBOLDT And you are prepared?

BOLÍVAR Absolutely.

HUMBOLDT It would be truly remarkable if those lands hoped for a hero from the Old World. If the situation so demands, they should have a liberator who springs from their own ranks. If, Monsieur Bolívar. If! Why should your enthusiasm touch me when your intractability angers me? Schiller already criticizes me in Germany for a lack of idealism. I stick to facts, he carps. Even though he's a historian and is no less interested in the Spanish than you are. The man is really not bad, but impractical. I can't be your partner.

BOLÍVAR He has offended you. Just as with mosquitoes—you never forget a sting, Baron. Show me the world that belongs to us, one we will love more deeply and take possession of.

HUMBOLDT A singular request to make of a tourist.

BOLÍVAR I stand corrected. You've experienced more than you reveal. Disclose yourself. You are the first European authority who was there after the Great Revolution. You must have observed some effects.

Humboldt remains silent.

You don't trust me. Demand proofs of my uprightness and discretion.

Humboldt remains silent.

Here is one who seeks the truth and you spurn him. Do you not believe in your heart that truth would be better upheld by those who need it for the establishment of their freedom, for an independent fortune? And do you not likewise fear that despite your precaution the old enemies of the people, the slaveholders and blood suckers, could wrest the truth from you and, under it as a new banner, crusade for plunder? Why would you not align yourself with the enemies of the enemies—with us?

HUMBOLDT Ah, Bolívar—the enemies of the enemies. You cannot make me attribute a higher moral standard to the blood letters than to the blood suckers. Change, if necessary, happens through metamorphosis, not through violence. Nature instructs us so. If you or others use her—I hate violence.

BOLÍVAR And your truth?

HUMBOLDT I humbly place in the treasury of mankind.

BOLÍVAR The truth lies poorly there.

HUMBOLDT But securely.

BOLÍVAR Secure from whom?

HUMBOLDT From the grasp of trespassers.

BOLÍVAR God, how alone you are!

Scene Seventeen

Humboldt before commencement of Napoleon's coronation. Also Bolívar.

HUMBOLDT (*putting on state dress*) I'm in a hurry, Monsieur Bolívar.

BOLÍVAR That you play along with this mummery.

HUMBOLDT I am a contemporary of this mummery. One must be there.

BOLÍVAR And Monsieur Bonpland?

HUMBOLDT Direct yourself toward Malmaison, in the winter garden of the Empress. Monsieur Bonpland is there. Monsieur Montúfar as well.

BOLÍVAR I've broken with my past.

HUMBOLDT So soon? And without any outlook for the future?

BOLÍVAR I've changed my residence. I'm studying the classics.

HUMBOLDT Who is your tutor?

BOLÍVAR Monsieur Rodríguez. He says that you have donated a sundial to my native city. Did you know that I was born in a house on the Place of the Sacred Hyacinth, upon which the sundial now marks the hour?

HUMBOLDT I wouldn't draw any conclusions from that.

BOLÍVAR I ask for your friendship.

HUMBOLDT Ask Monsieur Bonpland.

BOLÍVAR I am asking you, Baron Humboldt. Asking the "Second Discoverer of America." Asking the friend of the people. Asking the benefactor of the peoples of the New Continent.

HUMBOLDT I've done nothing to justify these titles.

BOLÍVAR I beseech you for your friendship. Help me.

HUMBOLDT You're dreaming, Bolívar. Follow me to Siberia and we may become friends. You're as good a European as you are an American. One can be even more. Travel, travel. See, see.

BOLÍVAR Return home.

HUMBOLDT You're well off, not tethered to a delegation. Return home—and then?

BOLÍVAR What would I do in Russia? What do you want in Russia? You are the dreamer, Baron. You want the earth, for which a lifetime is insufficient.

HUMBOLDT I want the cosmos, for which a thousand lifetimes are insufficient.

BOLÍVAR Next you'll want to consecrate the farce put on by Napoleon Bonaparte.

HUMBOLDT Not you?

BOLÍVAR I'll lock myself in my room and read the Charter of Human Rights.

HUMBOLDT Sounds noble but it's foolish and cowardly.

BOLÍVAR When I count myself among your pupils I'll allow you to adopt that tone with me, but not before.

HUMBOLDT You're already the pupil of a decent man. I myself must learn. Take a course at the Sorbonne.

BOLÍVAR I ask you for instruction. You. Teach me to know America as only you saw it: As it is and as it could be. Insult me if you wish, but compel me to understand just what is my America. I'll abandon selfishness, insolence, faintheartedness, arrogance, and false camaraderie. I am obedient. To become unbending, I will bend: to you. I place myself in your hands.

HUMBOLDT You'll make no political adviser out of me. America is politics. Or should I also fob off on you mountains, flowers, and rocks? These are my métier. These and nothing else. Nothing else.

BOLÍVAR Let us begin with mountains, flowers, and rocks.

HUMBOLDT Attend my lectures. Tomorrow I begin a series on ferns.

BOLÍVAR Excellent.

HUMBOLDT Then come the mosses.

BOLÍVAR The mosses.

HUMBOLDT The vegetation on the rims of volcanoes.

BOLÍVAR Vegetation on the rims of volcanoes. And then España.

HUMBOLDT España?

BOLÍVAR José España. The rebellion, Monsieur von Humboldt.

HUMBOLDT That was before I arrived, Monsieur Bolívar.

Scene Twenty

Napoleon Bonaparte is to be crowned Emperor of the French at Notre-Dame.

Pope Pius VII and his entourage enter amidst the joyous peals of a choir and grand organ. [...]

With the exception of Humboldt, Bolívar, and the anonymous female, all sink to their knees in homage. Humboldt approaches Bolívar.

HUMBOLDT One reads in the stars, masked friend? We heard "Vivat!" Have our hearts so changed? Do we now search for a sign from heaven that the usurper may be right? There is no sign. He is the sign himself.

BOLÍVAR He didn't prostrate himself! No bent knee! Rome didn't overcome!

HUMBOLDT A character. Carved from such wood, friend Bolívar, and to good purpose—who doesn't have this in mind?

BOLÍVAR The audacity! The effect! Zeal carries him aloft!

HUMBOLDT The ecstasy dissolves and fear remains.

BOLÍVAR To be such as he would be glorious! To bestow grace upon oneself in the name of the people and at the same time to crown the fatherland, thereby elevating oneself to its first servant!

HUMBOLDT He'll eventually want the fatherland to serve him. Hence the crown. Yet, he has long been serving, though not the fatherland.

All, with the exception of Humboldt, Bolívar, and the anonymous female, rise and sing amidst the ringing of bells the coronation hymn.

ALL Crowned for better opportunities
Of the merchants' guild: Napoleon
That was one of the inevitabilities
Of the French Revolution

The stage clears. Humboldt, Bolívar, the anonymous female, Don Pedro with his wooden Indian, and Isabey remain at different places.

DON PEDRO (*shakes the empty donation box*) No public spirit—everyone thinks only of himself. Outrageous.

ISABEY Wait. (*inserting a coin*) One never knows what it may be good for.

DON PEDRO You have our deepest sympathy, Monsieur Isabey.

ISABEY And take my coach. I'll go by foot and get some air. Soon all of Europe will go by foot and get some air. I am the first European.

Both off.

HUMBOLDT But what a man, after all, wouldn't you say?

BOLÍVAR A universal spirit!

HUMBOLDT One comparable only to universal spirit. Only universal spirit, friend Bolívar, and not the shortsightedness of ambitious patriots. To cling to a fatherland is to court disaster. The free mind loses the free vision, and an all-embracing love contracts and withers. Allow your mind to be focused upon a world-encompassing reason, which governs the great and small. Don't become bogged down in regions that finally overtax a perhaps hard-won freedom only to preserve its selfish miseries.

BOLÍVAR Today you call miserable what yesterday you considered unsurpassed in color and variety, in natural riches and the most glorious potential?

HUMBOLDT I call miserable the inability of the fatherlands to see beyond the horizon of their daily, private needs. I call miserable the lack of any overview and solidarity of reason. Miserable is the acknowledgment of limits by intelligent people, when they allow their musings to clip their own wings and give only the family their wit.

BOLÍVAR I believe you are mistaking the fatherland. If you want a reasonable world you must begin with the fatherland.

Both off.

RODRÍGUEZ (*appears and approaches the anonymous female*) I knew you are the People. The Eternal People.

ANONYMOUS FEMALE Did you recognize me?

RODRÍGUEZ I would recognize you whatever the color of your skin. But you are dearest to me in this one. (*He takes her in his arms*) The horse will appear to us. The white horse. But it may be that we won't recognize it. It may be that we'll beat it to death and eat its flesh. America, America. Should I reveal when the world will collapse? Not in eternity. For every nation must be happy once. At least once. There are still so many unhappy nations.

Scene Twenty-One

Atop Vesuvius, at the upper reaches of inhabitability, 12 August 1805. [...]

BOLÍVAR You forgot to bid me "adieu" when you left Paris.

HUMBOLDT I did not bid "adieu" to many. Only this way, I convinced myself, would I surely return.

BOLÍVAR You most likely would not have met me again. I've decided to go home.

HUMBOLDT Bon voyage, Simón Bolívar. And please don't hold it against me that I refused to do what you requested.

BOLÍVAR What I could use, I took. Come with me. I'll compensate you, that your mountain is now enveloped in silence. I'll hurl people from the craters of extinct volcanoes—volcanoes believed to be extinct, in whose shadows Spanish governors sip lemonade. Come with me, Monsieur Humboldt. Your book won't be complete before you've experienced and recorded what my friends and I set in motion.

HUMBOLDT Who arms you? Who gives you horses? Who will be your soldiers? You won't get far with mercenaries.

BOLÍVAR Stand with us. Once we've won, I'll make you president of the liberated New Continent.

HUMBOLDT You see, there lies the dark pit of your speculations, which so terrify even well-meaning people they no longer trust your projects.

BOLÍVAR Your good name would well serve a good cause. Monsieur Schiller was appointed an honorary citizen of the French Revolution—You'll be the honorary citizen of independence in my America.

HUMBOLDT That sounds much better. But I don't believe in the independence of your America. I desire it, but don't believe you'll create it. Not now—and not very soon. Wait a few years, my friend. We'll remain together in Paris. You, me, Bonpland, and the like-minded. Invest in my project. Together we'll construct an everlasting monument to your homeland, one that's exalted above party bickering and the murderous spirit of the times. You'll thereby guarantee attention and sympathy for your idea.

BOLÍVAR I can't wait. I'll die early. Yes, yes—die. And I don't want to die without having accomplished the most important thing that I recognize and shall fulfill. You began to give us back our self-respect. Freedom we'll capture ourselves.

HUMBOLDT Freedom. I'm on the way to Berlin. But I don't follow the call of the fatherland. I don't wish to discard the king's favor. One day I'll depend upon his money. What you call freedom doesn't exist. Every freedom brings new dependencies.

BOLÍVAR Every new dependency demands a new freedom. Until they're all equal.

HUMBOLDT I'm certain that I don't wish to be equal with all.

BOLÍVAR And yet you want to belong to all.

HUMBOLDT I want to be heard by all.

BOLÍVAR By the oppressed and the oppressors? Don't you need to place one before the other?

HUMBOLDT Why, Bolívar—when I can refine both?

BOLÍVAR That's impossible.

HUMBOLDT What could you possibly have taken from me that would be useful for so much narrow-mindedness, so much stubbornness?

BOLÍVAR Truth about the path of all development.

HUMBOLDT I proceed from harmony! From harmony!

BOLÍVAR Yet your description contains contradictions. I'll purchase weapons and horses. And my soldiers will be no mercenaries. And every one of your books that is useful to our cause, I'll have translated into Spanish. Thus will you fight on my side, without once having to set your foot outside the door of your self-chosen prison. Carry on. Don't exhaust yourself in the pursuit of eternal truths about rocks, flowers, beetles, and men. Don't you observe the sense and nonsense in this one word, "pursuit"? That it can mean to follow so as finally to reach and finally to enfold in one's arms and finally to unite with? Or, simply to pursue so as to capture and to rend and in the end to annihilate? Or simply to pursue with hope but without certainty of finally

attaining? You'll miss much if you don't come with me. You'll miss the success of your discoveries—or should I say, the consequences?

Vesuvius smokes more strongly.

HUMBOLDT Look, Bolívar! Look! I rouse the comrades!

BOLÍVAR Stay. This will be our last meeting.

HUMBOLDT Yes, I enter captivity, Simón. And I have chosen to do so myself. That's right. Perhaps it will not remain Berlin for long. Perhaps I will,
after all, manage to return to Paris, to this capital of my life. But that's uncertain. The currency exchange. And then Napoleon is also still here. Stay
by Bonpland in Paris. He regards you highly and knows as much about
America as I do.

BOLÍVAR He believes in me.

HUMBOLDT I wish I were born as he was: French. Please don't allow my
stuffiness to disturb you. That's the only Prussian inheritance that I shall
cultivate to the very end. You should marry, Simón. The responsibilities of
a wife and child would relieve even you of illusions.

BOLÍVAR I was married. My wife passed away. Of yellow fever.

HUMBOLDT When?

BOLÍVAR Last year.

HUMBOLDT In Europe?

BOLÍVAR Over there. When you were in Havana, I was in Caracas. When
you visited President Jefferson in Philadelphia, I sailed again for Spain.

Vesuvius smokes even more strongly.

HUMBOLDT There! There! The comrades snore? You're an astonishing character. Why did you conceal that from me? So as to feel me out?

BOLÍVAR I wanted to hear confirmation of my impressions from your own
mouth. I've seen the people agitated. And in the moments they feel the need
for freedom, the people are as strong as God because God pours His spirit
into them.

HUMBOLDT Leave God out of this. You mean yourself, Bolívar.

*Vesuvius spouts forth monstrous clouds of smoke. Flames also ignite and subside
again.*

Fire! We finally have fire! When you say "God" you mean yourself, Bolívar.
It's all the same to me. Probably no one can begin resolving difficulties in
any other way than by comparing himself to God.

BOLÍVAR There will be two free places upon the throne that I erect.

HUMBOLDT Take Bonpland instead of me. He would be happy. And he
wields the machete like one of you. He always cleared the paths for us in the
thick forests. The paths, yes ... the paths. ... (*off*)

BOLÍVAR Humboldt!—Humboldt!—Humboldt!

Chapter 84

CHRISTOPH HEIN

The Russian Letters of the Huntsman Johann Seifert

1980

With hesitation we are publishing the following letters of the huntsman Johann Seifert, the personal valet of Alexander von Humboldt and later the royal caretaker of the hunting lodge of Friedrich Wilhelm IV. The potential value of this publication has been considerably reduced by the lack of care of the transcription, such that we can not provide the usual historic authenticity verified and confirmed by scholarship. However, since our longtime transcriptionist has reached retirement age, and therefore we do not want to entrust such an important source as the Seifert letters to an inexperienced assistant, we find ourselves in the embarrassing situation of either withholding for years a substantial discovery, or immediately presenting it, though in a questionable form. Our Research Center has decided to agree to an initial, preliminary publication of the letters, which may be of interest to broader circles and, at least, announces the discovery of the letters to the academic world.

With this edition, which is inadequate and quasi more of belletristic than scholarly value, we would like to forthwith make known that before the end of a decade we intend to make the complete letters accessible to the academic world, annotated with historical-critical commentary.

The following letters of Seifert, which are addressed to his wife, and in which he oddly enough designates his employer Alexander von Humboldt as the "Prussian Prince Gumplot," were written during his travels in Russia in 1829. The let-

Translation by Rex Clark and Oliver Lubrich, from Christoph Hein, "Die russischen Briefe des Jägers Johann Seifert," in *Einladung zum Lever Bourgeois* (Berlin/Weimar: Aufbau, 1980), 104–105, 106, 107–108, 113–114, 115–116, 119–123, 131–134, 137–141, 177–183. Copyright © 2004 Suhrkamp Verlag Frankfurt am Main.

ters apparently did not reach their intended recipient. In 1946 they were found in the former archive of the disbanded Secret Police in the Prince-Albrecht-Street in Berlin. Classified at the time as innocuous and worthless, thirty years later they were discovered anew. The letters were located glued as wastepaper backing beneath the wallpaper of an apartment in the Tieck Street in Berlin.

~

To what extent we completely possess the outstanding letters of Seifert, remains for the time being unclear, since regretfully the apartment owner has not yet allowed our Research Center to examine the entire wallpaper for the wastepaper backing. At this time we are investigating several apartments in the vicinity of the site of the discovery, whereby the inconvenience of intruding into private quarters and removing wallpaper from walls is compensated by the hope of discovering similar treasures.

The documents which have been secured by us to date are in a dismal state of deterioration, which results in the above mentioned difficulties of descriptive analysis. On the back side of each of the last sheets is found the complete name of the writer and his travel location as well as the name of the recipient and her Berlin address. Next to the official postmarks all of the sheets show the stamps of the St. Petersburg secret police as well as various official seals of Prussia and the German Empire. From the stamps it must be concluded that the Seifert letters were intercepted in Russia and three years later were consigned by the St. Petersburg secret police to their Prussian colleagues. There is no evidence for the assumption that Ludmila (Mila) Seifert ever set eyes on the letters of her spouse.

With all of the aforementioned limitations we are nonetheless satisfied to have discovered these documents, which came out of the archives of the Gestapo through the collapse of the German Empire and through a fortuitous coincidence came into the public eye and into the light of academia from their condition as the wastepaper backing of wallpaper: per aspera historiae ad astra scientiae.

It remains to be added, that we had to undertake several necessary corrections for this first printing of the Seifert letters. The reader interested in the original text will be referred to the historical-critical edition.

Berlin, June, 1977.

Submitted by: C.H.

~

1st of August (hereabouts July 20)

I am rather tired, but the little letter for you will be written before slumbering. My Prussian prince himself is very keen on my letters, examines them occasionally with my permission and praises my progress. Even wants to fashion out of me a travel writer; but I told him right away, that's not something for a hunter and rather would haul ten wooden cases as ... (unreadable due to water damage) ... yet he argued that I had a natural talent for this business and a sense for the reading wishes of the public. In my letters appeared all sorts of famous personages, no matter whether I beheld their face or the heel of their shoe. Throughout they are treated in a familiar manner, the color of their coat excellently described, mention given to the turned-up cap, and the number of sugar cubes that they like with tea is not overlooked. Every pygmy of society is given due, and in the end the whole of Siberia appears like Charlottenburg and the arctic people like Herr Varnhagen. The slaves in the gold-sifting pits and marble quarries, the deported Poles, the famine and pestilence-ridden villages, so what? that part of Berlin which is interested in our journey wants to learn of the attachments of the St. Petersburg princesses. Years ago, he told me, he traveled through South America and discovered and described a few things worth mentioning, and the scientific world had conveyed to him thereof much that is agreeable. For Prussia as well his journey to the Orinoco had showed itself to be fruitful and stimulating. For thirty years the salons in Berlin puzzled about the children he supposedly fathered there.

～

When my prince mentioned the General von Gerlach, my body's shell shuddered. Hitherto I have not found the courage to confess to him and to tell him of the directive from Gerlach, nor of the adverse and for me fortunate circumstances whereby on my own I evaded the obligation, to ascertain personal facts and conversations of Prince Gumplot during the Siberia journey and to report on this. It was by no means for the lack of opportunity. Regarding a complaint from me on the exasperating absence of letters from you, he noted that it is the wisdom of the state to equally distribute abuse. My letters would probably not arrive in Berlin before the end of the half-year journey, his were expedited in three days to Tegel and received there, without neglecting in the interim to generate a Russian and a Prussian copy. And if my letters were read much later, his were read all too often. Both circumstances were unfortunate. And in summation there resulted a matching mathematical cipher, a so-called constant, that applied to me as well as my prince, which he named the constant of state security and safety. Therefore a suitable opening was presented to inform him about the non-implemented order for surveillance. But I was afraid that when he heard it he would, in spite of my assurances to the contrary, maintain an erroneous distrust and forthwith restrain outspoken conversations.

It's drizzling again. No boatman will risk taking us across. And since the Russian rivers are powerful and as such have no fords, we will have to be patient. It is getting dark, I'll have to finish my epistle. Underneath the name I press my lips and think of you and my daughter.

Your Johann who loves you

~

16th of September 1829
(hereabouts 4th September)
last night in Miass.

　　Back from a mountain climb on the Aushkul. The whole day and the previous night I was on my feet, since my prince repeatedly lent me out to Messrs. Ehrenberg and Rose. So I trotted behind the professors, boxes strapped on my back, and with both arms fighting the weeds, which are found there growing up to a height of six feet. A grass that made the gentlemen euphoric and only made me break out into sweat. Add to that fog and rain, marshes and swamp snakes, the occasional abandoned settlements and farmhouses, which are only used by their occupants in the winter, since these are Bashkirs who roam about in the summer. Enough of that. The party started in the early morning to reach the Ural River. My previous letter that I wrote you from Troitsk (not yet found or missing—C.H.), I showed to Prince Gumplot, who wished, unless private messages ruled it out, to take a look at. Finding in it his mockery of the Prussian Minister of Culture, Herr von Raumer, of the evening soirées of our king and the dinners with the family of the czar very much alarmed him, so that I feared that my marital gossip would cause him long-term chagrin and he might now or in the future on account of it have to put up with trouble, caused alone by my good-natured stupidity. Nevertheless in the end he only asked me to report with more care and moderation, so that a misdirected letter not cause all of us aggravation. He was obligated before the start of the expedition to submit a written assurance to the Russian court that the social institutions of Russia and its regions of influence and spheres of power would receive no notice, to renounce any comment in this regard and also to publish nothing in the future or even to notate privately anything that might resemble a criticism of what was observed. This assurance had become necessary, since his Essai politic of the America travels had not only angered Spain but also Sanssouci and London. Less because of the facts noted, which did not impact the latter royal houses; it was rather the method, that a naturalist would choose to look beyond the rocks and the animals and not abstain from commentary on institutions of the state. Quite possibly he had caused damage to the practice of research, as in the future one would deem to show less to the eye of the outsider, and he received proof of this, in that his trip to India was thwarted by the East India Company which had enough cause to fear a new Essai politic. Also he had considered it necessary, prompted by the comments of the expedition commander and the local military commanders, to give assurances in this matter anew to the Russian court, in order not to endanger the progression of the Siberian expedition. Through his word to the czar, through his responsibility to his occupation, and through the concern about the future work of each and every researcher, he was thus threefold compelled, to restrict himself to lifeless nature and to avoid everything that had to do with human institutions and above all the condition of the lower classes. To mention the rights, however acquired, of the upper ranks and the duties of the lower ranks had a provocative effect and helped no one. I was distraught to the utmost and embarrassed, but had nothing in response to his philippic and had to listen to it with red-hot face. Yet after he had paced back and forth several times with furrowed brow and not looking at or noticing me, he turned to me again and cheerfully said with a laugh, that I shouldn't look so tortured about it any further. It's fine the way it is. His letters, whenever and wherever they cross any border, are opened and copied. Whether Havana, Paris, Berlin, or Yekaterinburg, his fame and accomplishments were an occasion for hirelings of any persuasion to open and examine his papers with even more eagerness. And while in the beginning he took care and paused when writing, in order to consider all of the possible readers, those whose names were on the cover page, and those who had to keep their names concealed and their shabby doings until they have become entirely nameless, soon he abandoned all caution, mindful that in Sanssouci he would be denounced as the reddest Jacobin, yet, nevertheless, the chamberlain to Friedrich Wilhelm III and now bearing the title of Esteemed Privy Councilor with the distinction of Excellency. The Jacobin in the private correspondence would not be resented as long as he did not refuse to fawn like a cat for the court; some free-spiritedness was allowed if the epaulettes are correctly worn. Even more important in this matter were the annotations of a veteran spy who rather openly confided in him that the frivolous thought, the rebellious idea, the spoken or written insubordination alone would hardly make the individual in question appear suspicious, indeed almost unsuspicious, and would be regarded with only the lowest, quasi the lightest level of observation. Quite otherwise with someone who neither publicly nor privately complains; here there must be searching and investigating done, to see in which wicked corner he wears his true opinions, and with whom and about what he secretly confers. Further cause for higher-level observation is someone who takes all too much chatty and artificial pleasure in the political conditions and applauds them submissively with the most hackneyed phrases that even the eye of state order winces with pain; only too well would a modern Brutus decorate himself with this type of speech, he who with a deluge of songs of praise wants to drown out that he is already forging the dagger for autocracy. Such are the bits of philosophy of a Prussian spy, who characterized himself, as Prince Gumplot added, as a Kantian, which he didn't find particularly astounding. He recollected directly that the giant of Königsberg also published the dreams of a clairvoyant, which when read with the eyes of a Prussian spy must have been a charming spectacle. I stood there with open mouth and gaffed at him and I don't know even now, is it satire? But my prince gave me no explanation and so I take it as a fairy tale and won't rack my brains about it.

~

13th of October (hereabouts the 1st),
in Astrakhan

[...] Astrakhan is one big circus tent, it is swarming with people of all skin colors and languages, everyone bargains, yells, buys and sells, prays, fights and talking is done with hands and feet. The city is rich, the houses grand like in St. Petersburg. All of us are staying together in a huge building that is for the exclusive use of the expedition as lodging. The house belongs to a merchant with a massive beard, a Mr. Federov, a Russian. It's been pointed out to my prince that he's a millionaire. You couldn't tell by looking at him.

We're planning to stay here for a week and then will use the best post roads to reach Moscow, St. Petersburg, and finally Berlin. And if it can be combined with decency and Christian duty I will, and I write this down with a clear head, be able to carry in my luggage and drape around you a sable coat and some jewelry. It would please me and for this reason I want to include Herr von Menschenin in my prayers. The very same has approached me repeatedly and now yesterday offered the above-mentioned little purse. The favor that he wants from me he has kept to himself. Yet I think I will act casually and I'm thinking to myself that it can't be something scurrilous since he is old, sickly, and of high rank. Also something unchaste is impossible since I let him know in my initial confusion that for all the sable in Siberia I wouldn't agree to shine up his behind. Such things, he assured, was not his desire.

Two days ago we were invited to a Buddhist religious service that the Kalmyks celebrated in a temple a few miles from Astrakhan. [...] The Kalmyks are quiet and peaceful farmers who make their living within the czar's realm. [...] Altogether a more pleasant sight than the enslaved subjects which we observed in Siberia. More like animals than humans these people labored in the mines. Only from behind bars did we view their blackened faces, from which the whites of their eyeballs dreadfully shined on us. They sleep in the mineshafts in which they work since one dared not open them. With the same fear the exchange of the found gold for the meager supplies for subsistence takes place in the presence of armed Cossacks. As an unconscious sigh escaped me, my prince ordered me to be quiet, as the Russian government maintained only the wish to serve science. That evening he revealed to me that he was determined to exclude me forthwith from visiting places of work. He comprehended my outrage, shared it insofar as it required the eyes of a sixty year old in order to calmly observe the structures of this world. The imprudence of my presence however would endanger his projects. He was no less a slave than these Russian serfs and the deportees, albeit equipped with the Excellency title and outfitted with a half carriage from the Czar. This comfort stripped him of those rights which even a serf was entitled to. The gold, which the serf brought to the surface was needed; his scholarship one could easily do

without, and an inopportune word could ruin him. Only at the lowest level of
society and human institutions could the individual win back some part of the
freedoms, the acquisition and possession of which long ago raised him above
the animal kingdom. There, where a further descent is not possible, on the
boundary that divides us from the animal and inorganic world, the enslaved
finds solid ground. He himself, however, hovered in an untenable situation,
constrained from above and below. An indisposition of his king, an intrigue,
a glance construed with malice, a frivolous remark, a lack of self-censorship,
all of these can momentarily shatter him, he, whom one names in Berlin the
hero of the natural sciences, the new Aristotle, who is celebrated in Russia as
Prometheus. His Privy Councilor title, which has finally allowed him to fulfill
his thoroughly puritan needs, forces him to make the most foolish personal
appearances. Anyone if he is only nobly born and has scarcely learned to talk
takes the liberty of impertinent remarks and contemptible jests. To a bored
clique of the court he had to read aloud newspapers for evening entertainment, during which no one paid him any attention and they chatted, yawned,
or even slept. Also he was called to the palace at arbitrary times in order to
deliver state papers. Among them invitations to balls and dinners. The royal
sender required a privy councilor as letter carrier, and he, who for forty years
had not taken more than four hours a night as his scholarly work did not leave
him more time, he ran with these slips of paper all around Berlin in order to
wake some aristocratic fop out of bed around noontime to request an appearance at court. The real torture began however, when one started to speak with
these gentlemen. ... And then it was merciful when they would choose to gab
about the weather and didn't harass him to conduct a conversation on the sciences and fine arts. That was namely true tastelessness and incomparable in its
humiliation; just like an embarrassing inquiry that a pupil is subjected to by
the school principal when he catches him with a girl. And with all of this he
could speak of fortune not to be chased out of Berlin with a bare blade, which
a Herr Hinkeldey, the supervisor of police felt not a little desire to do, and
from which my prince was spared only because of his tormenting position at
the court.

19th October (hereabouts the 7th),
back in Astrakhan

My dear heart, we were out on the Caspian Sea for four days. The steam boat
which was hired for us lurched and wheezed and I was thankful to God that
I was able to arrive back on firm ground. Am I a fish? I'm fully satisfied with
Ehrenberg's grasses, Rose's rocks and Gumplot's pressure gauge. In the first
night on the boat I was awakened by loud children's sobbing. I had to think

about it for a long time and found out that it was the voice of my Alexandra. In my dream everything was alive and right in front of me. Only the small face of my little girl was unclear, a flowing pink cloud. I'm desirous to see my child.

Now we are preparing for departure. In two days we're leaving Astrakhan; I will hop with wild jumps towards Berlin.

God bless you and Alexandra.

The peculiar Herr von Menschenin asked me if he could take a look at my last letter to you. I acted astonished, moreover I had to explain, that my refusal resulted only from the private character of the letter. Whatever his desire might be, it doesn't seem to be of the dirty kind, and I am hopeful of hunting down the sable.

My three masters have promised me a bonus in Berlin. So I think I can advise you without concern that you can borrow an advance of fifteen Prussian Thaler from Rafaelson. If you can manage without that however, I would prefer it. Yet if need be, then do it. But try beforehand to borrow from someone else. There must surely be a Christian or decent German you can find who could extend the money to you. Because you know I have my opinions about Rafaelson and his people and even my prince can't escort me away from these. Quite the contrary, as I hope, quite the contrary! Gumplot on this point is very peculiar. He himself does not believe the murdering of children and atrocities of the Jews even though everybody talks about it and it is reported in the national papers. He asked me whether I really supposed that my Rafaelson, who is just living out his life, is conspiring against me and my country. As I replied to him that I didn't rule this out and that the merchant through his devious manner and shifty look very much seemed to be an agent of foreign, enemy powers, he became rough and abusive towards me. I said, I was not accustomed to being insulted. I wanted to leave the room, but he ordered me to stand still. Then he held a half-hour lecture such that I could almost believe he himself was an Israelite. He called the hatred of the Jews the considered philosophy of mediocrity. Incompetence and dilettantism seek their salvation in the denunciation of the other, of the alien. That could be the scholar, the sick, women, or anyone different. And the Jew is especially suited, since another religion, other facial features, other clothes are added on as well. There is, so said the peculiar prince, the possibility that arises to explain your own bad fortune as the fault of another. The uncaring and therefore shunned husband declares all women to be whores. The pupil who flunks out and his father who is infuriated by this, and who tried in vain to bribe the professor, characterize all teachers as corrupt individuals. The overfed bureaucrat who stares with little pig eyes at contemporary art images which remain for him incomprehensible as to why his own belching satisfaction with conditions is not shining back at him from all sides calls the artists on this account overblown or hysterical or even destructive. And with a certain special fondness the chorus of these scoundrels pounce at love (sic!) between men and the Jews in order to revenge their banal and unhappy lives. My prince believes in fact that the hatred of Jews originates in the disgust at one's own shabby doings. We are, he says, not able or willing to change ourselves and because of this bring the stranger to be burned at the stake. The murderous example of washing your own fur without getting wet. The invention of the devil is the prerequisite of canonizing saints. The holy fatherland, the holy idea, the deified ruler demand the crucifixion. A person, a minority must die for the unholy fatherland so that its misdeeds, its guilt can be explained. As the guilt of another. Always in this way have they been declared guilty, whether it is the women, the Jews, the scholars, the not normal, always they are therefore called dirty, sleazy, unclean. Thus mediocrity elevates itself. It denounces in order to be spotless. It beats the woman in order to be manly. It kicks the foreigner in order to elevate itself as master. It denounces reason in order to show off its healthy spirit.

So, Mila, the prince blabbered on like this for half an hour. Why should I write it down for you, washed-out old wives' tales and frail feebleness all of it. I ask myself to what extent he actually is attached to such bunk. If he doesn't share the healthy hatred of the Germans and all non-Welsh people towards Jewishness, I will now open his eyes and demonstrate to him the all-threatening conspiracy of these murderers of Jesus.

But I'm getting off topic, as I was about to advise you to borrow from others instead of from Rafaelson. If it's not to be avoided, then do it and tell him that I and only I will pay him the percentage owed and he should honorably leave you out of it. And if he only wants to lend with cash guaranteed by you or if he only hints at it or even wants to enter the house, I will circumcise him on my return, such that he will quickly be reunited with his Jewish ancestors. Just letting you know: my brother promised me by his own hand to be the guardian of my honor and to watch the comings and goings of my house.

But everything, Mila, everything, even the most hidden thing, the Lord sees and judges us accordingly. I commend you to Him. Think of me. Your Johann.

~

9th of December
(or the Russian 27th of November),
still in St. Petersburg

Mila, it is finally nighttime. I can't sleep, as much good as it would do me. The day was bad enough. In the morning I strolled around the market, of which there are several here, and where withered vegetables are offered for sale and icons of saints and candles, also equipment for the kitchen and stables, as well as rags for clothes, I didn't want to buy anything, but just amuse myself.

Suddenly a sleazy individual grabbed me on the coat, spoke to me in his gobbledygook, even wanted to hit me. I understood not a word and attempted to get free, but three, four brawny guys stopped me. They made gestures. Two uniformed officers arrived. My assailants let me loose and spoke with them, meanwhile I made known my cluelessness. The officers signaled that I empty my pockets, which I did very willingly to show my innocence. How great was my surprise, Mila, as I pulled from the depth of my coat pocket a wrapped paper covered with incomprehensible writing. Such a package was never before in my possession and how it was in my pocket—God only knows. The crowd howled, I was held tighter, the officers unwrapped the discovery from the paper and a gold and colored icon appeared, such as are traded at the market and hang in large number in every church. Yet how it came to be in my pocket—it is a mystery, Mila. Seized roughly, ringed by a shouting crowd, I was led to an office. I was given a sign to sit down. Meanwhile the Russians talked to each other and filled out papers. After three hours sweating on a chair, finally there arrived an official who knew German. He said that I was in custody on account of a crime and that on the next day I would be flogged—I protested, screamed, demanded Humboldt, demanded Count Cancrin, called all of the Russian names that were familiar to me. All for naught. A plea as well did not soften the grim faces. Neither did slipping to the office supervisor the Russian and German money I had along. I was laughed at, I was seized again in order to be put in a cell, where I was to stay the night, to be beaten the next day.

Before I was taken out of the room—and I was fighting like a animal, Mila—there appeared a new, apparently very important official, as everybody was deferential. This gentleman spoke my language with the best ability. After he scolded the Russians and completely reduced them to silence, he turned to me in a friendly way. He said that he regretted this incident, that undoubtedly an unfortunate mix-up had happened, that I could go on my way without concern and that nobody would do me any harm. I might take the trouble to call on Herr von Menschenin the next day in order to explain and describe the events.

Seconds later I was on the street. Alone, free. With a hurting head on account of all of the many incomprehensible matters. My way home took about three hours as I was too upset and constantly lost my way. I was sweating, shaking, and freezing, and comprehended nothing.

Once arrived I correctly reported to my Prince Gumplot. He was concerned and advised me not to leave the house again. Only Menschenin should I call upon, but then I should stay in my room until the journey home. I asked whether he could make any sense of my misfortune, since everything was devilishly confusing to me and I did not know how the icon of the saint got into my pocket nor the circumstances of my incredible rescue. I was also curious what Herr von Menschenin had to do with everything so that at the police station they so quickly had the name of our travel superintendent and chief lodging supervisor at hand. It might be a peculiar clustering of natural co-incidences, my prince said, and the superficial, incredibly, can also represent the actual cause. However other things might lurk behind it and it was appropriate to advise caution. A Herr von Menschenin, in any event, deserved consideration. In saying so Prince Gumplot smiled at me in such a special way, that I became very red in the face and my hands were sweaty. More so from this embarrassment—since I was again reminded of that directive—than from presence of mind, I contradicted him. Objecting to him that this Menschenin was only an insignificant official, who could not stand up to such a highly decorated travel expedition as ours. My prince replied, I should not behave like a fool and underestimate the small toads in front of temple doors where they preferably dwell. Even though they are not provided with much power, they can certainly have a remarkable bite. And their small amount of poison adds up over the years and is then capable of being deadly. Above all in the states ruled by absolutism these toads are dangerous since they disguise and mask their poisonous mouths and have all sorts of moral, political, and esthetic pretenses at hand so they can discharge their most private feelings. True criticism and even condemnation is, as always, open and thus expressible, if only the society itself is sound and the necessary evil of the state is not bloated, but rather a cozy wrap around the body of the people. However a government that misunderstands itself requires the slogan, and if a political dictatorship has developed enough practical phrases, any amount of garbage can be hidden. Many a person, who has had to suffer state displeasure, owes this alone to the look of his nose that a toad did not like. He was reminded of a privy councilor in Berlin, whose name he wanted to keep from me. This man was the worst fellow of the whole Prussian system, a repugnant sneak and dodger full of hate and poison. This fellow cultivated an antipathy towards Garcia, the most wonderful of all singers, and year after year knew how to prevent that the same be heard in Berlin. He maintained that she was too much of a red, which was egregious nonsense. But since the Garcia sang in Paris and in Italy, people believed him. To all objections, that her singing was not red, he countered with slogans of Prussian nationalism. This fellow, who with a deadly passion could not stand the glorious Garcia, declared far and wide that on account of this woman the fatherland was in danger only in order to help make a success of his aversion. Such toads, said the prince, sit in front of all entrances, garnish their idiotic opinions with the relevant court philosophy, cook their soup together with the state broth and call on the royal tribunals to lend the force of law to their stomach disorders. The best thing about these repulsive creatures was that they preferred to operate behind the backs of people, so that you did not also have to look at them even when you still had to suffer beneath them. He was not able to convince the same privy councilor otherwise about Garcia and finally said to him, he should send over to the Bethanian hospice and let the deaconesses sing for him.

Then my prince sat down at the desk which was a sign for me not to disturb anymore. I stood by the door as he called out to me once more to be careful with the toads.

I want to take the advice to heart, by God, dear Mila. My toads will get no pleasure out of me. Tomorrow I will go to him and write to you right away. In the days of waiting for the departure, the little letters are a pleasure and I want to spoil you with several additional sheets day by day in the remaining time.

Meanwhile it has turned night. I'll seal the letter and start off with a new page tomorrow.

Go to sleep, Mila. I'm right beside you. Your spouse.

13th of December

Mila, yesterday I was with von Menschenin. Today the invitation came for the second audience for the prince. On the 15th we will depart St. Petersburg. Now it is certain and unalterable.

Please excuse, my love, the pause in my little letters, as there was much to do and my fingers are bloody with writing.

I'm leaving Russia with no grudges since the Russians are true of heart and admirable people. But the grinning devil's face of Menschenin I never want to see for the rest of my days. A little sable critter from him was out of the question; I was not in the mood myself to speak to him about it, in spite of the pleasure that it would have brought you.

Keep in mind our evening meal together on the day of the birth of our Lord. One last little letter kiss from your Johann who loves you above all.

Postscript. The coachman said the 27th of December is the day that we will arrive in Berlin and when I may embrace my Mila and my Alexandra. Johann.

Chapter 85

Ibsen Martínez
Humboldt & Bonpland, Taxidermists
1981

BENEATH PALMS DRUNK WITH SUNSHINE

Open field in the so-called New World. The year is 1799. Wild noises. Bonpland, sweaty and breathless, makes his entrance. He parts the brush and looks up.

BONPLAND Well, I think you can see it better from here. What do you think it measures?

HUMBOLDT (*from offstage*) Height or width?

Bonpland shakes his head, discouraged.

HUMBOLDT (*still offstage*) Actually, it's hard to know. It's a tall mass, no doubt about it. Let's say, six hundred … seven hundred feet. … (*pause*) Maybe more.

BONPLAND The Royal Society of London will want data in meters. Could you be … more precise?

HUMBOLDT (*stubbornly from offstage*) Multiply by 230 or something like that and you'll have the sum in meters.

BONPLAND Alex, please!

Humboldt enters adjusting the buttons of his fly. He carries a retracting telescope in his hand.

HUMBOLDT (*unpleasant and perspiring*) The approximate measurement, of course. …

BONPLAND Alex, what kind of naturalists do you think we are?

Translation by Richard John Ascárate, from Ibsen Martínez, *Humboldt & Bonpland, Taxidermistas. Tragicomedia con naturalistas, en dos actos*, in *Humboldt & Bonpland, Taxidermistas. L.S.D. (Lucio in the Sky with Diamonds) (Teatro)* (Caracas: Fundarte, 1991), 13–19, 21–22, 23, 25, 31–32, 36–42. Copyright © 1981 by Ibsen Martínez.

HUMBOLDT Fairly approximate ones. I know they don't want approximations, but we're doing what we can. We're drawing as close as possible to the calcareous mass and calculating its measurements. This should be enough for them, this should quiet them for the next hundred years, when the next expedition comes to correct us. Besides, why do they want to know everything? It's promethean, absurd, indecent. ...

BONPLAND You were more meticulous with measurements before. ...

Humboldt looks at him in outraged amazement.

HUMBOLDT Of course, I can tease awhile with tangents and the goniometer. But really, *dear Bonpland,* it's not important if the error is a few hundred meters.

BONPLAND Oh, no?

HUMBOLDT They'll never come to verify it. Would you like to take the telescope for a while? It leaves an unbearable smell of copper.

Humboldt extends the telescope to his partner. He sits on a rough rock. He dries off his sweat. He sets about taking off his boots.

BONPLAND If you had put yourself into this we would've been finished today.

HUMBOLDT Do you have any of the Mosel, as you call it? I'd like to refresh myself.

BONPLAND One session of complete measurements and we can go home.

HUMBOLDT (*taking a long, exasperated pause*) Okay. A little of that Mosel and I promise you that I'll go back to the theodolite again. Maybe I'll take some readings of the heavens.

BONPLAND The heavens? It's not dark yet.

HUMBOLDT You're right. I'll drop the sextant. Measurements, Bonpland, I'm dying to take measurements. ...

BONPLAND (*with childlike enthusiasm*) And with the surface thermometer as well?

HUMBOLDT (*condescendingly*) As soon as I finish with this tick ... it's stuck between my second and third finger. ...

BONPLAND And the ambient humidity, too?

HUMBOLDT I don't understand this obsession you have with the ambient humidity. Everything is fairly humid, isn't it? That should be enough. (*he mimics giving a memorandum*) "Gentlemen of the Geognostic Circle: It gives me great pleasure now to inform you that the shores of the Orinoco are, in the main, inclined to be more humid than dry." That's it. But no. They insist on numbers.

BONPLAND Alex, you promised to do it. ...

HUMBOLDT (*putting on his boots again*) I said a few measurements. I said altitude. I said longitude. Maybe I even said luminous intensity. Maybe temperature … sure, measuring the temperature might be fairly interesting. But the humidity … ? What is this insistence of yours on the humidity?

BONPLAND Because it's not constant everywhere. For that reason you should measure it.

HUMBOLDT Pass the canteen with the Mosel.

BONPLAND Alex, you promised. …

HUMBOLDT I didn't want to leave today: I'm behind in my correspondence.

BONPLAND Behind? But if nobody writes to us. …

HUMBOLDT You mean nobody writes to you, you stupid Mason. I'm not a man who neglects his obligations.

BONPLAND Then measure the ambient humidity. You promised to do it.

HUMBOLDT Only from time to time. (*pause*) Besides, the hygrometer is damaged. Only a Swiss thinks of entrusting precision to the hair of a woman. Your humidity ended up soaking and breaking the hygrometer hair. It doesn't work. It doesn't measure the humidity today. Pass me the Mosel.

Bonpland runs up to the previously visible bundle with the instruments. He takes out a hygrometer. He shows it triumphantly.

BONPLAND Yesterday I obtained a woman's hair and fixed them. It's a little limp, true, a little too *Maquiritare*. But it'll work.

HUMBOLDT (*puffing breathlessly*) I don't believe it. Let me see it anyway.

Bonpland hands him the hygrometer. Humboldt examines it attentively.

HUMBOLDT You always get your way, Jean Claude. I'll also have to measure the ambient humidity. How do you foresee everything? How do you sleep in a hammock without falling out?

BONPLAND (*in all modesty*) One gets used to it.

Bonpland displays, temptingly, the canteen with wine.

BONPLAND What? I'm positioning the mechanism?

HUMBOLDT Go ahead, dear Jean Claude. And come here with the canteen!

Bonpland hurries in preparing extractors for geologic specimens, weathervanes that measure wind velocity, surface thermometers, herbariums, butterfly nets. … Humboldt watches him as he drinks.

HUMBOLDT How long has it been since we left La Coruña, Jean Claude?

BONPLAND (*without slowing his pace*) A few months. Don't call me Jean Claude. …

HUMBOLDT (*venomously*) A few months, eh? A month more, a month less. …

BONPLAND (*stops and, looking up, announces*) Four months, sixteen days. …

HUMBOLDT　A true man of your time, Jean Claude. The exactitude, the rigor. … (*pause*) I wonder how the revolutionary boys of the junta are doing? Will success spoil Gay-Lussac? Will they invade the Austrians again?

BONPLAND (*who appears indecisive*)　Do I also open the herbals? During the ascent I observed some unfamiliar gymnosperms.

HUMBOLDT (*with a guffaw*)　The herbarium, of course … set it up. What else?

Bonpland opens the herbarium with the utmost care.

HUMBOLDT　Where do you keep the key to the wine cellar?

BONPLAND　It's no more than a trunk with bottles.

Bonpland continues setting up the instruments. While toiling he avoids stumbling over Humboldt's extended, relaxed feet.

HUMBOLDT　I ask you because you never know what might happen. Everything is rather equinoctial in these parts. …

HUMBOLDT (*raising his voice*)　I said that anything can happen … !

BONPLAND　Huh?

HUMBOLDT　For example, suppose that some fine day you decide. …

BONPLAND (*looking around, to himself*)　Where did I put the magnetic register?

HUMBOLDT　… Once and for all to "go and see." Isn't this your motto? "To go and see" this ridiculous branch of the river that runs to the Orinoco in summer and to the Amazon the rest of the year. …

BONPLAND (*exasperated*)　Casiquiare … it's called the Casiquiare. And you have it backwards.

HUMBOLDT　Backwards? What's backwards?

BONPLAND　It runs to the Amazon in winter … the rest of the year it returns. …

HUMBOLDT (*disparagingly*)　Very edifying … very reasonable on your part … good, then you go and see the Casiquiare branch … and, what do I know … you suddenly fall out of the canoe … which probably won't happen because you always tie yourself to the bow. … But, what if this happens some night? You fall into the muddy water of the river without any of the Yanomamis, who paddle silently to the light of the stars, noticing. And so, without further ado, you go and drown. …

BONPLAND　It already did happen. I swam to the bank. I don't see your point. …

HUMBOLDT (*exploding, tossing aside the objection*)　You drown! You go and drown!

BONPLAND　Okay, Alex, I drown. Let's get to work. You do your part. Take the measurements.

Humboldt sets about taking measurements. He picks up a kind of case and approaches one of the instruments.

HUMBOLDT You drown ... and from scientific rigor you pass into *rigor mortis* and here I remain without the key to the wine cellar.

BONPLAND There's still light, but you have to hurry. ...

HUMBOLDT Or better ... I meant ... worse: You're eaten by the piranhas that obsess you so much ... and I'm left without the key to the chest full of bottles of Riesling, of Orvietto.

Bonpland now takes possession of the canteen. He gives it a long kiss. He lies down on the floor, reclining his head on the open herbarium. Humboldt copies down the readings with infinite carelessness. He whispers the measurements secretly. Bonpland now produces a box similar to the rest of the instrument cases.

HUMBOLDT (*intrigued*) What are your carrying there?

BONPLAND My flute (*pauses*), hurry up. The moon departs at 9:56 tonight and we still have to dismantle this platform and assemble the nocturnal instruments. ...

Bonpland clumsily attacks a chromatic scale: after making a mistake he begins again. Humboldt verifies the measurements.

HUMBOLDT (*musingly*) Sixteen degrees Réaumur ... Ridiculous! I think your thermometer is up to its old tricks, Jean Claude.

BONPLAND It's your thermometer. And don't call me Jean Claude.

HUMBOLDT Fine, I'll say that it's a question of an irregular climate ... for the amazement of the Academies.

HUMBOLDT (*taking careful note*) Sixteen degrees Réaumur. Remembering to translate to centigrade. ...

BONPLAND You exasperate me with your indifference. Are you really thinking of doing that?

HUMBOLDT And why not? It's the New World. The people will want to hear paradoxes, facts inconsistent with theory ... I can't speak of Amazons or Sirens. ... But indeed I can, how shall I put it ... hide certain imperfections of the instruments. ... After all, what are we? Hunters of inconsistencies ... seekers of irregularities ... like this idiotic branch of the river that interests you so much.

BONPLAND Casiquiare. It's called the Casiquiare.

HUMBOLDT Which flows to the Amazon in the summer. ...

BONPLAND (*correcting him*) To the Orinoco in the dry season. ...

HUMBOLDT What dry season? And to the Orinoco in the rainy season. ...

BONPLAND No, no ... it's the other way around. ...

HUMBOLDT (*exasperated*) It runs up here half of the time and over there the rest of the year. You like it better that way?

BONPLAND It's not very precise. ...

HUMBOLDT As precise as your river. (*pause*) We'd be better off in Egypt, old man. They don't have more than one season over there and the only irregularities are Napoleon's riflemen.

Meanwhile upstage, Humboldt has not stopped taking measurements. He finishes now and remains looking steadfastly at the herbarium, upon which Bonpland rests his head. Black poplars, ferns, and mimosas appear over the edge of the wood.

HUMBOLDT What's that viper doing in our herbarium, Jean Claude? You haven't been mixing up the containers, eh? I'd hate to run into a *Bothrops atrox,* otherwise known as the *mapanare,* among my collection of gymnosperms. ...

Bonpland turns pale from fright: the herbarium is right beside his neck.

BONPLAND (*terrified*) You know that I detest ophiology. That was one of my conditions, remember? No snake collections. I'm a botanist ... not a morbid snake handler.

Humboldt walks by the herbarium with exaggerated caution.

HUMBOLDT Well, a snake is there ... among your gymnosperms ... right by your neck. ...

BONPLAND (*paralyzed with fear*) What does it look like? Does it have an arrow-shaped head?

Humboldt notes something in his case. He murmurs the remark.

~

Camp headquarters of the Humboldt and Bonpland expedition. Hammocks side-by-side with the most sophisticated instruments and forest pets, and, almost always, exotic birds. Humboldt writes to the light of a candle on the table. His voice is heard through the sound system as he writes.

HUMBOLDT "In what ignorance we live, my dear Baron de Forell! Because of the war your note has still not arrived in Havana, and I have already sent Your Excellency more than one reminder since Tenerife, since Cumaná. I've written here a very bad letter, really very sterile. But I won't make excuses: I know that you esteem my person enough so as to be pleased merely by notice of my existence and good health. This will go to Madrid by way of the good fortune of the messenger of Havana. I'll send it from the neighboring mission of the Capuchin friars. I gave reports of myself in some letter for Saxony, to all my friends from Dresden and Freiberg. How I miss Dresden, Florence on the Elbe! In the cities they spoke here only of the terrible storm that the Spanish Armada suffered before Cartagena. ..."

Meanwhile upstage, Bonpland has discovered, foreseeably, the absence of serpents in his herbarium. He retreats to the thicket, panting from anger. He throws the herbarium at Humboldt's head. Humboldt happens to dodge it.

HUMBOLDT What the hell is wrong with you?

Bonpland throws himself at Humboldt and clutches the Baron's throat. [...]

Bonpland has not neglected to read Humboldt's writing.

BONPLAND What Capuchin mission are you talking about in this letter? There aren't any Capuchin missions for miles around. Why are you writing all of this to Baron de Forell? My god, Alex. ... [...]

HUMBOLDT "You have no idea of the dangers that we face, Baron. Poisonous vipers, overflowing rivers, and the malignant hostility of the native tribes, for the most part assumed to be cannibals, although I give no credit to these opinions. Father Junípero, from the neighboring Franciscan mission, confirmed the strange conduct of the Casiquiare branch, tributary of the Orinoco half the year and of the Amazon the rest of the time. ..."

A most sad air on the flute begins to be heard, played slowly. Humboldt stops his pen to listen. He looks up. He inhales profoundly.

Lights fade.

~

Noon light over Bonpland.

BONPLAND I, Aimé Bonpland, naturalist and Mason and in disconcerted maturity have sketched pieces, always incomplete but suggestive pieces, of the anatomy of the capybara, also called *chigüire;* sketches that to me are always fraying around the edges until turning into the scene, into rosy or bluish backdrops; the specimens always under the sun, always trying to stamp onto the physiognomy of the peccary a certain peaceful smile, an air of elegant gracefulness, over there, close to the flowers and tall weeds. I, who before any impertinence of the instruments, postpone judgment and confer benefit of doubt to her without equal, ineffable Mother Nature, saying to myself, perplexed: "she will know."

Because I, Aimé Bonpland, do nothing more than yield myself. I give myself up even to the moody scrutinizer, methodical about what I have declared the sinuous course of the Orinoco, and its wanderings and out-flows, notably the Casiquiare, so pendular and odd, the Casiquiare.

I have cornered the nocturnal habits of the Guácharo bird (curious little animal).

I have sensed the sea, slimy and Precambrian. Over there, on the other hand, where men today hang their hammocks and where they love and are tossed about I have seen the sea changing, enameled, foggy, in the middle of the jungle.

Finally, I have advanced by my deed the scientific knowledge of my time: I have not done so alone, truly: my faithful and well-intentioned collaborator Alex von Humboldt accompanies me and helps me: a little too German, he is, a little obstinate, a little pompous, but a good fellow, in the end.

In the end, I, Aimé Bonpland, remarkable man of the Spirit, Sentinel of Illustration, must not complain. No? I don't have any reason to complain. But it happens ... and I blush to confess it ... that I have gotten lost.

A most languishing pause in which sounds of the woods dominate. The wind, stirred up, howls without cease. End of the pause.

BONPLAND I wanted to say: I became lost in the jungle. This is horrible. This never happened to me before. My compass doesn't work. That's how things are: I, Aimé Bonpland, am lost!

HUMBOLDT (*offstage, asserting himself above the clamor of monkeys and cockatoos*) Jean Claude! Where are you?

⁓

Hotel D'Anjou, Paris, circa 1812 [...]

BONPLAND (*mildly*) I'm going to go back there.

HUMBOLDT You are about to tell me that you're going back there? To America? In the middle of the War of Independence? You must have gone crazy.

BONPLAND War of Independence? I thought that there were wars only here. At this time of the year, I mean.

HUMBOLDT Well, buddy, for having been a naval surgeon during the war you're not very perceptive. This fetid air of rotten spring that one breathes here ... is becoming popular in other latitudes. ...

BONPLAND I thought only Napoleon hatched wars. So they were conspiring. ...

HUMBOLDT They were conspiring. They were drinking chocolate and coffee ... and conspiring. You didn't realize it because you were busy watching the theodolite.

BONPLAND They're liberating themselves, then. I would have said that they were good people. ... (*pause*) You mean to say ... war?

HUMBOLDT Devastated land, mobilizations, rifles with bayonets and things like that ... (*pause*) War. It would be better if you went back to your watercolors of the laughing gulls ... they aren't there for safe conducts. If they can they'll melt your theodolite to make cannonballs. They don't travel very lightly, as we say.

Bonpland collapses into an armchair, overwhelmed.

BONPLAND And I came to ask you for a letter of recommendation for Schiller.

HUMBOLDT Schiller?

BONPLAND No. Schiller, the agent at the customs house of Schiller-Klopstock in Hamburg. I wanted him to be responsible for the charter fee ... and for the packing and the details. And new letters of recommendation for our friends from Caracas and Havana. (*recalling*) This fellow ... Vicente Emparán. ... Where will he go?

HUMBOLDT I don't know him.

BONPLAND And Bolívar? He visited us coming on two years ago, here in Paris.

HUMBOLDT You're talking about the arrogant fop who drinks coffee and speaks interminably about Montecuculli? I dropped the correspondence with this snob. He pretended certain interest in science but refused to climb the Ávila, feigning a gastric indisposition.

BONPLAND He had means, connections. ... I thought that you were keeping track of all those. You were always meticulous in taking down names, streets. ...

HUMBOLDT I threw it all into the sea, before Marseilles, upon returning.

BONPLAND Why? Didn't you think of going back?

HUMBOLDT I never really wanted to go. (*pause*) My idea was that we arrive in Egypt, collect some specimens under the protection of Napoleon and his soldiers ... you were the one who insisted (*imitating him*): "Spanish America, Alex, the unclassified species, Alex, the equinoctial regions, Alex. ..." (*pause*) Fine. So we went, didn't we? And here we are now. The best we can do is to put into order this assortment of stuffed ducks that are infested with lichens in my laboratory. (*pause*) I'm not very happy with your work, by the way ... furthermore. ... Oh, but why all this foolishness about returning to America?

BONPLAND (*solemn*) I was invited by the most excellent Don Bernardino Rivadavia to form part of the team of scientific assessors of the very new republic of Argentina.

Humboldt lets go with loud laughter.

HUMBOLDT "Bernardino" who?

BONPLAND "Ri-va-da-via." (*pause*) I informed Señor Rivadavia of my unfortunate dismissal from the Jardin des Plantes in Paris and, considering that I'm a liberal and facing the unavoidable fact that Napoleon has defrauded all republican expectations in Europe, he clearly had to invite me to live in that young, strong equinoctial nation. I'm considering, in turn, that I hadn't much knowledge to contribute to your peculiar conception of work. In short, I am finding myself very bored and overwhelmed by my economic misfortunes and, in the absence of incentives in postconsular France, I accepted. They offer me a botanical garden of my very own, none of that stinginess of Malmaison's where I had lunch with the grooms ... the climate is good ... the pay should be better ... everything is cheaper ... soon there will be republics ... I will be able to continue my modest study of mimosas. ... What's more, I'm getting married.

HUMBOLDT Oh, come on, Jean Claude. ... You're not about to ... ? I always warned you about them. Slick wordsmiths. They love only the public. What are you going to do with an actress in America?

BONPLAND I want to go. Here I have no more qualifications for life than that of a naval surgeon. And nobody wants a self-educated botanist. Over there everything begins anew. There won't be as many touchy persons as in the Botanical Garden. I want to go, that's all. If you're looking for a good botanist, a good artist, write me a note with the details. If you can, if you want. ...

HUMBOLDT I don't want. Don't go. They don't expect this of us.

BONPLAND Who?

HUMBOLDT All of them. The Académie Française. The Royal Society of London, the Saxony Department of Science.

BONPLAND They expect something from us?

Humboldt encircles the arms of his traveling companion and collaborator.

HUMBOLDT It so happens that we were dealt a bad hand and are screwed, old man. It's impossible to walk there, elegantly, picking up mimosas and naming crocodiles. Above all, for the peace of those who are unaware that the caiman of the Orinoco is not, strictly speaking, a crocodile.

BONPLAND They don't know it.

HUMBOLDT Of course they don't know it! But it calms them that someone knows it. That you and I know it. We're ready, skinny-boy. It occurs only to us to discover that curare is digestible, that the ceiba tree is self-pollinating, that the plantain is a healing agent.

BONPLAND We didn't discover it ourselves. Shamans already knew those things when we arrived.

HUMBOLDT True. But the Yanomami shamans don't travel on the Royal Society of London's dime. That's the difference. Consider that well. What are you going to do now that you know that the Casiquiare runs to the Amazon in winter and to the Orinoco in summer ... ?

BONPLAND It's the other way around ... over there in summer ... over the other way in winter. ...

HUMBOLDT You see? Even I myself am not clear about it. Don't you realize? The Casiquiare is an anomaly. And the unique ... how to phrase it ... the only exchange value of this anomaly realizes itself here, in Europe, in universities and academies. ... Is it that the naturalness with which all the Guahibos took it didn't upset you? (*he imitates them*) "Ah, yes ... the Orinoco ... has always been there." To whom are you going to sell what you know? To Bernardino Rivadavia? He's probably already going to buy rifles in Holland to inaugurate a civil war. To the Yekuana Indians? You're fooling yourself. You have to stay. You can't go. Even less now that Napoleon's going to Russia ... and us with him.

Bonpland returns, dispassionately, to look at him. Humboldt lowers his face.

HUMBOLDT I'm saying, if he succeeds. If he can stay there then it's very likely that we can go to Asiatic Russia, to the Ural regions, to the Altai Mountains ... the Caspian region. It's what we've been waiting for all these years; the chance to complete the work on the volcanic origin of earthquakes. We'll buy maps, instruments. ... I'll need a good technician. What's this about going to America? Nobody's going back to America!

BONPLAND (*perplexed*) The Altai Mountains?

HUMBOLDT (*enthusiastically*) What's more, it's this matter of 45,000 thaler. You can't go. I need a good technician when we go to Russia. ...

BONPLAND Forty-five thousand thaler? Russia?

HUMBOLDT (*dryly*) I've been talking to you about this trip for years, Jean Claude.

BONPLAND Don't call me Jean Claude.

HUMBOLDT And if this dwarf, Napoleon, is lucky and succeeds before setting out and they return the protectorate to the King of Freedonia-Ruritania, we could go to Russia and make geomagnetic measurements. It's very easy. With Napoleon and the forty-five thousand thaler from the Embassy the miles that separate us from Russia have never been shorter.

BONPLAND Do you realize that this fellow has complicated things since we have been in this business?

HUMBOLDT What fellow?

BONPLAND Napoleon, of course. In 1799 we were waiting for an expedition organized by the Revolutionary Directorate to take a trip around the world on a scientific mission. Who ruined everything?

HUMBOLDT The consul Bonaparte. But he was a little novice, one has to admit.

BONPLAND In the end it was necessary to settle for Egypt. And we couldn't even reach Tunis because that idiot had to go and declare war on Spain.

HUMBOLDT The idea of America wasn't Napoleon's. We should have waited. Champollion waited and had his stone.

BONPLAND "Fly to Russia with the Ambassador." Who has seen you, Alex ... !

HUMBOLDT And what's wrong with going to Russia? They speak French. They don't cut off heads like in Peru.

Bonpland gets ready to leave.

BONPLAND Good, that will spoil your trip to Russia.

HUMBOLDT What makes you so sure?

BONPLAND He can't always win. Like the saying goes. ...

HUMBOLDT and BONPLAND (*in unison*) ... "Winter is the Russian's best friend!"

BONPLAND (*hopelessly*) You don't know what temperance is. You've never formulated a sensible plan. Naming each rock on the planet, eh? Well, hurry up. You're already old for expeditions. You haven't even finished with the American exhibits. ... And you want to go to Russia! What's so bad about my returning, hmm?

HUMBOLDT They don't understand, they never understand. ... I'll spend my life explaining evidence (*raising his voice*): Someone has to go and give a name to the things and no one will do it if I don't go. As far as my relations with Napoleon. ...

BONPLAND You have none, apart from the subsidy from the Academy. Neither good nor bad. He treated you as a collector, remember? Not even as a spy. He didn't even extend his hand. He said only: "Ah, Humboldt ... I've heard tell that you collect plants."

HUMBOLDT And then he added that his wife, Josephine, collected them, too. And I say, what does it matter! This shows that we'll have to manage with this dwarf for a little bit and that progress cannot wait for the dawn of liberty and parliamentarianism. Bonaparte is the best travel agent that I know of.

BONPLAND Progress ... ! Liberty ... ! A nice pair of reasons to want to return to America, certainly not all of mine, I hasten to say.

HUMBOLDT You don't believe in progress?

BONPLAND Like an ascetic believes in demons. (*suddenly persuasive*) Alex ... I only ask you to lend me the instruments. ... I want to go from here. ... I'm fed up with invasions ... money of the occupation forces. ...

HUMBOLDT That's exactly what's happening over there.

BONPLAND I would like ... to be able to dedicate myself to a single aspect ... for the entire time necessary. Certainly I've been negligent ... but that's because you overwhelm me with your rhythm. You jump from a volcanic map to ... to a sketch of I don't know what emaciated eel of the Andes. ... (*pause*) And I don't want to see you growing old and to hear your liberal chatter while you serve in the court of Frederick Wilhelm.

HUMBOLDT The King of Prussia won't want to know anything of me.

BONPLAND He will want to know of you, that's for sure. They will offer you, that I know ... the Berlin Academy. ... Clearly, they'll first have to bind themselves together, Russians and Austrians and English, and roll up to Napoleon and his Oriental-trousered battalions. The question is ... How long will they delay? Will you travel again? Alex ... there won't be a republic or a free press or organized unions ... this is an American dream. Lend me your instruments.

HUMBOLDT Okay ... I'll give you those letters tomorrow. ... And I'll tell Seifert that he should help you to pack the equipment.

Humboldt rings the bell on his coat for sounding the time, a sign of leaving.

BONPLAND This ... is supposed to be a farewell ... a little more tearful. ...

HUMBOLDT I'm going to shave at Gay-Lussac's house. And it's not a farewell, it's a transfer of instruments.

BONPLAND You're not going to tell me anything more? The way things are there, we may never see each other again.

HUMBOLDT (*dryly*) Remember to leave ten percent for a tip. Now they're more sensitive with Europeans. Come back tomorrow and talk with Seifert.

Bonpland retires, oppressed and silent. Humboldt stops him just before he leaves.

HUMBOLDT Wait!

Humboldt goes to the bar. He takes a small rectangular object. He extends it to Bonpland.

HUMBOLDT You're going to need it. ...

BONPLAND No, thanks ... I don't take snuff. It seems like a filthy vice to me.

HUMBOLDT It's not a box of tobacco. It's a portable compass. It can be consulted without dismounting from your horse ... and without stopping the pirogue. ... I don't use it anymore ... only as a paperweight. ...

Bonpland takes it. He says goodbye movingly.

Alone, Humboldt gives free rein to his anger. He detaches objects from the scenery.

HUMBOLDT You'll see, Bonpland ... you're going to reckon with me ... !

Almost immediately the din of Phantom F-105s and of MIG-21s is heard. The nose-dives of bombers and the rat-a-tat-tat of 50-caliber machine guns. The blast of the incendiary bombs follows the vibration of the scenery.

Chapter 86

HANS CHRISTOPH BUCH
Caribbean Cold Breeze
1984

A German universal scholar of the early nineteenth century set standards for the scientific and literary assessment of the Latin American continent which remain valid today. Alexander von Humboldt's *Personal Narrative of a Journey to the Equinoctial Regions of the New Continent* has, even 150 years after its first appearance, lost none of its poetic freshness or political actuality and it still endures as a work of scholarship. That such a pioneering effort should no longer be replicable is not just a factor of the literary inaptitude of contemporary South American travelers or of their deficient education and geographical incompetence, but it also has to do with the aging of the object. In 1799, when Humboldt traveled the Orinoco together with Bonpland, South America was still largely terra incognita, plundered by conquistadors and colonists but it had not been made accessible to natural science and had not been described in literature. The classical educational ideal worked out by Lessing and Herder, by Goethe and Schiller bore the loveliest blooms and the richest fruits when transplanted to tropical land. Yet Humboldt's claim to totality, which incorporated flora and fauna just as much as geology and history, and which ran from prehistoric times to the political state of his own days, is today no longer possible. The synthesis of science and art that Humboldt sought has long since disintegrated into its components—even during his lifetime, the ever-increasing specialization had already displaced the comprehensive survey.

A traveler to South America today therefore finds himself in a situation akin to that of its first discoverers and conquerors: he stands there more or less awestruck before the "marvelous reality" of an unknown continent that disintegrates before his eyes into atomized units and unrelated image fragments. The traditional systems of reference of geography, sociology, and politics have lost their believability; they now contribute more to obscuring this reality than to revealing it. Perhaps the most accurate approach to truth under such circumstances is the one that foregoes a claim to objective truth. With this in mind, my texts pursue representation in ways diametrically opposed to the procedures practiced by Humboldt: they are subjective, personal to the point of private arbitrariness. The things that the author perceives and notes are as much a coincidence of time and place as a reflection of changing moods; his recordings are therefore dated and bear a diary character. The disadvantage of this representational method, its unreliability, is offset by a potential advantage: the traveler runs the risk of errors and misconceptions, but he perceives things that a local resident simply never (or at least no longer) registers because he regards them as insignificant. Both need each other: the traveler needs the local knowledge of the resident just as much as the latter needs the foreign gaze of the traveler. This note does not excuse errors or imprecisions, but does make clear one thing: I have attempted to change the actual wording as little as possible after the fact; where in doubt, I have given priority to uncertain perception over a reflection which intervenes with corrections. The reader will judge the legitimacy of this process.

Chapter 87

Eduardo Galeano

Memory of Fire

1985

1790: Paris

Humboldt

At age twenty, Alexander von Humboldt discovers the ocean and revolution.

At Dunkirk the ocean struck him dumb, and in Calais the moon blossoming from the waves drew a shout of wonder. Astonishment at the sea, revelation of the revolution: in Paris, a year after July Fourteenth, Humboldt lets himself go in the sweet whirlwind of streets in fiesta, merges into the people who dance and sing to their newborn liberty.

He has lived in search of answers and found questions. Without let-up he has inquired of books, of the heavens, and of the earth, pursuing the enigmas of the soul and the mysteries of the cosmos and the secrets of beetles and stones, always in love with the world and with men and women who fill him with dizziness and panic. *Alexander will never be happy,* says his brother Wilhelm, his mother's favorite child.

At twenty, fever of living, fever of going places, Humboldt swears eternal fealty to the banners of the French revolution and swears he will cross the ocean, like Balboa and Robinson Crusoe, to the lands where it is always noon.

1799: Cumaná

Two Wise Men on a Mule

The New World is too big for the eyes of the two Europeans who have just landed at Cumaná. The port sparkles on the river, set aflame by the sun, houses of white timber or bamboo beside the stone fort, and beyond, green sea, green land, the glowing bay. All truly new, never used, never seen: the plumage of the flamingos, the beaks of the pelicans, the sixty-foot coconut trees and the immense velvety flowers, tree trunks padded with lianas and foliage, the eternal siesta of the crocodiles, the skyblue, yellow, red crabs. ... There are Indians sleeping nude on the warm sand, and mulattas dressed in embroidered muslin, their bare feet caressing the places they head. Here there is no tree that does not offer forbidden fruit from the center of the lost garden.

Alexander von Humboldt and Aimé Bonpland rent a house facing the main plaza, with a good flat on which to stand the telescope. Looking upward from this roof they see an eclipse of the sun and a shower of meteors, the angry sky spitting fire through a whole night, and looking down they see how the buyers of slaves open the mouths of blacks newly arrived at the Cumaná market. In this house they experience the first earthquake of their lives; and from it they go out to explore the region. They classify ferns and rare birds and look for Francisco Loyano, who suckled his son for five months and had tits and pure, sweet milk as long as his woman was sick.

Later Humboldt and Bonpland set out for the southern high-lands. They carry their instruments: sextant, compass, thermometer, hygrometer, magnetometer. They also bring paper for drying flowers, bistouries for bird, fish, and crab autopsies; and ink and pen to sketch all the wonders. They go on muleback, weighed down with equipment, the German with the black top hat and blue eyes and the Frenchman with the insatiable magnifying glass.

Perplexed, the forests and mountains of America open up to these two lunatics.

~

1800: Apure River

To the Orinoco

America flames and spins, burned and dizzied by its suns. Giant trees embrace over the rivers and in their shade glows the canoe of the sages.

The canoe progresses pursued by birds and by hungry hordes of gnats and mosquitoes. Slapping continuously, Humboldt and Bonpland defend themselves against the onslaughts of the lancers, which penetrate clothing and skin and reach to the bone, while the German studies the anatomy of the manatee, the fat fish with hands, or the electricity of the eel or the teeth of the piranha, and the Frenchman collects and classifies plants or measures a crocodile or calculates its age. Together they draw maps, register the temperature of the water and the pressure of the air, analyze the mica in the sand and the conches of snails and the passage of Orion's belt across the sky. They want America to tell them all it knows and here not a leaf or pebble is dumb.

They camp in a small cove, unloading the troublesome instruments. They light a fire to ward off mosquitoes, and to cook. Suddenly, the dog harks as if to warn of an approaching jaguar, and runs to hide beneath Bonpland's legs. The toucan that Humboldt carries on his shoulder picks nervously at his straw hat. The undergrowth creaks and from among the trees appears a naked man, copper skin, Indian face, African hair:

"Welcome to my lands, gentlemen."

And he bows to them: "Don Ignacio, at your service."

Don Ignacio makes a face at the improvised fire. The sages are roasting a capybara rat. "That's Indian food," he says disdainfully, and invites them to sup in his house in splendid venison freshly hunted with an arrow.

Don Ignacio's house consists of three nets slung between trees not far from the river. There he presents them to his wife, Doña Isabela, and his daughter, Doña Manuela, not as naked as he is. He offers the travelers cigars. While the venison is browning, he riddles them with questions. Don Ignacio is hungry to know the news of tilt court of Madrid and the latest on those endless wars that are so wounding Europe.

~

1800: Esmeralda del Orinoco

Master of Poison

They sail on down river.

At the foot of a rocky mountain, at the remote Christian mission of Esmeralda, they meet the master of poison. His laboratory is the cleanest and neatest hut in the village. The old Indian, surrounded by smoking cauldrons and clay jugs, pours a yellowish juice into banana leaf cones and palm leaf funnels: the horrifying curare falls drop by drop, and bubbles. The arrow anointed with this curare will enter and kill better than the fang of a snake.

"Better than anything," says the old man, as he chews some liana and tree bark into a paste. "Better than anything you people make."

And Humboldt thinks: *He has the same pedantic tone and the same starchy manner as our pharmacists.*

"You people have invented black powder," the old man continues, as very slowly, with meticulous hand, he pours water onto the paste.

"I know it," he says after a pause, "that powder isn't worth a damn. It's noisy. It's unreliable. Powder can't kill silently and it kills even when you miss your aim."

He revives the fire under the kettles and pots. From within the smoke he asks, "Know how to make soap?"

"He knows," says Bonpland.

The old man looks at Humboldt with respect. "After curare," he says, "soap is the big thing."

~

1800: Uruana

Forever Earth

Opposite the island of Uruana, Humboldt meets the Indians who eat earth.

Every year the Orinoco rises, *the Father of rivers,* flooding its banks for two or three months. While the flood lasts, the Otomacos eat soft clay, slightly hardened by fire, and on that they live. It is pure earth, Humboldt confirms, not mixed with corn flour or turtle oil or crocodile fat.

So these *wandering Indians* travel through life toward death, clay wandering toward clay, erect clay eating the earth that will eat them.

~

1801: Lake Guatavita

The Goddess at the Bottom of the Waters

On the maps of America, El Dorado still occupies a good part of Guyana. The lake of gold takes flight when its hunters approach, and curses and kills them; but on the maps it is a tranquil blot of blue joined to the upper Orinoco.

Humboldt and Bonpland decipher the mystery of the elusive lake. In the glittering mica on a mountain which the Indians call Golden Mountain, they discover part of the hallucination; and another in a little lake which in the rainy season invades the vast plain neighboring the source waters of the Orinoco and then, when the rains cease, disappears.

In Guyana lies the phantom lake, that most tempting of America's deliriums. Far away, on the plateau of Bogotá, is the true El Dorado. After covering many leagues by canoe and mule, Humboldt and Bonpland discover it in the sacred Lake Guatavita. This mirror of waters faithfully reflects even the tiniest leaf in the woods surrounding it: at its bottom lie the treasures of the Muisca Indians.

To this sanctuary came princes, their naked bodies gleaming with gold dust, and at the center of the lake dropped their goldsmiths' finest works, then plunged in themselves. If they came up without a single speck of gold on the skin, the goddess Furatena had accepted their offerings. In those times the goddess Furatena, snake goddess, governed the world from the depths.

~

1801: Bogotá

Mutis

The old monk talks as he peels oranges and an unending shower of gold spirals down into a pan between his feet.

To see him, to listen to him, Humboldt and Bonpland have detoured from their southward route and have gone upriver for forty days. José Celestino Mutis, patriarch of America's botanists, is put to sleep by speeches but enjoys intimate chats as much as anyone.

The three men, sages ever astonished by the beauty and mystery of the universe, exchange plants, ideas, doubts, discoveries. Mutis is excited by talk of Lake Guatavita, the salt mines of Zipaquirá, and the Tequendama waterfall. He praises the map of the Magdalena River which Humboldt has just drawn, and discreetly suggests some changes with the sureness of one who has traveled much and knows much, and knows very deep inside himself that something of him will remain in the world.

And he shows everything and tells everything. While he eats and offers oranges, Mutis speaks of the letters that Linnaeus wrote him, and of how much those letters taught him, and of the problems he had with the Inquisition. And he recalls and shares his discoveries about the curative powers of quinine bark, and the influence of the moon on the barometer, and the cycles of flowers, which sleep as we do and stretch and wake up little by little, unfurling their petals.

~

1802: Chimborazo Volcano

On the Roofs of the World

They climb over clouds, amid abysses of snow, clinging to the rough body of Chimborazo, tearing their hands against the naked rock.

They have left the mules half-way up. Humboldt carries on his shoulder a bag full of stones that speak of the origin of the Andean cordillera, born of an unusual vomiting from the earth's incandescent belly. At seventeen thousand feet Bonpland has caught a butterfly, and higher up an incredible fly, and they have continued climbing, despite the bitter cold and vertigo and slippings and the blood that spurts from their eyes and gums and parted lips. Mist envelops them as they climb blindly up the volcano, until a shaft of light breaks through and strips bare the summit, that high white tower, before the astounded travelers. Is it real, could it be? Never has any man climbed so close to the sky, and it is said that on the roofs of the world appear horses flying to the clouds and colored stars at noon. Is it a hallucination, this cathedral of snow rearing up between north and south skies? Are not their bruised eyes deceiving them?

Humboldt feels an abundance of light more intense than any delirium: we are made of light, Humboldt feels, of light ourselves, and of light the earth and time, and he feels a tremendous urge to tell it right away to brother Goethe, over there at his home in Weimar.

~

1804: Mexico City

Spain's Richest Colony

Theology professors still earn five times more than their colleagues in surgery or astronomy, but Humboldt finds in Mexico City an astonishing nursery of young scientists. This is the heritage of some Jesuit priests, friends of experimental physics, the new chemistry, and certain theories of Descartes, who despite the Inquisition taught and contaminated here; and it is also the work of the viceroy Revillagigedo, a man open to the winds of time, defier of dogmas, who a few years ago governed these lands with anguished concern about the lack of machines and laboratories and modern books to read.

Humboldt discovers and praises the School of Mining and its learned professors, while Mexico produces more silver than all the rest of the world, a river of silver flowing to Europe through the port of Veracruz. At the same time, Humboldt warns that cultivated land is little and badly worked, and that the colonial monopoly of commerce and the poverty of the people block the development of manufacturing. *Mexico is the land of inequality,* he notes. *The monstrous inequality of rights and fortunes* hits one in the face. Counts and marquises paint newly purchased coats-of-arms on their carriages, and the people live in a misery that is the enemy of all industry. The Indians suffer atrocious penury. As in all of America, here too, *more or less white skin decides what class a man occupies in society.*

~

1804: Paris

Napoleon

The solemn chords of the organ invoke the sixty kings who have ruled France, and perhaps too the angels, while the pope offers the crown to Napoleon Bonaparte.

Napoleon wreathes his own brow with the laurel of the Caesars. Then he descends, slowly, majestic in ermine and purple, and places on Josephine the diadem that consecrates her as the first empress in France's history. In a gold and crystal coach they have reached the throne of this nation, the small foreigner, great warrior, sprouted from the harsh mountains of Corsica, and his wife Josephine, born in Martinique, an Antillean whose embrace they say will burn you to a crisp. Napoleone, the artillery lieutenant who hated Frenchmen, becomes Napoleon I.

The founder of the dynasty that is inaugurated today has rehearsed this coronation ceremony a thousand times. Each personage in the retinue, each actor, has dressed as he prescribed, has placed himself where he wanted, has moved the way he ordered.

"Oh, Joseph! If our father could see us. ..."

The voracious relatives, princes and princesses of France's new nobility, have done their duty. True, the mother, Laeticia, has refused to come, and is in the palace murmuring grudges, but Napoleon will order David, the official artist, to give Laeticia a prominent place in the painting which will tell posterity of these ceremonials.

The guests overflow the cathedral of Notre Dame. Among them, a young Venezuelan cranes his neck to miss no detail. At twenty, a hallucinated Simón Bolívar attends the birth of the Napoleonic monarchy: *I am no more than a diamond on the handle of Bonaparte's sword. ...*

During these days, in a gilded salon in Paris, Bolívar has met Alexander von Humboldt. The adventurer-sage, newly arrived from America, has said to him, *"I think your country is ripe for independence, but I don't see the man who can. ..."*

~

1858: San Borja

Let Death Die

His sore body is aching to mix itself with the American earth. Aimé Bonpland knew this was where he would end up and linger on, ever since that distant day when he landed with Humboldt on the Caribbean coast.

Bonpland dies of his death, in a mud and straw hut, serenely, knowing that the stars do not die; that ants and people will not stop being born; that there will be new cloverleaves, and new oranges or suns on the branches; and that foals, newly upright on their mosquito legs, will be stretching out their necks in search of a teat. The old man bids farewell to the world as a child does to the day at bedtime.

Afterwards, a drunk stabs the body; but this sinister imbecility of mankind is a detail of no importance.

~

1879: Chincha Islands

Guano

Pure shit were the hills that rose on these islands. For millennia, millions of birds had concluded their digestive process on the coast of southern Peru.

The Incas knew that this guano could revive any land, however dead it seemed; but Europe did not know the magical powers of the Peruvian fertilizer until Humboldt brought back the first samples.

Peru, which had gained worldwide prestige for silver and gold, perpetuated its glory thanks to the goodwill of the birds. Europeward sailed ships laden with malodorous guano, and returned bringing statues of pure Carrara marble to decorate Lima's boulevards. Their holds were also filled with English clothing, which ruined the textile mills of the southern sierra, and Bordeaux wines which bankrupted the national vineyards of Moquequa. Entire houses arrived at Callao from London. From Paris were imported whole luxury hotels complete with chefs.

After forty years, the islands are exhausted. Peru has sold twelve million tons of guano, has spent twice as much, and now owes a candle to every saint.

Chapter 88

RAINER SIMON

My Chimborazo Journals
1987–1988

27 June 1987

Thanks to Alexander von Humboldt, the film could become the first cooperative film and television production between both German states. [...]
 The time one otherwise sleeps away suffices to reach the other side of the
globe. It seems small and very vulnerable. One inevitably thinks about lost opportunities, about lifetime and purpose, stolen by a ban on travel. To produce
a film about Alexander von Humboldt means to think about a man who to the
utmost extent tried to give meaning to his life. One must be just toward this his
claim. Every single person has the right to this claim.

28 June 1987

During the night over the Atlantic I'm tormented by nearly unbearable stomach pains that I've never known before. I do know, however, that before all of
my travels to western countries I contract some kind of sickness. I call this
my GDR-travel syndrome. One always trembles to the very last minute: Will
I actually partake of the grace that allows one to travel? Will the passport, the
visa, the tickets be issued on time and not be left lying with some indifferent
bureaucrat? The body makes provision to cope with possible disappointment:
You couldn't have traveled anyway, because you'd gotten sick.

Translation by Richard John Ascárate, from Ranier Simon, *Meine Chimborazo-Tagebücher,* in Paul
Kanut Schäfer and Rainer Simon, *Die Besteigung des Chimborazo. Eine Filmexpedition auf Alexander
von Humboldts Spuren* (Köln: vgs, 1990), 120, 120–129, 130–132, 141–142, 143, 144, 146, 147–148,
151–152, 152, 153–154, 156, 156, 157. Used by permission of Rainer Simon.

3 July 1987

My first impression of Chimborazo is not only stamped with fascination, also by an awe-inspiring respect. And it will be the same as often as I see it. I understand very well that the Indians today—following the mythological tradition—still personify and call it *Tayta*, father, and offer it worshipful gifts. [...]

Beyond San Juan, before one arrives again at the endless Tierra del Fuego-Alaska Street, the *Carretera Panamericana*, white dust covers the eucalyptus and agave trees. The cement factory "Chimborazo" pollutes the air. We stop in Calpi. We're familiar with the place from Humboldt's travel diaries. From here he ascended to Chimborazo. A few years earlier, one of the most terrifying earthquakes had toppled the entire province. The ruins of the little old church serve as a constant reminder thereof. By the new, large church beside it a bronze tablet commemorates famous personalities who have visited the Calpi parish of Saint Jacob:

> Personajes ilustres que visitaron la parroquia de Calpi ("Eminent persons who have visited the church of Calpi")
> Alejandro Humboldt (22 June 1802)
> Simón Bolívar (5 July 1822) [...]

In the opening of one of the huts sits an ancient *indígena* woman. We greet one another. I ask if I may take some pictures. She consents. Then she refers me to her husband, who sits in the other *choza*. I want to explain to him why I am here, but receive no answer. The woman smiles: He hasn't heard a thing, she says, for the last twenty years. As usual whenever I have contact with the *indígenas*, I sense a great inner friendliness offered to me. I try to imagine how a European would react if a completely strange Indian were to suddenly stand there before the apartment door and ask for permission to look around inside just to suit his own purposes. Here in San Gerardo I first envision the scene of the encounter between Humboldt and an old, female highland Indian.

6 July 1988

Cotopaxi veils the rim of its crater, but the weather is agreeable. A few tourists are at the hut; three English youths coming with their skis from the peak; a family from Quito takes in the sun, the thirteen-year old boy films with a video camera. During a conversation we discuss his equipment and ours. When he hears that we want to make a film about Humboldt, he immediately knows all about it: Ah, Alejandro Humboldt, the famous explorer! The experience will repeat itself over and over. Humboldt seems to be better known in Ecuador than in Europe. We're approached on the street, in the market, in the villages: So you're the team making the Humboldt film! Television, press, and radio constantly give accounts of our work in live interviews, reports about film-making and such.

8 July 1988

A metaphoric setting, the black silhouettes of the *indígenas*. I, the European, explain to these foreign people why I have come to them. I know and they know that whites seldom came to them for honorable reasons. A young man from the village translates into Quechua because the women hardly understand Spanish. We're asked who Humboldt was. An older man wants to know how films were made two hundred years ago. The youths laugh at the question. Several of them have portable stereos and carry them around proudly as a status symbol. The terms of payment are discussed. They want me to confirm what was just negotiated. All the actors are supposed to receive the same daily wage, independent of the importance of their roles. More important, however, is that the entire community gains something from the making of the film, everyone is supposed to benefit: a pump house for watering the fields is to be built.

Illustration 88.1. Actors and members of the village cooperative on location in Ecuador.

11 July 1988

In our film, Humboldt's homosexuality—of which we're convinced—shall not
be taboo, as in almost all, including modern, biographies. Pedro Schütt proph-
esies to me: With this film you'll provoke the displeasure of the ideologues in
the GDR, frighten the commercially-oriented distributors in Western Europe,
and the Macho-Latinos will have a hard time tolerating a homosexual representation of Humboldt.

18 July 1988

We can't do any filming, because the trucks with the pack animals have not arrived. Hours go by. Tayta Fortunato shows me the props for his shaman rituals.
Little stones and knuckle bones, small dried plants, scraps of paper, matches,
pulverized materials, everything laid out on a sheet of newspaper. He is very
anxious, afraid of having forgotten something or incurring my displeasure.
Also we have to clarify whether rum or the home-distilled *puro* should be used
to *challate* [ritual of spraying a mouthful of liquor]. We carefully separate out all
that is modern, agree on the *puro,* and the ritual is explained to us. But I don't
want to rehearse it, I fear that some of the authenticity might be worn off. [...]

   We can begin. A look through the viewing glass promises a large hole in the
clouds. Tayta Fortunato addresses the mountains, but the first time he sprays

Illustration 88.2. The film crew at the base of the Chimborazo.

the *puro* over a long staff in the direction of the volcano, the young *caravane-ros* express amusement. They don't want us to assume that they still believe in such heathen customs. But once they've understood that they are to react as people from Humboldt's time, the invocation proceeds with great concentration, interrupted only by the changing of our film cartridges. As the shaman concluded with prolonged *challating* on all of the mountains, the older *caravaneros* call upon the mountains with the Quechua formula, *shamui*: Shamui Cotopaxi!—Shamui Rumiñahui!—Shamui Sangay!—Shamui Mama Tungurahua!—Shamui Tayta Chimborazo!

24 July 1988

The martyrdom at Cotopaxi continues. We've filmed on the glacier for two days in every kind of weather. Not without compromises. Each of us feels that he won't be able to make the ascent the next day. [...]

Questioning Jan Liefers, Olivier Pascalin, Luis Miguel Campos, and Pedro Sisa over and over: Can you do it? Can you still make it? Indeterminable whether their exhaustion is as real as they communicate to us. The sun breaks through, the next minute it snows again. Marco shouts to Pedro that he should close his eyes in the glistening light so as not to contract snow blindness. The others wear dark goggles. As they arrived where we were, Klaus Friedrich steps into action and aggravates—per Humboldt's description—the high altitude

Illustration 88.3. Crossing snow fields on the way to climb Chimborazo.

symptoms in their faces: bloody, swollen lips; red, haggard eyes; bleeding from the gums and nose. We haven't endured the extremes that Humboldt describes. In two hundred years of cumulative mountain climbing has the human constitution better adapted itself? Or did Humboldt exaggerate? All in all, his diaries don't give this impression. He never makes a display of what he suffered.

2 August 1988

First day of filming in La Moya. The evening before, Pocho and Alejandro once again spoke with us about the fundamental requirement of this work. Every member of the village cooperative has the same rights, even every child, yes, even every animal, every plant. While working, preserve peace, don't become nervous, no huts, no field entered without permission, no animals chased away, the children as respectfully handled as the adults. I don't believe there will be any difficulties. I suspect that our friends from ASOCINE exaggerate somewhat the precautions. For I believe that the *indígenas* exactly sense the inner condition of one who approaches them. At the same time, they also know of our open-mindedness to their culture and the self-evident respect that we show them. They see through every kind of arrogance and fawning.

3 August 1988

Filming at night occurs under the most difficult lighting conditions. Roland must improvise with three, four small lamps. Juan Guamán sings—following a self-written text—a song about Humboldt's arrival at Chimborazo. Then we film all of the scenes involving María Silveria, who plays the old woman. We film without rehearsals, but with retakes. I'm very happy how María makes the screenplay—conceived by us—thoroughly and openly her own existential concern. Afterwards, all of the scenes with Jan Liefers. I say to him, you can get through this only if you completely trust in yourself, I absolutely forbid you to act. He understood very well and surrenders his whole being to his emotions. As he approaches the woman, kneels before her, she strokes his head with hard motions of her hands as if in blessing. We understand this moment as far and away beyond mere film.

5 August 1988

The overwhelming warmth with which all thank us, young and old, embarrasses me. Why? We must thank them for their helpfulness, for our being accepted into another cultural world, one which could not be friendlier. We remain Europeans and will never really understand it, but it's nevertheless no longer foreign to us.

A sad, painful farewell. For as many times as I must promise Pedro, Alfonso, and Juanito to come again—we all know it would take a miracle for us ever to see each other again. And it remains the anxious question how life in La Moya will now go on after our film. Have we perhaps, especially among the youth, awakened hopes and desires that have no chance of ever being fulfilled? But are not hope and desire inalienable prerequisites in striving for change as well?

10 August 1988

We pass the time by exchanging German and Quechua terms with the natives, just the way the scene in the film is conceived. In the end, we film in fog a few scenes that take place at dawn.

11 August 1988

We're now filming the scene in which Humboldt and the *indígenas* learn Quechua and German from one other. I give both Jan and the *indígenas* different terms that they are supposed to make understandable to one another. It's

Illustration 88.4. Humboldt and the *indígenas* learn Quechua and German from one other.

filmed without rehearsal and with two cameras to achieve the utmost authenticity. Communication at that time between Humboldt and the natives can hardly have been different.

12 August 1988

Three hours we wait and implore the ice giant. He no longer allows the camera a view. He looms from eon to eon in the heavens and has had enough of us mayflies and our filmic vanities. We break up at noon. That doesn't bother him. As we are already on the way to Riobamba, he shines again in the most majestic light.

Chapter 89

PAUL KANUT SCHÄFER AND RAINER SIMON
The Ascent of Chimborazo
1988

A Literary Film Script

Scene 14 The Second Columbus

Madrid (1799)—The colossal mass of the royal palace stretches high and steep above the garden of Campo del Moro and must appear to the little man sitting on the grass below like an invincible fortress.

Not Humboldt.

"It's a bad joke!" he rages. "My life hangs from the silk thread of a decision by the Spanish king! Why must I ask a king where I am allowed to travel?"

"C'est la vie."

Bonpland shrugs his shoulders; with the magnifying glass he scrutinizes a leaf that he, undisturbed by the distrustful glance of a royal halberdier, had snapped from an overseas shrub.

"I travel using *my own* money! I travel solely and alone for scientific ends! For which humanity will one time be grateful to me!"

"Don't let the fathers of the Inquisition hear that. Good that you have patrons at court. Is the king even here?"

"Not here. The noble ladies and gentlemen are in Aranjuez, their spring residence. Tomorrow I'll take a coach there and stand before the face of His Catholic Majesties. But I won't kneel. And if they believe they sit at the left and right hand of God's throne, I'll speak to them like dear God Himself."

Translation by Richard John Ascárate, from Paul Kanut Schäfer and Rainer Simon, *Die Besteigung des Chimborazo. Literarische Filmerzählung*, in *Die Besteigung des Chimborazo. Eine Filmexpedition auf Alexander von Humboldts Spuren* (Köln: vgs, 1990), 94–95, 96–98, 109–110. Used by permission of Rainer Simon.

Illustration 89.1. Humboldt has an audience with Carlos IV of Spain to obtain permission to travel in the Spanish colonies.

Immensely self-aware, Humboldt strides into the dining hall, paying no attention to the gestures of the grandees who are supposed to indicate to him how far before the royal table he may stand. He knows his place.

The royals scrutinize him thoroughly and he, for his part, studies them in no less detail. They seem to have stepped from the painting of the master in the antechamber.

The breaking table is ravaged, dessert is already at hand: exotic fruits he has never seen before and *flan,* the Spanish custard with caramel sauce, which—since coming to Madrid—he gorges upon daily like a child. He loves confections and rolls his eyes a bit. Is the queen not smiling?

With a gesture of his hand, the king bids Humboldt speak.

"My wishes," he says, "are already known to your majesty."

Carlos IV is somewhat surprised. He is accustomed to the endless laments of petitioners. He taps the fruit knife on the table, upon which the long and tedious ritual of passing carafes to and fro takes place, so as to convey the desired glass of wine to the royal lips. Humboldt can look down upon all of them, the kneeling knight and the sitting royal couple. He alone stands. That suits his address, which is also as from above:

"Three hundred years have passed since Columbus's ships landed upon American coasts. Yet, the continent remains scientifically unexplored. Before you stands the rediscoverer of America, the second Columbus. Besides in my aims, I differ from the first in that I travel as a private person, supported by my own resources, without commission from any national power."

The king bids him be silent and listens mouth ajar to the chorus of his favorites, the clocks. One of the little voices rattles. All of a sudden, he acts quite ordinary and requires no one to assist him from his chair. He simply stands and opens the clock mechanism to repair the cause of the broken voice.

"Huulbald?" he asks, smiling.

"Humboldt, your Majesty." Alexander is accustomed to even more mangled pronunciations of his name. "Just Humboldt."

"Sí, sí. El Despacho Universal de Gracia y Justicia de España é Indias … The universal message of mercy and justice from Spain and the Indies … *Wie heißt deutsch?* What is German?" Proud and mischievous: "I can speak German!"

"*La gracia,* mercy—*die Gnade.*"

"Ah—!" The king allows the word to melt in his mouth: "*Die Gnade. …*"

"You have beautiful clocks, your Majesty."

"Sí, sí."

"Much more beautiful than my scientific instruments."

"Instrumentos?" María Luisa von Parma tears apart a piece of fruit with her fingers. The languid bedroom eyes of the fifty-year old have lingered upon this young, self-confident intruder since he entered. "Quiero ver sus instrumentos … I want to see your instruments."

"Nothing would afford me greater pleasure, your Majesty. If you so desire, I shall display for you *all* of my instruments."

While she allows a page to clean her sticky fingers, María Luisa exchanges a look with the king that he understands only too well. She has always governed him in the interest of her favorites. And so Humboldt hears from the lips of Carlos IV himself that overseas officials will carry every order, Mr. Humboldt—or Huulbald?—to be received with the utmost courtesy in all Spanish possessions.

Scene 15 Eye to Eye with Father Chimborazo: The Ascent

The four—Humboldt, Bonpland, Montúfar, Pacho—have stepped across the eternal snowline. Their heads are wrapped in scarves. The strain of the ascent has distorted their faces beyond recognition. Hearts rage, lungs draw air in ever faster rhythm. Bonpland attempts to insert a thermometer into the snow and loses so much energy through the simple act that he does not rise again for a long time. Arms outstretched, Montúfar leans with his chest on the glacier wall and lifts his head with infinite slowness to cast a look upwards at the peak.

Desperation grips him as he sees nothing more in the steep, towering wall than petrified snow with meter-long spears of ice aiming towards him.

Humboldt opens the large glass receptacle of the eudiometer to capture air samples so that he can later measure the oxygen level. The wind sweeps over the rim of the glass and makes it ring. All four bleed from the nose, the gums, but especially Montúfar; his teeth—blackened from blood—appear to be full of gaps. If you add to this his tasseled scarf, it makes him look like an old woman. But they smile, happy, enchanted by the singing of the Aeolian harp. Little Pacho, with what little breath he still can draw, tries to whistle and match the sound, he and the wind competing in the polyphonic song of Chimborazo.

In vain they search the skies for a condor. But if one were to fly over their heads and glance down at them, it would see them as we—the viewers of the film—are shown them from out of a helicopter: Along a ridge no wider than their feet four small men climb up the mountain, measuring their powers against infinite nature.

The last image shows Alexander von Humboldt's face once again. Large. His eyes greet Father Chimborazo with a look at once respectful and irreverently defiant and that wants to say: "Yes, you are stronger than I, but you have not conquered me. *My aim* is my measure, not *your* height!"

Illustration 89.2. Filming the high-altitude conditions of Humboldt's attempt to climb Chimborazo.

Chapter 90

Rainer Simon
Distant Land
2005

My relationship to Ecuador began with the Humboldt film.

In 1987, I was afforded the unbelievable privilege—for an East German—of traveling to South America to look for film locations. I flew for the first time into a land of the world which the West, in making a distinction from its own, called the "third." Until the last moment, I did not want to believe it. As I stepped into the airplane in Frankfurt am Main, a tugging ache tore at my body. I could not localize it, much less explain it. Just as we were aloft, far enough over the Atlantic, the pains vanished as suddenly as they had come. There was no going back now. *Tayta* Chimborazo was expecting me. *Papito* Chimborazo.

After filming in Ecuador my life began to change.

Two months after the film's premiere, the Wall fell and I could return sooner to Chimborazo, than I'd hoped for in my wildest dreams.

There it was—*Tayta* Chimborazo. A powerful white crest. As if the entire globe were suspended from this mountain, as if it alone carried the earth through the myriads of the cosmos and infinity. An *apu* was erected on the edge of the path, a small pyramid of stones. Each of us laid a stone on top. The mountain veiled itself again.

We visited the Indian village of San Gerardo, and it became ever clearer to me, that we had to infuse this other world more strongly into the film than was earlier intended. [...]

Translation by Richard John Ascárate, from Ranier Simon, *Fernes Land. Die DDR, die DEFA und der Ruf des Chimborazo* (Berlin: Aufbau, 2005), 21, 250, 254–255, 264–269, 269–270, 272, 275. Copyright © 2005 Aufbau Verlagsgruppe GmbH, Berlin

Off the path, at a hut made of mud and straw, I stood across from an old Indian woman. I asked her if I could take her picture, and noticed that she was nearly blind.

"Where do you come from, my son?"

"*De Alemania,* from Germany." This certainly meant nothing to her.

She made a gesture, which I understood, as if she were giving me a kind of blessing. This short encounter was the inspiration for one of the most important scenes of my film, in which an old woman implored *Tayta* Chimborazo to protect Humboldt, the stranger.

⌒

The one storyline described the life path of young Humboldt as he departed from his parents' house to his setting out upon the American journey. Now a story thread should come in that would tell of Humboldt's journey from the hacienda near Quito to the ascent of Chimborazo. It should stand as symbol of the entire American journey that Humboldt had taken across Venezuela, Cuba, Colombia, Ecuador, Peru, and Mexico and into the United States from 1799 to 1804. Of course, Humboldt's natural science achievements needed to play a part, but for me the encounter with the other, the Indian culture, stood center stage. We would not tell the story chronologically, but rather would fold both layers into each other.

⌒

We began the film at the end of June 1988 with two filming days in the vicinity of Potsdam. At the beginning of July we flew to Ecuador. In La Moya and Totorillas we had discussions that lasted for hours with the village inhabitants, who wanted us to assure them once more of what our Ecuadorian colleagues had negotiated regarding pay. For whites, as a rule, did not keep their promises. We had agreed that all of those working with us would receive the same daily pay, regardless of how large their roles were, and that every effort would be made to seek actors from each family, so as to prevent jealousy from arising. A larger sum would be paid to the community for a communal program, for the construction of a water pump station in La Moya and the construction of a water pipe in Totorillas.

We sat together in the school in La Moya. It became ever darker, we saw only silhouettes and later shadows and heard the translations of the negotiations in Quechua, sometimes interrupted by the crying of children, for the women carried their *huahuas* on their backs. As soon as they began to cry, they were given the breast. Older villagers sought explanations as to how it was possible to make a film about a man who had lived 200 years ago. Did television already exist then and how did this Humboldt get to be in it? The younger ones smiled at such questions. Finally, after all of the organizational business had been discussed, I was supposed to select the "actors." It was pitch black.

The car headlights were turned on and dazzled the faces. In this way I became acquainted with *Tayta* Fortunato, who was to play the shaman, *Doña* María Silveria, the old Indian woman, Pacho, the fifteen year old Pedro Sisa, who was to accompany Humboldt all the way to Chimborazo, and all of the other *caravaneros* of the expedition.

Filming began in Las Herrerías, hacienda of ex-President Ponce. Two Ponces would be engaged as extras; Javier, the diplomat, and Gonzalo, the journalist. Marco Cruz, the mountain guide, whose agency was also responsible for the onsite catering, had erected tents in the garden. Pretty girls served us. They were dressed in red costumes, presumably fit for the tastes of tourists, which seemed rather absurd to me. Usually, they looked after mountain climbers from Europe.

Pedro Sisa and Miguel Miñarcaja, who was supposed to work as Quechua translator, came from La Moya. Many of the older *indígenas* spoke either no Spanish or spoke it very badly, which in turn made my communication with them easier. They liked that Spanish didn't flow as smoothly from my tongue as it did from that of my Ecuadorian colleagues and that I made similar mistakes as they did. Miguel would soon come to be a kind of an additional director's assistant. When it came to film, he understood much more quickly than did many an assistant in Europe. I saw Pedro's and Miguel's eyes in regards to the wealth of Las Herrerías. They'd never seen anything like that. I also noticed their uncertainty, their caution. How should they move here among us? It was a completely different world for them. But they were not another world for us. They understood very quickly that our East German team treated white and indigenous Ecuadorians no differently. Such a thought would never have occurred to any of us.

As we filmed Humboldt's travel party setting out, all of those from La Moya came who were to play Humboldt's bearers and attendants. They skillfully took charge of the loading of the donkeys, mules, and llamas with the voluminous luggage of the expedition, and after it was explained once, they made sure that every day when loading they paid attention to continuity with the day before.

Every location brought us closer and closer to the Chimborazo. We filmed on the plateau of Cotopaxi. In the early mornings, when we awoke in ice cold rooms of the noble inn of "Rumipamba de las Rosas" near Salcedo, the volcano was enshrouded in an awesome, dark, infernal cloud. I *challated* [celebrated a ritual offering of rum]—beneath the gaze of confused tourists.

Then we drove onward and plunged into the cloud soup in the national park. Thoughts already circulated in my head about how to compensate for the filming day, which surely would be lost because of the miserable weather.

Then we reached the plateau beyond the tree line and drove out of the spooky clouds as if through a curtain. Beaming sunshine.

In the clear, high air Hirschmeier, the set designer, and his assistants had already set up Humboldt's sparkling measuring instruments: all of the sextants, quadrants, theodolites, levels, telescopes, thermometers, eudiometers, brass barometers, and the equally precious glass pipettes whose fragility Humboldt had even then lamented.

Tayta Fortunato prepared the ritual to call forth the mountains. He himself was no shaman, but he knew a few songs and ceremonies and which objects were necessary for them. These he spread out on a cloth and asked if that were all right with me and I had to convince him that modern utensils—such as cigarette packages and cola bottles—were not allowed to be included. He was very earnest about doing everything properly for us. He celebrated an hour-long ritual and the camera team feared that they would have to change the roll at just the decisive moment. But there is no point in interrupting a shaman. He cannot simply act, clown about, stage some mummery. He requires great concentration. This I experienced again and again.

The problems on the Cotopaxi volcano began as soon as we wanted to film a scene there, which actually took place on Chimborazo. For technical reasons, however, it was not possible to shoot there, so the scene of the ascent up the glacier was done where it is easier to reach at Cotopaxi. We laboriously climbed the zigzag path up to the foot of the glacier—just under 5,000 meters high—in freezing rain with the entire gear. Even the animals had difficulties. The clever donkeys sought their own ways and did not follow those laid out by humans. The llamas simply stood still after the carriers had saddled them with too much of a load.

But the entire day the clouds did not open up. We crawled into the tents, warmed ourselves with tea and hoped, and I *challated,* imploring the mountain to show some consideration for our plans. I also asked for forgiveness that we used it to film scenes that would play out on Chimborazo in the film. Of course, that seemed like a lie, perhaps it was even breaking a taboo.

Just as we were finally able to film on one of the following days, a rock avalanche came down the mountain, almost hitting our prop master. Luis Miguel Campos collapsed, shivering from cold. The radios no longer worked and we shouted our heads off in the heights to direct the actors as they climbed up the glacier, which we observed from a distance with the camera. But directions were superfluous anyway, there was nothing to perform, the physical exertion dominated everything. As we descended with the entire gear in the evening to our "parking place" at 4,600 meters high, a car nearly ran over the camera and the exposed rolls of film. Everyone's nerves were stretched to the limit.

I drove that night to the hotel in Latacunga, where the *indígenas* had been put up. We drank a bottle of rum with one another and I learned how much they were earning with us. Their pay had been kept secret from the western co-producers. Even compared to our low East German wages, what they were paid was so little that I wanted to throw away the whole film project, so shabby did I seem to myself. But our actors were most satisfied with what they received. It was, after all, double of what they could otherwise earn, assuming they could have earned anything at all. I needed to be convinced that higher *salarios* would be dangerous, they would increase envy immeasurably, which was impossible to prevent anyway, and upset the entire social structure of the community. Unfortunately, that was true, and it is always very hard to find a reasonably acceptable middle ground.

～

Pedro Sisa, the Indian boy, was doing poorly. He could hardly hold himself up. The native, of all people, had contracted altitude sickness. We climbed farther to the ridge. Everyone was now left completely to his own devices and went at his own pace, nothing would have been more foolish than to hurry behind the young carriers, who climbed on up like goats, with heavy packs on their backs. Arriving at higher altitude, the summit presented itself absolutely cloud-free. Pedro had tortured himself up this far, his face was bloated, his eyes bloodshot, he looked as Humboldt had described, and collapsed, tormented by stabbing headaches. Olivier Pascalin, our Bonpland, did not even arrive. No one had noticed that he had stayed behind. The carriers walked back and found him unconscious between boulders. He had to be carried back to the *refugio* and brought to the hotel in Riobamba. We always had a doctor with us during filming, but on that day he was not yet up above with us and could tend to Olivier at the mountain hut. Yet, I wanted for him to come up to help Pedro afterwards. A lively radio traffic developed and I noticed with what attentiveness the young carriers followed what Klaus-Pedro Schütt signaled to those below on my command. At some point he gave up, the doctor had driven with Olivier to Riobamba. "Oh, Rainer," he said, "you don't yet know that a white man here never helps an Indian when another white man is sick."

We filmed takes that were possible without Bonpland, someone brought his poncho up, so that we could double him in the long shots. Pacho recovered somewhat, but one sees in the film how sick he was on that day. He had a cold and ascended too quickly so as not to remain behind the foreigners. He paid dearly for that. He did in fact live at a height of about 4,000 meters, but the *indígenas* climbed higher only when they retrieved glacial ice or to accompany tourists. Otherwise, what would be the point of such a climb?

We then filmed in La Moya. The village welcomed us as Humboldt once had been.

～

In the film, a priest translates for Humboldt from Quechua to Spanish. Pedro Torres played the role and was himself a Catholic priest, a disciple of liberation theology from the diocese of Archbishop Proaño from Riobamba, who at that time was still living and had achieved very much for the liberation of the *indígenas* and for the relief of their great misery. It was no problem for such theologians that the *indígenas*—even when they were officially Catholics—never gave up the belief in their old gods. The reverence for *Pachamama*, Mother Earth, for *Inti*, the sun, for sacred animals and plants and tolerance for every living being was to be observed everywhere.

～

We wanted to film that day in Totorillas, but it had snowed so heavily that the snow lay all the way down to the little village and Chimborazo presented a completely different aspect. As the sun emerged, it quickly melted, but the important scene in which Humboldt exchanges linguistic knowledge with the *indígenas,* we did not get on film. We had yet just one more day, then the team had to go back to Quito. The return flight dates could not be postponed. I could only *challate* and implore the favor of *Tayta* Chimborazo. He guaranteed us a beautiful day.

We filmed with two cameras and without rehearsing. Humboldt asked about the Quechua words for eye, nose, mouth, hand, man, woman, child, family, and the *indígenas* asked him for the German words. Jan Josef Liefers knew as little as the nonprofessional actors what dialogue would develop out of that and had to improvise just as they did. It would become the most beautiful scene of the film and for me one of the best from all of my films.

Chapter 91

REDMOND O'HANLON
In Trouble Again
1988

Over the next few days we made short trips down the Río Negro with Old Valentine in his bongo, to test Charlie's outboard motors and to visit the few sites around San Carlos where Indian petroglyphs are found. On flat granite slabs at the head of half-hidden creeks, and on rocks at the edge of the river itself that were exposed by the exceptionally low waters, we photographed the engraved picture drawings of uncertain age and origin which Humboldt and Wallace and Spruce describe: matchstick men with multiple arms or box bodies, abstract designs of whorls and circles and lines, crude representations of iguanas or fish. Spruce thought such art had been "involved in unnecessary mystery," and tells us that having "carefully examined a good deal of the so-called picture writing, I am bound to come to the conclusion that it was executed by the ancestors of Indians who at this day inhabit the region where it is found; that their utensils, mode of life, etc., were similar to those still in use; and that their degree of civilisation was certainly not greater—probably less—than that of their existing descendants." But to me, then, standing beside Juan, whom I had only just met, and Simon, whom I momentarily felt I no longer knew, they seemed as enigmatic as the vast trees on the high bank above us, as impenetrable as Old Valentine's pock-marked face.

We kept close in to the banks of long forested islands in the middle of the great river, under the vast expanse of sky. But Charlie was right: the Río Negro was far too wide to show us much except the tall trees and thick lianas, the impenetrable-seeming, light-loving plants which crowd out over the water at the jungle's edge. We disturbed little but small flocks of White-winged swallows resting on overhanging branches, who simply resumed their zig-zagging flight low across the choppy surface of the river, hawking for insects; and an hour or so upstream we startled a different species, pairs of Black-collared swallows, neater, less approachable, perched on the rounded granite rocks. Simon pulled his pocket tape-recorder out of his bergen and began his devotional diary to Liz, his school-teacher-lady.

"Dateline May 3rd," he intoned. "We're on the move, Angel-drawers. Every boring mile brings me closer to you. I bite your bum. Simon."

"That's not the right spirit," I said. "Just think of it: Humboldt and Bonpland set off from San Carlos exactly like this—except that their Indians had to paddle—on 10 May 1800, on their way to prove that the Casiquiare really did connect the Orinoco and the Amazon."

"Update," said Simon, clicking his machine on again, "Redmond says that some crazy Kraut and his sidekick came this way 184 years ago. *Get that for a bundle of fun.* I grab your suspenders. Simon."

Valentine and Culimacaré, lookouts with no snags to look for in the deep water, surrendered to their hangovers and fell asleep. Simon put his recorder away and pulled out *War and Peace*. A giant white-fronted and black-bellied bird, standing halfway up a tangle of branches and lianas, grew increasingly agitated as we approached, raising and dipping its black-crowned, black-plumed head, and then, on broad grey wings, it laboured up over the trees and out of sight. I took Schauensee and Phelp's *Guide to the Birds of Venezuela* from its waterproof bag in the front pocket of my bergen and identified it at once—a White-necked heron. Shortly afterwards the right bank gave way to a great expanse of water. We turned east into the Casiquiare.

Humboldt estimated the Casiquiare to be "from two hundred and fifty to two hundred and eighty toises" wide, and Robert Schomburgk, passing on his way downstream in 1838 from the mission of Esmeralda, after becoming the first European to cross the mountains from British Guiana, put it at 550 yards. To me it just seemed as wide as the Río Negro, but mud-coloured rather than black. It was a white-water river, most of its flow deriving from the mountain-stream-fed Orinoco rather than from the low-lying rivers, stained with tannins from rotting vegetation, which supply the Negro network.

~

We swung into a straight stretch and a block of grey granite rose sheer on the right bank ahead of us, some three hundred feet above the forest canopy: the Rock of Culimacaré, from whose foot Humboldt fixed his position as 2° 0' 42" (slightly too far to the north) and which looked exactly as Spruce drew it in 1853. At its side was a smaller, chaotic assemblage of rocks, fractured towers, broken pinnacles, boulders perched one on top of the other. Further upstream, on the outer curve of a bend which swung the Casiquiare to the southeast, we passed the village of Culimacaré. From our low position, I could see nothing but the little landing-stage and two huts close by, their windows hung, as Humboldt described them, with palm-thatch and bamboo-frame defences against mosquitoes.

~

The air seemed remarkably free of mosquitoes. Humboldt, I decided, must have been exaggerating: his Journey on the Casiquiare, he tells us, was the most miserable of all his time in the Americas—the vicious clouds of biting insects were such a torment that he and Bonpland slept in their nets by day and travelled only at night. We were bothered by nothing worse than a lustrous, dark-green, persistent fly, as big as a horsefly and with a bite like one.

Occasional Large-billed terns and the much smaller, freshwater tern, the Yellow-billed, flew low and very white against the trees; as they quartered the surface their reflections skittered over the water, abruptly closing to meet them, at splash-point, as they plunge-dived for small fish. And by a rocky stretch of shore we passed a black, eagle-like bird, which disregarded us entirely, promenading thoughtfully on long yellow legs and stopping, every now and then, to hunch its shoulders, lower its head, and inspect something of consuming interest near its feet.

"Chimo!" I yelled, turning round and pointing. "What's that?"

"Aquila negra," said Chimo, unimpressed, but then brightening, clearing his throat and gobbing over the side. "That one eats well," he added as an afterthought, as the beach and the Great black hawk receded in our wake, "he eats like Chimo. He eats what you will eat with Chimo. Lizards, frogs and the babies of alligators."

~

The Pasimoni, wide, slow and black, began to narrow dramatically; trees no more than fifty feet high and ragged, thin-leaved shrubs replaced the great towering trunks; and small parties of Greater anis, magpie-like birds whose black plumage shone briefly purple or blue or bronze as they changed their position against the light, fussed from bush to bush in front of us, until their leader decided he had gone far enough, when they would all flap and glide back in the other direction, bubbling their collective annoyance as they went.

Just to look at such a group of swearing, quarrelling, thoroughly united anis would be enough to put you in mind of your friends, I thought, and those absurd birds alone should have saved Humboldt from his other, deeper unease in these regions—the loss which opened up inside him, the indifferent emptiness that threatened to draw out and engulf his—exceptionally rugged—sense of self. To begin with, he felt, in proportion as we draw near to an object we have long had in view, its interest seems to augment. The uninhabited banks of the Casiquiare, covered with forests, without memorials of times past, then occupied my imagination. ... In that interior part of the New Continent we almost accustomed ourselves to regard men as not being essential to the order of nature. The earth is loaded with plants, and nothing impedes their free development. An immense layer of mould manifests the uninterrupted action of organic powers. The crocodiles and the boas are masters of the river; the jaguar, the pecari, the dante, and the monkeys, traverse the forest without fear, and without danger; there they dwell as in an ancient inheritance. This aspect of animated nature, in which man is nothing, has something in it strange and sad. To this we reconcile ourselves with difficulty on the ocean, and amid the sands of Africa; though in these scenes, where nothing recalls to mind our fields, our woods, and our streams, we are less astonished at the vast solitude through which we pass. Here, in a fertile country adorned with eternal verdure, we seek in vain the traces of the power of man; we seem to be transported into a world different from that which gave us birth.

"These impressions," he added ominously, "are so much the more powerful, in proportion as they are of longer duration."

∿

Chimo and Pablo, driven inside by the blackfly, set up our primus in a corner of the hut and began to boil the strips of tapir meat. I drew up a log stool to the ex-mission table, and decided to comfort myself by imagining that all biting flies were still at a decent academic and historical distance. A passage in Humboldt had once seemed amusing. Relatively free of mosquitoes while travelling on the black-water rivers, he and Bonpland had discovered that "our sufferings recommenced as soon as we entered the Casiquiare." And in general:

Persons who have not navigated the great rivers of equinoctial America, for instance, the Oroonoko and the Río Magdalena, can scarcely conceive, how without interruption, at every instant of life, you may be tormented by insects flying in the air, and how the multitude of these little animals may render vast regions almost uninhabitable. However accustomed you may be to endure pain without complaint, however lively an interest you may take in the objects of your researches, it is impossible not to be constantly disturbed by the moschettoes, *zancudoes, jejens,* and *tempraneroes,* that cover the face and hands, pierce the clothes with their long sucker in the form of a needle, and, getting into the mouth and nostrils, set you coughing and sneezing whenever you attempt to speak in the open air.

∿

I must remember to remember, I thought, when lying on the jungle floor, porcupined with six-foot arrows (as the curare is telling the muscles of the diaphragm and the heart to relax, to take it easy after all these years) that the individual Yanomami did not really mean it. And anyway, no warning could be clearer than Chagnon's summary:

> The thing that impressed me most was the importance of aggression in their culture. I had the opportunity to witness a good many incidents that expressed individual vindictiveness on the one hand and collective bellicosity on the other. These ranged in seriousness from the ordinary incidents of wife beating and chest pounding to dueling and organized raiding by parties that set out with the intention of ambushing and killing men from enemy villages.

I also had with me Charlie's photocopy, in English translation, of Jacques Lizot's very different but equally impressive (and equally disturbing) account of Yanomami life and myth, *Le cercle des feux: Faits et dits des Indiens Yanomami* (1976). Lizot, unlike Chagnon, keeps himself well clear of his anthropological descriptions. And it was the sinister resonance of the explanation for this silence which reverberated in my skull: "I could of course have evoked my own experience of life among the Indians, but I wanted to speak of other things, for strictly personal reasons: I am not yet ready to speak of the terrible shock that this experience was for me ... perhaps I will never be able to speak of these experiences, for I would have to evoke so many harrowing things that touch my inner being. ..."

Well, whatever the terrible shocks that Lizot experienced may have been, I thought, the Indians have suffered worse. Humboldt's account of the exploits of the missionary of San Fernando could stand for them all, before and since. In 1797 this monk set out with his converted Indians on a soul-saving expedition to the banks of the Río Guaviare, where they found

> in an Indian hut a Guahiba mother with three children, two of whom were still infants. They were occupied in preparing the flour of cassava. Resistance was impossible; the father was gone to fish, and the mother tried in vain to flee with her children. Scarcely had she reached the savannah, when she was seized by the Indians of the mission, who go to *hunt men*. The mother and her children were bound, and dragged to the bank of the river. Had the mother made too violent a resistance, the Indians would have killed her, for every thing is permitted when they go to the conquest of souls (*a la conquista espiritual*), and it is children in particular they seek to capture, in order to treat them in the mission as *poitos*, or slaves of the Christians. The prisoners were carried to San Fernando in the hope, that the mother would be unable to find her way back to her home by land. Far from those children who had

accompanied their father on the day in which she had been carried off, this unhappy woman shewed signs of the deepest despair. She attempted to take back to her family the children, who had been snatched away by the missionary; and fled with them repeatedly from the village of San Fernando, but the Indians never failed to seize her anew; and the missionary, after having caused her to be mercilessly beaten, took the cruel resolution of separating the mother from the two children, who had been carried off with her. She was conveyed alone toward the missions of the Río Negro, going up the Atabapo. Slightly bound, she was seated at the bow of the boat, ignorant of the fate that awaited her; but she judged by the direction of the Sun, that she was removing farther and farther from her hut and her native country. She succeeded in breaking her bonds, threw herself into the water, and swam to the left bank of the Atabapo. The current carried her to a shelf of rock, which bears her name to this day. She landed, and took shelter in the woods, but the president of the missions ordered the Indians to row to the shore, and follow the traces of the Guahiba. In the evening she was brought back. Stretched upon the rock (*la Piedra de la Madre*) a cruel punishment was inflicted on her with those straps of manatee leather, which serve for whips in that country, and with which the alcaldes are always furnished. This unhappy woman, her hands tied behind her back with strong stalks of *mavacure,* was then dragged to the mission of Javita.

She was there thrown into one of the caravanseras that are called *Casa del Rey.* It was the rainy season, and the night was profoundly dark. Forests till then believed to be impenetrable separated the mission of Javita from that of San Fernando, which was twenty-five leagues distant in a straight line. No other path is known than that of the rivers; no man ever attempted to go by land from one village to another, were they only a few leagues apart. But such difficulties do not stop a mother, who is separated from her children. Her children are at San Fernando de Atabapo; she must find them again, she must execute her project of delivering them from the hands of Christians, of bringing them back to their father on the banks of the Guaviare. The Guahiba was carelessly guarded in the caravansera. Her arms being wounded, the Indians of Javita had loosened her bonds, unknown to the missionary and the alcaldes. She succeeded by the help of her teeth in breaking them entirely; disappeared during the night; and at the fourth rising Sun was seen at the mission of San Fernando, hovering around the hut where her children were confined. We pressed the missionary to tell us, whether the Guahiba had peacefully enjoyed the happiness of remaining with her children; and if any repentance had followed this excess of cruelty. He would not satisfy our curiosity; but at our return from the Río Negro we learnt that the Indian mother was not allowed time to cure her wounds, but was again separated from her children, and sent to one of the missions of the Upper Oroonoko. There she died, refusing all kind of nourishment, as the savages do in great calamities.

Chapter 92

GABRIEL GARCÍA MÁRQUEZ
The General in his Labyrinth
1989

The worst part of the voyage was forced immobility. One afternoon the General was so desperate with pacing the narrow confines of the canvas tent that he had the boat stop so he could take a walk. In the hardened mud they saw tracks that seemed to be those of a bird as large as an ostrich and at least as heavy as an ox, but this seemed normal to the oarsmen, who said there were men roaming that desolate place who were as big as ceiba trees and had the crests and claws of roosters. He scoffed at the legend, as he scoffed at everything that had the slightest glimmer of the supernatural, but his walk took longer than expected and they had to make camp against the judgment of the captain and even his military aides, who considered the place dangerous and unhealthy. He spent a sleepless night, tortured by the heat and the clouds of mosquitoes that seemed to fly through the suffocating nets, unsettled by the fearful roars of a puma that kept them on the alert all night. At about two o'clock in the morning he went to chat with the groups standing watch around the bonfires. Only at dawn, as he contemplated the vast swamps gilded by the rising sun, did he renounce the dream that had kept him awake.

"All right," he said, "we'll have to leave without seeing our friends with the rooster claws."

Just as they weighed anchor a filthy, emaciated dog, suffering from mange and a paralyzed paw, leaped onto the barge. The General's two dogs attacked him, but the invalid defended himself with suicidal ferocity and refused to surrender even when he was covered with blood and his throat had been torn open. The General gave orders to keep him, and José Palacios took charge of him, as he had done so many times with so many other stray dogs.

That same day they rescued a German who had been abandoned on an island of sand for beating one of his oarsmen. When he came on board he represented himself as an astronomer and a botanist, but in conversation it became evident he knew nothing about either science. On the other hand, he had seen with his own eyes the men with rooster claws, and he was determined to capture one alive, put it in a cage, and exhibit it in Europe as a phenomenon comparable only to the Spider Woman of the Americas, who had caused such a sensation in the ports of Andalusia a century before.

"Take me instead," the General said to him. "I assure you you'll earn more money showing me in a cage as the biggest damn fool in history."

At first he had thought him an agreeable charlatan, but that changed when the German began to tell indecent jokes about the shameless pederasty of Baron Alexander von Humboldt. "We should leave him on the beach again," he said to José Palacios. In the afternoon they came across the mail launch sailing upstream, and the General used all his charm to have the mail agent open the sacks of official correspondence and give him his letters. And then he asked him to please take the German to the port of Nare, and the agent agreed even though the launch was overloaded. That night, while Fernando was reading the letters to him, the General growled:

"That motherfucker isn't worth a single hair on Humboldt's head."

He had been thinking about the Baron even before they rescued the German, for he could not imagine how he had survived in that untamed wild. He had met him during his years in Paris, after Humboldt's return from his trip through the equinoctial countries, and he had been as astonished by the splendor of his beauty, the likes of which he had never seen in any woman, as by his intelligence and erudition. On the other hand, what he had found least convincing was the Baron's certainty that the Spanish colonies in America were ripe for independence. He had said as much without a tremor in his voice, at a time when the thought had not occurred to the General even as an idle Sunday fantasy.

"All that's missing is the man," Humboldt said.

He told José Palacios about it many years later, in Cuzco, perhaps because he found himself at the top of the world at a moment when history had just demonstrated that he was the man. He did not tell anyone else, but each time the Baron was mentioned he took the opportunity to pay tribute to his prescience:

"Humboldt opened my eyes."

Chapter 93

LUIS ARMANDO ROCHE AND JACQUES ESPAGNE
Aire Libre
1996

INTERIOR, DAY—Latin American church

INTERTITLE: Paso de Hombres Libres, Argentina—May 1858

Tropical atmosphere. The camera advances inside the church from behind a dark wall. It enters a church illuminated by candles, all around which flutter thousands of insects forming "trees of light" from one side of a casket to another, wherein rests the cadaver of a very old man. The embalmers have made up his face in an exaggerated fashion, giving the man an artificial and somewhat "carnivalesque" look. Careful observation reveals that one of the "saints" found on the side of the church is a replica of Father Zea. ... Will he pray? Men and women are found seated on chairs or kneeling on the floor, murmuring prayers that recall the sound of the insects. A man, apparently drunk, enters the nave of the church astride a horse. The noise of the hooves on the tiles interrupts the murmuring. The man approaches without dismounting and is followed by dozens of disquieted and condemning eyes. The women rise and separate themselves from the men, as if they were the first to realize that something terrible were about to happen.

MAN ON THE HORSE Doctor Bonpland!

Receiving no response, he comes closer and repeats in an increasingly stronger voice.

MAN ON THE HORSE Quiet!

Translation by Richard John Ascárate, from Luis Armando Roche and Jacques Espagne, *Aire libre (Passage des hommes libres). Un filme de Luis Armando Roche* (Mérida, Venezuela: Fundación del Nuevo Cine Latinoamericano, 1996), 11–13, 18–21, 65–70, 93–103. Copyright © 1996 by Jacques Espagne and Luis Armando Roche. The film *Aire Libre* and other films by Luis Armando Roche can be acquired at www.amazon.com.

The horse bucks, slips, and rears, upset by the light and odor of the candles and embalming medium. Apparently, there is no possible response. The men slowly rise. . . . The man on the horse does not appear to see them.

Furious, he draws a machete and loudly begins to hack at the cadaver.

MAN ON THE HORSE Doctor Bonpland, your "scee-ence" don't do a damn thing for you now!

From the thorax, from the belly of the dead, lacerated by the machete, cloth strips full of blood and embalming agents escape. A woman, followed by others, reacts and falls upon the man on the horse. Some take him by the boots and try to knock him off, others pull on the reins of the animal while repeating a strange and hallucinatory litany. ... Bonpland's cadaver seems to observe what is happening with singular indifference. Stimulated by the boldness of the women, the men in their turn rush headlong, armed with chairs and candelabras. The man frightens no one in spite of the machete that still hangs from his arm. Men and women try to reach him and knock him to the ground. The violence increases. Frozen with panic, the man half turns around on his horse, overturning chairs and saints, and leaves the church pursued through the village.

~

EXTERIOR, DAY—beach near Cumaná

INTERTITLE: Cumaná, Venezuela—May 1799

An almost savage beach at a little distance from the colonial village of Cumaná. Close up of the letter "A" sketched in the sand. All around are found a group of children and the school teachers PEDRO and LUISA (who appears pregnant). They teach the alphabet to the students. The children say the letter "A" in unison. ... Pedro then follows up by writing the letter "B" in the sand. The camera zooms out. In the distance, a canoe approaches the beach.

CHILDREN A ... B ... C ... D ... E ...

An athletic young man, agitated, face reddened by the wind, heat, and excitation, supports himself on the prow of the canoe. It is Aimé Bonpland. Humboldt, equally young, rides seated, astern. Two natives row. The boat is loaded with the equipment of the two explorers. Bonpland jumps to shore with an almost childlike joy.

BONPLAND [*in French*] AMERICA! ... ALEXANDER, WE'RE IN AMERICA!

The teachers interrupt the class and little by little stop reciting the alphabet to approach and see who has come. They draw close to the new arrivals. The keel of the boat brushes against the sand. Two natives carry Humboldt on their shoulders to the beach. The moment the explorer is about to set foot on land, Bonpland stops him.

BONPLAND [*in French*] Careful! Your foot!

Humboldt remains with foot suspended. Bonpland throws himself to the ground and uproots a small plant that he finds at his feet.

BONPLAND [*in French*] Look! It doesn't resemble any of ours! I would swear that it's never been recorded.

Alexander observes distractedly. Takes a large thermometer out. Inserts it into the sand. He then lifts his face to observe the group surrounding him. He rises and addresses them.

HUMBOLDT Good day! Allow me to introduce my friend and colleague, Doctor Aimé Bonpland. I am Alexander Humboldt and we come on a scientific mission with a letter of safe conduct from His Majesty, King Carlos IV of Spain.

The natives begin unloading the canoe. The children run and play around the new arrivals, examining and touching everything. Bonpland is pleased to see that Pedro carries a chameleon on his shoulder.

BONPLAND [*in French*] A chameleon! ... I would love to verify what Linnaeus wrote about its ability to change color.
PEDRO If you wish, take it as a gift.
BONPLAND Thank you!
PEDRO Pedro Montañar. This is my wife, Luisa. ...
LUISA We are teachers in the village school.
HUMBOLDT (*anxious, concerned about the scientific equipment*) Excuse me ... can you tell them that those things are rather fragile?
PEDRO Hmm, oh ... Be careful, children ... !

Each carries what he or she can and they begin to walk along the beach toward the village.

~

INTERTITLE: San Fernando de Apure, Venezuela

A few months later, 1800, the century changes. ...

Bonpland, naked, throws himself into the river.

BONPLAND (*to Humboldt* [*in French*]) Oh! Come on!
HUMBOLDT [*in French*] I can't swim!
BONPLAND [*in French*] The water is not deep!
HUMBOLDT (*to Pedro*) And you, are you going for a swim?

PEDRO No ... I'll stay here. ...

Humboldt finishes undressing and lowers himself carefully into the channel. A long conversation begins in which the two "walk about," exchanging intimacies with one another in the semitransparent space of the water.

HUMBOLDT [*in French*] Do you remember when we fought for the bathtub at the Hotel Boston in Paris?

BONPLAND [*in French*] How odd you should speak about that here ... !

HUMBOLDT [*in French*] Undoubtedly an effect of our nudity. ... When I was a boy, in Tegel Castle, we would bathe together in the basin, my brother, my cousins, and myself, completely nude. The female cousins weren't allowed, of course. ... I remember how the cold water nearly congealed my blood ... but not as much as my mother did. My father had already passed away. ... She told me that I was a delicate boy, incapable of the least physical exertion.

BONPLAND [*in French*] Ha! How wrong she was!

HUMBOLDT [*in French*] Later they tried to marry me to Amelie von Imhoff ... an enchanting woman. She was beautiful. You'd have gone mad for her ... but I couldn't decide. ... If I recall these memories it's just ... I know that at times you ... you question my ... manhood. ...

Bonpland interrupts him.

BONPLAND [*in French*] ... Um, excuse me for interrupting, but if you value your memories and manhood in the very least, we should swiftly return to the bank. I see a caiman preparing to enjoy a few memories of human flesh!

An enormous Orinoco caiman lowers itself into the channel.

HUMBOLDT [*in French*] A caiman? Where?

BONPLAND [*in French*] On the bank!

BONPLAND (*frightened* [*in French*]) Good God! He thinks I'm calling him! Let's go!

They leave the water hastily and go towards Pedro.

HUMBOLDT Is this why you didn't want to go for a swim?

PEDRO The caiman, I saw it. ...

HUMBOLDT If you knew there was danger, why didn't you say something?

PEDRO Well ... ever since you set foot in this country, you've been through dangerous situations and nothing terrible has ever happened. I just wanted to know if you were immortal. ...

HUMBOLDT Mortal?

PEDRO Immortal. ...

BONPLAND Immortal. ...

PEDRO I make my own observations as well!

Suddenly, a strong, threatening voice is heard. The three jump. Humboldt and Bonpland, completely naked, are seen from behind. Pedro, clothed, puts his hands behind his back, imitating a "certain José Gregorio Hernández." ...

ZEA Good afternoon, gentlemen! I see that you've made the acquaintance of the grand caiman, ruler of this channel. ...

It is Father Zea, an old missionary accompanied by a small donkey.

Illustration 93.1. The Humboldt expedition on the Orinoco.

~

EXTERIOR, DAY—native camp

An Indian, visibly excited, enters the native house. This consists of a wood hut with a palm roof.

NATIVE [*in Yanomami*] Strangers, strangers!

Expecting hostilities, the men forcefully exit the large hut with their arrows. Pedro and Bonpland, who have just arrived at the camp, are questioned by the natives.

WALIMA [*in Yanomami*] What is this? A sword?
WANADI [*in Yanomami*] Yes! It is a sword!
HEPEWE [*in Yanomami*] No, not a sword. ...

The natives calm themselves.

The first moment of hostility has already passed. Bonpland tries to begin measuring Walima, who, displeased at this, tries to walk away.

WALIMA [*in Yanomami*] No!

Bonpland detains him and convinces him that there is no danger. Walima removes the hand Bonpland uses to lower the gauge and grasps it by the end. The gauge sticks a few centimeters above the head of the warrior, who becomes uneasy and impatient.

BONPLAND [*in French*] I agree … it's downward … downward … I agree, you do it yourself.

The gauge loosens and falls forcefully on the native's skull with a dry sound. Walima lets loose a growl that unleashes a new wave of hilarity among the group.

GROUP OF INDIANS [*in Yanomami*] Careful!
WALIMA (*furious* [*in Yanomami*]) Idiot!
BONPLAND [*in French*] No… don't go. It's not dangerous. …

Tries to hold him back.

WALIMA [*in Yanomami*] No.
BONPLAND [*in French*] It's not dangerous … Look, come. …

Bonpland is extremely busy and we see that he is not going to be able to do everything alone. All at once we hear Humboldt's voice offscreen.

HUMBOLDT (*offscreen* [*in French*]) Wait … You won't be able to do it alone.
   …
BONPLAND (*without even seeing him* [*in French*]) Ah … it's you. … There should be at least three of us. …

He discovers at the same time as the spectator *the naked arm of Humboldt completely painted with annatto coloring. He dared not paint his entire body and does protect his pants and boots, but from the waistline up he is the same "savage scarlet" as Bonpland.*

BONPLAND (*to Humboldt, surprised* [*in French*]) YOU!
HUMBOLDT [*in French*] Yes, so?
BONPLAND [*in French*] Umm, it's just that … I … I wasn't expecting this. …
HUMBOLDT [*in French*] Please, don't say anything. … You'll make me regret. …
BONPLAND [*in French*] Oh, no, Alexander! To regret is to die a little!

At this moment a warrior, Hepewe, draws near, turning around suspiciously. … Suddenly, the native goes up to Humboldt and carries the sage like a sack of potatoes. While shouting, he carries his load to the edge of the clearing and lowers him to the ground. … Humboldt does not know what to do and looks petrified. … Suddenly he imitates what Hepewe has done, lifts the native and carries him back to where Bonpland and the others are! Everyone laughs uncontrollably.

BONPLAND (*euphoric* [*in French*]) Bravo, Alexander! We're in the heart of the world, at the source of all beginnings of humor!

Even Alexander seems to "loosen up." ... He shouts like the others. The children imitate everything in the background in a bacchanal of games: pushing and pulling, tumbling and laughter, while the water from a gentle rain falls from above.

Illustration 93.2. Scene with members of the Yanomami tribe and Roy Dupuis as Bonpland, center, with Christian Vadim as Humboldt on the right.

EXTERIOR, DAY—native camp

Once more, measurements are recorded. Humboldt is found sitting and transcribing what Bonpland dictates to him.

BONPLAND [*in French*] Forty-two pounds, let's say nine years old. ...
HUMBOLDT [*in French*] Nine years. ...
PEDRO Three feet, a little over ten inches. ...
HUMBOLDT [*in French*] Three feet, ten-and-a-quarter ... Agreed. ... And what is his name?

Father Zea suddenly appears, dressed in an old and worn-out ecclesiastical apron.

ZEA It's useless, they won't tell. ... They don't give their names. ... Something that has to do with "death." ...

Father Zea calls the boy that they are about to measure.

ZEA COME HERE!

PEDRO Four feet, nine inches. …
HUMBOLDT [*in French*] Four feet, nine inches. …

Meanwhile, Bonpland receives into the scale a beautiful and completely nude female native. Her face and torso are adorned with simple and refined tattoos. Bonpland—possibly for the first time in his life—is literally intimidated by the natural beauty, the grace, and the radiant smile of the young woman.

BONPLAND [*in French*] Are not here beauty, innocence, and sensuality embodied as woman?
HUMBOLDT [*in French*] Eve before original sin! This is the first time I've ever seen a woman intimidate you. … You dare not even touch her skin … !

As he sees that Bonpland does not know what to do, he rises, approaches the young woman, extends his hands, and the young woman places hers in them. Humboldt presents the young woman's hands to Bonpland.

HUMBOLDT [*in French*] Take them, my friend. …

Bonpland continues observing the woman in a quasi-catatonic state.

HUMBOLDT [*in French*] Her weight?
BONPLAND (*returning to reality* [*in French*]) Oh, yes … Her weight. …

While the scientists weigh and measure, Zea and Rivera prepare to baptize the natives.

ZEA (*to Rivera*) Choose a name that we haven't used!
RIVERA A name … a name. … What about Bernardo? I had an uncle named Bernardo who was bookkeeper in the government of Madrid. …
ZEA Well, Bernardo it will be then. … *In nomine Patris, Filii et Spiritus Sancti.* …

Rivera lifts the boy and helps Zea to baptize him.

RIVERA Amen. …
ZEA Bernardo, do you reject Satan and his splendor and all of his works?
RIVERA I do reject. …
ZEA And do you unite yourself with Jesus Christ for all eternity?
RIVERA I do. …
ZEA Therefore, I baptize you *Bernardus, in religionem Catholicam, Apostolicam Romanamque, in nomine Patris, Filii et Spiritus Sancti … Amen!*

Pedro is finishing the measurement of Orasimi, the beautiful young woman.

PEDRO Five feet, four inches.
HUMBOLDT [*in French*] Five feet, four inches.
RIVERA ANOTHER!
ZEA Another? She's ANOTHER!

With a natural gait, the female native walks over to Zea and Rivera, thinking like the rest of the tribe that the activities of these other persons are neither more nor less strange than those of the painted "gentlemen." ... Pedro tries to stop the young woman.

PEDRO No, not you!

RIVERA (*forceful, he approaches*) Careful, bastard!

ZEA Calm yourself, Rivera!

RIVERA (*to the priest*) Do you want to leave him to his old tricks?

PEDRO (*to Humboldt and Bonpland*) And does it not bother you that they give them names, that they baptize them in this way ... without explaining anything to them ... ?

HUMBOLDT The natives have their traditions, their gods: nature, the trees, the river, the rain. ...

BONPLAND I refuse to be an accomplice!

ZEA For the love of God! So much discussion over a few little drops of holy water! By baptizing them I hope to give them a name, an identity. ...

RIVERA (*to Pedro*) Why do you fear baptism so, mestizo?

PEDRO I have a name! You are the only one who calls me thus! ... And it is not so much baptism that I fear as the way in which you practice it, and what goes along with it. ...

RIVERA Quiet, fool! Our conquest is: Civilization first ... Civilization ... or death!

Illustration 93.3 Carlos Cruz as Pedro Montañar collecting materials after the dugout canoe overturns in the Orinoco.

Illustration 93.4. Roy Dupuis as Bonpland with some of the animal menagerie collected by the expedition.

Illustration 93.5. Bringing the plant collection to safety, Roy Dupuis as Bonpland.

Chapter 94

Denzil Romero
Equinoctial Recurrence
1998

The First Historical Discoveries of the Orinoco

The worst thing for Humboldt was joining the group of Indians (those of the tribe of the salacious girl, the patron of the launch, the rowers) who—excessively and lustfully—observed with satisfaction the sexual gymnastics of the two turtledoves. At times he felt he could no longer endure the humiliation the act itself signified to him. A lack of decency on the part of Bonpland, this, a contemptible thoughtlessness towards him. This is a shame. A disgrace. ... The outburst passed, I will protest this very seriously; I will certainly raise this matter with him. ...

In the meantime, he prefers to keep his distance.

This time, Alexander von Humboldt wanted to keep up with his historical account just to that point. To tell the truth, he was tired. And he did not stop thinking about the absurdity of Mr. Bonpland, delighted with the little Indian girl. ... But, already, already can be heard the voice of Bonpland, who is looking for him and calling all around. He now goes up to the bend where Humboldt tied his hammock. In no way does he want to confront that gentleman now. He will fall completely asleep. ... Yes, he will fall completely asleep or pretend to sleep. ... He in no way wants to face him. Nothing to do with this gentleman. He will not even pop her cherry. Let him go somewhere else with his music! Let him go and continue his hanky-panky with the little Indian girl! Him and his *ass* and *crap*! Him and his *slacking off* of the Patagonian giant!

Translation by Richard John Ascárate, from Denzil Romero, "Los primeros descubrimientos históricos del Orinoco (II)," in *Recurrencia equinoccial. Novela*, ed. Karl Kohut (Frankfurt/Madrid: Vervuert/ Iberoamericana, 2002), 167, 169. Copyright © 2002 Iberoamericana, Vervuert Verlagsgesellschaft.

Him and his *testicles*! Him and his *sperm*! Let them go to hell! It's better that they go to hell! Better to pretend to sleep and avoid a fight. No fights over sex now or later, Baron Friedrich Wilhelm Heinrich Alexander von Humboldt. Don't forget that, in the end, you're a baron and a man as well. Better to pretend to sleep. Yes. You'll fall completely asleep. … You'll fall completely asleep or pretend to sleep. … "Goodbye." "Good night." "A pleasure." … "Ciao, to you, you big wild rodent." … I don't recall if I've seen you. … Ciao. … I haven't seen you, and I haven't seen you, and I haven't seen you, and I don't ever want to see you again … I never want to see you again. … Agreed? … Continue stirring the fire of your little Indian! … Continue stirring it! …

Chapter 95

César Aira

An Episode in the Life
of a Landscape Painter

2000

Rugendas was a genre painter. His genre was the physiognomy of nature, based on a procedure invented by Humboldt. The great naturalist was the father of a discipline that virtually died with him: *Erdtheorie* or *La Physique du monde,* a kind of artistic geography, an aesthetic understanding of the world, a science of landscape. Alexander von Humboldt (1769–1859) was an all-embracing scholar, perhaps the last of his kind: his aim was to apprehend the world in its totality; and the way to do this, he believed, in conformity with a long tradition, was through vision. Yet his approach was new in that, rather than isolating images and treating them as "emblems" of knowledge, his aim was to accumulate and coordinate them within a broad framework, for which landscape provided the model. The artistic geographer had to capture the "physiognomy" of the landscape (Humboldt had borrowed this concept from Lavater) by picking out its characteristic "physiognomic" traits, which his scholarly studies in natural science would enable him to recognize. The precise arrangement of physiognomic elements in the picture would speak volumes to the observer's sensibility, conveying information not in the form of isolated features but features systematically interrelated so as to be intuitively grasped: climate, history, customs, economy, race, fauna, flora, rainfall, prevailing winds. ... The key to it all was "natural growth," which is why the vegetable element occupied the foreground, and why, in search of physiognomic landscapes, Humboldt went to the tropics, which were incomparably superior to Europe in terms of plant variety and rates of growth. He lived for many years in tropical regions of Asia and America, and encouraged the artists who had adopted his approach to do likewise. Thus he established a circuit, stimulating curiosity in Europe about regions that were still little known and creating a market for the works of the traveling painters.

Humboldt had the highest admiration for the young Rugendas, whom he dubbed the "founding father of the art of pictorial presentation of the physiognomy of nature," a description that could well have applied to himself. He played an advisory role in the painter's second great voyage, and the only point on which they disagreed was the decision to include Argentina in the itinerary. Humboldt did not want his disciple to waste his efforts south of the tropical zone, and in his letters he was generous with recommendations such as the following: "Do not squander your talent, which is suited above all to the depiction of that which is truly exceptional in landscape, such as snowy mountain peaks, bamboo, tropical jungle flora, groups composed of a single plant species at different ages; filiceae, lataniae, feathery-fronded palms, bamboo, cylindrical cactuses, red-flowered mimosas, the inga tree with its long branches and broad leaves, shrub-sized malvaceous plants with digitate leaves, particularly the Mexican hand plant (Chiranthodendron) in Toluca; the famous ahuehuete of Atlixco (the thousand-year-old Cupressus disticha) in the environs of Mexico City; the species of orchids that flower beautifully on the rounded, moss-covered protuberances of tree-trunks, surrounded in turn by mossy bulbs of dendrobium; the forms of fallen mahogany branches covered with orchids, banisteriae and climbing plants; gramineous species from the bamboo family reaching heights of twenty to thirty feet, bignoniaceae and the varieties of foliis distichis; studies of pothos and dracontium; a trunk of Crescentia cujete laden with calabashes; a flowering Theobroma cacao with flowers springing up from the roots; the external roots of Cupressus disticha, up to four feet tall, shaped like stakes or planks; studies of a rock covered with fucus; blue water lilies in water; guastavia (pirigara) and flowering lecitis; a tropical jungle viewed from a vantage point high on a mountain, showing only the broad crowns of flowering trees, from which the bare trunks of the palms rise like a colonnade, another jungle on top of the jungle; the differing material physiognomies of pisang and heliconium. ..."

The excess of primary forms required to characterize a landscape could only be found in the tropics. In so far as vegetation was concerned, Humboldt had reduced these forms to nineteen: nineteen physiognomic types that had nothing to do with Linnaean classification, which is based on the abstraction and isolation of minimal differences. The Humboldtian naturalist was not a botanist but a landscape artist sensitive to the processes of growth operative in all forms of life. This system provided the basis for the "genre" of painting in which Rugendas specialized.

Chapter 96

Mattias Gerwald
[Berndt Schulz]
The Explorer
2001

Condors

Unexpectedly the setting sun sent glittering rays up through the dissolving mist. A west wind picked up. And Alexander saw how the sky was speckled with white shapes. Were they birds' feathers reflecting in the sunlight? The shapes soared with great speed from the valley and moved over the crest of the neighboring peaks. Some fell back onto the southern slope.

"Do you see that?"

"Yes!"

"What is that?"

"Birds?"

"No."

"Oh I think it is. It's condors. They're gliding in a thermal updraft."

The climbers' boots were soaked through with snow-water. It froze quickly. None of the three could feel his feet any longer. Each step grew heavy. And the burden pressed down still more when the men took account of the sad solitude around them. On these steep slopes everything cried out with ill will and repulsion. It was no place for humans.

Now the temperature sank quickly to five degrees below freezing. The hair, eyebrows and beards of the mountain climbers had long been frozen, crusted blood stuck to their faces. They had to wipe ice-crystals from their eyes and

Translation by James Adam Redfield, from Mattias Gerwald, *Der Entdecker. Historischer Roman über Alexander von Humboldt* (Bergisch Gladbach: Bastei Lübbe, 2001), 354–357, 362–364. Copyright © 2001 by Verlagsgruppe Lübbe GmbH & Co. KG.

could no longer breathe through their noses. The ice-cold air burned their lungs with each gasp of breath.

It was now seven at night. Visibility was getting worse. The climbers couldn't even see the crest nor any of the nearby snowy mountains, not to mention the Quito plateau. They felt infinitely alone and isolated. "Like in a Blanchard balloon. Higher and higher, into air ever thinner and more silent," Alexander thought as he forced one foot in front of another.

And then everything happened very fast.

Alexander broke through a snowdrift. He fell down flat and was horrified to feel the ground give way under him. Bonpland cried out:

"Alexander … !"

Then he too began to slide downwards. Next to him he noticed Carlos, whose cry of fear called forth an unpleasant realization of his own situation. They toppled over the spur of a rock into the depths, slid further. But after thirty meters the sliding game came to an end. When they landed roughly next to each other, they looked up and saw that a sparkling, dripping, ice-cold roof had closed over them. They were trapped at the bottom of a cave.

*

They had tried everything. They had run around the cave like men possessed, had hammered against the ice and searched for an opening. With their hands and feet they had crawled up on the loose snow that had delivered them down, only to come sliding down again and again with piles of snow. They had scratched rungs in the ice with their knives, dug a diagonal tunnel, tried to grab onto an icicle with the rope. All in vain. They had knocked themselves out trying everything in the ten- by twenty-meter crevasse, and failed. Ultimately nothing remained but the terrifying knowledge that they were stuck.

Shortly after nightfall the three men sat huddled together on the frozen floor of the ice crevasse. The realization of having done everything and accomplished nothing was doubly exhausting to them. The rum that they passed around in a tube didn't heighten their spirits either, but it warmed them.

Suddenly large shapes appeared above them, throwing shadows in the clear moonlight. They fluttered here and there. The fog was gone.

"What is that?" Carlos whispered.

"Condors. Vultures. They smell carrion," Bonpland said in a tight voice.

Humboldt cleared his throat. "Let's review. We survived the fall unharmed and didn't break any bones, that's the most important thing. It might even be better to spend the night here. It's definitely less cold. We have to make the best of it, we're stuck here for the time being. As soon as it's light we'll look for a way out."

"If we aren't frozen by then!"

"I don't think so, Carlos. Up there, with the wind and the frost, the danger of that would definitely be greater. At night the temperature goes down to at least 15 degrees."

"And the vultures?" Bonpland asked.

"That doesn't concern us," said Humboldt with confidence. "They're not coming down. If they do—well, we still have our strength and we can defend ourselves."

"Still, wouldn't it be better to use every minute instead of sitting around?"

"We shouldn't fall into a panic," Alexander countered. "Let's calmly consider what we can do. That way we can relax for a few hours. Let's gather all our strength for tomorrow morning."

"If only these cursed vultures weren't here!"

The three men moved close together to warm themselves. With the thick ponchos and the schnapps there was enough heat to withstand a few hours.

"Read us something, Alexander. I know you brought along the little book with your notes in it."

"No, please don't," Carlos retorted. "I don't want to listen. Then the silence of this terrible mountain will just get louder."

"It's fine, Carlos. It's really all right," Humboldt consoled him.

"I just don't want to die, you know, Baron? I am twenty-one and I still have a lot ahead of me. I want to join up with Bolívar, we'll create a just world! If only those birds weren't up there. ..."

"You don't die that quickly," Alexander said in an exaggerated jovial tone, although his courage too was ebbing. "The condors don't mean anything at all. They're everywhere in these parts."

No one said anything else. They all looked up, towards—it seemed to Alexander—freedom and death. "We can't give up," he said to himself. "When we give up, we're lost. But maybe everything really is over—how quickly it can happen, how banal it is." He was angry, but not too much, he was too tired for it. At the same time thoughts rumbled rough and loud in his head.

~

"Has anything occurred to you?" Humboldt asked.

"All sorts of things," Bonpland said, "but honestly nothing that helps us."

Carlos just shook his head.

"That's it!"

The two others turned to look at Humboldt as if electrified. The despair in their eyes frightened him. "Listen," he said. "Let's think about the location of this cave. It has a diagonal elevation, even as much as sixty percent downwards. Right?"

"Yeah, sure. Probably. So?"

"Until now we've been trying to get up over the sloping walls, to go the direct way. This seemed obvious, but it didn't work for us. And it also wasn't thought-through. Then we tried a tunnel—but in the wrong direction."

"Humboldt! Mining Inspector Humboldt! Don't keep us on tenterhooks!"

"We have to go the indirect way. A detour often gets you there faster. We don't have to go up, but down. ..."

His companions looked at him skeptically.

"Are you serious?" Aimé asked.

Humboldt ignored the objection. "We have to dig! *There!*" Alexander pointed with his finger at the side towards the valley. "It looks like we'll be digging into the mountain, but actually we'll be digging out of it. Think about it! The wall can't be so thick. As I said, the mountain has at least a 60 percent downhill incline."

"Ingenious!" Bonpland was perplexed.

A little color came back to Carlos' face. "You could be right there. So, what are we waiting for?"

Doggedly they set to work. Each of them had a knife and, separated by a meter, they carved the ice out of the wall. But their hopes didn't come true. It went so slowly that it seemed they would need days to break through. Bonpland's knife-blade almost broke off and he had cut himself badly. Aimé let himself fall in the snow, exhausted. "We won't make it. ..."

"Take a break. We'll keep going."

"But there's just no point!"

"Aimé! We just have this one chance!"

Humboldt and Carlos Montúfar hacked doggedly on. Aimé, too, joined in after a long moment of resignation.

From disappointment and exhaustion they dug slower and slower. And yet suddenly they noticed that it was nevertheless going faster. The knives cut more deeply into the snow and they could scoop out larger amounts.

Dumbfounded, with new hope, they looked at each other. "It can only have to do with the fact that the ice is getting more porous," Humboldt conjectured.

The success doubled their strength. Now they were doing five meters an hour. And after four hours of hard work, a white wall in front of them suddenly collapsed. They looked out—and saw the rising sun, edging whitish-gold over a low mountain-ridge in the valley of Quito.

The men broke into exultation. Carlos struck the ice under him with his fist again and again. Alexander just smiled, content. Bonpland babbled senselessly.

"We did it, Inspector! You're a genius!" he cried.

They crawled into the open air. Now the ball of sun stood swelled to fullness over Quito, but it took the three men a few seconds to grasp why it was at their feet. "We're at the very top, almost in heaven," Bonpland said.

The vultures had disappeared.

Chapter 97

GÜNTER HERBURGER

Humboldt. Travel-Novella

2001

It was said that when the elderly Alexander von Humboldt was in Berlin he hurried in the evenings up flights of stairs from one salon to another; then dispensing hand-kisses, a few tender complements and several courteous denigrations, and he was gone again, the thriving old man; downstairs the coach with coachman and servant was waiting. The four lanterns of the springy carriage, one on each corner, never went out, not even in storm and rain.

It will never be that way again, now that we're stuck in the atomic zoo of particularized sciences, even cautiously now and then inch towards sundry theologies in light of the big bang gap of God, which even set a little lithium free as a third element, chemical refreshment for those lost in reverie.

Humboldt was the last universal scholar, he could even draw very well, organize at the same time, on the road in cold and heat, the researcher and spy in countries that were very distant back then. At the same time the social mission was just as important to him as the aesthetic one. He condemned slaveholders, painted watercolors of rotting bits of skin with the same curiosity and consideration of beauty as flower petals. He also ate everything, trusted his intestinal flora, which silently adapted to each climate, which meant: ego and immune system depend on each other.

Only with music did he accomplish little, never sang, let alone imitated, but listened: to extreme locusts, to icy boulder clay or to an old Cuban woman, and there, on that island, he nearly stayed, but his maternal inheritance of millions came to an end. Additionally he chose to bring home stones, pictures, hundredweight herbariums and draw up the work to end all works, which he

Translation by James Adam Redfield, from Günter Herburger, *Humboldt. Reise-Novellen* (München: A1 Verlag, 2001), 5–22. Copyright © 2001 A1 Verlag München. The fifteen images from this photo essay are reproduced without figure captions in accordance with the original format.

did, in French. He did not live to see the presentation of the collected edition; 34 volumes, Paris.

He had no children, would have been exceedingly odd in light of the Hegelian syllogism: when, where, how?

Towards the end of his life he was in Siberia, again enthusiastic, so many new things to discover, that are closer to us, for, as he said, whoever doesn't value the hybrid can only become misanthropic and come to false judgments at home, the most familiar place.

Nostalgia creeps up. Why is the era of the pioneers, of the troops of genius now past? Must we now begin to apprentice ourselves?

He would probably have recommended: sans le présent ne pas des pronoms interrogatifs; without the present there are no interrogative pronouns.

Illustration 97.1

When he looked out the window and discovered the Barrio, the settlement of small blocks, he was happy to have fled from what he called the cold, Buddhist hell of the Potsdam royal court. He wore a neck scarf, a Prussian overcoat and was accompanied by a bulldog in the European manner.

Illustration 97.2

In his Paris lecture series on popular science, held from 1825 to 1827, he in-sisted on an aesthetic treatment of objects of natural history. He was good on his feet, was a steadfast rider and mastered the dugout canoe. Thanks to his mother's estate he remained largely independent, after expeditions he could therefore afford to give free lectures at the Berlin Choral Academy.

Illustration 97.3

Humboldt's curiosity never wore itself out. Inhospitable alien places especially attracted him. He didn't just want to get acquainted, he wanted to understand them. His folded sheets of cartography and water colors of plants and animals are first rate.

Illustration 97.4

Yes, he mastered eleven languages, but here he stopped short, he didn't want to consider the possibly Indian symbols of fertility and sexuality; he wrote that sometimes among unsophisticated natives the confusion of taste is accompanied by cannibalism.

Illustration 97.5

This swing reminded him of the preparation of thick-flowing curare arrow poison. He said it tasted pleasantly bitter, and he often swallowed small quantities. No danger, you just have to be careful that you're not bleeding on the lips and gums. After being struck a chicken dies within three minutes, it takes four times as long for a pig.

Illustration 97.6

Lavish abundance spreads itself out as on the upper Orinoco. Humboldt discovered the remains of a Guácharo bird, probably brought down by murderous Potsdam pigeons. Urban culture, he noted, likewise holds onto secrets. And with the plantago vulgata, the common plantain, it occurred to him that the nakedness of the blossoms was abnormal.

Illustration 97.7

For a long time there was a Siberian colony on a small knoll on the palace grounds, which served as a refuge for a few refugees during wars. Alexander von Humboldt ate dried fruits there, tasting of horsehair, and a kind of raisins which, according to him, bore the name Kischmisch. His gifts were boots, leggings he designed himself and a bundle of shawls.

Illustration 97.8

The Russian-German friendship, which has since been reinstated, was a matter nearest his heart. On his journey from Dorpat through St. Petersburg and the Urals to the Altai, he celebrated his 60th birthday. He wrote in a letter that he had danced at night with Kalmyk oarsmen, but had, because of much indulgence in firewater, confused them with sled dogs. Rattling hard-backed bugs also pushed their way in.

Illustration 97.9

Ruined cities of the Mayas, Incas and Aztecs were known to the researcher. He sketched them and contemplated the details that he vainly tried to compare with Greek capitals. The atrocious scenery in stone, he noted, signified grandeur and tragedy, but his confidence remains a flight into the finite. Goethe and Schiller raved about a flight, an escape into the infinite.

Illustration 97.10

There are hotels, pharmacies, universities, liqueurs, shoulder bags, even subway stations with the name of the last universal scholar. In Venezuela, Humboldt mania reigns. There they assert that the country was first invented by the German's five-year journey.

Illustration 97.11

When he visited Peruvian silver mines he was horrified by the working conditions. There are no higher and no lower races of men, he wrote. He denounced slavery as an abomination. What we were presented with from it, turns out to be trivial artwork in the public space.

Illustration 97.12

He never ventured into the colony of the pure Lutheran church. From the design of the brickwork, it was built later. It housed workshops, families, a school, a kindergarten and government offices. The Blumenau settlement in Brazil could be one of its offshoots.

Illustration 97.13

This trail doesn't lead to the foot of the Chimborazo, which Humboldt scaled with his friend Bonpland, the botanist. The two bold classifiers almost managed to reach the crater of the frozen volcano. A fastidiously drawn profile of the vegetation with the side of a mountain covered in Latin plant names in miniscule writing, like flurries of snow, attests to it.

Illustration 97.14

The sign reads: This oak was planted in the year 1796 by the pupil Friedrich Martel. He came from a district not far from the Dordogne, attended the school for cadets of the old-fashioned Potsdam royal residence, perhaps wanted a token to be left of his newly-acquired nationality and subservience.

Illustration 97.15

Alexander von Humboldt, whose painstaking hand-crafted sextants, theodolites, thermo-, baro-, and hygrometers are legendary, was devoted to the future and to the beginning industrialization. He designated it as expansive diversity and a muse, if only we endeavored to value the colors of aesthetics.

Chapter 98

LAUREN GUNDERSON
Wide World
2004

DOLLEY MADISON An adventurer of your caliber in this house. My, what a world. You must know you are the absolute talk of the town. As soon as we heard you were coming the whole town just lit up. All the ladies are sure they love you already, and are desperate to follow you just about anywhere … but not everywhere!

Humboldt forces a smile. Bonpland stifles a giggle.

And you're Prussian! That is something, isn't it.
BONPLAND Quite something.
JEFFERSON Something I'm sure the good Baron is too exhausted to spend much time discussing.
DOLLEY You're not going to take the Baron away from us before we hear the terrifying tales from the South, are you Mister President?
JEFFERSON I'm sure he's very tired.
DOLLEY Well he could at least sum it up.
BONPLAND *smiling* Yes, why don't you "sum it up."

Humboldt eyes Bonpland, and thinks nervously.

HUMBOLDT *In one breath* Sea voyage, fever, inland trek, snakes, more fever, forests, forests, mountains, river, waterfall, near drowning, mosquitoes the size of that ham, fever, poison, jaguar, to the ocean, back to the mountains, up to the top, volcano, fever, Mexico City, storm that almost sunk us, Philadelphia, fever, here.

Lauren Gunderson, *Wide World,* first public staged reading 14 October 2004, Break A Leg Productions, commissioned by City University of New York Graduate Center for the *Alexander von Humboldt: From the Americas to the Cosmos International Conference.* Copyright © 2004 Lauren Gunderson Production; rights for "Wide World" are available through www.LaurenGunderson.com.

A moment.

DOLLEY That is something, isn't it.

~

PEALE Fascinating. You are a hero of reason.

JEFFERSON Truly a scholar and a gentleman.

HUMBOLDT Then Monsieur Bonpland is my sanity.

BONPLAND Or his Sancho, depending on the situation.

JEFFERSON I find it a pleasant thought to be that optimistic when I approach
   Señor Quixote's age. Something to aim for, at least.

HUMBOLDT I have seen enough of the world to trust its optimism, myself.
   There are too many incredible events happening in every corner of the universe to believe it has no sense of hope.

PEALE And the people. The indigenous men and women. What were they
   like? So different from us?

HUMBOLDT They ate and slept like we do.

PEALE Yes?

HUMBOLDT The cultures are so varied it is hard to make generalizations.
   Some of them wore little more than animal skins, some full cloaks. Some
   painted clothes on their bodies.

PEALE Oh my.

DOLLEY How barbaric.

HUMBOLDT Actually I found most of the barbarians to be quite civilized.

DOLLEY Really? Civilized in the jungles?

HUMBOLDT Quite. They have simple but sufficient industry, medicine,
   fashion, even.

DOLLEY Fashionable barbarians, too?

HUMBOLDT It's another way of life for sure, but not altogether a foreign one.

DOLLEY You wonder what sort of real civilization a country like that could
   have if they would accept the missionaries and properly apply the Negroes.

A moment for this to register.

HUMBOLDT I would fain to suggest it.

DOLLEY You'd think it would be obvious, wouldn't you. They could really be
   something.

Another careful moment.

HUMBOLDT I think it would be obvious in this country above all others that
   it's barbaric to ground a state in the rhetoric of freedom and equality only to
   enslave half the population. I think the real barbarism comes in the form of
   the educated hypocrisy. One that allows the obvious and profound disgrace
   of a people for the purpose of extracting a profit and forgoing a life.

A moment.

DOLLEY *coldly* That is something, isn't it.
HUMBOLDT I'm sorry. That may have been a bit—
DOLLEY Baron. I understand your reference, and coming from the jungles of the South I can only imagine the social structure you encountered. But I don't think you understand how things work here.
HUMBOLDT Yes. I try to understand how they work *everywhere*. That universality is the world's promise to us as human beings. Biased oppression is simply out of fashion, Madam.

∼

ANNABELLE JEFFERSON You're a scientist?
HUMBOLDT I am, yes.
ANNABELLE Of what?
HUMBOLDT Well. …
ANNABELLE Geography? Geology? Astronomy? Botany?
BONPLAND Yes.

∼

JEFFERSON Your discoveries can be invaluable to us.
HUMBOLDT I'm sure they can, sir.
JEFFERSON I speak of Mexico. You have maps, information, sketches of what we might find as our explorers go west.

Bonpland coughs in the direction of Humboldt.

HUMBOLDT I do. Meant for Spain of course.
JEFFERSON I see.

Bonpland coughs again. Humboldt ignores it.

HUMBOLDT But they, happily, do not. I have the maps in my trunk and will be happy to explain them. Aimé, please go to the carriage––
BONPLAND If you think this is right. … Yes, I'll be right back.

Bonpland leaves.

JEFFERSON This will be a great help to myself and Monsieurs Clark and Lewis.
HUMBOLDT I am sad to have missed them. It is a great journey they've begun.
JEFFERSON Someone's got to know what all we've got in this country.
HUMBOLDT Twice as big all of a sudden.
JEFFERSON Twice as rich.
HUMBOLDT And these new states. What is their position?

JEFFERSON West.

HUMBOLDT No. I mean, position ... on the slaves.

A moment.

JEFFERSON Yes.

And we have come back to your initial interest.

HUMBOLDT Fear more than interest, Mister President. I am concerned for the stability of this great country.

JEFFERSON As am I. It is a difficult wind to chart. I understand your issue, and I hope you know the lengths to which I have gone to alleviate the effect of slavery on this country.

HUMBOLDT Except on your own farm?

JEFFERSON There are several issues here.

HUMBOLDT There are thousands of issues here.

JEFFERSON There always are when dealing with profits, populations, and philosophy. . . .

HUMBOLDT In that order? In *that* order. Sir. When we were stationed on the coast of Venezuela I rented a house on the town square. Three, four times a week I would wake up to a sight I can only describe to you with clinched hands. A slave trade. Men from Africa, fresh off a boat, lathered in coconut oil to make them gleam like fruit. Pranced around like horses, sold like livestock. Hand-cuffed and chained together. That is the earthly opposite of humanity. And I saw it on every shore in South America, in Cuba, and most disturbingly, in your great country. I cannot imagine a less appropriate way to follow your country's edict of "all men created equal."

JEFFERSON I thought you a man of science, not politics.

HUMBOLDT I am a man of the world. And this corner of the world needs more than science. It needs heart.

Silence.

I don't mean to directly chastise. I just ... need to understand. From the man I've respected since I was young. How this continues?

JEFFERSON It won't. I've pressed law after law trying to ensure a gradual but eventual emancipation of the slaves. I've tried to outlaw slavery in our new territories. Trying to progress toward another system to sustain this country's livelihood.

HUMBOLDT Nothing has come of these attempts?

JEFFERSON That is hard to answer. I seem to be resigned to lay the ground-work for future activists.

HUMBOLDT I wish you would not give up. I fear this issue will bite, if left too long.

JEFFERSON It's not the only thing that will bite if I try to disband it too soon. We are a young country. You must appreciate its delicacy.

HUMBOLDT Souls are rather delicate, aren't they.

JEFFERSON So is mass stability.

HUMBOLDT There will be wars fought for this.

JEFFERSON They're fought everyday.

HUMBOLDT Injustice anywhere is a threat to it everywhere.

JEFFERSON Sometimes *everywhere* is not prepared to be *any*where.

HUMBOLDT Does this not sting of hypocrisy, Mister President?

JEFFERSON Only when you look from just one side.

HUMBOLDT Then you allow the right questions to be answered with the wrong logic.

Annabelle enters with tea. The men stop. She sets down the tea. Silence.

ANNABELLE You're welcome.

JEFFERSON Baron. Why don't I go help Monsieur Bonpland prepare the maps for our viewing. We can compare your drawings to our initial ones, and see where we stand.

HUMBOLDT I would like that.

JEFFERSON I'll be back in just a moment. Enjoy some tea.

Humboldt stands. Jefferson stops.

HUMBOLDT Mister President.
My experience with the Negroes is the only thing I know that I didn't have to study to confirm.

Jefferson nods and leaves.

ANNABELLE I said, you're welcome.

HUMBOLDT Thank you.

She sits next to him. Silence.

ANNABELLE Well. What do you think?

He takes a sip of tea.

HUMBOLDT Oh … It's very … hot.

ANNABELLE Not the tea, the country. Do you like it here?

HUMBOLDT Parts of it.

ANNABELLE Me too.

HUMBOLDT Parts of it are very difficult to accept.

ANNABELLE Hm. I hope I will grow up one day and be able to help make things better. Like Grandfather. Plus, I tend to be right a lot. That helps.

HUMBOLDT Sometimes seeing what's right and being right are very different things.

ANNABELLE I suppose you're right. Or did you just see yourself being right and know that what you saw was you being right.

Giggles.

　　Right?

More giggling.

HUMBOLDT *Laughs a bit himself. An idea.* Miss. I have something to ask you. Something I wish to speak to you about.

ANNABELLE Yes?

HUMBOLDT A proposal.

ANNABELLE Oh my. …

HUMBOLDT I've been talking to your Grandfather as you know.

ANNABELLE Yes. …

HUMBOLDT And he agrees. This is really quite important.

ANNABELLE Well, we just met but—

HUMBOLDT Something that could mightily move your country, an essential part of life. …

ANNABELLE My goodness, I didn't think it could happen so fast—

HUMBOLDT A perfect use of your time—

ANNABELLE I should hope so. …

HUMBOLDT A union—

ANNABELLE Oh my!

HUMBOLDT Of justice and legacy.

ANNABELLE Of—what?

HUMBOLDT Of humanity and national security.

ANNABELLE Wait. What are you talking about?

HUMBOLDT What are *you* talking about?

Pause.

ANNABELLE Marriage.

HUMBOLDT Slavery.

Chapter 99

HANS MAGNUS ENZENSBERGER

Alexander von Humboldt and François Arago

2004

∽

A scientific tête-à-tête in the Paris Observatory

ARAGO Welcome to this shabby temple of science! If you knew, Alexander, just how ramshackle this observatory is! Abysmal instruments, a half-blind doorman, making our observations in a mice-ridden annex because the main building is unusable. ...

HUMBOLDT And you in the seat reserved for the lord of the manor. From here you'll not just conquer Paris, but rather the most unfamiliar stellar nebulae and most distant of galaxies.

ARAGO We will! You and I. Even though you've already arrived at the very top and I remain no more than the clerk of this establishment. A handy-man. My aged master is sitting up there at the telescope, same as every night. He calculates and calculates in the cold. I wish I had his patience. Here, those are his computations. The libration of the moon. You know, there really is something very tricky about those irregularities. A mess of numbers that I can't fathom.

HUMBOLDT But he lets you alone, and you can pursue your own star.

ARAGO Thank God. The dear Bouvard!

HUMBOLDT He has no ideas. It's a good fit.

ARAGO But you do.

Translation by Steven Sidore, from Hans Magnus Enzensberger, "Präsidenten, Konsuln und Kaiser kommen und gehen, aber die Natur ist unbesiegbar. Alexander von Humboldt und François Arago: Ein wissenschaftliches Tête-à-tête in der Sternwarte zu Paris," in *Frankfurter Allgemeine Zeitung*, 16 September 2004, 33. Copyright © Hans Magnus Enzensberger.

HUMBOLDT Unfortunately, I have too many. That's a bit of a disadvantage in the academic world.

~

HUMBOLDT I fear that things are not well in France.

ARAGO The Corsican will ruin it with his delusions of grandeur.

HUMBOLDT Naturally. And then he'll wreck, like all of his ilk. The history of mankind is full with such figures. But have no fears, we'll survive him.

ARAGO You say that so cold-bloodedly. But I hate him and his regime.

HUMBOLDT You are and will remain a hothead. And I love that about you. Yet you should always remember one thing: It's better for us to stick to our work. Science lives longer than power. The presidents, consuls, and emperors come and go, but the natural forces that we research are invincible. We are fortunate people, because we have an enormous task before us; and if we can accomplish something, then it's not thanks to, but rather in spite of the governments breathing down our necks.

ARAGO Yes, you've already proved just what you're capable of. You've measured an entire continent, and the fruits of your labor will occupy generations to come. But I . . .

HUMBOLDT Shall I recount your own adventures for you? The measurement of the meridian, the Spanish jails, the intermezzo with the Bey of Algiers, the pirate attack, the quarantine? You were declared dead! I shudder to think of it!

ARAGO That was then. Now I sit here, clerk of a second-rate observatory, dependent on the benevolence of a self-declared majesty.

HUMBOLDT Yes, and so the world turns, my dear friend. Do you think that I've had it any differently? To reach your goals you must think in the long term, like a strategist. And in a pinch, stick to the Bible. Be soft as a dove, cunning as a snake.

ARAGO Yes, you know your way there, Alexander. I'm not sure whether I should admire you for it. This diplomatic talent, this discretion, this subtlety! Whether it's your own king or Spain's, you always manage to get your way with these lords. Even Napoleon hasn't been able to get the better of you. It's fantastic, but frightening as well. One day you'll become a minister and have run of the royal court.

HUMBOLDT But François, you know perfectly well that I've always refused such offers. Just recently, in fact, my unfortunate king offered me just such a position. But I prefer to simply remain my own master. I cannot change that, nor do I want to.

ARAGO You can afford to do so.

HUMBOLDT Yes, that's true. I've inherited a lot of money. That helps my work. For myself, I just need a desk, a chair, and a bed. But I am glad that I can finance my travel volumes. I am a buccaneer of the sciences and require no man's leave. But as far as politics is concerned, my dear friend, I already sense that your passion for the republic will be your downfall some day. Though it would be tantalizing to have a man like you at the top, wouldn't it?

⌣

ARAGO What does the King of Prussia have to do with us, or Marshall Ney, or the campaign in Spain? We need weather stations in all parts of the earth to measure air pressure, temperatures, relative humidity, wind direction and strength, amounts and distribution of precipitation. …

HUMBOLDT And what about magnetism? The entire earth is a magnet. But—what does that really mean? Is it the same power as electricity? Wherever you look, it's all the same: We're only just getting started.

ARAGO I know precisely what I'll begin with. With light. I've got a theory. Well, theory is perhaps a bit of a stretch. A hunch. I believe Newton will be proven wrong on this matter. He claims that light beams consist of corpuscles much smaller than any atom. Until now, almost everyone believes this; no one cares to heed the teachings of old Huygens: light is wave-like by nature. I'm convinced that he was right. Deflection, refraction in various media. Interference, polarization, light speed. Someday you'll be able to calculate all these things with mathematic precision.

HUMBOLDT And gravitation? How do you explain that? We know its laws, but nobody knows just what gravity really is. Coincidentally, I'm also curious as to why the sky is blue and why the stars twinkle. But you're the astronomer of the two of us. You need to ask the right questions, even if the answer appears to be nowhere on the horizon.

ARAGO Not with our laughably weak telescopes.

HUMBOLDT The atmosphere of Mars and Venus.

ARAGO The rings of Saturn.

HUMBOLDT Uranus' satellites and its perturbations.

ARAGO Whether there are planets we've not yet recognized.

HUMBOLDT The composition of comets.

ARAGO The sun and its spots, its corona.

HUMBOLDT Where its energy comes from, the energy from which we live.

ARAGO The classes of the fixed stars, their births, development, and demise.

HUMBOLDT Novas that appear suddenly in the heavens. The grand spiral nebula. Perhaps there are thousands of Milky Ways out there. Dark clouds and holes that no telescope can penetrate.

ARAGO Whether our universe is the only one?

HUMBOLDT And how did it begin? I don't believe in the Bible. You, perhaps?

ARAGO Stop it! My head is spinning! I can't go on.

HUMBOLDT You see where it's headed. We and our science—in the end perhaps we are the crazy ones. What do you think?

ARAGO Perhaps. But to use the words of the English poet: Though this be madness, yet there is method in 't.

HUMBOLDT Between us, my dear François—I've got a terrific idea. Do you know what we'll do once we get old? With combined powers, we'll depict the entire natural world, everything that we know about the phenomena of the heavenly spaces, of the stellar nebulae, right down to the geography of moss on granite, all in one single large work that is comprehensible to all. Every idea of significance and importance, wherever it has arisen, must be documented there.

ARAGO It's good that no one is listening to us. Who knows, otherwise they'd perhaps end up sticking us in the madhouse.

Things never progressed that far. Neither did the two friends ever realize their plans to travel together. François Arago made several significant contributions to optics and to magnetism, but his creative period as a researcher ended shortly after he turned forty-five. Thereafter he became a grand promoter of science. He fostered countless talented figures and was unrivaled in helping natural science achieve a public resonance. He would later get caught in the pull of French politics. Following the Revolution of 1848, he was made a member of the provisional government—by and large without any action on his part—first as a war and maritime minister, and then, if only for a few weeks, as the very head of government. He actually managed during this brief time to end slavery in the French colonies. But the February Revolution famously ended in debacle, one from which Arago never recovered. When Louis Napoléon carried out a coup shortly thereafter, an era of European political dreams was extinguished. Arago died in October 1853, blind and racked by incurable disease.

Alexander von Humboldt outlived his much younger friend by six years. In his old age, he lived as a chamberlain to the Prussian king in Berlin. "Evenings at court," he said, means "clawing at the walls from sheer monotony." Yet Friedrich Wilhelm IV at least protected him from his numerous enviers and antagonists. Lavished with honors but emotionally isolated, he did indeed implement his "terrific idea." He worked on his masterpiece, the *Kosmos*, up until he drew his last breath in his nineties in 1859. As to his friendship with Arago, one that spanned more than four decades, he said: "Not a single cloud ever darkened it in more than forty years."

Chapter 100

Daniel Kehlmann
Measuring the World
2005

Alexander von Humboldt was famous in all of Europe for an expedition to the tropics he had led twenty-five years earlier. He had been in New Spain, New Granada, New Barcelona, New Andalusia, and the United States; he had discovered the natural canal that connects the Orinoco and the Amazon; he had climbed the highest mountain in the known world; he had collected thousands of plants and hundreds of animals, some living, the majority dead; he had talked to parrots, disinterred corpses, measured every river, every mountain, and every lake in his path, had crawled into burrows and had tasted more berries and climbed more trees than anyone could begin to imagine.

He was the younger of two brothers. Their father, a wealthy man of the minor nobility, had died early. When seeking advice on how to educate her sons, his mother had turned to no less a figure than Goethe.

The latter's response was that a pair of brothers in whom the whole panoply of human aspirations so manifested itself, thus promising that the richest possibilities both of action and aesthetic appreciation might become exemplary reality, presented as it were a drama capable of filling the mind with hope and feeding the spirit with much to reflect upon.

Nobody could make head or tail of this sentence. Not their mother, not Kunth the majordomo, a rail of a man with large ears. He took it to mean, he said finally, that it was a kind of experiment. The one should be educated to be a man of culture, and the other a man of science.

And which was which?

Kunth thought. Then he shrugged his shoulders and suggested that they toss a coin.

Fifteen highly paid experts came to lecture them at university level. For the younger brother it was chemistry, physics, and mathematics, for the elder it was languages and literature, and for them both it was Greek, Latin, and philosophy. Twelve hours a day, seven days a week, with no time off and no holidays.

The younger brother, Alexander, was taciturn and frail; he needed encouragement in everything he did and his marks were mediocre. When left to his own devices, he wandered in the woods, collecting beetles and ordering them in categories he made up himself. At the age of nine he followed Benjamin Franklin's design and built a lightning conductor and attached it to the roof of the castle they lived in near the capital. It was only the second anywhere in Germany; the other was in Göttingen, mounted on physics professor Lichtenberg's roof. These were the only two places where one was safe from the heavens.

The elder brother looked like an angel. He could talk like a poet and from the earliest age wrote precocious letters to the most famous men in the country. Everyone who met him was dazzled, almost overcome. By thirteen he had mastered two languages, by fourteen four, by fifteen seven. He had never been punished; nobody could even remember him doing anything wrong. With English envoys he talked about economic policy, with the French the dangers of insurrection. Once he locked his younger brother in a cupboard in a distant room. When a servant found the little boy half-unconscious the next day, he swore he'd locked himself in; he knew nobody would believe the truth. Another time he discovered a white powder in his food. He knew enough about chemistry to identify it as rat poison. With trembling hands he pushed the plate away. From the other side of the table his elder brother watched him knowingly, his pale eyes impenetrable.

Nobody could deny that the castle was haunted. Nothing spectacular, just footsteps in empty corridors, sounds of children crying out of nowhere, and sometimes a shadowy man who asked in a rasping voice to buy shoelaces, little toy magnets, or a glass of lemonade. But the stories about the spirits were even eerier than the spirits themselves. Kunth gave the two boys books to read full of monks and open graves and hands reaching up out of the depths and potions brewed in the underworld and seances where the dead talked to terrified listeners. This kind of thing was just becoming fashionable and was still so novel that there was no familiarity that could inure people to the feelings of horror. And horror was necessary, according to Kunth, encountering the dark side of things was part of growing up; anyone innocent of metaphysical anxiety would never achieve German manhood. Once they stumbled on a story about Aguirre the Mad, who had renounced his king and declared himself emperor. He and his men traveled the length of the Orinoco in a journey that was the stuff of nightmares, past riverbanks so thick with undergrowth that it was impossible to land. Birds screamed in the language of extinct tribes, and when one looked up, the sky reflected cities whose architecture never came from human hands. Hardly any scholars had ever penetrated this region, and there was no reliable map.

But he would, said the younger brother. He would make the journey.

Naturally, the elder brother replied.

He really meant it!

Yes he understood that, said the elder brother and summoned a servant to note down the day and the exact time. The day would come when they would be glad they had fixed this moment.

Their teacher in physics and philosophy was Markus Herz, Immanuel Kant's favorite pupil and husband of the famed beauty Henriette. He poured two substances into a beaker: the liquid did nothing for a moment, then suddenly changed color. He poured hydrogen out of a little tube, held a flame to its mouth, and there was a joyous explosion of fire. Half a gram, he said, produced a twelve-centimeter flame. Whenever things were frightening, it was a good idea to measure them.

Henriette held a salon every week for intellectual sophisticates who talked of God and their feelings, wept a little, wrote one another letters, and called themselves the Assembled Virtues. No one could remember how this name had come about. Their conversations were kept secret from outsiders, but all impulses of the soul were to be shared completely openly with other Assembled Virtues. If the soul failed to experience impulses, they had to be invented. The two brothers were the youngest. This too was an essential part of their upbringing, said Kunth, and they must never miss a single gathering. It served to educate the emotions. Specifically, he encouraged them to write to Henriette. A neglect of one's sentimental education early in life could bear the most unfortunate fruit. It went without saying that every letter must be shown to him first. As expected, the elder brother's letters were finer.

Henriette's replies were courteous, and written in an unsure child's hand. She herself was barely nineteen. A book that the younger brother had lent to her was returned unread: *Man a Machine* by La Mettrie. A proscribed work, an abominable pamphlet! She could not bring herself to so much as open it.

What a pity, said the younger brother to the elder. It was a notable book. The author was insistent that man was a machine, a highly sophisticated automaton.

And no soul, answered the elder brother. They were walking through a park that surrounded the castle; a thin layer of snow coated the bare trees.

No, the younger boy contradicted him. With a soul. With intimations and a poetic feel for expanse and beauty. Nonetheless this soul itself was no more than a part, even if the most complex one, of the machine. And he asked himself if this didn't correspond to the truth.

All human beings are machines?

Perhaps not all, said the younger boy thoughtfully. But we are.

The pond was frozen over, and the late afternoon dusk was turning the snow and the icicles to blue. He had something to tell him, said the older boy. People were worried about him. His silences, his reserve. His laborious progress at his lessons. A great experiment would either stand or fall with them. Neither of them had the right to let go of things. He paused for a moment. The ice looks quite solid.

Really?

Yes of course.

The younger boy nodded, took a deep breath, and stepped onto the ice. He wondered if he should recite Klopstock's ode to skating. Arms swinging wide, he glided to the middle and turned in a circle. His brother was standing bent slightly forward on the bank, watching him.

Suddenly everything was silent. He couldn't see anything any more and the cold knocked him almost unconscious. Only now did he realize that he was underwater. He kicked out. His head banged against something hard, the ice. His sheepskin hat came off and floated away, his hair was loose and his feet hit bottom. Now his eyes were accustoming themselves to the darkness. For a moment he saw a frozen landscape: trembling stalks, things growing above them, transparent as a veil, a lone fish, there for a moment then gone, like a hallucination. He made swimming motions, rose in the water, banged into the ice again. He realized he only had a few more seconds to live. He groped, and at the moment when he ran out of air, he saw a dark patch above him, the opening; he dragged himself up, gasped in air, breathed out again and spat, the sharp angles of the ice cut into his hands, he heaved himself out, rolled away, pulling his legs up after him, and lay there, panting and sobbing. Turning onto his stomach, he belly-flopped toward the bank. His brother was still standing there, bent forward the way he had been, hands in his pockets, his cap pulled down over his face. He reached out a hand and helped him to his feet.

That night the fever started. He was aware of voices and didn't know whether they belonged to figures in his dreams or the people who were standing round his bed, and he could still feel the cold of the ice. A man who must be the doctor was pacing up and down the room, and said it's up to you, you'll either make it or you won't, it's your decision, all you have to do is hold on, you know. But when he tried to answer, he could no longer remember what had been said; instead he was looking at the wide expanse of a sea under skies flickering with electricity, and when he opened his eyes again it was noon two days later, the winter sun was hanging all pale in the window and his fever had broken.

From now on his marks improved. He concentrated when he worked and began a habit of balling his fists while thinking, as if there were an enemy to conquer. He had changed, Henriette said in a letter to him, and now he made her a little fearful. He asked permission to spend a night in the empty room which was the most frequent source of nocturnal sounds. In the morning he was white and quiet, and the first vertical line had appeared in his brow.

Kunth decided that the elder brother should study jurisprudence, and the younger, public administration. Of course he traveled with them when they went to university at Frankfurt-on-the-Oder; he accompanied them to lectures and oversaw their progress. It was not a good higher education. If someone incompetent wanted to earn his doctorate, the elder boy wrote to Henriette, he could come here in full confidence. And for some unknown reason there was also a large dog which attended lectures most of the time, scratching incessantly and making noises.

It was the botanist Willdenow who introduced the younger boy to his first dried plants from the tropics. They had protuberances that looked like feelers, buds like eyes, and leaves with upper surfaces that felt like human skin. They seemed familiar to him from his dreams. He dissected them, made careful sketches, tested their reaction to acids and alkalis, and worked them up cleanly into preparations.

He knew now, he said to Kunth, what he wanted to concern himself with: Life.

He couldn't give his approval, said Kunth. One had more tasks on earth than mere existence. Life in and of itself did not supply the content for existence.

That wasn't what he'd meant, he replied. He wanted to investigate Life, to understand its strange grip on the world. He wanted to uncover its tricks!

So he was allowed to stay and study with Willdenow. Next semester the elder brother transferred to the University of Göttingen. While he was finding his first friends there, trying his first alcohol, and touching his first woman, the younger boy was writing his first scientific paper.

Good, said Kunth, but not yet good enough to be printed under the name of Humboldt. Publication would have to wait.

During the holidays he visited his elder brother. At a reception given by the French consul, he met Kästner the mathematician, his friend Privy Councilor Zimmerman, and Professor Georg Christoph Lichtenberg, the most important experimental physicist in Germany. The latter, a hunchback, a clotted mass of flesh and intellect, with a flawlessly beautiful face, pressed his hand softly and stared up at him with a twinkle. Humboldt asked him if it was true he was working on a novel.

Yes and no, said Lichtenberg with a look that suggested he could see something beyond Humboldt's understanding. The work was called *About Gunkel*, had no story, and was making no progress.

Writing a novel, said Humboldt, seemed to him the perfect way to capture the most fleeting essence of the present for the future.

Aha, said Lichtenberg.

Humboldt blushed. It must be a foolish undertaking for an author, as was becoming the fashion these days, to choose some already distant past as his setting.

Lichtenberg observed him with narrowed eyes. No, he said. And yes.

On the way home, the brothers saw a second slice of silver, only slightly larger, alongside the newly risen moon. A hot-air balloon, the elder explained. Pilâtre de Rozier, a collaborator of the Montgolfier brothers, was in nearby Brunswick for the moment. The whole town was talking about it. Soon everyone would be going up in the air.

But they wouldn't want to, said the younger boy. They would be too afraid.

Shortly before leaving, he was introduced to the famous Georg Forster, a thin man with a cough and an unhealthy pallor. He had circumnavigated the globe with Cook and seen more than any German had ever seen; now he was a legend, his book was world-famous, and he worked as the librarian in Mainz. He told tales of dragons and the living dead, of supremely well-mannered cannibals, of days when the sea was so clear that one seemed to be rocking over an abyss, of storms so fierce that one didn't even dare pray. Melancholy enveloped him like a fine mist. He had seen too much, he said. That was the meaning of the simile about Odysseus and the Sirens. It was no good tying oneself to the mast; even when one escaped, one couldn't recover from the brush with the unknown. He could hardly sleep any more, he said, his memories were too strong. Recently he had had the news that his captain, the great saturnine Cook, had been boiled and eaten on Hawaii.

He rubbed his forehead and looked at the buckles on his shoes. Boiled and eaten, he said again.

He too wanted to go on voyages, said Humboldt.

Forster nodded. Quite a few had that wish. And every one of them regretted it later.

Why?

Because one could never come back.

Forster recommended him to the school of mining in Freiberg. It was where Abraham Werner worked. The earth's interior, he taught, was cold and hard. Mountain ranges were created by the chemical precipitations left as the primordial oceans shrank. The fire in volcanoes didn't come from deep in the earth, it was fed by burning coalfields. The core of the earth was solid rock. This theory was called Neptunism and was championed by both churches and Johann Wolfgang von Goethe. In the chapel at Freiberg Werner had masses said for the souls of his opponents who still denied the truth. Once he had broken the nose of a doubting student, and supposedly bitten off the ear of another years before. He was one of the last alchemists: member of secret lodges, expert in the signs that commanded the obedience of demons. He had the power to reassemble what had been destroyed, to re-create what had been burned from its smoke, and to make pulverized objects take shape again; he had also talked to the Devil and made gold. But he didn't give the impression of being an intelligent man. He leaned back, squeezed his eyes shut, and asked Humboldt if he was a Neptunist and believed in a cold earth's core.

Humboldt said yes.

Then he should get married.

Humboldt went red.

Werner puffed out his cheeks, looked conspiratorial, and asked if he had a sweetheart.

That was only an impediment, said Humboldt. One got married when one had nothing essential to do in life.

Werner stared at him.

Or so it was said, added Humboldt hurriedly. Of course that was wrong!

No unmarried man, said Werner, had ever made a good Neptunist.

Humboldt ran through the entire curriculum of the mining school in three months. In the mornings he spent six hours underground, in the afternoons he went to lectures, in the evenings and for half the night he learned what he needed for the next day. He had no friends, and when his brother invited him to his wedding—he had found a woman, he said, who suited him perfectly, there was no one like her in the world— he answered politely that he couldn't come, he had no time. He crawled through the lowest tunnels until he had accustomed himself to his claustrophobia as one would make peace with a relentless pain that slowly became bearable. He measured temperatures: the deeper one went, the warmer it got, which contradicted Abraham Werner's every teaching. He noticed that even in the deepest, darkest caves there was vegetation. Life seemed to have no boundary, some new form of moss or other growth occurred everywhere, or some kind of rudimentary plant. They struck him as sinister, which is why he dissected and examined them, classified them, and wrote an essay on each. Years later, when he saw similar plants in the Cavern of the Dead, he was prepared.

He took the final examinations and was given a uniform. He was supposed to wear it wherever he went. His official title was Assessor in the Department of Mines. He was embarrassed, he wrote to his brother, to be so pleased.

Not many months later he was already the most reliable inspector of mines in Prussia. He went on inspection tours of foundries, peat bogs, and the firing chimneys of the Royal Porcelain Factory; wherever he went, he scared the workers by the speed of his note-taking. He was always on the road, barely ate or slept, and had no idea himself what it was all supposed to be for. There was something in him, he wrote to his brother, that made him afraid he was losing his mind.

By chance he stumbled upon Galvani's book on electrical current and frogs. Galvani had removed the legs from frogs, then attached two different metals to them, and they had twitched as if alive. Was this something inherent in the legs themselves, which retained some life force, or was the movement of external origin, produced by the difference between the metals, and merely made manifest by the frog parts? Humboldt decided to find out.

He took off his shirt, lay down on the bed, and instructed a servant to attach two cupping glasses to his back. The servant obeyed, and Humboldt's skin produced two large blisters. And now please cut the blisters open! The servant hesitated, Humboldt had to raise his voice, the servant took up the scalpel. It was so sharp that the cut caused almost no pain. Blood dripped onto the floor. Humboldt ordered a piece of zinc to be laid on one of the wounds.

The servant asked if he could stop for a moment, he wasn't feeling well.

Humboldt told him not to be so stupid. As a piece of silver touched the second wound, a painful spasm shot through his back muscles and up into his head. With a shaking hand he made a note: *Musculus cucullaris,* ongoing prickling sensation in dorsal vertebrae. No doubt about it, this was electricity! Repeat with the silver! He counted four shocks, regularly spaced, then the objects around him lost their color.

When he regained consciousness, the servant was sitting white-faced on the floor, his hands bloody.

Onward, said Humboldt, and with a strange shiver of apprehension he realized that something in him was finding pleasure in this. Now for the frogs!

Oh no, said the servant.

Humboldt asked if he was intending to look for a new job.

The servant laid four dead, meticulously cleaned frogs on Humboldt's bloodied back. But this was quite enough, he said, after all they were both good Christians.

Humboldt ignored him and ordered silver again. The shocks began immediately. With each one, as he saw in the mirror, the frogs jumped as if alive. He bit down into the pillow, the cloth was wet from his tears. The servant giggled hysterically. Humboldt wanted to make notes, but his hands were too weak. Laboriously he got to his feet. The two wounds were running and the liquid coming out of them was so corrosive it was inflaming his skin. Humboldt tried to capture some of it in a glass tube, but his shoulder was swollen up and he couldn't turn round. He looked at the servant.

The servant shook his head.

Very well, said Humboldt, in that case in God's name would he please get the doctor! He wiped his face and waited until he regained the use of his hands so that he could jot down the essentials. There had been a flow of current, he had felt it, and it hadn't come from his body or the frogs, it had come from the chemical antagonism between the metals.

It wasn't easy to explain to the doctor what had been going on. The servant gave notice the same week, two scars remained, and the treatise on living muscle fiber as a conductor established Humboldt's reputation as a scientist.

He seemed to be showing some evidence of confusion, said his brother in a letter from Jena. He should really bear in mind that one also had moral obligations to one's own body, which wasn't just some random object among many; I'm begging you, do come, Schiller wants to meet you.

You misunderstand me, Humboldt replied, I have established that a human being is prepared to endure insult, but that a great deal of knowledge escapes him because he is afraid of pain. The man who deliberately undergoes pain nonetheless learns things he didn't... He laid down his pen, rubbed his shoulder, and crumpled the paper into a ball. Why, I wonder, he began again, does the fact that we are brothers strike me as the real riddle? That the two of us are alone, that we're doubles, that you are what I was never intended to be, and I am what you cannot be, that we must go through existence as a pair, together, whether we want it or not, closer all our lives than either of us will ever be to someone else. And why do I imagine that the greatness we each achieve will have no future, no matter what successes we have, and that it will vanish as if it were nothing until our names, which competed against each other in their fame, melt back into one and fade to a blank? He faltered, then tore the sheet into little pieces.

To examine the plants in the Freiberg mines, he developed the miner's lamp: a flame fed by a gas canister which worked in places even where there was no air. It almost killed him. He climbed down into a chamber in the rock that had never been explored before, set down the lamp, and within a matter of minutes lost consciousness. Dying, he saw tropical creepers which turned to women's bodies as he watched, and came back to his senses with a scream. A Spaniard named Andrés del Río, a former classmate at the Freiberg School of Mines, had found him and got him up to the surface again. Humboldt was almost too ashamed to thank him properly.

It took him a month of hard work to develop a breathing machine: two pipes led from an airbag to a breathing mask.

He strapped the apparatus on and went down. Stony-faced he endured the onset of hallucinations. Then first his knees began to buckle and dizziness multiplied the single flame to a blaze; he opened the air valve and watched grimly as the women turned back into plants and the plants into mere nothings. He stayed down in the cool darkness for hours. When he emerged into the daylight, he was met with a letter from Kunth, summoning him to his mother's deathbed.

As was appropriate, he found the fastest horse and rode out. Rain lashed his face, his coat flapped behind him, twice he slipped from the saddle and landed in the dirt. He arrived filthy and unshaven, and because he knew what was correct behavior, he pretended to be out of breath. Kunth nodded his approval; they sat together at her bedside and watched as the pain transformed her face into something unknown. Consumption had burned her up inside, her cheeks had fallen in, her chin was long, and her nose was suddenly hooked; so much blood had been let that she had almost died of it. While Humboldt held her hand, afternoon passed over into evening and a messenger brought a letter from his brother, excusing himself on the grounds of urgent business in Weimar. As night set in, his mother struggled erect in bed and began to emit sharp screams. The sleeping draught was having no effect, even another bleeding brought no relief, and Humboldt could not believe the fact that she was capable of such improper behavior. Around midnight her screams became so unbridled and loud and seemed to be coming from so deep in her body as it arched upward that she seemed to be in ecstasy. He waited with closed eyes. It took two hours for her to fall quiet. At first light, she murmured something incomprehensible; as the sun rose in the morning sky she looked at her son and said he must control himself, that was no way to be lolling about. Then she turned her head away, her eyes seemed to turn to glass, and he was looking at the first corpse he had ever seen in his life.

Kunth put a hand on his shoulder. No one could begin to measure what this family had meant to him.

No, said Humboldt, as if someone were whispering to him, he could measure it and he would never forget.

Kunth was moved, and sighed. Now he knew he would continue to receive his keep.

In the afternoon the servants watched Humboldt waiting up and down in front of the castle, over the hills, round the pond, mouth wide open, face turned up to the sky, looking like an idiot. They had never seen him this way. He must surely, they said to one another, be awfully shaken. And he was: he had never been so happy.

SOURCE BIBLIOGRAPHY

The sources are listed with the first publication in any form, which is the basis for the texts or translations for this volume, followed where appropriate by a historical edition or collected works edition, followed by a modern standard edition for convenient reference. If a published translation has been used, this citation follows the references for the original language edition. If this volume includes multiple pieces by the same author, the sources pertaining to each piece are separated by ***, and the entries appear in the order in which the pieces appear in the volume.

CÉSAR AIRA
(1949–)

Un episodio en la vida del pintor viajero, Rosario (Argentina): Beatriz Viterbo 2000, pp. 11–14.
An Episode in the Life of a Landscape Painter, trans. Chris Andrews, New York: New Directions 2006, pp. 5–8.

HANS CHRISTIAN ANDERSEN
(1805–1875)

Dagbøger 1825–1875, eds. Kåre Olsen and H. Topsøe-Jensen, 12 vols., vol. 1: *Dagbøger 1825–1834,* ed. Helga Vang Lauridsen, Copenhagen: G. E. C. Gad 1971, p. 440.
***
Dagbøger 1825–1875, eds. Kåre Olsen and H. Topsøe-Jensen, 12 vols., vol. 3: *Dagbøger 1845–1850,* eds. Helga Vang Lauridsen and Tue Gad, Copenhagen: G. E. C. Gad 1974, pp. 38–39, 39–40.

MÁRIO DE ANDRADE
(1893–1945)

Macunaíma o heroi sem nenhum caracter, São Paulo: [Oficinas graficas de E. Cupolo] 1928, pp. 281–283.
"Epílogo," in: *Macunaíma o herói sem nenhum caráter,* ed. Telê Porto Ancona Lopez, Florianópolis: Coleção Arquivos 1988, pp. 167–168.
"Epilogue," in: *Macunaíma,* trans. E. A. Goodland, New York: Random House 1984, pp. 167–168.

REINALDO ARENAS
(1943–1990)
El mundo alucinante (Una novela de aventuras), [prize submission, Cuba, 1966], Mexico:
Diógenes 1969, pp. 128–133.
El mundo alucinante. Una novela de aventuras, Barcelona: Tusquets 2001 [corrected edition
of 1997], pp. 179–184.
Hallucinations or, the Ill-Fated Peregrinations of Fray Servando, trans. Andrew Hurley
[1987], New York: Penguin 2002, pp. 132–136.

LUDWIG ACHIM VON ARNIM
(1781–1831)
Der Wintergarten. Novellen. Berlin: Realschulbuchhandlung, 1809, pp. 481–485.
Werke in sechs Bänden, eds. Roswitha Burwick, et al., 6 vols., Frankfurt am Main: Deutscher
Klassiker, 1989–1994. *Der Wintergarten*, in *Sämtliche Erzählungen 1802–1817*. Ed. Re-
nate Moering. Frankfurt a. M.: 1990, vol. 3, pp. 69–423, here: pp. 418–21.

BETTINA VON ARNIM
(1785–1859)
Dies Buch gehört dem König, 2 vols., Berlin: E. H. Schröder 1843, vol. 1, pp. V–VIII.
Dies Buch gehört dem König, in: *Werke und Briefe*, 4 vols., eds. Walter Schmitz and Sibylle
von Steinsdorff, vol. 3: *Politische Schriften*, eds. Wolfgang Bunzel, Ulrike Landfester,
Walter Schmitz and Sibylle von Steinsdorff, Frankfurt: Deutscher Klassiker Verlag
1995, pp. 11–13 ("Vorrede").

HONORÉ DE BALZAC
(1799–1850)
"Aventures administratives D'une Idée heureuse," in: *Causeries du monde*, Paris: Vincent
Deberny (10 March 1834), pp. 97–111, here: pp. 97–101, 107–111.
"Aventures administratives d'une idée heureuse," in: *La Comédie humaine*, Bibliothèque de
la Pléiade, ed. Pierre-Georges Castex and others, 12 vols., Paris: Gallimard 1976–81,
vol. 12, pp. 767–779, here: pp. 768–770, 775–778 (annotations: pp. 1100–1103).
                                             ***
"Un des trois grands coiffeurs de Paris" in: *Le Courrier français*, 14–18 and 22–24 April
1846.
La Comédie humaine, 20 vols., Paris: Furne 1842–1852, vol. 12, *Études de moeurs: Scènes de
la vie parisienne. Les Comédiens sans le savoir* 1846, pp. 155–208, here: 186–187.
La Comédie humaine, Bibliothèque de la Pléiade, ed. Pierre-Georges Castex and others,
12 vols., Paris: Gallimard 1976–1981, vol. 7, *Études de moeurs: Scènes de la vie parisi-
enne. Les Comédiens sans le savoir*, pp. 1153–1213, here: 1185–1186 (annotations: pp.
1670–1737).
The Unconscious Mummers. Trans. Ellen Marriage. *The Novels of Balzac. Seraphita and other
Stories*. Ed. George Saintsbury. 32 vols. Philadelphia: The Gebbie Publishing Co., 1899.
Vol. 28: 339–406, here: 377–379.

KAROLINE BAUER
(1807–1877)

Aus meinem Bühnenleben. Erinnerungen. Ed. Arnold Wellmer. 2nd ed. 2 vols. Berlin: R. v. Decker, 1876–1877. Vol 1, pp. 272–274.

ANDRÉS BELLO
(1781–1865)

"Alocución a la poesía," in: *Biblioteca Americana*, London: G. Marchant 1823, vol. 1, pp. 3–16; vol. 2, pp. 1–12, here: vol. 1, pp. 3–10.

"Alocución a la poesía," in: *Obras completas*, 22 vols., vol. 1: *Poesías*, Caracas: Ministerio de Educación/Biblioteca Nacional 1952, pp. 43–64, here: pp. 43–49.

[For a comparison to the translation in this edition]: *Selected Writings of Andrés Bello*, trans. Frances M. López-Morillas, ed. Ivan Jaksic, New York/Oxford: Oxford University Press 1997, pp. 7–13, here: pp. 7–12.

"Allocution to Poetry," in: *Anthology of Andrés Bello*, trans. Barbara D. Huntley and Pilar Liria, ed. Pedro Grases, Washington: Organization of American States 1981, pp. 9–12 [excerpts].

SAUL BELLOW
(1915–2005)

Humboldt's Gift. New York: Viking 1975, p. 333.

ERNST BLOCH
(1885–1977)

"Erstaunen am Rheinfall," in: *Frankfurter Zeitung* 78:853, 7 December 1933, p. 1.

"Erstaunen am Rheinfall" [expanded version], in: *Literarische Aufsätze*, Frankfurt: Suhrkamp 1965, pp. 427–433.

Der unbemerkte Augenblick. Feuilletons für die Frankfurter Zeitung *1916–1934*, ed. Ralf Becker, Frankfurt: Suhrkamp 2007, pp. 349–353.

"Astonishment at the Rhine Falls," trans. Andrew Joron in: *Literary Essays*, trans. Andrew Joron and others, Stanford: Stanford University Press 1998, pp. 378–383.

SIMÓN BOLÍVAR
(1783–1830)

Manuscript (facsimile and transcription): Ángel Grisanti, *Bolívar. Sí escaló el Chimborazo, y escribió su Delirio en Ríobamba*, Caracas: Tipografía Principios 1964, pp. 75–81.

Papeles de Bolívar, ed. Vicente Lecuna, Caracas: Litografía del Comercio 1917, pp. 231–234.

"My Delirium on Chimborazo," in: *El Libertador: Writings of Simón Bolívar*, trans. Frederick H. Fornoff, ed. David Bushnell, Oxford/New York: Oxford University Press 2003, pp. 135–136 (annotations: p. 226).

Ludwig Börne
(1786–1837)

Quoted in: Hermann Reinganum. *Aus Börnes Leben*. In: Ludwig Börne. *Gesammelte Schriften Neue vollständige Ausgabe*. 12 vols., Hamburg/Frankfurt a. M.: Verlag der Börne'schen Schriften, 1862, vol. 12: *Briefe aus Paris,* 219–399, here pp. 360, 363–364, 371.

Sämtliche Schriften, eds. Inge Rippmann and Peter Rippmann, 5 vols., Düsseldorf: Joseph Melzer 1968, vol. 4: *Briefe I,* pp. 870–871, 889, 906, 929, 936–937, 945, 1157 (editorial information: pp. IXX–XX, XXII).

Volker Braun
(1939–)

Guevara oder Der Sonnenstaat. Schauspiel, in: *Spectaculum. Moderne Theaterstücke,* 27 (1977) pp. 67–109, here: 69–71, 90–92, 102–104; author notes: pp. 282.

Guevara oder Der Sonnenstaat, in: *Gesammelte Stücke,* 2 vols., Frankfurt: Suhrkamp 1989, vol. 1, pp. 159–210, here: pp. 161–164, 182–184, 202–204.

Guevara oder Der Sonnenstaat, in: *Texte in zeitlicher Folge,* 10 vols., Halle: Mitteldeutscher Verlag 1989–1993, vol. 5, 1990, pp. 111–179, here: pp. 115–119, 141–144, 165–167.

Hans Christoph Buch
(1944–)

"Nachwort," in: *Karibische Kaltluft. Berichte und Reportagen,* Frankfurt: Suhrkamp 1985, pp. 191–200, here: pp. 198–200.

George Gordon Byron
(1788–1824)

Don Juan, 6 vols., London: Thomas Davison/John Hunt 1821–1824, vol. 2: *Cantos III, IV, and V,* London: Thomas Davison 1821, p. 127 (Canto IV, 112).

Don Juan. A Variorum Edition, eds. Truman Guy Steffan and Willis Winslow Pratt, 4 vols., Austin: University of Texas Press 1957, vol. 2, p. 406 (Canto IV, 112).

Don Juan, in: *Poetical Works,* ed. Frederick Page, revised by John Jump, Oxford/New York: Oxford University Press 1970, pp. 635–858, here: p. 711 (Canto IV, 112).

Frances Calderón de la Barca
(1804–1882)

Life in Mexico During a Residence of Two Years in That Country, 2 vols., Boston: Charles C. Little and James Brown 1843, vol. 1, pp. 132, 133–134 (Letter 9), 192–196 (Letter 13); vol. 2, pp. 97–98 (Letter 34), 156–158 (Letter 40), 343–345 (Letter 49).

Life in Mexico, Berkeley/Los Angeles/London: University of California Press 1982, pp. 98, 98–99 (Letter 9), 135–137 (Letter 13), 349–341 (Letter 340–341), 377–379 (Letter 40), 495–497 (Letter 49).

ALEJO CARPENTIER
(1904–1980)

Los pasos perdidos, novela. México, D.F.: Edición y Distribución Ibero-Americana de Publicaciones 1953, pp. 175–176, 214, 216–217, 246–247, 253–254.

Los pasos perdidos, ed., Roberto González Echevarría, Madrid: Cátedra 1985, pp. 205–206, 238, 240, 264–265, 269–270.

The Lost Steps, trans. Harriet de Onís, New York: Knopf 1956, pp. 144–145, 176, 178, 202–203, 208.

ADELBERT VON CHAMISSO
(1781–1838)

Werke, 1836–39, 6 vols., vol. 1: *Reise um die Welt, erster Theil.* Leipzig: Weidmann'sche Buchhandlung 1836, pp. 375–376.

Sämtliche Werke, eds. Jost Perfahl and Volker Hoffmann, 2 vols., München: Winkler 1975, vol. 2, pp. 5–503, here: p. 224.

***

"Der Stein der Mutter oder der Guahiba-Indianerin," *Der Gesellschafter oder Blätter für Geist und Herz. Ein Volksblatt,* Berlin: Maurer 1817–1850, vol. 12, no. 64 (21 April 1828), pp. 317–318.

"Der Stein der Mutter oder der Guahiba-Indianerin," in: *Gedichte,* Leipzig: Weidmann'sche Buchhandlung 1831, pp. 292–297.

"Der Stein der Mutter oder der Guahiba-Indianerin," in: *Sämtliche Werke,* eds. Jost Perfahl and Volker Hoffmann, 2 vols., München: Winkler 1975, vol. 1, pp. 414–417.

FREDERIC EDWIN CHURCH
(1826–1900)

Letter to mother, Bogota, 7 July 1853. Winterthur Library, Collection 66, Folder 20.36, Accession no. 57x18, *Mrs. Joseph Carson Autograph Collection 1785–1945.*

WINSTON CHURCHILL
(1871–1947)

The Crisis, New York: Macmillan 1901, pp. 137–138.

CHARLES DARWIN
(1809–1882)

The Life and Letters of Charles Darwin, Including an Autobiographical Chapter, ed. Francis Darwin, 3 vols., London: John Murray 1887, vol. 1, pp. 190 (Fox), 190 (Henslow), 212–213, 231–232, 233–234, 237, 255.

***

Charles Darwin's Diary of the Voyage of H.M.S. "Beagle", ed. from the MS. by Nora Barlow. Cambridge: Cambridge University Press, 1933, pp. 24–25, 39.

Charles Darwin's Beagle *Diary,* ed. Richard Darwin Keynes, Cambridge: Cambridge University Press, 1988, pp. 23, 41–42.

***

Journal of Researches Into the Natural History and Geology of the Countries Visited During the Voyage of H. M. S. Beagle Round the World, Under the Command of Capt. Fitz Roy, R. N., 3 vols., London: John Murray, 1st ed., 1837, parts of text here only in: 2nd ed., corrected, with additions, 1845, vol. 3, pp. 500–506.

***

The Life and Letters of Charles Darwin, Including an Autobiographical Chapter, ed. Francis Darwin, 3 vols., London: John Murray 1887, vol. 1, p. 336; vol. 2, pp. 30, 43.

***

The Life and Letters of Charles Darwin, Including an Autobiographical Chapter, ed. Francis Darwin, 3 vols., London: John Murray 1887, vol. 3, p. 247.

***

The Life and Letters of Charles Darwin, Including an Autobiographical Chapter, ed. Francis Darwin, 3 vols., London: John Murray 1887, vol. 1, pp. 55–56, 74.

EUGEN HERMANN [VON DEDENROTH]
(1829–1887)

Ein Sohn Alexander's von Humboldt oder der Indianer von Maypures, in: *Gesammelte Novellen und Skizzen,* Leipzig: Rollmann / Philadelphia: John Weik 1858, pp. 1–138, here: pp. 3–4, 4–12, 16–18, 19, 20–22, 53, 126, 128–129, 129–138.

TANKRED DORST
(1925–)

Auf dem Chimborazo: eine Komödie, in: *Theater heute* 16:3 (March 1975), pp. 40–48, here: pp. 40, 42, 42–43, 44, 45, 46, 46, 46–47, 47, 47, 48.
Auf dem Chimborazo. Eine Komödie. Frankfurt: Suhrkamp 1975, pp. 9, 23, 26–27, 36–37, 49, 50, 55–56, 57, 60, 64.

RALPH WALDO EMERSON
(1803–1882)

"On the Relation of Man to the Globe," in: *Early Lectures,* 3 vols., eds. Stephen E. Whicher and Robert E. Spiller, Cambridge, MA: Harvard University Press 1959, vol. 1, pp. 27–49, here: pp. 38–39.

***

The Journals and Miscellaneous Notebooks, 16 vols., vol. 9: *1843–1847,* eds. Ralph H. Orth and Alfred R. Ferguson, Cambridge, MA: The Belknap Press of Harvard University Press 1971, p. 270.

***

The Conduct of Life, Boston: Ticknor and Fields 1860, pp. 80–83.
The Conduct of Life. The Collected Works of Ralph Waldo Emerson, eds. Barbara L. Parker, Joseph Slater and Douglas Emory Wilson, 10 vols., vol. 6, Cambridge, MA: Belknap Press of Harvard University Press 2003, pp. 50–52.

***

The Journals and Miscellaneous Notebooks, 16 vols., vol. 16: *1866–1882,* eds. Ronald A. Bosco and Glen M. Johnson, Cambridge, MA: The Belknap Press of Harvard University Press 1982, pp. 160–161.

HANS MAGNUS ENZENSBERGER
(1929–)

"A. v. H. (1769–1859)," in: *Mausoleum. Siebenunddreißig Balladen aus der Geschichte des Fortschritts.* Frankfurt: Suhrkamp 1975, pp. 56–58.

"A. v. H. (1769–1859)," in: *Mausoleum: Thirty-seven Ballads from the History of Progress,* trans. Joachim Neugroschel, New York: Urizen 1976, pp. 62–66.

***

"Präsidenten, Konsuln und Kaiser kommen und gehen, aber die Natur ist unbesiegbar. Alexander von Humboldt und François Arago: Ein wissenschaftliches Tête-à-tête in der Sternwarte zu Paris," in: *Frankfurter Allgemeine Zeitung,* 16 September 2004, p. 33.

THEODOR FONTANE
(1819–1898)

Wanderungen durch die Mark Brandenburg, 4 vols., Berlin: Hertz, 1862–1882. vol 1: *Die Grafschaft Ruppin, Der Barnim, Der Teltow.* Berlin: Hertz, 1862, "Tegel," pp. 189–205, here: pp. 189, 203–205.

Sämtliche Werke, ed. Edgar Gross, 24 vols., München: Nymphenburger 1959–1975, vol. 11: *Wanderungen durch die Mark Brandenburg,* 4 vols., vol. 3: *Havelland. Die Landschaft um Spandau, Potsdam, Brandenburg,* "Tegel" [moved by Fontane in later editons from vol. 1 to vol. 3]: pp. 152–165, here: pp. 152, 163–165.

Wanderungen durch die Mark Brandenburg, ed. Helmuth Nürnberger, 3 vols., München: dtv 2006, vol. 2: *Havelland. Spreeland,* "Tegel," pp. 156–170, here: pp. 156, 168–170.

ERICH FRIED
(1921–1988)

"Der Guacharo," in: *Die Beine der größeren Lügen. Einundfünfzig Gedichte,* Berlin: Klaus Wagenbach 1969, p. 26.

"Der Guacharo," in: Gesammelte Werke, eds. Volker Kaukoreit and Klaus Wagenbach, 4 vols., Berlin: Klaus Wagenbach 1993, vol. 1, pp. 609–610. (See "Quellen und Anmerkungen," pp. 639ff.)

EDUARDO GALEANO
(1940–)

Memoria del fuego, 3 vols., vol. 2: *Las caras y las máscaras,* Mexico: Siglo Veintiuno 1982, "Humboldt. 1790, París": p. 89; "Un par de sabios a lomo de mula. 1799, Cumaná": pp. 104–105; "Hacia el Orinoco. 1800, Río Apure": pp. 107–108; "El amo del veneno. 1800, Esmeralda del Orinoco": pp. 108–109; "Tierra y siempre. 1800, Uruana": p. 110; "La diosa en el fondo de las aguas. 1801, Laguna Guatavita": pp. 110–111; "Mutis. 1801,

Bogotá": pp. 111–112; "En las cumbres del mundo. 1802, Volcán Chimborazo": p. 114; "La más rica colonia de España. 1804, Ciudad de México": p. 115; "Napoleón. 1804, París": pp. 117–118; "Que se muera la muerte. 1858, San Borja": p. 223; "El guano. 1879, Islas Chinchas": p. 265.

Memory of Fire, 3 vols., trans. Cedric Belfrage, vol. 2: *Faces and Masks*, New York: Pantheon 1985, "Humboldt. 1790: Paris": pp. 72–73, "Two Wise Men on a Mule. 1799: Cumaná": pp. 84–85, "To the Orinoco. 1800: Apure River": pp. 87–88, "Master of Poison. 1800: Esmeralda del Orinoco": pp. 88–89, "Forever Earth. 1800: Uruana": pp. 89–90, "The Goddess at the Bottom of the Waters. 1801: Lake Guatavita": p. 90, "Mutis. 1801: Bogotá": pp. 90–91, "On the Roofs of the World. 1802: Chimborazo Volcano": pp. 92–93, "Spain's Richest Colony. 1804: Mexico City": pp. 93–94, "Napoleon. 1804: Paris": pp. 95–96, "Let Death Die. 1858: San Borja": p. 182, "Guano. 1879: Chincha Islands": p. 217.

GABRIEL GARCÍA MÁRQUEZ
(1928–)

El general en su laberinto, Bogotá: Oveja Negra 1989, pp. 99–102.
The General in his Labyrinth, trans. Edith Grossman, New York: Alfred A. Knopf 1990, pp. 94–97.

MATTIAS GERWALD [BERNDT SCHULZ]
(1942–)

Der Entdecker. Historischer Roman über Alexander von Humboldt, Bergisch Gladbach: Bastei Lübbe 2001, pp. 354–357, 362–364.

JOHANN WOLFGANG VON GOETHE
(1749–1832)

Die Wahlverwandtschaften. Ein Roman, 2 vols., Tübingen: J. G. Cotta 1809, vol. 2, pp. 147–151.
Die Wahlverwandtschaften, in: *Goethes Werke* (Weimarer Ausgabe), 133 in 143 vols., section 1, vol. 20, Weimar: Hermann Böhlau 1892 = München: dtv 1987, pp. 290–293.
Revised translation based on: *Elective Affinities*, trans. James Anthony Froude, in: *Novels and Tales*, trans. R. Dillon Boylan and James Anthony Froude, London: Henry G. Bohn 1854, pp. 1–245, here: pp. 170–172.

FRANZ GRILLPARZER
(1791–1872)

Sämtliche Werke. Historisch-kritische Gesamtausgabe, ed. August Sauer, 42 vols. 1909–1948, part 2, vol. 11: *Tagebücher und literarische Skizzenhefte V, vom Frühjahr 1842 bis gegen Ende 1856*, Vienna: Kunstverlag Anton Schroll & Co. 1924, pp. 173, 175.
Tagebücher und Reiseberichte, ed. Klaus Geißler, Berlin: Verlag der Nation 1980, p. 212.

***

Sämtliche Werke. Historisch-kritische Gesamtausgabe, ed. August Sauer, 42 vols. 1909–1948, part 2, vol. 11: *Tagebücher und literarische Skizzenhefte V, vom Frühjahr 1842 bis gegen Ende 1856*, Vienna: Kunstverlag Anton Schroll & Co. 1924, p. 232.

Tagebücher und Reiseberichte, ed. Klaus Geißler, Berlin: Verlag der Nation 1980, p. 228.

LAUREN GUNDERSON
(1982–)

Wide World. First public staged reading 14 October 2004 by Break A Leg Productions, commissioned by City University of New York Graduate Center for the *Alexander von Humboldt: From the Americas to the Cosmos International Conference.*

KARL GUTZKOW
(1811–1878)

Die Ritter vom Geiste. Roman in neun Büchern, 9 vols., Leipzig: Brockhaus 1850–1851, vol. 3 (1850), pp. 41–44; vol. 5 (1851), pp. 79–80.

***

Ein Mädchen aus dem Volke in: *Unterhaltungen am häuslichen Herd*, ed. Karl Gutzkow, vol. 1, Leipzig: Brockhaus 1853, issues 1–7 [dated 1852], pp. 3–111, here: issue 7, pp. 108–109.

Ein Mädchen aus dem Volke. Bilder der Wirklichkeit. Leipzig: Heinrich Hübner, 1855, pp. 182–184.

Republished with new title: *Der Emporblick. Novelle aus dem Volksleben der Großstädte*, in: *Gesammelte Werke. Erste vollständige Gesammt-Ausgabe*, 12 vols., part 1, vol. 2: *Kleine Romane und Erzählungen, I: Das Johannisfeuer. Der Wärwolf. Der Emporblick. Eine Phantasieliebe. Seraphine*, Jena: Hermann Costenoble 1873, pp. 141–245, here: pp. 240–241.

Der Emporblick. Novelle aus dem Volksleben der Großstädte, in: *Gutzkows Werke. Auswahl in zwölf Teilen*, ed. Reinhold Gensel, 12 vols., vol. 5: *Die Selbsttaufe – Der Emporblick – Die Kurstauben – Die Nihilisten – Der Werwolf*, Berlin/Leipzig/Wien/Stuttgart: Deutsches Verlagshaus Bong & Co. 1910, pp. 65–148, here: pp. 144–145.

***

Rückblicke auf mein Leben, Berlin: A. Hofmann & Co. 1875, pp. 242–244.

Gutzkows Werke und Briefe. Kommentierte digitale Ausgabe. Autobiographische Schriften, vol. 2: *Rückblicke auf mein Leben*, ed., Peter Hasubek. Münster in Westfalen: Oktober Verlag, 2006, pp. 278–280.

PETER HACKS
(1928–2003)

Ein Gespräch im Hause Stein über den abwesenden Herrn von Goethe. Schauspiel, München: Drei Masken 1975, pp. 12–14.

Ein Gespräch im Hause Stein über den abwesenden Herrn von Goethe. Schauspiel, in *Werke*, 15 vols., Berlin: Eulenspiegel 2003, vol. 5, *Die Dramen III*, pp. 97–151, here: 105–107.

CLAUS HAMMEL
(1932–1990)
Humboldt und Bolivar oder Der neue Contintent. Schauspiel, Berlin (GDR): Aufbau 1980, pp. 9, 11–12, 13, 18, 22–24, 39–43, 64–66, 71–72, 77, 78–84, 108–110, 117, 118–121, 122, 131–136.

CHRISTOPH HEIN
(1944–)
"Die russischen Briefe des Jägers Johann Seifert," in: *Einladung zum Lever Bourgeois,* Berlin/Weimar: Aufbau 1980, pp. 104–183, here: pp. 104–105, 106, 107–108, 113–114, 115–116, 119–123, 131–134, 137–141, 177–183.
"Die russischen Briefe des Jägers Johann Seifert," in: *Nachtfahrt und früher Morgen,* Frankfurt: Suhrkamp 2004, pp. 91–159, here: pp. 91, 93, 93–94, 99–100, 101–102, 104–107, 113–117, 120–123, 155–159.

HEINRICH HEINE
(1797–1856)
Lutezia. Berichte über Politik, Kunst und Volksleben, in: *Vermischte Schriften,* 3 vols., Hamburg: Hoffmann und Campe 1854, here: *Lutezia* II, vol. 3, pp. 108–125 (chap. LVII), here: pp. 120–125.
Historisch-kritische Gesamtausgabe der Werke, ed. Manfred Windfuhr, 16 vols., 1973–97, vol. 14/1: *Lutezia* II, ed. Volkmar Hansen, Hamburg: Hoffmann und Campe 1990, pp. 56–64 (chap. LVII), here: pp. 62–64 (editorial information: pp. 629–690).

WILLIAM HERBERT
(1788–1847)
The Guahiba. A Tale, London: John Murray 1822.
Works. Excepting those on botany and natural science; with additions and corrections by the author, 3 vols., vol. 1, London: H. G. Bohn 1842, pp. 47–74.

GÜNTER HERBURGER
(1932–)
Humboldt. Reise-Novellen, München: A1 Verlag 2001, "Einführung," pp. 5–6; "Humboldt," pp. 7–22.

JOSÉ MARÍA HEREDIA
(1803–1839)
"En el teocalli de Cholula," composed in 1820, first publication with the title of "Fragmentos descriptivos de un poema mexicano," in: *Poesías de José María Heredia,* New York: Behr & Kahl 1825, pp. 100–104. Revised version here from: *Poesías del ciudadano José María Heredia,* 2 vols., Toluca: Imprenta del Estado/Juan Matute, 2nd ed., 1832, vol. 2, pp. 37–42.

Poesías líricas, Paris: Garnier Hermanos, 2nd ed., 1832, pp. 153–158.

Poesías completas. Homenaje de la ciudad de la Habana en el centenario de la muerte de He-redia, 1839–1939, ed. Emilio Roig de Leuchsenring, 2 vols., Havana: Municipio de la Habana 1940/1941, vol. 2, pp. 150–153 (editorial information: pp. 153–154).

Poesía completa, ed. Carmen Alemany Bay, Madrid: Verbum 2004, pp. 79–84.

"On the Teocalli of Cholula," trans. Daniel Charles Thomas and Luisa Elena Ruiz Pulido, in: *Un pasado visible. Antología de poemas y crónicas sobre vestigios del México Antiguo.* Universidad Nacional Autónoma de México, Instituto de Investigaciones Filológicas. <http://unpasadovisible.com/htmlingles/heredia1_ing.html>

***

"Viage al Nevado de Toluca," in: *Calendario de las Señoritas Megicanas para el año de 1838,* ed. Mariano Galván [Rivera], Mexico: Mariano Galván Rivera [1837], pp. 241–254.

"Viaje al Nevado de Toluca," in: *Crítica literaria,* ed. José María Chacón y Calvo, Havana: Pablo de la Torriente 2002, pp. 236–243.

Oliver Wendell Holmes
(1809–1894)

"Bonaparte, Aug. 15th, 1769—Humboldt, Sept. 14th, 1769," in: Louis Agassiz, *Address Delivered on the Centennial Anniversary of the Birth of Alexander von Humboldt. Under the Auspices of the Boston Society of Natural History; with an Account of the Evening Reception,* Boston: Boston Society of Natural History 1869, pp. 86–88.

"Bonaparte, Aug. 15, 1769—Humboldt , Sept. 14, 1769," *The Atlantic Monthly* 24:145, November 1869, pp. 637–638.

"Humboldt's Birthday," *Songs of Many Seasons. 1862–1874,* Boston: James R. Osgood 1875, pp. 116–119.

Aldous Huxley
(1894–1963)

Beyond the Mexique Bay. New York: Harper & Brothers, 1934. "Cholula," pp. 272–279, here: pp. 275–276.

Ernst Jünger
(1895–1998)

Siebzig verweht, 5 vols., Stuttgart: Klett-Cotta 1980–1997, vol. 1: *Siebzig verweht I,* 1980, "22 October 1966," pp. 308–310.

Sämtliche Werke, 22 vols., Stuttgart: Klett-Cotta 1978–2003, vol. 4: *Erste Abteilung: Tagebücher IV, Strahlungen III, Siebzig verweht I,* 1982, pp. 307–309.

***

Siebzig verweht, 5 vols., Stuttgart: Klett-Cotta 1980–1997, vol. 1: *Siebzig verweht I,* 1980, "7 June 1970," pp. 584–585.

Sämtliche Werke, 22 vols., Stuttgart: Klett-Cotta 1978–2003, vol. 4: *Erste Abteilung: Tagebücher IV, Strahlungen III, Siebzig verweht I,* 1982, pp. 596–597.

Daniel Kehlmann
(1975–)

"Das Meer," in: *Die Vermessung der Welt. Roman*, Reinbek: Rowohlt 2005, pp. 19–51, here: 19–36.
"The Sea," in: *Measuring the World*, trans. Carol Brown Janeway, New York: Pantheon 2006, pp. 13–41, here: pp. 13–28.

Egon Erwin Kisch
(1885–1948)

"Zwiegespräch mit einem Nazi. Zum 14. September 1944, dem 175. Geburtstag Alexander von Humboldts," in: *Demokratische Post* 2.3 [Mexico], 15 September 1944, p. 5.
[Translations of the Humboldt quotations used by Kisch in this essay have been taken from: Alexander von Humboldt, *Cosmos*, trans. E. C. Otté, 5 vols., London: Bohn 1849–1858 and *Political Essay on the Kingdom of New Spain*, trans. John Black, 4 vols., London: Longman, Hurst, Rees, Orme, and Brown 1811.]
"Zwiegespräch mit einem Nazi," in: *Gesammelte Werke in Einzelausgaben*, eds. Bodo Uhse and Gisela Kisch, Fritz Hofmann and Josef Polácek, 11 vols. in 10, vol. 10: *Läuse auf dem Markt. Vermischte Prosa*, Berlin/Weimar (GDR): Aufbau 1985, pp. 273–277.

Heinrich Laube
(1806–1884)

Gesammelte Schriften, 16 vols., Wien: Braumüller 1875–1882. *Erinnerungen 1810–1840*, vol. 1, pp. 329–334.
Gesammelte Werke, 50 vols. in 20 vols., eds. Heinrich Hubert Houben and Albert Hänel, vol. 40: *Erinnerungen 1810–1840*, Leipzig: Max Hesse 1909, pp. 344–349.

Bernhard von Lepel
(1818–1885)

An Humboldt. Ode, Berlin: Alexander Duncker 1847.

Friedrich Adolf Maercker
(1804–1889)

"An Alexander v. Humboldt," in: *Gedichte*, 2nd ed., 2 vols., Berlin: Verlag der Königlichen Geheimen Ober-Hofbuchdruckerei R. Decker 1858, vol. 1, pp. 13–15.
"An Alexander von Humboldt," in: *Gedichte*, 2nd ed., 2 vols., Berlin: Verlag der Königlichen Geheimen Ober-Hofbuchdruckerei R. Decker 1858, vol. 2, p. 157.

***

"Alexander von Humboldt unter den Urwählern des 170. Berliner Wahlbezirks, am 12. November 1858," in: *Erinnerungen. Gesammelte Gedichte*, Berlin: Verlag der Königlichen Geheimen Ober-Hofbuchdruckerei R. Decker 1862, p. 74.

"Am Sterbebette Alexanders von Humboldt. Den 6. Mai 1859," in: *Erinnerungen. Gesammelte Gedichte,* Berlin: Verlag der Königlichen Geheimen Ober-Hofbuchdruckerei R. Decker 1862, p. 75.

JOSÉ MARTÍ
(1853–1895)
"Un Voyage à Venezuela," in: *Obras completas,* 74 vols., Havana: Editorial Trópico, 1936–53, vol. 55, *Viaje 1,* 1944, pp. 171–197, here: pp. 180–182, 193–194.
"Un Voyage à Venezuela," in: *Obras completas,* 2nd. ed., 27 vols., Havana: Editorial de Ciencias Sociales, 1975, vol. 19: *Viajes, Diarios, Crónicas, Juicios,* pp. 137–153, here: pp. 143–144, 150–151.

IBSEN MARTÍNEZ
(1951–)
Humboldt & Bonpland, Taxidermistas. Tragicomedia con naturalistas, en dos actos, in: *Humboldt & Bonpland, Taxidermistas. L.S.D. (Lucio in the Sky with Diamonds) (Teatro),* Caracas: Fundarte 1991, pp. 5–59, here: pp. 13–19, 21–22, 23, 25, 31–32, 36–42.

WILLIAM MCJIMSEY
(1797–1881)
The Memory of Humboldt. Born in Berlin, Germany, September 14th, 1769, Finished His Work Entitled Cosmos, or the World, *September 14th, 1858. Died in Berlin, Prussia, May 6, 1859. A Poem On the occasion of the unveiling of the Statue of Alexander von Humboldt, on the Celebration of his Centennial Birth-day in the Central Park, City of New York, September 14, 1869,* New York: [n.p.], 1869.

PABLO NERUDA
(1904–1973)
"El pájaro Colorario," in: *Arte de pájaros,* Santiago de Chile: Sociedad de Amigos del Arte Contemporaneo, 1966, p. 95.
"El pájaro Colorario, *Minus Cothapa,*" in: *Obras completas,* ed. Hernán Loyola, 5 vols., Barcelona: Galaxia Gutemberg / Círculo de Lectores 2001–2002, vol. 3: *De "Arte de pájaros" a "El mar y las campanas" 1966–1973,* 2000, pp. 96–97.
"Corollary Bird," in: *Art of Birds,* trans. Jack Schmitt, Austin: University of Texas Press 1985, p. 78.

REDMOND O'HANLON
(1947–)
In Trouble Again: A Journey Between the Orinoco and the Amazon, London: Hamish Hamilton 1988, pp. 44–45, 49–50, 55, 58–59, 60–61, 124, 134–136.

In Trouble Again: A Journey Between the Orinoco and the Amazon, New York: Vintage 1990, pp. 44–45, 49–50, 55, 58–59, 60–61, 124, 134–136.

THEO PIANA AND HORST SCHÖNFELDER
(1914–1969; n.d.)

Alexander von Humboldt. Ein deutscher Weltreisender und Naturforscher, Berlin (GDR): Altberliner Verlag Lucie Groszer 1959, no pagination [44 pages, here: pp. 32–37].

EDGAR ALLEN POE
(1809–1849)

Eureka: A Prose Poem, New York: Geo. P. Putnam 1848, pp. 3 (Dedication), 7–10.
Eureka: A Prose Poem, Amherst: Prometheus 1997, pp. 3 (Dedication), 5–7.

EZRA POUND
(1885–1972)

The Cantos 1–95, New York: New Directions 1956, Canto 89: pp. 50–64, here: pp. 56–58. [Sections paginated separately. Pagination is from "Section: Rock-Drill. 85–95 de los Cantares."]
The Cantos of Ezra Pound, New York: New Directions 1970 = 1998, Canto LXXXIX: pp. 610–624, here: pp. 616–618.

WILHELM RAABE
(1831–1910)

Abu Telfan oder die Heimkehr vom Mondgebirge. Ein Roman in drei Theilen, 3 vols., Stuttgart: Eduard Hallberger 1868, vol 2, pp. 21–31.
Sämtliche Werke, 26 vols., ed. Karl Hoppe, vol. 7: *Abu Telfan oder die Heimkehr vom Mondgebirge,* ed. Werner Röpke, Freiburg/Braunschweig: Hermann Klemm 1951, pp. 140–146.
Abu Telfan: or, The Return From the Mountains of the Moon, trans. Sofie Delffs. 3 vols., London: Chapman and Hall 1882, vol. 2, pp. 27–40.

CARL RITTER
(1779–1859)

Gustav Kramer. *Carl Ritter: ein Lebensbild nach seinem handschriftlichen Nachlaß dargestellt.* 2 vols. Halle: Buchhandlung des Waisenhauses, 1864–70, vol. 2, pp. 185–186.

EMIL RITTERSHAUS
(1834–1897)

Fest-Gedicht für die Humboldt-Feier in Amerika am 14. September 1869 [German/English], New York: L. W. Schmidt 1869, 7 pp., here: pp. 2, 4, 6.
Neue Gedichte, Leipzig: Ernst Keil 1871, pp. 223–230.

Neue Gedichte, Stuttgart/Berlin/Leipzig: Union Deutsche Verlagsgesellschaft 1913 (7th edition), pp. 178–183.
Fest-Gedicht für die Humboldt-Feier in Amerika am 14. September 1869 [German/English], trans. Kate Kroeker-Freiligrath, New York: L. W. Schmidt 1869, 7 pp., here: pp. 3, 5, 7.

LUIS ARMANDO ROCHE AND JACQUES ESPAGNE
(1938– ; n.d.)
Aire libre (Passage des hommes libres). Un filme de Luis Armando Roche, Mérida (Venezuela): Fundación del Nuevo Cine Latinoamericano 1996, pp. 11–13, 18–21, 65–70, 93–103.

DENZIL ROMERO
(1938–1999)
"Los primeros descubrimientos históricos del Orinoco (II)," in: *Recurrencia equinoccial. Novela,* ed. Karl Kohut, Frankfurt/Madrid: Vervuert/Iberoamericana 2002, pp. 167–169, here: pp. 167, 169.

THEODORE ROOSEVELT
(1858–1919)
Through the Brazilian Wilderness, New York: Charles Scribner's Sons 1914, pp. 343–346.
Through the Brazilian Wilderness, London: John Murray 1914, pp. 331–334.

PAUL KANUT SCHÄFER AND RAINER SIMON
(1922–; 1941–)
Die Besteigung des Chimborazo. Literarische Filmerzählung, in: Paul Kanut Schäfer and Rainer Simon, *Die Besteigung des Chimborazo. Eine Filmexpedition auf Alexander von Humboldts Spuren.* Köln: vgs 1990, pp. 10–110, here: pp. 94–95, 96–98, 109–110.

RAINER SIMON
(1941–)
Meine Chimborazo-Tagebücher, in: Paul Kanut Schäfer and Rainer Simon, *Die Besteigung des Chimborazo. Eine Filmexpedition auf Alexander von Humboldts Spuren,* Köln: vgs 1990, pp. 120–157, here: pp. 120, 120–129, 130–132, 141–142, 143, 144, 146, 147–148, 151–152, 152, 153–154, 156, 156, 157.
***
Fernes Land. Die DDR, die DEFA und der Ruf des Chimborazo. Berlin: Aufbau 2005, pp. 21, 250, 254–255, 264–269, 269–270, 272, 275.

JOAQUIM DE SOUSÂNDRADE [JOAQUIM DE SOUSA ANDRADE]
(1833–1902)
O Guesa, London: Cooke & Halsted/Moorfields Press, n.d. [1884], pp. 1–2, 320 (Canto XII).

O Guesa, facsimile edition, ed. Jomar Moraes, São Luís, MA: SIOGE 1979, pp. 26, 186 (Canto XII).

JORDAN HERBERT STABLER
(1885–1938)

Bolivar. December 1830–December 1930. In Memoriam. The Spirit of Chimborazo Speaks, Caracas: Vargas 1930, here: pp. 7–8, 17–20.

ADALBERT STIFTER
(1805–1868)

Der Nachsommer, 3 vols., Pesth: Gustav Heckenast 1857, vol. 1, pp. 66–67, 69–70, 74, 78–79, 91, 110–111, 116–118.

Werke und Briefe. Historisch-Kritische Gesamtausgabe, 32 vols. to date, eds. Alfred Doppler and Hartmut Laufhütte, Stuttgart: Kohlhammer 1978–, vols. 4.1–4.3: *Der Nachsommer* 1997–2000, here: vol. 4.1, pp. 49–50, 51, 54, 57, 65, 78, 82–83.

Der Nachsommer. Roman, München: dtv 2005, pp. 42–43, 44–45, 47, 49–50, 56, 67, 71–72.

JULIUS STINDE
(1841–1905)

Die Familie Buchholz. Aus dem Leben der Hauptstadt, Berlin: Freund & Jeckel 1884, pp. 138–141.

[For a comparison to the translation in this edition]: *The Buchholz Family. Sketches of Berlin Life,* trans. L. Dora Schmitz, London: George Bell and Sons 1886, pp. 158–162.

AUGUST STRINDBERG
(1849–1912)

"Triumfatorn och narren," in: *Sagor.* Stockholm: Hugo Geber 1903, pp. 87–101.

"Triumfatorn och narren," in: *Samlade Skrifter,* 55 vols., Stockholm: Albert Bonnier 1912–, vol. 38: *Sagor och Ensam,* 1916, pp. 54–62.

"Triumfatorn och narren," in: *Ensam. Sagor,* ed. Ola Östin, Stockholm: Norstedt 1994, pp. 135–143 (annotations: pp. 326–328).

"Conquering Hero and Fool," in: *In Midsummer Days, and Other Tales,* trans. Ellie Schleussner, London: H. Latimer, 1913. pp. 79–89.

JOSÉ SERVANDO TERESA DE MIER
(1763–1827)

Relación de lo que sucedió en Europa al Doctor D. Servando Teresa de Mier después que fue trasladado allá por resultas de lo actuado contra él en México: desde Julio de 1795 hasta Octubre de 1805, manuscript first published in: José Eleuterio González, *Biografía del benemérito mexicano d. Servando Teresa de Mier Noriega y Guerra,* Monterey: Impresa de la calle de Dr. Mier Número 37/José Saenz 1876, pp. 142–328, here: p. 201.

Memorias, ed. Antonio Castro Leal, 2 vols., Mexico: Porrúa 1946, vol. 2, pp. 44–45.
The Memoirs of Fray Servando Teresa de Mier, trans. Helen Lane, ed. Susana Rotker, New York/Oxford: Oxford University Press 1998, p. 32 (annotations: p. 229).

HENRY DAVID THOREAU
(1817–1862)
"A Walk to Wachusett," in: *The Boston Miscellany of Literature and Fashion,* January 1843, pp. 31–36, here: p. 31.
"A Walk to Wachusett," in: *The Writings of Henry David Thoreau. Excursions and Poems,* Boston/New York: Houghton Mifflin and Company 1906, pp. 133–152, here: pp. 133–134.

ARTEMIO DE VALLE-ARIZPE
(1884–1961)
La güera Rodríguez, Mexico: Porrúa 1950, 4th ed., pp. 119–138 (Jornada Novena: "De lo humano de la ciencia a lo divino del amor").
Obras, 2 vols., Mexico: Fondo de Cultura Económica 2000, vol. 1, pp. 165–177 (Jornada Novena: "De lo humano de la ciencia a lo divino del amor").

JULES VERNE
(1828–1905)
Voyage au centre de la terre, Paris: J. Hetzel [1864], here from 1867 edition, p. 140.
Voyage au centre de la terre, Paris: Le Livre de Poche, 1966, p. 196.
A Journey into the Interior of the Earth. Trans. Frederick Amadeus Malleson. London: Ward, Lock and Hall, 1877, chapter XXX.

***

"Les Anglais au pôle Nord. Le désert de glace," *Magasin d'Éducation et de Récréation,* vol. 1, no. 1 (20 March 1864); vol.4, no. 42 (5 December 1865).
Voyages et aventures du capitaine Hatteras: Les Anglais au pôle nord–Le Désert de glace, Paris: J. Hetzel [1866], Seconde Partie, *Le Désert de glace,* chapter XXIV, pp. 439–440.
Voyages et aventures du capitaine Hatteras. Les Anglais au pôle nord. Le Désert de glace, ed. Roger Borderie, Paris: Gallimard 2005, chapter XXIV, pp. 622–623.
The Voyages and Adventures of Captain Hatteras. Boston: J. R. Osgood, 1876. Part II, *The Desert of Ice,* chapter XXIV, pp. 419–420.

***

"Les Enfants du capitaine Grant," *Magasin d'Éducation et de Récréation,* vol. 4, no. 43 (20 December 1865); vol. 8, no. 90 (5 December 1867).
Les enfants du capitaine Grant. Voyage autour du monde, Paris: J. Hetzel [1867], chapter VIII, pp. 70–74.
Les enfants du capitaine Grant. Voyage autour du monde, vol. 1, Paris: Le Livre de Poche/Librairie Générale Franaise 2004, pp. 75–79.
A Voyage Round the World. 3 vols. [1] South America, [2] Australia, [3] New Zealand. London; New York: Routledge, 1876. Vol. 1, *South America,* chapter VIII, pp. 73–77.

***

"Vingt Mille Lieues sous les mers. Tour du monde sous-marin," *Magasin d'Éducation et de Récréation*, vol. 11, no. 121 (20 March 1869); vol. 13, no. 151 (20 June 1870).
Vingt mille lieues sous les mers, Paris: J. Hetzel [1869], pp.75–76.
Vingt mille lieues sous les mers, ed. Jacques Noiray, Paris: Gallimard 2005, pp. 151–154.
Twenty Thousand Leagues under the Seas. Trans. Louis Mercier. London: Sampson Low Marston Low & Searle, 1872, chapter XI.

***

"La Jangada. Huit Cents Lieues sur l'Amazone," *Magasin d'Éducation et de Récréation*, vol. 33, no. 385 (1 January 1881); vol. 34, no. 407 (1 December 1881).
La Jangada. Huit cents lieues sur l'Amazone, Paris: J. Hetzel [1881]. Première Partie, chapter V, pp. 64, 67–68; chapter VII, pp. 99–100; chapter XIV, pp. 195–196.
La Jangada. Huit cents lieues sur l'Amazone, ed. Michel Tournier, Monaco: Alphée/Motifs/ Le Serpent à Plumes 2005, pp. 81–82, 84–85, 114–115, 201–202.
The Giant Raft. (Part I) Eight Hundred Leagues on the Amazon. (Part II) The Cryptogram. Trans. W. J. Gordon. 2 vols. New York: Scribner's, 1881–1882, part 1, chapter V, pp. 56, 59–60; chapter VII, pp. 86–87; chapter XIV, pp. 168–169.

***

"Le Superbe Orénoque," *Magasin d'Éducation et de Récréation*, (seconde série), vol. 7, no. 73 (1 January 1898); vol. 8, no. 96 (15 December 1898).
Le superbe Orénoque, Paris: J. Hetzel [1898]. Première Partie, chapter VII, pp. 85–89; chapter VIII, pp. 102–114.
Le superbe Orénoque. Roman, Monaco: Alphée/Motifs/Le Serpent à Plumes 2005, Première Partie, chapter VII, pp 137–143; chapter VIII, pp.163–181.
The Mighty Orinoco, trans. Stanford L. Luce, eds. Arthur B. Evans and Walter James Miller, Middletown, CT: Wesleyan University Press 2002, part 1, chapter VII, pp. 76–79; chapter VIII, 91–101.

WALT WHITMAN
(1819–1892)

"Kosmos," in: *Leaves of Grass*, Boston: Thayer and Eldridge, 1860/1861, pp. 414–415.
"Kosmos," in: *The Complete Poems*, ed. Francis Murphy, London/New York: Penguin Classics 1986, p. 413.

Index of Names

INDEX OF PLACES